Goddesses in World Culture

Goddesses in World Culture

Volume 3
Australia and the Americas

Patricia Monaghan, Editor

PRAEGER

AN IMPRINT OF ABC-CLIO, LLC
Santa Barbara, California • Denver, Colorado • Oxford, England

Library of Congress Cataloging-in-Publication Data

Goddesses in world culture / Patricia Monaghan, editor.
  p. cm.
Includes bibliographical references and indexes.
ISBN 978-0-313-35465-6 (set : alk. paper) — ISBN 978-0-313-35466-3 (ebook)
1. Goddesses. I. Monaghan, Patricia.
BL473.5.G64   2011
202′.11409—dc22   2010017298

ISBN: 978-0-313-35465-6
EISBN: 978-0-313-35466-3

15   14   13   12   11   1   2   3   4   5

This book is also available on the World Wide Web as an eBook.
Visit www.abc-clio.com for details.

Praeger
An Imprint of ABC-CLIO, LLC

ABC-CLIO, LLC
130 Cremona Drive, P.O. Box 1911
Santa Barbara, California 93116-1911

This book is printed on acid-free paper ∞

Manufactured in the United States of America

Contents

Introduction

Patricia Monaghan

Any museum in which great art is exhibited includes statuesque women, some nakedly beautiful, some clothed in symbols of power and prestige. Some bear names of historically known goddesses, like Isis and Hera, Xiwang Mu and Epona, but others remain nameless or are labeled as "fertility figures" or "ancestor idols." The earliest of these artworks go back to the dawn of humanity's emergence in the Paleolithic or Old Stone Age, approximately 35,000 years ago. The latest might be only a few years old, crafted by an artist in one of the many lands where feminine divinity is still honored.

Goddesses have been part of human culture for millennia. They appear not only in visual art but also in literature, both oral and written. At times they are clearly divine powers such as Greek Athena in *The Iliad* or White Buffalo Calf Woman in the sacred stories of the Lakota. Or they may be disguised and diminished, appearing as queens and other heroines: Guinevere in the legends of King Arthur and Vashti in the Hebrew scriptures. Alternatively, they may be so removed from cultural centrality that they have become figures of folklore, appearing in children's stories as the fierce witch Baba Yaga in Russian tales or in local legend to explain names of places, as does the Irish cow of abundance, the Glas Ghaibhleann.

These powerful female figures also appear in religious rituals and liturgies. In some cases, the rituals remain only in historical records, for worship of the goddess in question died out or was suppressed. Such is the case with the great goddesses of Greece and Rome, known now only through ancient literature and archaeological remains. No one alive has seen a man castrate himself with a stone knife in honor of the Magna Mater, the "great mother" Cybele, or seen the vast procession of worshipers seeking initiation into the mysteries, threading their way to the shrine of Greek Demeter at Eleusis. The number of goddesses lost to history through deliberate persecution is impossible to know, although historical evidence points to the elimination of some divinities such as Berecynthia in Gaul, known only through documentation that her wagon-borne procession ceased when the Christian Martin of Tours destroyed all her images and threatened her followers. In other cases, as with many indigenous peoples around the globe, colonization and forced conversion, together with destruction of culturally important sites and monuments, have meant that the name and mythology of the goddess have been lost to history.

But in many cases, goddess rituals are still celebrated today. Such is the case with Divali, the Indian feast of the goddess of wealth, Lakshmi, which is part of the yearly cycle of Hindu devotion in Chicago as well as Calcutta. In Ireland the old Celtic feast of the goddess Brigit continues to be marked on February 1; although she now appears as a Christian abbess and saint, the same holy wells are visited in her honor as when she was acknowledged as divine. Finally, some goddesses are honored in reconstructed rituals, such as that dedicated to Isis in Southern California or those to Diana across the United States. Far removed in time and place from earliest worshipers, these new devotees create rituals; they walk to the Pacific Ocean rather than to the Nile, wearing gold lamé rather than hand-woven linen, chanting the name of Isis the all-mother; or they join in drum circles on a midwestern farm and call down to Diana to empower their daily lives. Even more startlingly, a worldwide movement to honor Celtic Brigit's ancient fire worship exists entirely online; people who never see or speak to each other share a living vigil by a virtual flame.

When scholars address the role of the feminine in religion today, they do so most frequently from the point of view of monotheistic religions. Annually, hundreds of articles and books, both learned and popular, address questions of the status of women in Judaism, Christianity, and Islam. But an underlying question arises among scholars who question how women can ever be equal in religion based on a single male divinity. Although orthodox believers argue that such a god represents all humanity, male and female, others point out that monotheism is almost invariably associated with a male clerical hierarchy whose edicts impact the lives of countless voiceless women. While the presence of a goddess within a religion is no guarantee of better status for women, her absence provides an opportunity for oppression. In countries that offer a vote to their citizens, only two do not allow women to vote: Saudi Arabia and Vatican City, both centers of monotheistic patriarchal religions.

Monotheism is based on a male divine image. The opposite is not, how-ever, true. There is no known case of a monotheistic religion based on a goddess; all religions where goddesses are honored employ both male and female imagery in describing divinity. Scholars of goddess religion have argued that by creating a "god/nongod" dualism, monotheisms encourage an exclusionary and divisive worldview. When "woman" is placed on the side of "nongod," spiritual gender segregation can result, with women excluded from religious power.

Yet even within monotheisms, images remain of powerful women: moth-ers, sisters, lovers, warriors. Although not accepted as divine, these figures hold much the same place in art and narrative as goddesses in nonmonothe-istic cultures do. Christianity deliberately adopted the images and symbols of powerful goddesses for saints and the Virgin Mary. Slavic Europe still honors many "black Madonnas" in areas where the black-skinned earth goddess Mokosh was once worshiped; when the Spanish conquered Mexico, the figure of Aztec Tonan was absorbed into the Christian Guadalupe. Such goddess-like figures often attract more popular devotion than the official male divinity, as is suggested by the fact that more Catholic churches in America are named for the Virgin Mary than for her divine son.

These volumes offer an introduction to the ways in which images of the feminine divine have appeared in world culture. Rather than attempting to discuss only the best-known figures in world religion, the chapters address figures of varying centrality within their cultures. Sedna, the "great food-dish" who assures survival to the Inuit, appears here, but so does Sôlmundae Halmang, a Korean goddess who exists only in place-name sto-ries of the island of Cheju. Some goddesses suggest a bridge between several cultures; the Matronae, for instance, were honored in Roman-occupied areas where Celtic and Germanic peoples lived and thus reveal some of all three cultures; and Cinderella, familiar to readers from Germanic fairy tales, is shown to have come originally from Asia by way of Egypt. Some cultures that are especially rich in goddess lore, such as India, are represented by more than one chapter, while due to limitations of space, other cultures are not covered. In every case, the figure is not intended to represent all aspects of the female divine in a specific culture; rather, each offers an illuminating view of a culture's views of the feminine.

Similarly, the chapters exemplify a variety of methods for goddess study, from new translations of liturgical hymns to the living goddess Lakshmi to interpretation of archaeological remains in examination of the related Egyp-tian goddesses Bast, Sekhmet, and Hathor. Among the methods employed by the authors of these chapters are ethnography, textual analysis, and visual reconstruction. Several authors are primarily poets and bring a trained poetic sensibility to the examination of goddesses, such as Greek Helen and Mexican Guadalupe. Others employ a psychological framework, especially relying on archetypal theories articulated by Carl Jung and Toni Wolff in examining the feminine divine. Many of the contributors deliberately select or create cross-disciplinary methods in order to better define and describe their topics. The writers themselves include both women and men from various religious and ethnic backgrounds. Within these volumes are Christians and Mormons, Jews and pagans, women in religious orders and those who follow indigenous religions. Some approach their subjects as devoted followers of the goddess in question, others as disinterested observers, but all employ critical analysis in discussing their subjects.

Volume 1 discusses figures from Asia and Africa. Here several important Hindu divinities are found, including the wealth-goddess Lakshmi and the death-dancer Kali. As well as orthodox Hinduism, this volume includes discussion of goddesses from pre-Hindu traditions, the "village goddesses" known only with a limited geographical area and perceived as protectors of both land and people. In the nearby lands of Tibet and Nepal, female Buddhist figures appear who hold great power, both spiritual and political. Similar imagery is found in China, where the "goddess of mercy" Guanyin melds an indigenous tradition with images from the immigrant Buddhism. In Japan and Korea, contributors describe geographically located goddesses who are seen as embodied in the land itself. In Egypt and Africa scholars attest to important female divinities whose influence continues despite recent attempts to discourage their worship.

Volume 2 discusses goddesses from the eastern Mediterranean and Europe. Goddesses of the Babylonians and the Assyrians, such as Inanna-Ishtar and Nisaba, testify to the power and prestige such deities had among people of the lands that are now Iraq and Iran. Another chapter describes the controversial Asherah, now believed by many scholars of the Old Testament to be an original primary divinity of the Hebrews, consort to Jehovah. That a now-monotheistic religion may have once honored a goddess is unsettling to some believers, but contemporary archaeological evidence points to monotheism as having been created during the Babylonian captivity. Similarly, the figure of Mary Magdalene, either a saint or sinner (or both) in Christian legend, is shown to hold the power of earlier goddesses despite being positioned within a monotheistic religion, while Lilith, "Adam's first wife," shows how female power was demonized with the rise of monotheism. In Europe, despite a common assumption of an overarching "Western way of thinking" that upholds linear and patriarchal values, our authors reveal an ongoing and powerful substrata of goddess worship. Even such an apparently familiar figure as Helen of Troy is revealed to descend from a powerful earth divinity. From the Celtic lands, evidence of several important goddesses appears in iconography and literature, suggesting the power of the feminine in that ancient culture, while in the Germanic culture we find a number of similarly powerful figures including the fate-goddesses called Norns who sit at the foot of the world-tree and control human destiny. In the Alps, place-names and legends hold in memory an ancient goddess of the white peaks, whose worshipers may have included the "Ice Man" found sacrificed on her glaciers.

Volume 3 brings together myths of Australia and the Americas. The volume begins with reflections on goddesses of Australia, including an indigenous figure rarely discussed in scholarly literature and the unnamed goddesses who appear in pre-Aboriginal rock art; these chapters only graze the surface of a rich and complex goddess mythology in the world's most ancient continent. The volume then explores some of the goddesses of North, Central, and South America. These range from White Buffalo Calf Woman, whose myth is today used to inspire a new generation of Lakota with reverence towards living women, to the frightening snake-skirted Aztec goddess Coatlicue, whose visage can be seen in magnificent ancient art. Several chapters reflect the syncretic impulse that led, in Mexico and the Caribbean, to the emergence of figures that include aspects of ancient goddesses under the guise of Christian figures. The volume also includes chapters on contemporary American interpretations of goddess myths: the adoption of Roman Diana as the matron divinity of women's religious groups in America, the self-creation as a goddess of a Wiccan priestess, the creation of a temple to Egyptian Sekhmet on the western American desert. The volume also includes commentary on the use of goddess imagery by contemporary American writers, whose projects of reclamation suggest the importance of the feminine divine to the creative artist.

Were all the world's important goddesses to be discussed in such depth, dozens more volumes would be needed; were we to add the intriguing but lesser-known divinities, the volumes would cover many shelves. Goddesses and goddess-like figures have been known in every culture and every era. Their stories and images offer an immense variety of possibilities for ways to interpret women's realities. They speak both to men and to women about human as well as divine potential. These volumes offer a glimpse of the richness of goddess mythology throughout the world and, it is hoped, will inspire more such efforts as well as more general awareness of the diversity of approaches possible in study of such mythic figures.

1

Jillinya: Great Mother of the Kimberley

Munya Andrews

Long ago in the Kimberley region of northern Australia, there lived a goddess who helped create the first peoples, called the Gwion Gwion, ancestors of the Ngarinyin who revere her as Jillinya or Mumuu, the great mother "who gave women their genitals and the gift of motherhood."[1] Her fecund and procreative powers are still celebrated in art, song, ritual, and dance. Her totemic symbol is that of the *mandzu* (praying mantis) whose insect image adorns caves and other rock art galleries, while all Ngarinyin women remain living manifestations of her deity.

Her cultural and spiritual influences on Ngarinyin people, as among their neighboring tribes the Worora and Wunambul, are profound. Her enduring presence is central to their existence. Like mothers everywhere, Jillinya is primarily responsible for feeding, nurturing, and sustaining her children. Gwion worshiped the great mother and brought *lulwa* (gifts) to honor and appreciate her for supplying her children with *mangarri* (food). She is seen as the female embodiment of the *wunan* ("sharing system": land and all its resources), the cornucopia of life. As one male elder remarked, "She is the greatest mother of all."[2]

Jillinya's Supreme Authority and Her Powers

To make sense of these gendered divisions, writers such as Robert Lawlor and Hannah Rachel Bell explore the Aboriginal cultural and spiritual philosophy known as Dreamtime that explains creation and provides a moral blueprint of life. Those raised in this cultural tradition are immersed in Dreamtime from the moment they are born and continue to learn in staged cycles throughout their lives. This ongoing process of learning and gaining knowledge through periods of initiation is referred to as "going through the law." In this instance, the English term *law* does not refer to legal precedent or the common law system, but to an ordered, cultural, and spiritual existence that is largely predetermined by spiritual and human ancestors during the creative epoch of the Dreaming.

Taking a cosmic view of Dreamtime concepts of the earth as a living being and of gendered polarities, Lawlor draws on these traditions to better understand the "cyclic patterns" that govern human lives. He refers to these binary influences as "cultural oscillations" or alternating cycles flowing throughout history. These cycles, says Lawlor, operate over much larger time frames than commonly understood. Primarily energetic in nature, these cycles relate to and are influenced by other energy cycles that affect humanity such as the earth's magnetic field. Thus, in his view, the "two archetypal polarities, the 'All-Mother' (Universal Feminine) and the 'All-Father' (Universal Masculine) alternate their primary/secondary influence on humanity and nature, reflecting the earth's alternating magnetic polarity."[3]

These alternating cycles have at different times been primary or secondary in their influence. Neither is therefore necessarily "better" or "worse" than the other. Whether or not one accepts Lawlor's understanding of these cycles on a grand planetary scale, the reality of strict gendered division of Aboriginal spiritual organization into what is commonly referred to as "men's and women's business" is unavoidable. The English word *business* in an Aboriginal-English context does not refer to monetary transactions but rather to spiritual matters arising from the Dreamtime.

Focusing on the pragmatic, spiritual, and cultural experiences of Ngarinyin men and women in daily life, Hannah Rachel Bell offers valuable insight into the "two-way thinking" underlying this gendered cultural division. A feminist, she found her political views challenged, then changed, over a twenty-five year involvement with Ngarinyin people. When first introduced to the gendered concept, she "thought it was a quaint but outdated code of conduct for human behaviour." But over time, Bell began to see "a fantastic depth, consistency, and wisdom in this ancient knowledge and its behavioural protocol." What struck her most was the continued emphasis placed on the binary gendered nature of the Ngarinyin universe. She discovered that in Ngarinyin philosophy and cosmology, as in Ngarinyin law, "there are *always* two . . . two moieties [groups], two energies, two genders, two dimensions of existence such as above and below, seen and unseen, action and idea, generative and receptive. Neither division can exist without the other." As in nature, just like the "dual strands of DNA" both "survival and increase are dependent upon their interactivity."[4] The dynamic of relationship holds that neither one is viable without the other, that survival and increase are dependent upon their interactivity, like the strands of DNA whose chemical bonds govern the growth and life of an organism.

Jillinya's Authority over Sacred Sites

However that ongoing theological and political debate is analyzed, there is no question as to Jillinya's authority in regards to specific sacred sites or circumstances. Aboriginal men in this region of Australia (at least those who are initiated and who have gone through "the law") remain fully cognizant and in awe of her primordial powers. It is she whom they invoke in male initiation ceremonies and to whom they offer performance of her ring dance when young novitiates are carried in the arms of older men.

She is seen as the "Big Boss" of winds and can directly influence the weather. Children are warned not to harm or hurt her physical manifestation, the praying mantis, lest they incur her wrath in the form of storms with raging winds or, worse, cyclones. Men are especially mindful that Jillinya can influence or temporarily control their minds "in dramatic and profound ways." Even more danger lurks for the uninitiated man who dares to look directly at her sacred images, the penalty for which includes an inexplicable loss of memory for a few days or so. Above all, Jillinya remains custodian of the Tree of Knowledge and gatekeeper of the *dulwan nimindi mamaa* ("pathway of sacred knowledge"). In this sense, she is regarded as a great spiritual teacher who demands respect. So, when Aboriginal lawmen "talk of Jillinya and her influence today, they always show deep respect for *munumburra* women (law women), who carry their authority from the great mother with great vitality."[5]

Jillinya's Sacred Sites in Wandjina Country

The Wandjina tribes (Ngarinyin, Worora, and Wunambul) are, as Bell points out, unique, not just because they formed a recognized confederacy but because of their cultural identity. What binds them together as one people, says Bell, is their spirituality and law based on the Wandjina "icon or image that repeats itself throughout their country."[6] Although land and sites are shared between the three tribal nations, Ngarinyin country pre-dominantly lies north and west of the Gibb River road that runs between the small townships of Derby and Wyndham. The Worora are largely based along the west coast, while Wunambul country is further inland to the east.

Like all other Dreamtime creators who traversed the land, naming and making life, Jillinya's *wungud* (life essence) lies encoded within the land, wait-ing to be reactivated and "pulled out" by Aboriginal law men and women or the spiritually aware, (i.e., non-Aboriginal people sensitive to the spirits of the land) to gain insight and self-empowerment.[7] Her adventures, exploits and journeys are remembered in story, song and dance. Places she visited and inhabited remain as sacred sites along a vast array or network of "song-lines."[8] As part of communal and women's spiritual business, Jillinya's steps are retraced and recounted in rituals that celebrate her achievements. Her tales are recorded on stone and cave walls that mark her sites. The three best-known locations in the coastal regions are at Alyaguma, Anaut gnarri, and Guringi. At Guringi she is depicted in as praying mantis, at Anaut gnarri in her naked form (which young children are forbidden from viewing) and at Alyaguma as head matriarch Algi where she stamps her authority over the Tree of Life and Knowledge, an image that may sound Christian but is much older.

The Tree of Knowledge and the Sacred Pathway

High above the waterhole at Alyaguma, on the rock wall, are a number of ancient paintings depicting sacred beings and other significant icons. Nowhere is the great mother's presence more palpable or authoritative than at this special place. Here along an east-west axis, Jillinya is depicted both singularly as head matriarch, and as a collective of women, each with indi-vidual names albeit all incarnations of the same goddess. All of the female beings stand upright. Most have raised arms with hands outstretched. Ngari-nyin people interpret these images as saying, "Stop. Do not trespass. Listen to what we have to say."[9] The single large female figure, lying horizontally below the others with her head in the east and her feet pointing to the west, is the matriarch Algi. Like the other women she has her arms raised, with outstretched palms signaling viewers to halt. Unlike the others, she has clearly defined lines radiating out of her body that Ngarinyin say are spears given as gifts to honor Jillinya.

This gift of a weapon, what is now perceived as the domain of men, is not surprising given that many Aboriginal nations across Australia have similar stories of women once possessing hunting weapons, including weapons of warfare. While nowadays hunting and warfare are strictly perceived as men's activities, the old practice of women offering spears to this goddess suggests they may have once possessed these weapons, as the old tales suggest. These strong and imposing icons, says Jeff Doring, attest to the fact that these women "had great authority from the earliest days."[10]

Although Alyaguma is associated with one of the Wandjina beings who passed through this location, the absence of Wandjina paintings suggest that Jillinya's connections are superior and much older. What is more, her depictions alongside the iconic Tree of Life suggest that all knowledge comes through her. Or as the late Ngarinyin elder David Mowaljarlai explains, the spiritual roles of men and women differ, with important consequences for both genders. Because a woman gives life, she is seen as being tied to the land and is therefore sacred, while men do not automatically return to the creator, having a task that is far more onerous and exacting. Unlike women they have "to tend the spiritual aspects and maintain the connection with the cosmic regions where the Law of Creation is manifest." As such, men are "held to ceremony, sacrifices, judging and guidance with the community," says Mowaljarlai. "Without these constant services, a man cannot be assured of his passage through death into a new life cycle. He must earn it."[11]

During her childbearing years, a woman is tied to the cycles of the earth. Her roles are identical with the functions of the earth: life-giving, nurturing, healing, continuing, maintaining, and giving service to living things. For that she is *mahmah* (sacred). When a woman dies, no ceremony is needed. She automatically goes back to the *Wungud* ("life essence"), the snake cycle of life-death-rebirth. The earth is her own womb as she belongs to the snake. The role of man differs. He has to tend the spiritual aspects and maintain the connection with the cosmic regions where the Law of Creation is manifest. He is held to ceremony, sacrifices, judging, and guidance with the community. Without these constant services, a man cannot be assured of his passage through death into a new life cycle. He must earn it.

As with other cultural trees of life such as that in the Jewish esoteric tradition of Kabbalah, the Ngarinyin icon is a spiritual tool that teaches spiritual insight and enlightenment along life's journey. With the use of specific Ngarinyin cultural symbols such as the native plum tree known as *golai* (*Terminalia carpentariae*), the "seed language" that Lawlor discusses provides visual metaphors for teaching young and old alike, while maintaining and preserving culture. "All forms of life spring from a tiny seed," says Lawlor. Therefore it is a perfect symbol of creation and of life. Aboriginal people have drawn parallels between the "seeds' separation and externalization into leaf and root" and that of "the division of mind and body, as well as the separation of the child from the womb of the mother." These parallels reflect the creation process from birth (initiation) through to death (a return to the infinite). From an esoteric viewpoint, "life is a process of dissolving the boundaries of comprehension, the self-centredness of being, the isolation of embodiment, and the fears and neediness of separation."[12]

The Ngarinyin Tree of Life clearly extols these human virtues. The Tree not only reflects these separations of growth as one journeys through life as proscribed by Ngarinyin cultural rules, but it is also viewed as a sacred pathway that has "implications for a personal moral direction," says Doring.[13] The notion of a pathway is clearly posted with the drawing of a footprint at its trunk and, just a little way up the base, a forked branch jutting out from the right side that represents "the wider social identity gained from the Wunan." Its orientation from east to west "matches the actual direction from which the four main groups of people came to the law table at Dudu ngarri to originate Wunan law." The tree diagram is used as an educational tool throughout life. During youth, young initiates climb the tree where it is marked by "a series of small rings connected to the lower trunk." As they progress through subsequent initiations they obtain adult or senior knowledge. This level of spiritual mastery is marked higher up the tree by three long paths that lead to larger rings. Immediately above these large rings is an unusual image of "two straight branches with human feet on their ends" that represent the Gwion ancestors Wodoi and Jungun, who split their society into two groups or moieties (from French meaning "halves"). From this celebrated division marriage laws and other social obligations and responsibilities were proscribed. It is here at this point on the tree that people are introduced to the Ngarinyin binary viewpoint or two-way thinking. From there onwards, a branch growing outwards with leaves ending in forked stems. Says Doring, "Painted lines of vertical rain descend from above the branch, suggesting the arrival of *winjin* [monsoon rains] when lightening triggers the ripe fruit to swell and burst, before cracking open to release new seed."[14] The realistic depiction of the bush plum is essential to survival skills of living in the bush but, as Doring's analysis reveals, its esoteric associations remain fundamental to Ngarinyin wisdom.

Jillinya's guardianship of the Ngarinyin Tree of Life and Sacred Pathway is made abundantly clear at Alyaguma by prolific visual icons. That she is intimately connected to the Wunan system is further emphasized by her looming presence as Algi that directly hovers above a Wunan painting. It may be that the spears covering her reclining body are symbolic of the time and energy sustained in hunting and gathering food to be shared among family and friends.

Wunan: The Sharing Law

Reciprocity and kinship are the principal foundations of the Wunan system that stretches across the northern Kimberley from west to east reaching into the Northern Territory. It governs marriage and skin systems that determine the basis of kin and sharing all of life's resources—land, culture, stories, songs, dances, animals and other objects.[15] Everything is considered part of Wunan. Everyone and everything is related to one another and everyone belongs. No one is left outside the Wunan. As David Mowaljarlai puts it, "Wunan is created from the beginning to share everything in life. It's a total care of life that Wunan." When expressed in visual terms, the Wunan appears as a series of interlocking, interwoven lines that form part of a vast network grid across the land. Many Ngarinyin refer to that picture as an underlying pattern that speaks to them of complex relationships and interconnections. The Wunan also provides "a graphic model for the larger network of Wunan trading routes." Although the system came into being through the actions of the Gwion ancestors Jungun and Wodoi, for whom the binary moiety system is named, Jillinya is regarded as being primarily responsible for providing her children with food. It is she who taught them to share food with one another. It is for this reason the Wunan is depicted under her sacred figure of Algi. There on a white background are red lines that form curved pocket-like pouches joined together much like a patchwork quilt. Here "the abstraction of the social principles of sharing demonstrates the fundamental influence of Jillinya," says Doring.[16]

Mother Mantis

Throughout many world cultures divinities have been depicted in zoomorphic form. In Africa, among the Khoisan or Kalahari Bushmen, the praying mantis is regarded as their supreme creator Kaang.[17] Like Jillinya, he is associated with wind and rain that he controls. One can only wonder at the praying mantis's significance in ancient Egypt, where a mummified body of the insect was found wrapped in cloth in a burial tomb.[18] The insect is mentioned in the Book of the Dead in connection to the "Opening of the Mouth" ritual. Of perhaps more significance is the following statement found on papyrus in the tomb of Seti I: "I have seen my father in his every form—the form of the [drawing of a praying mantis]."[19]

Jillinya's depiction as praying mantis is intriguing given the apparent rarity of this insect in world mythology. What is it about the praying mantis that lends itself to Jillinya being portrayed in this fashion? What does her totemic association with that insect reveal about motherhood and of the goddess? Doring says it is because the praying mantis "releases and stands guard over a multitude of fully formed but miniature offspring" that explains why it is "revered as a natural manifestation of the primordial mother's power and prolific fecundity."[20] The fact that all Ngarinyin women are regarded as earthly manifestations of Jillinya affirms that.

Beyond that immediate observation one may adduce other symbolism drawn from the insect's physical and biological appearances that relate to the Tree of Life. First, its long, thin body is very plant-like. When its color is largely brown, it becomes wooden-like, resembling a dried-out stick. When green, it can camouflage itself among more verdant, luxurious foliage. Its articulated joints resemble branch stems that suggest growth, directions, or pathways. Its bulbous eyes may be likened to the fruit of native plums and, when viewed from the side, give the appearance of seed sprouting new life. The two antennae also suggest two directions or two roads that emphasize the moiety division of Ngarinyin society. Above all, its stillness teaches the importance of listening to nature, of meditating and being open to spiritual messages.

Doring's description of the Gwion Gwion images at the Guringi sanctuary is especially revealing of the metaphoric association between Jillinya and the praying mantis in terms of her shamanic influence on Ngarinyin people. Alongside a painting of the goddess are two black dancing figures wearing huge, triangular-shaped, mud wigs called *mudurra*. The taller dancer's wig has a triangular shape that, to Doring, represents the praying mantis's head complete with "bulbous eyes." Adding to this insect likeness are two feathers or *yululun* extending upwards that represent the insect's antennae. Doring becomes mesmerized as he observes the following:

> The pair of *yululun* sweep away as if swaying in unison to the dancer's movement. This *mandzu mudurra* (praying mantis wig) virtually replaces the human head of the figure as befits a trance dancer revealing Jillinya the great mother herself. Holding two *mandi* (boomerangs) in one hand implies songs associating Jillinya with *mandzu* (praying mantis).[21]

The taller of the two black residual images is a particularly enigmatic mantis-human figure partially submerged beneath layers of surface stains and other superimposed images. This impressive black mandzu dancer has several female features found in Gwion representations of women; rounded legs and thighs and the typical women's *wangarra* (girdle made from fiber or hide string) that hangs to make a long skirt. The most significant feature is the unique triangular mudurra representing the head of the praying mantis. The bulbous eyes of a mantis round out the base of the triangle and a pointed beak shapes the apex of this uniquely formed wig. Also extending upwards from this mandzu mudurra are two very long *yululun* (feathers) representing the two antennae of the living mantis. The pair of yululun sweeps away as if swaying in unison to the dancer's movement. This mandzu mudurra virtually replaces the human head of the figure as befits a trance dancer revealing Jillinya the great mother herself. Holding two *mandi* in one hand implies songs associating Jillinya with *mandzu*.

This observation reveals the role played by Jillinya in ritual and ceremonies of the Gwion Gwion and of the Ngarinyin. Her spiritual presence is without doubt a central component of Ngarinyin practices that speak of altered states and other dimensions. Without her willing participation there can be no access to knowledge and other worlds. One engages the great mother's involvement by honoring her through art, dance, and ritual and bringing gifts to demonstrate that allegiance.

Helen Payne and Lynne Hume have both written of the shamanic powers inherent in Aboriginal ritual, song, and dance. Hume describes the overwhelming sense of timelessness and transformation that these engender: "Dance aids in the transformation of a Dreaming event into a *now* event." Within that process, living descendants become reincarnations of Dreaming ancestors. Powers once possessed by these ancestors are conferred upon singers and dancers. More important, perhaps, is the empowering result of invoking certain deities to draw their strengths by "pulling out" these powers where their essence is saturated. Thus, these rituals, songs and dances "are used to change aspects of women's lives, such as to restore health, engender a sense of well-being, or to change weather conditions."[22]

While Jillinya's deity is specifically cultural to the Wandjina tribes, her spiritual voice and messages have real meaning and purpose for all women everywhere. She teaches human virtues of patience, stillness, and meditation, and of the need to think before acting. She reminds women of their primary duties to motherhood and guarding offspring. As Barbara Walker says, the word *mantos* in Greek, from which the praying mantis derives its name, means "prophet" or "prophetess."[23] Like all goddesses, she imparts wisdom to those who beseech and seek her guidance.

In a land largely dominated by images of male gods, Jillinya holds her own. Like many of the other great earth mothers across northern Australia (Einganna, Gudjeri, Gunabibi, Imberombera, Ungulla, and Waramurrugundji), she remains a "symbol of fertility and creator of life."[24] Her legacy lives on in the Kimberley where she continues to affect the minds of men (and women), to influence the weather, to provide food, to steer and guide people on life's pathway. Little wonder David Mowaljarlai proclaimed with unabashed pride: "Jillinya. She was the *biggest* woman in this coastline!"[25]

Notes

1. Jeff Doring, ed., *Gwion Gwion* (Köhn: Könemann Verlaggesellschaft, 2000), 65.

2. Ibid., 37, 45, 54.

3. Robert Lawlor, *Voices of the First Day: Awakening in the Aboriginal Dreamtime* (Rochester, VT: Inner Traditions, 1991), 92.

4. Hannah Rachel Bell, *Men's Business, Women's Business: The Spiritual Role of Gender in the World's Oldest Culture* (Rochester, VT: Inner Traditions, 1998), 121–128.

5. Doring, *Gwion Gwion*, 66, 73.

6. Bell, *Men's Business, Women's Business,* 18.

7. Lynne Hume, *Ancestral Power* (Carlton: Melbourne University Press, 2002), 42.

8. The English term "songlines" was popularized in Bruce Chatwin's book of the same name. It refers to the cultural practice of Aboriginal people "singing" the land or country as part of their spiritual duties that include cultural maintenance and transmission of rituals and stories about ancestral creator beings. These songs "travel" across tribal territories in grid-like patterns that unite different tribes who share in that mythology, hence the reference to song lines.

9. Doring, *Gwion Gwion,* 42.

10. Ibid., 65.

11. David Mowarljarlai and Jutta Malnic, *Yorro Yorro: Aboriginal Creation and the Renewal of Nature* (Rochester, VT: Inner Traditions, 1993), 144.

12. Lawlor, *Voices of the First Day,* 154.

13. Doring, *Gwion Gwion,* 26.

14. Ibid., 316.

15. *Skin* is another of those English words that have an entirely different meaning within an Aboriginal-English context. It translates as "skin" from various indigenous terms that refer to the division of Aboriginal society into moieties (halves)

and then into further divisions of 4, 8, 16 and 32 or more groups within the one culture. Membership of these groups determines social and classificatory kinship. It determines who can marry whom and other social obligations and responsibilities.

16. Doring, *Gwion Gwion*, 59, 73.

17. Roy Willis, ed., *World Mythology* (New York: Duncan Baird, 1993), 31.

18. Gene Kritsky and Ron Cherry, *Insect Mythology* (Lincoln, NE: Writers Club Press, 2000), 57.

19. Linda Evans, "The Praying Mantis in Ancient Egypt," *Bulletin of the Australian Centre for Egyptology* 15 (2004): 10.

20. Doring, *Gwion Gwion,* 69.

21. Ibid.

22. Hume, *Ancestral Power,* 41, 42.

23. Barbara Walker, *Women's Encyclopedia of Myths and Secrets* (New York: HarperCollins, 1983), 173, 417.

24. Jennifer Isaacs, ed., *Australian Dreaming: 40,000 Years of Aboriginal History* (Sydney: Lansdowne Press, 1980), 58.

25. Doring, *Gwion Gwion,* 46.

Bibliography

Bell, Hannah Rachel. *Men's Business, Women's Business: The Spiritual Role of Gender in the World's Oldest Culture.* Rochester, VT: Inner Traditions, 1998.

Berndt, Ronald, and Catherine Berndt. *The Speaking Land: Myth and Story in Aboriginal Australia.* Australia: Penguin Books, Australia, 1977.

Berndt, Ronald, and Catherine Berndt. *The World of the First Australians.* Canberra: Aboriginal Studies Press, Canberra, 1977.

Chatwin, Bruce. *Songlines.* London: Jonathon Cape, 1987.

Doring, Jeff, ed. *Gwion Gwion.* Köhn: Könemann Verlaggesellschaft, 2000.

Evans, Linda. "The Praying Mantis in Ancient Egypt." *Bulletin of the Australian Centre for Egyptology* 15 (2004): 7–18.

Hume, Lynne. *Ancestral Power, the Dreaming, Consciousness, and Aboriginal Australians.* Carlton: Melbourne University Press, 2002.

Isaacs, Jennifer, ed. *Australian Dreaming: 40,000 Years of Aboriginal History.* Sydney: Lansdowne Press, 1980.

Kritsky, Gene, and Ron Cherry. *Insect Mythology.* Lincoln, NE: Writers Club Press, 2000.

Lawlor, Robert. *Voices of the First Day: Awakening in the Aboriginal Dreamtime.* Rochester, VT: Inner Traditions, 1991.

Mowaljarlai, David, and Jutta Malnic. *Yorro Yorro: Aboriginal Creation and the Renewal of Nature.* Rochester, VT: Inner Traditions, 1993.

Payne, Helen. "The Presence of the Possessed: A Parameter in the Performance Practice of the Music of Australian Aboriginal Women." In *Rediscovering the Muses: Women's Musical Traditions,* ed. K. Marshall. Boston: Northeastern University Press, 1993.

Walker, Barbara. *The Women's Encyclopedia of Myths and Secrets.* New York: HarperCollins, 1983.

Willis, Roy, ed. *World Mythology.* New York: Duncan Baird, 1993.

2

Rock Goddesses: Australia's First Creator Beings

Margaret Grove

Think of Australia, a vast continent floating in the swirling convergence of the Indian and Pacific oceans, spanning the equatorial hot zone of Papua New Guinea on one edge and the freezing Antarctic shelf on the other. Australia is a primordial continent that surfaced over 4.5 billion years ago. Formed by upthrusts from the deep, hot, turbulent vents in the ocean, the continent was shaped by these violent ocean waters. The shores off the northern coast flanking the Arafur Sea are the habitat of giant crocodiles, deadly sea snakes, and miles and miles of stinging jelly-fish. Where the Arafur Sea merges with the Timor Trough, chaotic ocean activity marks the separation of plant and animal life between Asia and Australia. This transition point in the ocean, which severs traditional species from each other only to encourage new and unusual variations, is known as the Wallacea line, after the 19th-century naturalist Alfred Russel Wallace. Because of Australia's location, this continent has an unusual array of life forms, unlike any other part of the world.

Early migration by humans occurred under the most difficult of circum-stances. Because of changing ocean levels and hard-to-negotiate currents, no other outsiders were able to repeat this migration until recently. This splendid isolation allowed not only the development of animals found nowhere else in the world, it also allowed the human migrants to remain separate from the rest of the world and to develop a unique religious belief

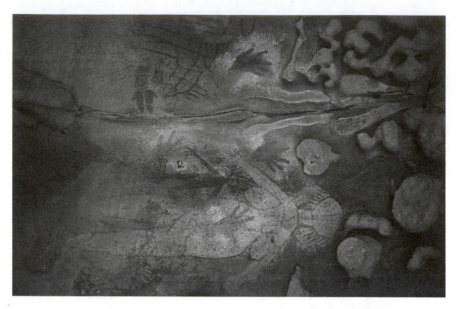

Figure 2.1 Australia is the world's most ancient continent. Early people there emblazoned rocks with goddess figures, such as the Deighton Lady, that are still kept as sacred by aboriginal people today. (Photograph © Margaret Grove. Reprinted with permission.)

system, known as the Dreamtime, which flourishes all over Australia to this day. This principle holds that life forms and topographical features are manifestations of ancestral beings who were present during the creation era and who remain active today. The Dreamtime beings traveled across the turbulent oceans on rays of the rising sun, creating the land formations as they traveled.

Indigenous people remember and pass on their history and the laws set forth in the Dreamtime to future generations in two ways: by oral stories and by marking important locales with engravings or paintings. The rocks record the activities of the creator beings. Many of the paintings honor the women who were once goddesses and are now spirits in the rocks. They are considered to be the rock goddesses of the creation era.

The Creator Beings of Australia

Rocks, gullies, hills, and rivers did not exist in Australia until the arrival of the Dreamtime beings. Significant features in the landscape began to appear as these creators traveled across the continent, inscribing the once-flat land with their activities. Aboriginal storytellers know that, for those who listen closely, the rocks, hills, caves, and other landscape features exhale and give away their secrets. They release ancient memories of the travels of the first creators and of the ancestor beings who followed. The divine women who created the original landscape and those women who followed, including all who today create land formations, are part of the Dreamtime. They have left their distinctive imprint on the land.

In southern and central Australia, the vestiges of ancestral travels across the land are referred to as songlines, for the creator beings sang the landscape into its present configuration as they traveled. In northern Australia the patterns in the landscape are created by footprints or body impressions that creator beings left in their trek across the country. These prints have become known as the Dreamtime Tracks.

The oral portion of the creation story is still sung and chanted today and recalled in spoken and murmured mythology. Australia is not just a flat blank canvas, as it was prior to the initial creation period. It has become a rocky shore with undulating interior landmasses rift by rivers and valleys, caves and shelters, hills and mountains. The ravines and upthrusts are layered with life and with art. Perhaps most important for those interested in ancient belief systems, Australia is covered with painted remembrances, depicting prehistoric events, plants, animals, and beings.

Portraits in the Rocks

Aboriginal people keep the Dreamtime stories alive by adding mineral pigments to the surface of the continent's primeval rocks. The paintings mark the spot where a creator being resides for eternity or where she traveled during the creation era. Australian scholar George Chaloupka notes that these creator beings "sat down at the localities where their last acts took place or returned to one or other of the sites which mark their journey. Here they now remain as a living essence."[1] The creator and ancestor beings take on defined visual aspects when Aboriginal artists paint the rocks with images, applying naturally occurring minerals found on the land, such as ochre, manganese, and carbonate. These paintings, placed where the creator beings entered the rocks, are portraits of the spiritual beings who continue to exist. In many instances, the portraits contain the essence or spirit of the rock goddesses of Australia.

The intense, incandescent power of those who created this land is tapped by the Aboriginal people if, first, they find the likeness of the spirit where she entered the rock, and then, second, if they rub the rock. These activities are considered a way to release the essence of the sacred being. Rubbing the paintings increases the species of plant, animal, or insect painted at that particular location. Touching marks or making paintings where the ancestor being resides provides contact with the power of the spirit. Aboriginal elder Bill Harney says, "We didn't paint the rocks to start with—all the paintings are just the many animals who put themselves into the rock in the Dreaming times, the Buwarraja, and today we just touch the painting up every now and again to keep them going."[2]

The First Rock Goddess

The first female creator being, Warramurrunggundji, came to this continent from far away, traveling across the sea on the rays of the setting sun. The late Big Bill Neidjie, Aboriginal elder and spokesperson, recorded the origin of Warramurrunggundji across the waters.

> This story is one of the Women, from Macassa I think,
> Her name . . . Warramurrunggundji,
> So that story . . . [sh]e came from the sea.
> Came up Mali Bay, north from here.[3]

She created children in her own likeness and carried them in her dilly bag (a bag woven of natural fibers). From the dilly bag, a metaphoric uterus, the goddess was able to place children across the northern landscape. She created the landscape, she created the children, and then she decided where they were to grow up and what languages they would speak. She also planted the yams they would eat.

Warramurrunggundji is visible today as the first of the rock goddesses of Australia. Rock paintings in the Aboriginal reserve of Arnhem Land along the northern coast of Australia show her likeness. One depicts a pregnant woman carrying a digging stick, with a dilly bag hanging from her head. Another shows a female figure with fifteen dilly bags hanging from her head ring. Aboriginal experts have identified both of these paintings as portraits of Warramurrunggundji.

Baldwin Spencer, a pioneering anthropologist who spent time in Arnhem Land in the early 1900s, recorded that Warramurrunggundji

> was recognized as the creator of all the people in the Alligator Rivers region and responsible for many features of the present landscape, which she then populated with animals and planted with vegetable foods. Although at a later period there were other mythical characters

who took part in the continuing creation process, they were said to have derived all their powers from (her) and were guided by her in everything they did.[4]

Fertility is essential in the lives of the creator beings and in the lives of Aboriginal people. In fact, the concept of a fertility mother is widely distributed over the Australian continent. The sacred uterus of the first female and her act of creation are symbolically incorporated into almost every human ritual, particularly in Arnhem Land where Warramurrunggundji began her creative activities. The sacred objects used in these rituals often refer to the reproductive parts of the female body. The venerated dilly bag that Warramurrunggundji wears is often used in ritual or depicted by artists with lengths of feathered string hanging from it, representing either the rays of the sun on which Warramurrunggundji traveled across the ocean or the umbilical cord that provides sustenance to a fetus. Ronald Berndt, who with his wife Catherine Berndt spent half a century living and studying with the Aboriginal people, notes that men hold small woven dilly bags in their clenched teeth during certain rituals because they and their ancestors emerged from the uteri that the bags symbolize.[5]

The ubiquitous digging stick is also sacrosanct. Rock paintings clearly show it as an object carried by Warramurrunggundji, and the digging stick also is evident in many mythological references regarding fertility. The oral stories say that the digging stick, plunged into the ground, could bring forth water, a metaphorical reference to the act of having coitus. Frequently, in Aboriginal lore and in Aboriginal ritual, a digging stick is used as an equivalent to the male reproductive organ. Bodies of water or wells and indentations containing water are references to the female reproductive system.

During the Dreaming period, a grasshopper named Yamidj, who represents the quest for abundance, accompanied a group of women as they traveled across the land planting yams for food. The women were searching for the most fertile ground in which to plant their yams. It is in the context of the images of the digging stick and the water gushing forth from where the digging stick is plunged that the reference to intercourse and the ensuing abundance it brings to the Aboriginal people appears:

The circular stone arrangements . . . represent the last holes Yamidj dug with her digging stick . . . it was at this place . . . that some of the women accompanying Yamidj menstruated. Their menstrual blood seeped deep into the ground, and this now is the source of a highly valued red ochre.[6]

Aborginal women today carry digging sticks, implements useful for living on the land, for planting and foraging for food. These wooden poles, fashioned from tree limbs, represent survival to the Aboriginal people.

The Second Generation of Goddesses

Warramurrunggundji is followed by other women created in her likeness. These ancient culture heroines, the first female ancestors, still exist in the ongoing, ever-unfolding Dreamtime activities. They continue to form features of the landscape, which gives the land a powerful ontological resonance with the Aboriginal people and sets the foundation for an earth-based religion. The existence of these culture heroines also imbues the people with a spiritual life based on the body of the female and her reproductive abilities.

During Warramurrunggundji's journeys across the land, she gives birth to children who formed the Aboriginal clans. Her daughter and granddaughters then initiate more creative acts that accentuate the reproductive power of the female. These second- and third-generation female ancestors continue Warramurrunggundji's initial quest to shape the landscape and bring fertility and abundance to the Aboriginal people. These goddesses—the Kunapipi Mother and her daughters, the Wawalag sisters, as well as the Djanggawul sisters—are all invoked during ritual. They, along with the Rainbow Serpent, are the basis of the Aboriginal religion along the northern shores of Australia. Over fifty years ago an Australian anthropologist observed how intense the relationship was between the Kunapipi Mother and the Aboriginal people and how fully they used her likeness in their rituals. His records of this relationship showed the Kunapipi Mother to be like the Rainbow Serpent who has been a source of spirituality for over 6000 years.

She was the source of life in humans and nature both in the Dreamtime or creative past and now. In this activity, she was associated with a great serpent, usually the Rainbow Serpent, who "made the road" into the womb for the pre-existent spirits to be incarnated and reincarnated. She was also the very earth itself, that from which living things came and on which they depended for sustenance. This doctrine was expressed in the Kunapipi ritual.[7]

Complete ceremonies are built around the concept of the female as an extraordinary essential being in the Aboriginal quest to continue the cyclical wonders of the universe. Remembrances of these culture heroines' travels, representations of their *maarien* or sacred objects, invocations of them through songs and chants commemorating them, and the inclusion and replication of their awe-inspiring reproductive capabilities in ritual grounds or sacred earth sites reveal these females as the pinnacle in Aboriginal spirituality.

Like Warramurrunggundji and her dilly bag, the Kunapipi mother has a sacred object: the *ubar*, a long wooden log or gong, also considered the uterus of the mother. This gong is played at the beginning of the *ubar* ritual to call the mother into consciousness and then is constantly sounded by musicians with flat sticks made from the center rib of the pandanas palm frond. Should the sound stop, it means that the mother's spirit has departed. The Berndts note that the *ubar* can be considered a representation of the Rainbow Serpent and, at the same time, the mother. The ritual ground where the *ubar* is played can also be considered a representation of the uterus. A triangle-shaped trench is carved out of the earth to represent the pubic area of the female. A metaphoric uterus is then formed from which the ritual participants emerge. Men "coming onto the ground are re-enacting their original spiritual conception and birth from the Mother."[8]

In keeping with the doctrine of Kunapipi being essential in the "coming and going of the seasons, the appearance and disappearance of vegetable and plant matter, and the propagation of other natural species," Berndt continues this explanation, centering the concept of fertility with the importance of these cultural heroines: "a natural development has been the stress on procreation—the importance of pregnancy and childbirth, and the essential sequence of sexual intercourse and conception, expressed particularly in ritual and long song cycles."[9]

The Deighton River Goddesses

The mythology of the Kunapipi mother eventually became integrated with that of her daughters, the Wawalag sisters.[10] The images of the mother and her two daughters can be seen painted in earth-toned ochre pigments in a spectacular rock shelter along a steep river canyon in Queensland.[11] The major figure is recognized in anthropological terminology as the Deighton Lady, her name derived from the Deighton River Valley where she is located.

Percy Trezise, who discovered this painting, considered the major female figure to represent Wongabel, the first beehive, for she wears the branching headdress that symbolizes the original honey tree.[12] Mary Haginikitas mentions that Percy Trezise felt Wongabel "alluded to the feminine in its aspect of honey, sweetness, and light."[13] She was one of the first goddesses associated with the nourishment of the clans. Others say the grouping of three women at this site, one large and two small, may be the Palpalpi sisters, a pair of ancestral beings. The Kunapipi mother and her daughters, or the Palpalpi sisters or Wongabel, are fully realized as rock goddesses at this extraordinary site.

These female ancestor beings have selected a very special rock shelter in which to retire for eternity. This shelter is delineated by a background of most unusual natural shapes. The contours have been created through the eons by the action of rainwater dripping down the limestone cave wall. The undulating rock formation running along the side of the mother and her daughters appears to reference the external genitalia of the female. An outline of a human hand has been placed over the uterus of this larger figure, indicating the power within this part of the female body, according to local Aboriginal people. The shimmering white pigment surrounding the hand was blown onto the rock by the artist who understood the spirituality of this place and created these startling depictions of myth. Blown handprints impart the artist's spirit into the rock in order to meld with the goddesses already living there.

Under one arm of the mother is an outline in vivid red ochre of the younger Wawalag sister. To her left is the older Wawalag sister. One of their dogs accompanies them. Complex religious and fertility concepts behind the Wawalag sisters and their interactions with the Rainbow Serpent are seen in this ancient oral tradition:

> The elder Sister gave birth to a child, and the afterbirth blood or menstrual blood attracted the attention of a great python which lived in the waterhole. . . . The sisters realized that something was wrong. "Oh, elder sister, a snake! Quick, let's go!" . . . They crouched in the hut by the fire while the rain poured down outside, taking it in turns to dance and call ritually in an effort to drive away the storm. . . . Then they sang Kunapipi songs, and the storm died down, but he was there, waiting. . . . He raised himself up, standing erect, then lowered himself again. His head went into the hut; he wrapped his body around it, around the molg, the banagaga (two words for the sacred mound used in ritual). Then he swallowed them. . . . But an ant bit him; he jumped and vomited them all.[14]

Several versions of the myth stress the importance of the sister's blood reaching the waterhole of the Rainbow Serpent and the awakening that occurred when he smelled the blood. Some versions of the myth have the second sister beginning her blood flow in synchronicity with her elder sister's. Judy Grahn has called the consciousness that arises from the realization of the power of menstrual blood "metaformic theory." Blood synchrony between women, their seclusion rites, the rhythms of the female body with the lunar cycles, all allowed for this consciousness. The resulting parallel consciousness of males in learning the patterns of the "menstrual mind" lead them to go "one further step, and mirror it back to the females: an ongoing dance of mind between the genders."[15] Ritual arose, with the males re-enacting the biological powers of the female.

Astonishing images of the Wawalag sisters have also been discovered in Arnhem Land, correlating with the myth of the sisters painted on the rock in the Queensland shelter. These very specific anatomical paintings in brilliant red ochre and white dolomite depict menstrual blood flowing into the waterhole of the sleeping Rainbow Serpent, a particular and detailed rendering of the Wawalag mythology.[16]

The Djanggawul sisters, granddaughters of Warramurrunggundji, daughters of Kunapipi and sisters of the Wawalag, also became holders of the quest for fertility and creation. These sisters are also known as "Mother Goddesses in the true sense of the term, for although they were allegedly instrumental in populating the greater part of eastern Arnhem Land, they are responsible also for all subsequent fertility."[17] Their sacred emblems continue to be metaphors for the female body and her reproductive capabilities. One such object is the *ngainmara,* a round plaited mat shaped like a shallow stone rising to a peak in the center. Bordered with a fringe, this additional accoutrement represents the Djanggawul sisters' pubic hair.

Contemporary Aboriginal Women and Ancient String Games

Women as well as men dance in the Kunapipi rituals. Women often hold a long piece of string in their hands, moving it to the pulse of the drums and chants. This activity commemorates the string games performed by young girls who have just reached puberty. In mythoreligious song cycles, string weaving suggests female puberty and menarche; the string may represent the umbilical cord and the rays of the setting sun on Warramurrunggundji's original journey. Male dancers often wear decorated woven dilly bags around their necks in honor of the essence of the original mother. Rock-art paintings throughout the area of Arnhem Land and also the Upper Yule River show numerous examples of women holding string during dance rituals, invoking a woman's ability to add to the continuity of the clan.

Women participating in ritual in recent times have become part of the rock goddess tradition of the past. Instead of having their individual and clan markings painted on their bodies in the pictographs of the region, contemporary Aboriginal women in ritual are now adorned across their actual physical bodies with the same ancient symbols seen on the paintings of women in the rocks. These symbols, representative of women of a certain age and of definite importance, reference the Rainbow Serpent, the grasshopper, the praying mantis, and other creatures imbued with fertility and the power to give birth. Women carry creation stories on their bodies.

Rock painting in this area generally ceased approximately forty years ago. Ritual painting on bodies still continues today. Both types of painting, on the rocks of the past and in the rituals of the present, document the story of women of power. Ancient goddesses painted on the rocks are depicted as holding ritual dilly bags in which they carried the children who were to populate their world. They also are painted carrying strings above their heads, known as talking strings, which hold the stories of the clans. Today, women still dance in ritual with their strings held high over their head. They still carry dilly bags. These living goddesses hold their string accessories and move their painted bodies in ritual, honoring the long line of women before them, portraying the stories of their lives. When men cut the fringe of their sacred dilly bags or perform ritual, they are called the "sons of the Djanggawul"; when they enter the sacred ground, marked out in a special way, they are returning to their mothers' uteri; when they enter the sacred hut on the ritual ground, they are also returning to their mothers' uteri.[18]

Women and children place themselves under the *ngainmara* mats during ritual, emerging from them as though coming from the womb. Berndt shows the similarity of the Djanggawul sisters with their Kunapipi mother and with their grandmother Warramurrunggundji by saying, "This concept of people flowing from the Mothers' uteri is used in western-central Northern Territory in reference to the Kunapipi Mother, who is also said to 'let postulants out from her womb during ceremonial time.'"[19]

These various icons—the *ngainmara* mat, the strings for dance and weaving—plus other sacred objects such as *rangga* poles, relate to fertility. Aboriginal people describe the sisters walking across northern Australia using *rangga* poles to help them navigate difficult rock formations. In ritual, the *rangga* poles "are kept hidden within the *ngainmara*, and removed from time to time for drying, thus symbolizing coitus. . . . Or the *mauwulan* (a type of *rangga* pole or digging stick) is plunged into the earth so that water gushes forth at its removal: this is compared to coitus."[20] This moves a full circle from grandmother to granddaughters, from ancient mythology to contemporary ritual.

The Dating Game

How old are these rock goddesses? As noted in the beginning, spoken and sung mythological evidence has been carried on since the beginning of human life in Australia. Aboriginal people, carried across the sea in the uterus of

Warramurrunggundji, were given the gift of language and the chanting of myths began. When Warramurrunggundji and her offspring retired into the earth, their images appeared and have been retouched and painted ever since. Warramurrunggundji and the Kunapipi mother inhabit the same myths as the Rainbow Serpent. They mimic mythic activities in order to form the landscape. And they exhibit the same zigzag, rhomboid, and circular body patterns as each other, archetypal shapes that are said to imitate the shimmer of the snake's skin or the eggs of the serpent. The related myths of Warramurrunggundji and the Rainbow Serpent have been in existence for at least six millennia.

In western Arnhem Land, where Warramurrunggundji first came ashore, rock shelters have been explored and pieces of ochre have been found in occupation levels dating to 50,000 to 60,000 years ago. Was her image painted on the rocks that long ago? A mineral-stained grindstone was found in one of these same sites in an archaeological level dating to 18,000 years ago. Perhaps the ochre ground on that red-stained grindstone during that time was used to paint her reflection onto rock.

The oldest archaeological evidence to date for an actual rock painting comes from the Carpenter Gap shelter in the Kimberley region. A slab of limestone that formed the roof of the shelter collapsed 39,700 years ago. It had been coated with bits of red ochre pigment and represents the oldest trace of rock art presently known. Red paint also shows up under the organic oxalates that formed a crust in a cave in Cape York. Here the earliest layer of red pigment dates to an antiquity of over 28,000 years before present time. Was the myth of the Wawalag sisters present at that time and were their images seared into the rock inside this cave at Cape York? It is impossible to know.[21]

Scientific dating shows that during the Late Holocene period, approximately 3000–4000 years ago, geological deposits containing salt-like substances of oxalic acid formed on the floor of the Deighton River site. Before that crust percolated into being, Aboriginal artists had pecked nonfigurative engravings on the shelter floor. Although this does not give the actual age of the Kunapipi mother/Wawalag sisters painting, it does show that there was human activity in this location at least three millennia ago. In this region alone, excavations have shown occupation by Aboriginal people from approximately 34,000 years ago until today. However, the inclusion of the dog or dingo figure in the Kunapipi/Wawalag panel would set the maximum date of the creation of these images at approximately 3000 years ago, the probable date for the arrival of the dingo in Australia, assuming the panel was painted all at one time.

Understanding the antiquity of these rock paintings offers one criteria for understanding the enormously long-lived Aboriginal spirituality based on the female. The songs and paintings surrounding these myths still take place today, thus elongating the spiritual tradition of the Aboriginal people. Although most rock-art painting in the traditional sense has ceased since the 1970s, in the world of the contemporary Aboriginal artist, images of the Rainbow Serpent and of the creator beings are still continuously painted, now on more portable backgrounds such as paper, wood, or canvas.

Culture Heroines and Increase Rituals

There area the four major religious patterns of Australia: the fertility cults of Arnhem Land; the religious complex of the desert, which pertains to the songlines of the ancestor beings; the magic of the mythical beings in the *bora* complex of southeast Australia, a *bora* consisting of rocks placed on the ground as a ceremonial demarcation; and the ancestral-mythic cults of Queensland.[22] All these religious belief systems hold in prime regard the mythological travels, creation stories, and the fertile essence of the creator beings. In both Aboriginal mythology and Aboriginal spirituality, increase is vital. In fact, many rites and rituals are called "increase rituals." Among certain clans, "the increase of the various valuable animal and plant species and the maintenance of the regular operation of various natural phenomena like the sun, moon, stars, wind and rain, is assured" by "retouching the paintings in the various Wondjina [creative ancestor beings] galleries, where large groups of mythic beings" have retreated into the rock and left their images.[23]

In Australia, males and females both have roles in the mythology of creation. Yet it is the female of the species who is the embodiment of increase and fertility and who holds the cycles of life within her body. It is the female who is considered the essential creator and the culture heroine. She has brought life and consciousness into this world. She permeates Aboriginal religion, and aboriginal religion replicates her. As Warramurrunggundji, Kunapipi, the Wawalag sisters, and the Djanggawul sisters, she marries the spiritual importance of the land with the fertility of the clan.[24] And she is fully celebrated in paintings of the rock goddesses of Australia.

Notes

1. George Chaloupka, *Journey in Time* (Chatswood, NSW: Reed Press, 1993), 45.
2. Bill Y. Harney and J. Yositsky, *Born under the Paperbark Tree: A Man's Life* (Sydney: ABC Books, 1996), 85.
3. Bill Neidjie, *Story about Feeling*, ed. K. Taylor (Broom, Western Australia: Magabala Books, 1989), 2.

4. Chaloupka, *Journey in Time*, 46.

5. Ronald M. Berndt, *Australian Aboriginal Religion*, Fascicle Four (Leiden: E. J. Brill 1974), 50.

6. Chaloupka, *Journey in Time,* 83–84.

7. L. R. Hiatt, introduction to Ronald Berndt, *Kunapipi: A Study of an Australian Aboriginal Religious Cult* (Melbourne: F. W. Cheshire, 1951), xvii.

8. Ronald Berndt and Catherine Berndt, *The World of the First Australians* (Canberra: Aboriginal Studies Press, 1996), 279.

9. Berndt, *Kunapipi,* 7.

10. A. P. Elkin, *The Australian Aborigines* (reprint; Sydney: Angus and Robertson, 1956), 215–216.

11. Copyright photograph taken of the Deighton Lady by Margaret Grove in the Deighton River Valley, Queensland, Australia, 1995.

12. For other interpretations of the Kunapipi myth, see Percy Trezise, *Dream Road: A Journey of Discovery* (Sydney: Allen and Unwin, 1994).

13. Mary Haginikitas, personal communication (e-mail), August 3, 2009.

14. Berndt and Berndt, *The World of the First Australians,* 255.

15. Judy Grahn, *Blood, Bread, and Roses* (Boston: Beacon Press, 1993), 9–23.

16. For a deeper development of the Wawalag sisters myth, including documentation of pictographs depicting the myth, see Margaret Grove, *An Iconographic and Mythological Convergence: Gender Motifs in Northern Australian Aboriginal Rock Art* (Ann Arbor: UMI Press, 1999).

17. Ronald Berndt, *Djanggawaul* (Melbourne: F. W. Cheshire, 1952), 10.

18. Ibid.

19. Ibid.

20. Ibid.

21. For an extensive explanation of dating techniques and ancient findings throughout Australia, see Michael J. Morwood, *Visions from the Past: The Archaeology of Australian Aboriginal Art* (Crows Nest, NSW: Allen and Unwin, 2002).

22. John Mulvaney and Johan Kamminga, *Prehistory of Australia* (Sydney: Allen and Unwin, 1999), 25; Berndt, *Australian Aboriginal Religion*, 22.

23. Quote from A. P. Elkin, in Berndt and Berndt, *The World of the First Australians,* 271.

24. For a deeper understanding of the Aboriginal relationship to landscape features and religion, including the concept behind ritual ground formations which duplicate the female reproductive system, see Margaret Grove, "Woman, Man, Land: An Example from Arnhem Land, North Australia," in *Before Farming,* ed. P. S. C. Taçon et al. (Liverpool: Western Academic and Specialist Press, 2003).

Bibliography

Berndt, Ronald M. *Australian Aboriginal Religion*. Leiden: E. J. Brill, 1974.
Berndt, Ronald M. *Djanggawaul*. Melbourne: F. W. Cheshire, 1952.

Berndt, Ronald M. *Kunapipi: A Study of an Australian Aboriginal Religious Cult.* Melbourne: F. W. Cheshire, 1951.

Berndt, Ronald M., and Catherine Berndt. *The World of the First Australians.* Reprint. Canberra: Aboriginal Studies Press, 1996.

Chaloupka, George. *Journey in Time.* Chatswood, NSW: Reed Press, 1993.

Elkin, A. P. *The Australian Aborigines.* Reprint. Sydney: Angus and Robertson, 1956.

Grahn, Judith. *Blood, Bread, and Roses.* Boston: Beacon Press, 1993.

Grove, Margaret. *An Iconographic and Mythological Convergence: Gender Motifs in Northern Australian Aboriginal Rock Art.* Ann Arbor: UMI Press, 1999.

Grove, Margaret. "Woman, Man, Land: An Example from Arnhem Land, North Australia." In *Before Farming,* ed. P. S. C. Taçon et al. Liverpool: Western Academic and Specialist Press, 2003.

Harney, Bill Y., and J. Yositsky. *Born under the Paperbark Tree: A Man's Life.* Crows Nest, NSW: ABC Books, 1996.

Morwood, Michael J. *Visions from the Past: The Archaeology of Australian Aboriginal Art.* Crows Nest, NSW: Allen and Unwin, 2002.

Mulvaney, John, and Johan Kamminga. *Prehistory of Australia.* Sydney: Allen and Unwin, 1999.

Neidjie, Bill. *Story about Feeling.* Edited by K. Taylor. Broom, Western Australia: Magabala Books, 1989.

Tresize, Percy. *The Dreamtime.* New South Wales: Allen and Unwin, 1993.

3

The Native American Earth Mother: From the Inuit to the Inca

Jordan Paper

In virtually all traditions, save the interrelated monotheistic ones, Earth is sacred. Indeed, in Christianity, the earth as Hell is the locus of evil, and only the sky or Heaven is considered the abode of the holy. It is there that the female sacred being, Mary, is to be found. In other traditions, Earth is usually understood as a female cosmic deity in a complementary relationship with male Sky. From the conjoining of the two comes the creation of all beings, for humans have always understood that creation requires the combining of opposing sexual energies. Where creation is understood to arise from a single primordial deity, aside from the Abrahamic traditions, that deity is always female, as only females give birth and nurture the newborn. Frequently Earth is portrayed as a beautiful woman, while Sky is depicted symbolically, such as zigzag lines indicative of lightning. Human females are understood to be coterminous with Earth, for they too birth and nurture.

Throughout the history of Chinese civilization until a century ago, for example, only the emperor and his consort, as the chief priests of Chinese society, could sacrifice to Sky and Earth, as they were the most powerful deities. In a 17th-century Chinese anti-Christian tract, objection was made with regard to the Christian missionaries criticizing the sacrifice to Earth. So this difference between Christian and non-Christian religions was noted long ago.[1]

Outside of China with its long continuous written history, the understanding of Earth as a deity has in large part been lost, particularly in traditions that have been overwhelmed by monotheistic Christianity and Islam. But in Native American traditions, many of which survived Christian persecution and are presently undergoing revitalization, the hermeneutics of Earth in her various manifestations is still present. These understandings can help articulate how Earth was understood in the distant past.

It should be noted that in the long denial of Native American religions, even as ubiquitous a concept as the Earth Mother has been denied. One well-known scholar of Native religious traditions argued that the Native American understanding of the Earth Mother was recent and primarily due to Euroamerican influence.[2] The presumption that Native peoples learned about the Earth Mother from Christian culture is mindboggling. Yet that understanding has become general. As shall be discussed in the following, the concept of the Earth Mother came with the people who populated the Americas and has remained with the indigenous peoples here to the present day.

The Manifestations of the Earth Mother

Until the development of urban habitations, humans literally lived on the earth: walking and sitting directly on her, sleeping on her under bark or skin tents and on earthen floor lodges. And all that provided nourishment either walked on her, slid through her, grew on her, flew low over her, or swam through her blood, the waters. Typical of polytheistic cultures where deities can be found in several manifestations, in Native American traditions Earth can be understood as incarnated in those animals on which humans depend or the garden as the major source of food.[3] The following are but some of the many forms in which the Earth Mother is perceived.

Earth Spirit in the Arctic and Subarctic

Throughout the world, there are many myths of hunted animals being released from the bowels of the earth. Often a culture hero brings forth the animals from a cave, for it is Earth who produces the animals. For the Chugach Alutiiq (Sugpiaq) of southwestern Alaska, she is known as *numamshua*, the Earth Spirit. She is a woman who can appear to humans wearing a coat from which hang miniatures of all the terrestrial animals, similar to the amulets worn by the Chugach on their own coats. For the Copper and Netsilik Inuit of northern Canada, the Earth Spirit warns against working with soil and stones during the season when the migrating caribou herds pass by, lest the hunters fail to obtain caribou, the essential feature of their diet. The Iglulik Inuit have a similar myth in which a person made a hole in the ground from which the caribou emerged.

The coastal Inuit are a maritime people, who often understand the sea to be the equivalent of Earth, while terrestrial cultures understand lakes and rivers to be the blood of Earth. For maritime gathering-hunting traditions, the major source of food, especially throughout the long winter, are sea mammals. Thus, the Sea Mother is the equivalent of and functions as the Earth Mother. Hence, the Chugach reverence not only the Earth Spirit but the Sea Spirit as well. To her they pray for a successful maritime hunt. Sometimes, she too is seen wearing a coat with the maritime animals hanging from it. She may take off some of these animals and give it to the person who perceives her for success in hunting. Others have seen her transform into a sea otter.

Among some Siberian Inuit, she is known as the Big Woman, and sacrifices are offered to her. Among the Inuit of North America's far north, she is called the One Who is Wife by the Mackenzie Inuit, the Sea Mother by the Copper Inuit, or the One Below by the Netsilik. The latter is a circumlocution, since for many Native American traditions, out of awe and respect, the deity is never directly named. The Inuit in eastern Greenland refer to her directly as the Sea Mother. She controls both sea and earth and all of the animals. Major ceremonies are directed toward her. She also determines the winter weather; that is, whether the weather will be amenable to kayak hunting.

Often she is perceived in form as half-human and half-seal, the major hunted maritime mammal. In this mode she is often known as Sedna ("the One Down There"). When the ice conditions are not right for seal hunting or the seals do not come to the hunters, it is assumed that someone in the community has transgressed the customs of the seal-hunting season. During a shamanistic ceremony, the offender is found out and confesses. The shaman in trance will then descend under the sea to her. There he first wrestles Sedna and then placates her by combing her hair; because she has flippers, Sedna cannot do it herself. Once Sedna is placated, the seals return to be hunted and feed the people.[4]

Earth as Bear Mother

From the earliest times, humans have had not only an ecological relationship with bears but a spiritual one as well. There is clear evidence in

European caves of rituals directed toward Bear over 15,000 years ago. A specific sacrificial ritual toward Bear can be found throughout the circumpolar regions.[5] In Native North American traditions Bear is understood in two different gender-determined aspects. Particularly in the Plains, the now-extinct Plains grizzly was known for its ferocity. Bear, in his male aspect, was accordingly sought for warrior power. Throughout the continent, however, the black bear is understood as a female spirit of fertility and healing.

As humans migrated around the continent, they noted the habits of the omnivorous black bears, who are similar to humans in many regards. Humans observed what they ate, for then they could eat the same food without concern. They noted what plants and minerals the bears ate when they were sick and thus were guided to healing herbs and other substances. Most important, they saw female bears emerge from their winter dens in the earth with new life, their cubs. Bear came to be understood as a theriomorphic manifestation of Earth herself and spiritually the most powerful of the animals. Those who have Bear power from a special relationship with Bear have warrior power and/or healing power. For the Anishnaabe, Bear symbolizes the Earth Mother when young women merge with her during the menarche ritual.[6]

White Bison (Buffalo) Woman

The Lakota were originally a horticulture-hunting tradition located in present-day Minnesota. The intertribal wars for a trading monopoly with Europeans due to the fur trade pushed the Lakota onto the Plains, where they adapted to the horse introduced by the Spanish. The horse allowed them to live on the Plains year round, following and hunting the bison during their slow seasonal migration. The bison became their major source of subsistence. From them they received not only food, but hides for teepee covers and blankets, bones for tools, sinew for sewing, and so forth. From the bison, they also received spiritual power. For warriors, the strong male Bison provided warrior power. More important, Bison as their source of life took on the role of the Garden Mother, from when they were horticultural. Female Bison became a manifestation of the Earth Mother, a relationship that can be seen visually as bison are prone to roll in the prairie dust and cover themselves with earth.

The most important tribal sacred bundle of the Lakota contains a pipe given them by White Bison Woman. This myth is best known through the recorded narration of Nicholas Black Elk.[7] The following synopsis leaves off the Christian aspects—Black Elk was both a Lakota holy man and a Catholic catechist—which conflated "White Buffalo Calf Woman" with aspects of the Virgin Mary.[8]

A Lakota warrior is traveling on the plains and has a vision of a woman dressed in a whitened-skin dress (usually reserved for ceremonies) rising from a bison dust wallow. Carrying on her back a ritual bundle, she asks to be taken to his village. There she gives directions for forming a ceremonial teepee and then proceeds to reveal the contents of the bundle with its myths and songs. She passes on to the community the sacred pipe within the bundle with teachings on the ritual for smoking it. She then walks away from the community sequentially turning into bison of four colors (representing the sacred Four Directions—the entirety of the earth) as she recedes into the distance.

The Garden Mother

For horticulturists, the Earth Mother is often approached from her functional role as the Garden Mother. For many traditions this understanding has been lost as horticultural traditions tended to be Christianized earlier than gathering-hunting ones. Until the last half of the 20th century, many cultures in the Amazon region remained free from Christian missionaries until logging, mining, and other industries destroyed the forests and opened roads. But the understanding of the Garden Mother still remained inaccessible until female ethnologists took the religious lives of the women seriously.

The Aguaruna are a Jivaroan-speaking people living at the western end of the Amazon rainforest in northeastern Peru. In these cultures, men are commonly hunters and warriors, and women are horticulturists. The two most important deities are similarly divided by gender, as women relate to Nugkui, the Earth, while males relate to Etsa, the Sun. Nugkui lives in the soil and in caves, and she controls the garden plants. Women pray to her in gardening rituals, when making pottery, and when caring for domestic animals.

Men's hunting rituals are paralleled by women's horticultural rituals. As animals are spirits, so too are the plants; both are understood to have similar feelings as humans. Sometimes the largest plant in the garden is understood to be Mother Manioc (*mama dukuji*), who walks about the garden. Sacred songs are sung to the plant spirits day and night during the most vulnerable time of the manioc plant's life cycle, the first three to six months.

A second type of horticultural ritual involves the use of sacred stones, often red, that are acquired through visions and dreams and passed on matrilineally. Many of these visions involve Nugkui informing women where a stone will be found. The stones are used in planting rituals, together with pods of the red-staining achiote and other plants. On arriving at the garden, the women crush an achiote pod and paint red lines on their cheeks, those of their children and anyone else with them. This is to let the stone and the manioc plants recognize them as friends. The stones are placed in a bowl with mashed achiote pods, other special plants, and water, creating a red liquid. This liquid, referred to as "blood," is poured on the root cuttings to be planted and on the hands of the women. This is an explicit paralleling between the blood of hunting and raiding and the "blood" involved in manioc gardening.[9]

Imaging the Earth Mother

Save for Judaism and Islam, human cultures have a propensity to create visual images of their deities. These may be used as a focus for rituals and for concentrating one's thoughts on the deity. Thus, the Earth Mother's image is ubiquitous in most cultures. In Christian cultures, there is a tendency for the Earth Mother to be hidden within the image of another deity or other sacred concept, such as the Black Madonna in Europe. Two interrelated images that are found over much of the globe go back to the earliest human cultures. Their interpretation is controversial in that not all scholars agree on the same meaning, but for the Native American religious traditions, major elements of which continue into the present from the distant past, general meanings appear more certain.[10]

In European caves with engraved or painted images from the Paleolithic period, a common design motif is an upside-down triangle, often with interior lines. Few would doubt that these represent the human vulvae, although the interpretation of their purpose varies. Similar images are found in Asian and African caves. They are mainly found in caves simply because images engraved or drawn elsewhere are less likely to have survived the elements after many thousands of years.

These images are also found throughout the Americas. A few meters from Bear Creek in northeastern Iowa—an area famous for large "effigy mounds" or mounds in the shape of animals—there is a vagina-shaped cave with sandstone walls. It is just tall enough to walk in without stooping, just wide enough to walk through without touching the walls, save where it tapers at the end, and just long enough to lie down and be sheltered from the elements. Each of the walls is inscribed over and over again with the same symbol, and there is no other design. The image consists of two vertical ellipses with a straight vertical line in between.

In Anishnaabe pictographs, that sign signifies Earth, pronounced *aki* in at least one dialect. Adding the suffix *tun* ("motion") to *aki* to form *akitun* ("a moving Earth) signifies "woman." In other words, Earth and human women are virtually one and the same. The only difference is that Earth is still and human women move. According to an Anishnaabe male elder from a Minnesota community not far from the cave, during the menarche ritual young women painted this image on rock faces with their own menstrual blood.

Archeologists have found a village site near the above cave that was inhabited a couple of centuries ago. There can be little doubt that the cave was used in lieu of a menarche hut. There the young women sat on the earthen floor, their fresh menstrual blood seeping into the earthen floor and bonding them to Earth, as they heard the flow of her blood, the waters of Bear Creek, outside the cave. Each pubescent girl scratched the vulva image on the cave wall to memorialize her becoming a woman; that is, becoming one with the Earth Mother.

In another shallower cave close by, along with the vulva images, bear paws are incised on the walls. If one sits on the natural shelf at the rear of the cave and outstretches one's arms, each hand will fit into a bear paw. In this cave, not only do the images link Earth and Bear, but make explicit the meaning of the ritual called "Becoming a Bear" (see below).

Beautiful Woman

In some versions of the Anishnaabe myth cycle of the culture hero, Nanabush is the child of West Wind, the most powerful of the Four Winds, and Winona, a beautiful human woman closely linked to Earth. Winona dies in childbirth, and her son Nanabush is raised by his grandmother, Nokomis, closely linked to Moon. Culture heroes tend to be universally understood as the child of a sacred spirit who impregnates a human woman, such as Hercules in Hellenic culture and the Lord of Grain in early Chinese culture. Imaging the Earth Mother as a beautiful woman, particularly in her fertility aspect, is universal, just as in her capacity as a healer she is often imaged, as by the Maya, as a crone.

Just north of Lake Ontario, there is a very large flat rock on which has been pecked many images, now called the Peterborough Petroglyphs. Included among these images are those of the vulva made by forming an oblong around a small vertical cleft in the rock face. The largest figure is of a woman with prominent breasts formed around a large cleft in the rock face serving as the vagina of the figure. In the spring, the sound of water can be heard from this cleft as the high water flows through the interior of the rock. For those who wish to interpret the Earth Mother as a monotheistic deity, it should be understood that many deities and semi-deities are pecked into the rock face, including a human-like male with an erect penis. Other images are those of Turtle, another female deity, and Nanabush in his most common theriomorphic form, that of a hare.

An archeological artifact frequently found in the Andes, particularly from the Inca (the last major culture), is a small image of a young woman cast from silver or an amalgam of copper, silver, and gold. The image generally has straight legs, arms with the hands clenched and touching each other under slight female breasts, an obvious vulva, and straight hair that is combed down from a part in the middle. When found *in situ*—in burial bundles or as an offering—she is fully dressed in tiny, beautiful robes of woven llama wool. Remarkably, exactly the same image of the same general size made of pottery is common in Valdivia culture sites of the same region of Ecuador dating from 5000 to 4000 years ago. This is perhaps the longest continuing specific religious image in the human experience.

Andean peoples have made offerings to the mothers of subsistence: Potato Mother, Corn Mother, and especially Pachamama ("Earth Mother") from the early archeological sites to the present day. In Incan times, offerings were miniature replicas of the food: potato for the Potato Mother, an ear of corn for the Corn Mother, and so forth. What image was offered to Pachamama? The only image not otherwise accounted for is of the lovely woman; hence, by elimination, she must be the Earth Mother. These small sculptures of a woman, made differently with the common feature being the clenched hands touching under the breasts, have been found elsewhere in the Americas, including those of stone in Mesoamerica, clay in the Great Lakes area, and of walrus ivory in Alaska, as well as many other places in the world. One can assume, at least for the Americas, the image represents the Earth Mother; Chinese archeologists assume the same for similar early images found in northern China.

Becoming the Earth Mother

The Christian doctrine of original sin determined that women were the source of human evil. This understanding when applied to female physiology meant that menstruation came to be considered unclean and shameful, to be either hidden or ignored. Native American rituals regarding menarche and menstruation, particularly the sequestering of females, came to be understood as confirming that women were considered dirty and impure. Nothing could be further from reality.

In Native American traditions, menstruating women isolate themselves to varying degrees, usually for four days, because it is understood that at the time of flowing blood women are particularly sacred (and, as Native traditionalist women have said, it gives them a monthly four-day vacation). Since sacredness is coterminous with spiritual power, women's power at this time could overwhelm male power, which would be detrimental to all. It is at menarche, at the first menses, that female spiritual power is considered particularly dangerous, because the young women have not yet learned how to control and utilize it. Hence, pubescent girls fast at menarche to gain spirit helpers and to learn to control their spiritual power. It also was a time when they bonded to Earth and Moon.

Becoming a Bear

In some Anishnaabe traditions, the menarche ritual is called "Becoming a Bear." In traditional times, and where it is possible to maintain the tradition in a rural setting today, when a girl feels the onset of puberty with the first flow of blood, she immediately leaves the village and sets off for a prearranged place in the woods. There she waits for the elder women of the village to come to her. When the girl is nowhere to be found, it will be understood what is happening. Her mother, an aunt, or a grandmother will seek her out and help build a small wigwam—the traditional living structure in gathering-hunting times—exactly as built for the isolated vision quest fasts by males and for the Spirit ("sweat") Lodge. In urban areas, she may retreat to a prearranged room of the house or apartment. There she will fast alone for four days, with no water, food, or sleep, awaiting the vision that will create a relationship with a spirit that will be of utmost importance to her for the rest of her life.

At this time, she will also receive visits from female elders who will instruct her regarding her becoming a woman, as well as providing guidance regarding her visions. At a distance from the fast lodge, her brothers will stand guard so those who do not respect the traditions will not bother her. At this time, she bonds with Earth as her blood seeps into the earthen floor of the fast lodge. She becomes for the time of the fast the female Bear, a manifestation of the Earth Mother, due to her increased spiritual power.

The Sunset Dance

The most elaborate menarche rituals are found among the Athapaskan-speaking Dené and Diné. The Dené live in present-day Yukon and

Northwest Territories, and aspects of the menarche ritual can continue for a full year. Rather than speak of individual spirits with regard to the spirit realm, they speak of Power in general, and men understand women to be spiritually more powerful than themselves.

The Dené were the last to migrate from northeastern Asia to the Americas, and some later moved south to as far as present-day New Mexico and Arizona, arriving about 500 years ago. The Pueblo people there successfully revolted against the Spanish colonists in 1680, but in 1696 the Spanish retook the area. Many fled and joined the Diné (the Southeast dialectical version of Dené). Intermarriage took place, and there was a fusion of the traditions. One group of Diné, the Navajo, became semi-sedentary and took up horticulture and sheep raising. Another group, the Apache (including the Chiricahua, Jicarilla, and Mescalero), continued a foraging-raiding lifestyle.

Fusing the Dené focus on female spiritual power with the matrilineal, matrilocal, and matrifocal Pueblo elaborate ceremonialism, with masked dancers embodying the deities, the Diné created powerful menarche rituals. In these rituals, the girl becoming a young woman does not just merge with or embody the Earth Mother as among the Anishnaabe, but for a short period of time she *is* Changing Woman / White Shell Woman, the Earth Mother, and has the power to heal. The menarche rituals do not take place during the first menses, in that they require considerable time for preparation, as well as time to accumulate the necessary wealth to pay for ritual specialists, the feasts, and gifts for all who honor the young woman by coming to the ceremony.

The Navajo version is called Kinaaldá, part of the great Blessingway, the Navajo ceremonial that celebrates creation and life.[11] The Navajo female puberty ceremony involves four days of public ritual, followed by a further four days of private teachings and rituals. This is the most important ceremony of these cultures. No man who has taken part can possibly disrespect a woman who has undergone these rituals, and no girl who has endured the ceremony can ever lose her empowerment in being a woman. For during the time of the ceremony, the young woman becomes a deity.

The Apache maintained a nomadic lifestyle until the late 19th century; a Chiricahua band was the last Native American group forced onto reservations when Geronimo surrendered in 1886. The men raided into Mexico well into the 20th century. They remain a matrifocal tradition, whose single major ceremony is the one that celebrates a girl's menarche. For it is this ritual that brings the presence of the Earth Mother, called Changing Woman (known as White Shell Woman / White Clay Woman in some Apache traditions), into the community to heal the sick and renew social harmony. Often called the Sunset Dance, it has different names among the Apache tribes, such as *Na'ii'ees* ("preparing her").

Two elders are asked to lead the ritual: a woman, who dresses, leads, and sings over the girl, called "she who makes the sound," and a man who sings the public songs and supervises the construction of the Gowa'a. The Gowa'a is a ritual structure of four poles tied at the top, each leg aligned with one of the Four Directions, to which eagle feathers and other sacred objects are attached, creating a sacred space. In choosing elders to lead the ritual, a woman who learned the ritual directly from Moon or had a vision of Changing Woman is preferred, as is a man who sang for women-to-be who subsequently led a good life. A third ritual leader arranges for the Ga'an, the masked dancers who assume the power of the Mountain Spirits, to take part. A fourth participant to support the pubescent girl is a friend who has already completed the ceremony. This friend supports the girl by dancing with her and encouraging her as she carries out the arduous tasks.

The Na'ii'ees takes place over four days, with four further days of private reflection for the girl-changed-into-woman. The following description is but a brief outline and generalized from several sources and several of the Apache traditions. It is intended to present the spirit of the ceremony only. What happens on which day is not fixed and can vary among the Apache tribes.

The ceremony begins with a Spirit Lodge for the male ritualists, the raising of the Gowa'a, and the making of the ritual items for the girl. These include a scratching stick, as the girl is not to touch herself with her fingernails during the eight days, and a reed drinking tube, from which the girl will drink for the eight days. Both of these ritual paraphernalia survived the migration from the Northwest to the Southwest. On the evening of the first day, the ritual items are brought to the girl, prayers are sung, and she is instructed on their use.

Before sunrise on the second day, the female singer places pollen on the girl as a blessing and prays for her. She arranges the girl's hair and dresses her. The girl, who has now become Changing Woman, faces the rising sun, for Sun is the husband of Changing Woman. The men sing the songs of Changing Woman, and she begins to dance facing the sun. Often she dances with the friend mentioned above and dances for several hours to four sets of four songs. She must not show any signs of fatigue, for she is becoming an Apache woman. Any deviation from proper form will lead to correction by the singer or any of the women present. She can then sit or kneel on a deerskin placed over several blankets, but she will sway with hand movements to the continuing songs. After several more hours, she lays down on the deerskin and is "molded," as was Changing Woman, into the proper shape, while further sets of songs are chanted.

A prepared sacred cane has been placed to the east, and after the molding she races to it and back; running is a common means for eliciting trance among Native traditions in the Southwest. The cane is then moved to each of the other four directions. After each set of races, the canes are moved further and further away. Young boys and old men run behind her, praying for long life and good health, but she must stay ahead of them. Those who tire of chasing her are replaced by others, but she must continually run.

At the end of the runs, gifts for the crowd are poured from baskets over her, while all rush in to grab them. Food has been placed along the ground of the run toward the east which is eaten by the crowd while she continues to dance in place, although the young woman fasts for the four days of the ritual. Then while she is dancing, the singer and all attending one by one bless her with pollen and pray over her. While they are praying for her, the pubescent girl as Changing Woman is healing them, while all the time dancing in place.

Toward evening a fire is lit in a traditional way in the Gowa'a, which will be kept burning through the remaining days of the ceremony. When the sun sets, the Ga'an arrive with the sound of a bullroarer, frightening away all negative energy. The Ga'an are treated in a most reverential manner as they embody, although do not actually become, the Mountain Spirits. They dance around the fire in the Gowa'a four times. During the dancing, men beat the rhythm on rawhide skins as is done on the Plains or with pottery water drums as used in the Pueblos. Later people retire to their campsites where they engage in social dancing, gambling, and otherwise having a good time.

Before dawn of the third day, the singer mixes a white clay paint, praying all the while. At sunrise Changing Woman will again be found dancing facing the sun. The Ga'an reappear, banishing all negativity, and dance facing her. Everyone lines up to bless the Ga'an with pollen and be healed by them in turn. When the Ga'an feel all have been purified, the painting begins.

The paint is thickly applied all over the girl by the singers and the Ga'an. The girl then walks through the crowd carrying the bowl of paint while the male singer dabs and sprays it on everyone. When the paint is used up, the onlookers line up behind Changing Woman, the Ga'an, the sponsor, and the singers, and all dance through each of the four doorways, the sacred directions, of the Gowa'a. The final act is for Changing Woman to throw the blankets on which she lay toward each of the four directions. The onlookers then return to their campsites for more dancing and fun. On the fourth day, Changing Woman, the Earth Mother, remains available for all those who need healing; this concludes the ceremony.

For those women who have undergone the ceremony, it remains the most important and empowering event of their lives. The ritual not only benefits the young women and their families but the entire community. It is the occasion for the appearance of the Earth Mother and the Ga'an, for the community to come into contact with the deities and be blessed and healed by them. It is also a means for the continuation of tradition and for the community to reaffirm its solidarity in the presence of the sacred.[12]

An Earth Mother Creation Story

Most Native American traditions do not have creation stories per se, but virtually all have origin stories. Often these are migration or emergence from the earth myths. One of the most accessible of the few creation stories is found within the Navajo Blessingway.

In this myth, the Earth Mother is found in two aspects. One is White Shell Woman, whose name refers to the substance of the earth as well as to the vagina, whose shape is echoed in such shells as the cowrie, which is sacred in many cultures around the world. The second is Changing Woman, referring to the changing seasons of Earth and the changing aspects of woman from child (spring) to young, fertile woman (summer), to mature woman (autumn), to an old woman (winter), and back again to a child (spring).[13] Thus, Changing Woman represents the aspect of Earth in its cosmic relationship to Sky/ Sun and the ongoing cycle of the seasons; White Shell Woman represents the material aspect of Earth. Together as the Earth Mother they give birth to humans and nourish them with the animals that surround her and the plants that grow on her. The following is but a brief synopsis of a rich and beautiful story:

Long ago, when the spirits were emerging from the different realms, Talking God and Growling God instructed some spirits to place two figurines, of turquoise and white shell, together with yellow and white ears of corn on a buckskin and cover them with another buckskin. While the spirits sang a sacred song, the deities lifted one end of the buckskin cover so Wind could enter. On the fourth entry of wind, the turquoise and shell figurines were transformed into Changing Woman and White Shell Woman, respectively, while the corn was transformed into White Corn Boy and Yellow Corn Girl.

After four days, White Shell Woman impregnated by a waterfall gave birth to Born for Water, and Changing Woman impregnated by Sun's rays gave birth to Monster Slayer. The twins—for many elders consider Changing Woman and White Shell Woman, both being the Earth Mother, to be one—instructed by Spider Woman and armed by Sun, kill many dangerous monsters.

Following these events, Sun returns, wanting to marry Changing Woman and have a home in the West. Sun claims that their son, Monster Slayer, promised her to him, but she refuses. Only she can promise herself; only she can speak for herself; only she can decide what she will do.

Sun pleads that he is lonely and that male and female belong together. She replies that she wants him to build her a house in the west as nice as his in the east. She wants it built out on the water, so that when the Earth Surface People (humans) are created, they will not bother her with their petty quarreling. She wants the house surrounded by many types of gems so she can live in beauty. She wants the animals hunted by humans around so she will not be lonely while Sun makes his daily journey across the sky. He asks why he should give her all of this. She tells him he is male and she female. He is of the sky, and she is of the earth. He is constant in his brightness, and she changes with the seasons. He constantly moves across the sky, and she must remain solid and unmoving. Most important, she is to give her body to him, endure the trouble of pregnancy and the pain of birth, nurture the child and raise him to serve the people, and what will he do in return?

Sun agrees. On the fourth day of their journey westward, on top of a sacred mountain, Changing Woman lies down facing west. Her body is massaged and her limbs stretched. Thus, human girls are massaged during the menarche ritual; their bodies are molded into the perfect shape of Changing Woman.

White Shell Woman is now lonely. Talking God returns, and she asks him if he is lonely. He is not, as he lives with other deities elsewhere. But White Shell Woman, being Earth, cannot leave and join them. Talking God tells her to wait four days. He then comes back with Growling God, Changing Woman, and other Holy People. They are carrying sacred items and two ears of corn: white and yellow. After a complex ritual, the ears of corn are placed between sacred buckskins and Wind enters. Wind gives life to the ears of corn; the white ear becoming a human man, and the yellow ear a human woman. These are the five-fingered Earth Surface People. White Shell Woman happily leads them to her home, and she is no longer lonely. The other deities return to their homes.[14]

The Apache have similar myths, although they are not as available fully articulated as they are in the Navajo songs. In these myths, White Painted Woman appears as another variation of the Earth Mother. She is the basis for the white clay with which the pubescent girl is painted in the Apache menarche ritual.

A Final Note

It should not be understood from the above that only women in Native American religious traditions spiritually relate to the Earth Mother. In all the traditions discussed above, males and females ritually interact with her, but only women, because of their physiology, are one with her. In the common pan-Indian ritual of the sacred pipe, for example, tobacco smoke is offered to the Four Directions, Sky, and Earth. This pipe itself is sacred because the bowl symbolizes the Earth Mother, while the stem that is inserted into the bowl part during ceremonies symbolizes the entry of the male into the female. Whenever offerings are made to Sky, they are equally made to Earth, and vice versa, regardless of whether the one making the offering is female or male.[15]

Notes

1. Jordan Paper, *The Spirits Are Drunk: Comparative Approaches to Chinese Religion* (Albany: SUNY Press, 1995).

2. See Sam D. Gill, *Mother Earth: An American Story* (Chicago: University of Chicago Press, 1987), and the critique by Jordan Paper, "Review of Sam D. Gill, *Mother Earth: An American Story*," in *Studies in Religion* 17 (1988): 488–489.

3. For an introduction to polytheistic theology, see Jordan Paper, *The Deities Are Many: A Polytheistic Theology* (Albany: SUNY Press, 2005).

4. For an excellent summary of the ethnological material, as well as an interesting analysis, see Daniel Merkur, *Powers Which We Do Not Know: The Gods and Spirits of the Inuit* (Moscow: University of Idaho Press, 1991).

5. A. Irving Hallowell, "Bear Ceremonialism in the Northern Hemisphere," *American Anthropologist* 28 (1926): 1–175.

6. For more on Bear, see Jordan Paper "Bear" in *Wo(men) and Bears: The Gifts of Nature, Culture and Gender Revisited*, ed. Kaarina Kailo (Toronto: Innana Press, 2008), 235–241.

7. Joseph E. Brown, *The Sacred Pipe: Black Elk's Account of the Seven Rites of the Oglala Sioux* (1953; New York: Penguin Books, 1971).

8. Clyde Holler, *Black Elk's Religion: The Sun Dance and Lakota Catholicism* (Syracuse, NY: Syracuse University Press, 1995.)

9. This understanding was extracted from Michael E. Brown, *Tsuwa's Gift: Magic and Meaning in Amazonian Society* (Washington, DC: Smithsonian Institution Press, 1985); for an analysis, see Jordan Paper, *Through the Earth Darkly: Female Spirituality in Comparative Perspective* (New York: Continuum, 1997).

10. See Paper, *Through the Earth Darkly*, for a more detailed description.

11. Charlotte Johnson Frisbie, *Kinaaldá: A Study of the Navajo Girl's Puberty Ceremony* (Middletown, CT: Wesleyan Press, 1967; Leland C. Wyman, *Blessingway* (Tucson: University of Arizona Press, 1987).

12. Jordan Paper, *Native American Religious Traditions: Dancing for Life* (Westport, CT: Praeger, 2007) for a fuller version.

13. Wyman, *Blessingway*, 32.

14. Paul G. Zolbrod, *Diné Bahane: The Navajo Creation Story* (Albuquerque: University of New Mexico Press, 1984), for the complete myth.

15. Jordan Paper, *Offering Smoke: The Sacred Pipe and Native American Religion* (Moscow: University of Idaho Press, 1988).

Bibliography

Brown, Joseph E. *The Sacred Pipe: Balck Elk's Account of the Seven Rites of the Oglala Sioux.* New York: Penguin Books, 1971.

Brown, Michael E. *Tsuwa's Gift: Magic and Meaning in Amazonian Society.* Washington, DC: Smithsonian Institution Press, 1985.

Frisbie, Charlotte Johnson. *Kinaaldá: A Study of the Navajo Girl's Puberty Ceremony.* Middletown, CT: Wesleyan Press, 1967.

Gill, Sam D. *Mother Earth: An American Story.* Chicago: University of Chicago Press, 1987.

Hallowell, A. Irving. "Bear Ceremonialism in the Northern Hemisphere." *American Anthropologist* 28 (1926): 1–175.

Holler, Clyde. *Black Elk's Religion: The Sun Dance and Lakota Catholicism.* Syracuse, NY: Syracuse University Press, 1995.

Merkur, Daniel. *Powers Which We Do Not Know: The Gods and Spirits of the Inuit.* Moscow: University of Idaho Press, 1991.

Paper, Jordan. "Bear." In *Wo(men) and Bears: The Gifts of Nature, Culture and Gender Revisited*, ed. Kaarina Kailo, 235–241. Toronto: Innana Press, 2008.

Paper, Jordan. *The Deities Are Many: A Polytheistic Theology.* Albany: SUNY Press, 2005.

Paper, Jordan. *Native American Religious Traditions: Dancing for Life.* Westport, CT: Praeger, 2007.

Paper, Jordan. *Offering Smoke: The Sacred Pipe and Native American Religion.* Moscow: University of Idaho Press, 1988.

Paper, Jordan. "Review of Sam D. Gill, *Mother Earth: An American Story.*" *Studies in Religion* 17 (1988): 488–489.

Paper, Jordan. *The Spirits Are Drunk: Comparative Approaches to Chinese Religion.* Albany: SUNY Press, 1995.

Paper, Jordan. *Through the Earth Darkly: Female Spirituality in Comparative Perspective.* New York: Continuum, 1997.

Wyman, Leland C. *Blessingway.* Tucson: University of Arizona Press, 1987.

Zolbrod, Paul G. *Diné Bahane: The Navajo Creation Story.* Albuquerque: University of New Mexico Press, 1984.

4

Mother and Origin: Female Divinity in South America

Max Dashu

First there was the sea. All was dark. There was no sun, no moon, nor people, animals or plants. Only the sea was everywhere. The sea was the Mother. She was water and water in every direction and she was river, pool, waterfall and sea and so she was everywhere. So, at the beginning, only the Mother was. She was named Gaulchováng.[1]

So say the matrilineal Kogi people of the Santa Marta mountains of Colombia. Descendants of the rich Tairona civilization, they base their cosmology on a primordial Mother Essence from whom everything originates, in darkness and deep awareness. She is the unborn and eternal source. She is the Mother of Songs. "The Mother was not human, or nothing, or anything. She was aluna. She was the spirit of what was to come and she was thought and memory. So the Mother existed only in alúna, in the lowest world, in the ultimate depths, alone."[2]

The Kogi say that the power of *alúna* exists in everything and gives rise to all that exists. After long ages, the Mother brought the first world into being. Lands began to form above in the darkness, and in successive worlds, spirit people without bones, then people with limbs and heads and blood. In the fifth world, the Mother commanded that the

Figure 4.1 Sinú women facing the four directions, ceramic vessel from the great mound temple at Betancí, Colombia. Dated before 1000 CE. (© 2005 Max Dashu.)

ancestral beings speak. In the ninth world, the ancestral pair found a great tree and heavens above the waters and built a great house there.[3]

The Kogi (or Kágaba) say that their ceremonial "house of the sun" is like this first house, circular with a womblike opening in the roof. They call it *cansamaría* ("house of [the virgin] Mary"), although they never converted to Catholicism. Another account says that the Kogi "believe that the world was created by the great mother Gauteovan who created the sun from her own menstrual blood, and who is also the origin of everything else in the world."[4]

On the Guajira peninsula, the matrilineal Wayúu say that Night was the Great Mother, and heaven's Light the Great Father. Each had twins: his were Sun and Moon; hers were Earth and Sea. Sun fertilized Sea, and her son Rain fertilized Earth, from whom all the spirits, plants, animals, and humans came forth. The Wayúu speak of her as "the great mother Mma, the earth."[5] Renilda Martinez explains, "Wayúu elders tell us that we are children of Juya (rain) and Mma (Earth) and that the trees, mountains and animals are our relatives. We conceive of the earth as a fountain of sustenance. She is the creator of life."[6]

In the Isthmus region of Colombia, Dabeiba was the primary deity, a storm goddess and culture-giver. A river and the country Dabeiba were named after her. People made pilgrimages to the "house of Dabeiba," a temple full of gold and precious stones, said to be guarded by a puma.[7] Like other Spanish missionaries, Petrus Martyr fixated on a masculine creator, but admitted, "They believe that Dabeiba, the divinity universally venerated in the country, is the mother of this creator." He noted that he was much less worshiped than she was.[8] Modern Catío people described Dabeiba as a beautiful woman who in the beginning taught the people agriculture, how to weave baskets, mats, and firefans; how to make pots, to body-paint and dye their teeth black. Then she ascended back to the sky. She brings storms and earthquakes.[9]

The Chibcha revered an ancestral goddess Bachué ("big-breasted"), also called Fura-Choguá ("good woman"). Soon after light appeared and the world came into being, she emerged from a mountain lake, carrying a three-year-old child. Bachué made her home in Iguaque and raised her son there. After he matured, she married him and bore four to six children at each birth. Their descendants populated the earth. She taught her people how to live: agriculture, arts, and ceremonies.

After a long time, Bachué and her consort left Iguaque, calling the people to follow them to their mountain lake. There, "she made a speech exhorting the people to live in peace and conservation, to keep the laws and precepts she had given, which were not few, especially in the matter of the divine rites." Then Bachué and her consort turned themselves into huge snakes and returned to the sacred lake. But people said that she appeared again in many places. The snake spirits of the sacred lakes belonged to her veneration. All the Chibcha worshiped her, especially in agricultural ceremonies, and made images of her and her son. The only other offering to Bachué was resinous incense burned at sacred springs.[10]

The Chibcha also revered the moon goddess Chía. Her temple in Cundinamarca was an important religious center.[11] Chía was also known as Huitaca, who challenged the patriarchal prophet Bochica when he established institutions favoring men: "The goddess Huitaca appeared in this new situation that gave men more power, a beautiful woman of great resplendence who preached her rebellion against patriarchy and the necessity of a broad life, open, full of games, pleasure and drunkenness." Bochica turned her into an owl, or alternatively, threw her into the sky where she became the moon.[12]

Another Chibchan-speaking people, the Kuna of Panama, speak of the Great Mother Nana Dumat as the "Path on which we have come." Her partner Baba helped her in the creation, and they form a divine unity. Nana Dumat gives birth to all life. The Nila, three beautiful women who descended from the sky, were prophets who brought culture to the Kuna.[13]

In Brazil, the Paressí creation story begins with the stone woman Maisö, who existed before earth and water and light. By placing a piece of wood in her vagina, she caused the muddy Cuyaba River to flow forth, followed by the clear waters of the Paressí. Then Maisö created the earth by putting land in the water. She gave birth to many stone people. Among them were Daru-kavaitere and Uarahiulu, who procreated the sun, moon, and stars and placed them in the heavens. They also brought forth parrots and snakes and the first human, ancestor of the Paressí.[14]

In Ecuador the people of Manta venerated a goddess who lived in a huge emerald and healed diseases. The early Spanish writer Velasco said that she was called Umiña.[15] Garcilaso de la Vega wrote that this emerald was the size of an ostrich egg, and was displayed in the great festivals. People came from great distances to worship the goddess and make offerings, including emeralds that were regarded as her "daughters." The Spanish looted the gems, but the Manteños had already hidden the goddess away.[16]

During colonization, Catholic names were affixed to indigenous goddesses. A famous example is the assimilation of Pachamama, the Quechua Earth Mother, to the Virgin Mary or her mother Santa Ana. A 1526 Spanish account refers to a goddess on Salango Island off the coast of Ecuador. Her tent sanctuary was

> draped with rich embroidered mantles, where they have an image of a woman with a child in her arms whom they call María Meseia: when someone has an affliction in some part [of the body], they make a copy of the part in silver or gold, and offer it to her, and they sacrifice sheep [alpacas] before this image at certain times.[17]

Venezuela and the Guyanas

Early in the 20th century, a member of the Yaruno nation of Venezuela's Rio Capanaparo described their goddess thus: "Everything sprang from Kuma, and everything that the Yaruro do was arranged so by her—the other gods and culture heroes act according to her laws." She created the world with the help of two brothers, the water serpent Puaná and the jaguar Itciai. Kuma lives in a western paradise that the shamans see in visions, and visit in spirit journeys. Their rattles depict her with upraised arms.[18]

In the Orinoco delta, the Warao say the forest is a tribe of trees, bushes, and palms. The red *cachicamo* tree is Dauarani, the Mother of the Forest, and its guardian. Anyone who wants to fell a tree to make a canoe must seek her permission, and the consent of the tree, her daughter. Shamans ritually approach the tree-woman, who appears as a maiden wearing a comb and beaded necklace, and sing to her. The canoe carved from her wood is vulva-shaped, and the Warao compare its cargo to the fruits created by the Mother of the Forest.[19]

The Cariña Caribs revere Amaná, a self-conceiving mother whose essence is time. She was never born, but exists eternally. Amaná has borne all beings, including the twins of light and dark, and can take any shape. She lives in the watery Pleiades in the form of a woman-serpent, renewing herself continually by sloughing off her skin. Amaná is called a sun serpent, and another name for her is Wala Yumu, "spirit of the kinds [species]." She especially governs all water spirits. Powerful rocks at the rivers' headwaters are called Mothers. Shamans commune with them and with Amaná for visions and healing.[20]

In Cariña philosophy, spirit precedes matter: "If there were no spirit to cause everything to be as it is, there would be nothing." The Cariña emphasize the creative power of sound: "We believe that the *aula* [word, speech] of every *wala* [species] has existed from the very beginning, and that it created the physical aspect. Every *wala* in the visible world is the physical counterpart of a flowing *wala* [melody] which gives it life."[21]

The Arawaks of Guyana spoke of a creator pair: the male Kururumany formed men, and the female Kulimina formed women. After people populated the land, they fell into corruption, and so death was decreed for them. Kulimina may have been the sister of the masculine creator, since he is described as having two wives, Wurekaddo ("She who works in the dark") and Emisiwaddo ("She who bores through the earth"). The second name refers to the cushi ant, a red burrowing insect.[22]

Brazilian lore may provide a clue to the ant's significance. The Kayapó say that the little red ant is the relative of manioc and guardian of the women's fields. She keeps the bean vines from choking the manioc by chewing through them. So Kayapó women often paint their faces with the ant pattern.[23]

Mothers of Manioc, Mothers of Animals

Manioc or cassava is a tuber that is a primary food in tropical South America. Many rainforest peoples hold ceremony to honor the Manioc Mothers. In Brazil the Mundurucú shamans invoke her thus: "Mother of manioc, show favor to us. Let us suffer no famine; we call on you each year with our prayers. We have not forgotten you."[24]

In Ecuador, the Canelos Quichua honor Ningui as the soil of their fields, as *chagra mama* ("Garden Mother"). She is equally Mother of Clay, for ceramics is also women's work, and is the very spirit of culture. For their neighbors the Shuar or Jívaro, Ningui is the Earth Mother. Long ago she taught women agriculture. Shuar women plant their crops and then hold dances and ceremonies for five nights for Ningui, asking her to make their manioc grow. They also call on her in tobacco feasts which women host for each other, to give young women strength after their first menses and to reinvigorate older women. They plant manioc during these ceremonies while chanting incantations.[25]

The Manioc Mother belongs to a broad spectrum of guardian spirits. Every kind of animal has a mother who nurtures and protects it. The Arawakans "use either the suffix *oyo* ('mother') or *kuyu* or *kuyuha* ('wildness or shyness of an animal')." The Camayura of Brazil call these Mothers *mama'e*. Manioc has three Mothers, represented by posts that stand for manioc farming tools and the fishy *mama'e* who gave the people manioc and farming technology long ago.[26]

Among the Tupí peoples of Brazil, the title Cy ("mother") belongs to female spirits of land, water, and heavenly bodies. In the 1750s the missionary João Daniel wrote about sacred stones in a forest sanctuary, which the colonials destroyed. He said people venerated the sun as Coara Cy, "mother of day," and the moon as Ja Cy, "mother of fruits." They celebrated when the new moon appeared: "These two heavenly bodies were regarded as divinities, creators."[27]

For the Mundurucú, Putch Ŝi ("mother of game") lives in upland springs where rivers originate. She roars when she moves, and the animals follow her. She appears as a tortoise or coatá monkey, as well as in stone *wirakuá*. Shamans keep tortoises as her avatars, feeding them *möri* paste of manioc and scented water in order to propitiate Putch Ŝi. The most gifted shamans make shamanic journeys to visit her, making offerings and calling her for successful hunting. The Game Mother kills those who break her law by eating her special animals, disrespecting animals they kill, or wasting their flesh.[28]

The Mundurucú also propitiate Asima Ŝi, "the mother of fish" who rides on an alligator. She is guardian of all aquatic animals, including mammals. The Canelos of Ecuador say that a certain kind of tick attracts animals, and call it Aischa mama, "mother of game."[29]

Women, Serpents, and the Waters

Across South America, divine women are connected to sacred lakes and serpents. Brazilians speak of the water-mother (*mae d'agoa*). Sacred lakes figure in Brazilian legends about amazons called Icamiabas. Many indigenous peoples of the Amazon speak of the Women-Living-Alone, the Women-Without-Husbands, the Masterful-Women.[30] The Waurá of the Xingu river still celebrate rituals in their memory.[31] The Amazon River itself is named after the women warriors encountered by the Spanish soldier Orellana. The chief Aparia asked him whether he had seen the Amazons, "whom in his language they call Coniapuyara, meaning Great Ladies."[32] This name could be rendered as "masterful women."[33] Other sources translate it as "Great Lord" or as "mighty chieftains," ignoring the meaning of *conia* or *cunha*, "the Tupí word for woman."[34] The "mighty women" title, like the Waurá ritual, suggests a supernatural status.

A widespread Tupí legend tells of a sacred lake near the source of the Nhamundá River. It is called Yaci-uaruá ("mirror of the moon"). Every year the Icamiabas hold a ceremony to honor the moon and the Mother of the Muiraquitãs who lives in the lake. The women purify themselves and under the moonlight plunge deep into the lake to receive *muiraquitãs*. These are jade amulets in the form of frogs, fish, tortoises, and other shapes. Some say that the Icamiabas scooped up clay from the lake bed and shaped it into these forms. In another version, the Icamiabas caught little underwater animals and froze their forms by dropping a little of their own blood onto them. Once exposed to air or moonlight, the *muiraquitãs* hardened into stone.[35]

These "greenstones" or "amazon stones" were sacred, and worn, gifted, and traded as far north as the Guyanas. Early colonial reports place the *muiraquitã*s around the Jamundá and Tapajós rivers and often refer to their healing properties. In 1851 the traveler Castlenau wrote, "The Indians attribute to them the greatest medicinal powers." Tapajós women used them to prevent disease and to conceive. Nursing mothers preferred pale and yellowish stones, which were said to increase the flow of milk.[36] In Guyana, chiefly women often wore them: "commonly every king or cacique hath one, *which their wives for the most part wear*; and they esteem them as great jewels."[37] Centuries later, Fernando Sampaio called the *muiraquitā* "a symbol of feminine power."[38]

Guaraní Cosmology: Paraguay and Gran Chao

The various Guaraní peoples tell several versions of the creation story. Accounts of a sole masculine creator are common, thanks to Christian missionary influence, but others say that creation was a joint effort of Tupã the sun and Arasy the moon. They descended to earth, to the sacred hill Arigua, where they created seas and rivers, woods, stars, and all living beings. They formed humans from clay mixed with water and various natural elixirs, each making a statue in his or her own likeness. The people came to life with the sun's rays, and sat before their creators who named them.[39]

Arasy spoke first, and when the humans replied, it was again the woman Sypavê who spoke first. Tupã told both to love each other, have many children, care for them, and then they would have everything they needed. Arasy protested, saying that people need to work, or their life would be a slow death. Tupã agreed. They instructed the first people on how to live, avoiding unnecessary harm to living things, and to tattoo their faces to remind them of the sacred. They told them, "Earth is your mother and the Moon is her sister."[40]

The Tavyterã speak of an earlier divine generation, Our Great Grand-father, who "suckled himself" and raised his wife out of his ceremonial crown. She was Ñande Jari Jusu, Our Great Grandmother, also titled Great Golden Flaming Ritual Staff. The pair quarreled, and Grandfather decided to leave. In his anger he wanted to destroy the earth with a flood, but Ñande Jari succeeded in protecting it by singing the first sacred song, to the beat of the *takuára* ("women's rhythm staff").[41]

Another Guaraní story says that a great flood destroyed the previous world, but the ancient grandmother Chary Pire survived through her shamanic power. "As the floodwaters rose, Chary Piré stamped out a dance beat with her rhythm stick and sang a powerful chant without stopping." She caused a palm to grow between heaven and earth, and took refuge at its top with her son.[42]

As the divine Grandparents had quarreled, so their children also dis-agreed. Our Father left Our Mother, Ñandecy.[43] Some stories say they fought over her making love with another man. In one version, it was his brother. In another, Ñandecy told her husband that another man had fathered her child, and he left. She and her child went looking for him on the path of tigers. The Tiger Grandmother gave them shelter and hid them from her grandchildren. But the young tigers found Ñandecy and killed her. Later her son with his magical twin avenged her death by killing the tigers.[44] This theme of a divine woman who has twin sons and then dies is a common theme in stories across the Americas. The Guyana Caribs tell a very similar story about a mother slain by tigers and avenged by her twin sons.[45]

Ñandecy went to the world of the ancestors, and she rules the land-without-evil, over the eastern waters. A parrot meets all comers with food and only allows the humble to enter. While the male creator withdrew far away, Ñandecy cares about humans. From the 1530s on, she inspired waves of Guaraní spiritual movements confronting European colonization.[46]

Sun and Other Sky Women

In north Argentina, the Toba say that in the beginning women lived in the sky and the stars were their houses. Men lived as half-animals on the earth below. One day the sky women decided to go down to earth to taste its fruits. They descended by long cords many times. While the men were out hunting, the sky-women came and ate all their food. The men couldn't figure out what had happened, so they set someone to keep watch. The rabbit-man fell asleep and didn't see what happened. The parrot-man saw how the women came down from the sky, but one of them threw a stone and broke his beak, so he was unable to tell what he saw. The eagle-man was stunned by the brilliance created by the cord brushing against the earth, and his speech was too confused to understand. Then the bird-man stood guard. When he saw the women descending, he flew and cut the cords, trapping those who had landed.

The men wanted to have sex with the sky-women. The fox man grabbed the prettiest and carried her to his hut, but soon came out screaming and holding his crotch. He said the woman had bitten him with the teeth in her vulva. The men saw that the women used these lower teeth to chew their fruit. The bird-man invited the women to sit cross legged on the ground in a circle. Then the men built a fire and danced hard all night, beating the ground with their feet and making the ground vibrate. At dawn they collapsed in exhaustion. The women got up and went over to them, but the teeth remained stuck in the ground where they had sat. Then men and women got together and had human children.

As for the women who remained in the sky, the sun woman Aquehua stayed close to the earth near her sisters. Sometimes she moves quickly, like a young person, which makes the days short and cool. Other times she goes slowly like an old woman, and the days are long and hot. She regenerates herself, turning from young to old and then young again, as she will until the end of time.[47] The Toba say that the belt stars in Orion are "three old women who live in a large house with a garden." They are also known as the Tres Marías. Star Woman (the planet Venus) produces the Magellanic Clouds by pounding carob flour in her heavenly mortar.[48]

Patriarchal Coups: The Goddess Appropriated

Stories of men seizing the sacred ceremonies, instruments, and masks from women are widespread in South America. The Yamana of Tierra del Fuego say that Húanaxu was the leader of women, who once ruled and controlled ceremonial life. Men killed all the women in a patriarchal coup. Furious, Húanaxu rose into the sky as the Moon, and sent a great flood to punish the gynocide.[49]

The Selk'nam told a similar story: the moon, Kreeh, was a powerful shaman who led the women's ceremonies and decided who would play which spirits. One of the greatest was the chthonic serpent Xalpen who arose from deep in the earth, causing the ceremonial hut to shake and flames to spit forth. But the men found out the women's secret and violently overthrew them. Moon became a despised figure, though her power was still feared.[50]

In Venezuela, the Arawakan Wakuénai tell how Amáru and her women took the sacred flutes away from her trickster brother and the men. This act opened up the world after an earlier destruction, and the women played the flutes as they traveled along the Orinoco, Vaupés, Negro, and Amazon rivers. The trickster tracked down Amáru at a lake, but she escaped through a secret underground passage and returned to the mythic center. (Women also flee through underground tunnels in Brazilian amazon legends.) Finally the men regained control over the sacred flutes and tricked Amáru into thinking that the instruments turned into wild animals and birds. Yet Amáru retains great power, being "strongly associated with the eastern horizon, the sun's heat as it rises to light up the day, and the biological power of fertility and giving birth."[51] Here the overthrown female power is sun, not moon.

In Paraguay, the Ishir or Chamacoco describe a male overthrow that killed not only the women, but the spirits themselves (*ajnábsero*). Only the most powerful survives, the goddess Ashnuwerta. Her name can be translated as "Lightning, Brilliance," or as "Flower, Intensely Red." For humans she is the Great Teacher, the Giver of Words, who reveals the law and brings culture. She protects the land and animals by regulating hunters and food distribution. She is Ashnuwerta of the Red Splendor, of the Black Brilliance, Mistress of Water and Fire, Mother of the Birds of the Benign Rain, Mistress of the Dark Blue Storm. She is all knowing, present everywhere, and beyond time.

Then how could she be killed? The men's tradition says that it was done at her own instruction, because the women had looked down on men and tricked them. In early times it was women who performed the sacred rites that renewed the bonds between all beings. Once men had learned the ways of the *ajnábsero*, they no longer needed them and wanted to get rid of them. Inexplicably, Ashnuwerta revealed to the chief (her lover) how to kill the *ajnábsero*, herself included, by striking the mouths hidden in the fur on their left ankles.

The women's overthrow began with the men seizing boys and subjecting them to such severe tests in the initiation house that some died. Among them was the chief's son, and he vowed revenge on the spirits. With Ashnuwerta's help, the men killed the *ajnábsero*. Then Ashnuwerta told them that they must take the spirits' ceremonial places, with each slayer acquiring the clan identity of his victim. She taught them their costumes, paints, dances, and rites.

According to the legend, it was Ashnuwerta who imposed the Great Secret: keeping women ignorant that the dancing *ajnábsero* were really their men. But the women rejected the fiction: "Doubled over with laughter, they ridiculed the actors, mocking their attempt to supplant the gods."[52] The men complained to Ashnuwerta who instructed them to kill all the women. She promised that they would be resurrected but would remember nothing. So the slaughter began, and one man came after the goddess herself with a club. She turned into a doe and escaped into the forest. Later she instructed the men to kill her, each taking a piece of her body. At nightfall the women would rise again from her dismembered flesh.[53]

The women were not the same. Their memories had been erased; they knew nothing. Since then, Ishir women believe that the men in ritual costumes are really the *ajnábsero*—or so it is said. What the women thought of all this remains unspoken, though in Tierra del Fuego Selk'nam women were well aware of the "secret."[54] Ashnuwerta never returned, but her immortal and eternal being lives on in the Milky Way with the "invincible shamanic souls."

María Lionza

In Venezuela, a thriving modern tradition has coalesced around María de la Onza ("of the tapir"). A bronze statue in Caracas depicts her as a wildwoman riding a tapir. María Lionza reigns over wild animals, a benevolent goddess of nature, love, and peace. She lives in a palace by the headwaters of the Yaracuy River, on a throne of snakes and turtles, flanked by lions and goats. Her devotees make a pilgrimage up Mount Sorte on October 12, to make offerings, purify themselves in her spring, and trance-dance over red-hot coals.

Her origins are Indian, blended with African and European strands. She was the daughter of a Caquetío or Jirjana chief in the Yaracuy valley. Beyond this, her story branches out in many directions. Her green eyes were taken as a dangerous sign, so her father threw her into the lake for the anaconda. But she reemerged as a goddess surrounded by animals, plants, and waters. Or, a prophecy warned against the birth of a green-eyed girl: if she ever saw her reflection in the lake, a giant snake would come out of her and cause destruction. She was to be sacrificed to the lake anaconda, but her father hid her away. One day she saw herself in the lake, turned into a snake, and began expanding. Her body burst, releasing a flood. Or, the lake anaconda carried her off, and he swelled up and burst open as a flood. Then María Lionza became mistress of the waters, fish, and all the surrounding lands.

Or, Yara's dazzling green eyes were a good omen for the Caquetío during the Spanish conquest. She became a diplomat in talks with the Spanish, but they refused to make a treaty, and she returned to the mountains. The modern priestess Veit-Tané says that María Lionza was chosen as priestess for her spiritual powers. When the Spanish invaded, she fled to the mountains and tried to rouse her people to resist. They called her a witch, but she used her divine power to help them anyway. The missionaries recast her as the Virgin Mary, baptizing her as María de la Onza.

This syncretic goddess incorporates Ave Marías, spirit mediums, and African influences from Cuba and Haiti. She heads a Venezuelan Trinity with the Indian warrior Guaicapuro and Black Felipe, a Cuban who joined the Venezuelan revolution. She is surrounded by spirit courts of river and mountain spirits, saints, and historical figures like Simon Bolívar, and has acquired Indian, African, Hindu, and Arab courts, medical, political, and Venezuelan folk courts. Her religion is popular, egalitarian, participatory, and gift-giving.[55]

South American peoples have a large number of stories about female founders and culture-makers. The goddesses run the gamut from moon to sun, stone to plant to serpent and animals. They are creators, ancestors, and protectors. Although colonial conquest and forced conversions have taken a big bite out of the original South American religions, the Kogi, Brazilians, and other indigenous people have kept their traditions alive. They have influenced both European and African-descended cultures, as in the example of María Lionza.

Notes

Portions of this chapter are adapted from Max Dashu, "Female Divinity in South America," http://www.suppressedhistories.net/goddess/fdivsa.html.

1. Javier Montoya Sanchez, *Antología de creencias, mitos, teogónias, cosmogonías, leyendas y tradiciones de algunos grupos aborigines colombianos* (Bogotá: Concejo de Medellín, 1973), 63.

2. Ibid.

3. Ibid.

4. Hermann Trimborn, "South Central America and the Andean Civilizations," in *Pre-Columbian American Religions*, ed. Walter Krickenberg et al. (New York: Holt, Rinehart and Winston, 1969), 86–87.

5. Eden E. Vizcaino, *Sociologia del Derecho y la Cultura Wayúu* (Baranquilla, Colombia: Editorial Antillas. 1999), 13, 83.

6. Renilda Martinez, "Children of Rain and Earth: Respecting All That Lives," in *Woman of Power*, No. 23 (Cambridge MA, 1992), 9.

7. Montoya Sanchez, *Antología de creencias*, 102–103.

8. Hartley Burr Alexander, *Mythology of All Races: Latin American* (Boston: Marshall Jones, 1920), 191.

9. Montoya Sanchez, *Antología de creencias*, 60–61.

10. Ibid., 77; Trimborn, "South Central America and the Andean Civilizations," 92.

11. Trimborn, "South Central America and the Andean Civilizations," 90.

12. Javier Ocampo Lopez, *Mitos y leyendas latinoamericanos* (Bogotá, Colombia: Plaza y Janes Editores, 2006), 58; Max Dashu, "Female Divinity in South America," http://www.suppressedhistories.net/goddess/fdivsa.html.

13. Antje Olowaili, "Goldmother Created Her Children on Earth," Address, Second International Matriarchal Studies Congress, San Marcos, TX, September 29, 2005.

14. Robert Lowie, "Cosmogony and Cosmology (Mexican and South American)," in *Encyclopedia of Religion and Ethics* (Whitefish, MT: Kessinger, 2003), 7:172.

15. Emilio Estrada, *Las culturas pre-clasicas, formativas o arcaicas del Ecuador*, pub. 5 (Guayaquil: Museo Victor Emilio Estrada, 1958), 76ff.

16. Marshall H. Saville, *The Antiquities of Manabi, Ecuador* (New York: Irving Press, 1907), 105.

17. Elizabeth Currie, *Prehistory of the Southern Manabi Coast, Ecuador* (Oxford: BAR International, 1995).

18. Otto Zerries, "Primitive South America and the West Indies," in *Pre-Columbian American Religions*, ed. Walter Krickenberg et al. (New York: Holt, Rinehart and Winston, 1969), 252–253.

19. Joan Halifax, *The Fruitful Darkness* (San Francisco: Harper, 1994), 144–145.

20. Zerries, "Primitive South America and the West Indies," 245–247.

21. Ibid., 267–269.

22. Alexander, *Mythology of All Races*, 259.

23. Nimuendaju, "Kayapó (Horda Irãamráyre) Mitos coletados por Nimuendaju," http://www.terrabrasileira.net/indigena/index.html.

24. Zerries, "Primitive South America and the West Indies," 276.

25. Ibid., 277.

26. Ibid., 267–280.

27. Helen Constance Palmatary, "The Archaeology of the Lower Tapajos Valley, Brazil," *Transactions of the American Philosophical Society* 50, no. 3 (1960): 15–16.

28. Zerries, "Primitive South America and the West Indies," 260–261.

29. Ibid., 262–265.

30. Alexander, *Mythology of All Races*, 285.

31. Harald Schultz, "The Waurá: Brazilian Indians of the Hidden Xingu," *National Geographic* 129, no. 1 (1966): 142.

32. Van Heuvel, Jacob Adrien, and Sir Walter Raleigh, *El Dorado* (New York: J. Winchester, 1844), 117.

33. Richard Spruce, *Notes of a Botanist on the Amazon and Andes* (London: Macmillan, 1908), 457.

34. Alexander, *Mythology of All Races*, 285; Robert Southey, *History of Brazil* (London: Longman, Hurst, Rees and Orme, 1810), 86.

35. Palmatary, "Archaeology of the Lower Tapajos Valley," 75.

36. Ibid., 79–80.

37. Sir Walter Raleigh, "The Discovery of . . . El Dorado," in *Voyages of the Elizabethan Seamen to America: Select Narratives*, ed. Edward John Payne (Oxford: Clarendon, 1900), 202; emphasis added.

38. Zoe de Camaris, "A Muiraquitã, o Talismã das Amazonas," *Mitologia Brasileira*, http://www.heramagica.com.br/zoe_muiraquitã.htm.

39. Narcizo Colmán, *Nuestros Antepasados (Ñande Ypy Kuéra)*, http://www.bvp.org.py/biblio_htm/colman/indice.htm.

40. Ibid.

41. Friedl Paz Grünberg, "Guarani (notas)," http://www.guarani.roguata.com/articles/spa/gruenberg_notas_guarani_2004.pdf, 4.

42. Lawrence E. Sullivan, "The World and Its End," in *Religions and Cultures of Central and South America: Anthropology of the Sacred*, ed. Sullivan (New York: Continuum, 2002), 187.

43. Grünberg, "Guarani (notas)," 4.

44. Colmán, *Nuestros Antepasados.*

45. Walter E. Roth, "An Inquiry into the Animism and Folk-Lore of the Guiana Indians," in *Thirtieth Annual Report of the Bureau of American Ethnology, 1908–1909* (Washington, DC, 1915), http://www.sacred-texts.com/nam/sa/aflg/aflg02.htm and aflg12.htm.

46. Zerries, "Primitive South America and the West Indies," 241.

47. Analía Bernardo, "Taller de Mitos y Cuentos para Mujeres," http://agenda delasmujeres.com.ar/notadesplegada.php?id=1078.

48. Alfred Metraux, "Indians of the Gran Chaco," in *Handbook of South American Indians*, ed. Julian Steward, vol. 1, *The Marginal Tribes* (Washington, DC: Smithsonian Institution, 1950), 365.

49. Patricia Monaghan, *The Encylopedia of Goddesses and Heroines* (Santa Barbara, CA: Greenwood, 2009).

50. Anne MacKaye Chapman, *Drama and Power in a Hunting Society: The Selknam of Tierra del Fuego* (Cambridge: Cambridge University Press, 1982), 67–73.

51. Jonathan Hill, "Shamanism, Colonialism, and the Wild Woman," in *Comparative Arawakan Histories: Rethinking Language Family and Culture Area in Amazonia* (Urbana: University of Illinois Press, 2002), 237–240.

52. Ticio Escobar, *The Curse of Nemur: In Search of the Art, Myth and Ritual of the Ishir* (Pittsburgh, PA: University of Pittsburgh Press, 2007), 53.

53. Ibid., 30–61; Edgardo Jorge Cordeu, "The Religion of the Chamacoco (Ishir) Indians," in *Religions and Cultures of Central and South America*, ed. Sullivan, 268–271.

54. Chapman, *Drama and Power in a Hunting* Society, 74–75.

55. Sabrina Mervin and Carol Prunhuber, *Women Around the World and Through the Ages* (Wilmington DE: Atomium, 1990), 61; Gabriel Ernesto Andrade, "A Girardian Reading of the Myth of Maria Lionza," http://www.anthrobase.com/txt/A/Andrade_G_E_01.htm.

Bibliography

Alexander, Hartley Burr. *Mythology of All Races: Latin American.* Boston: Marshall Jones, 1920.

Andrade, Gabriel Ernesto. "A Girardian Reading of the Myth of Maria Lionza." http://www.anthrobase.com/txt/A/Andrade_G_E_01.htm.

Bernardo, Analía. "Taller de Mitos y Cuentos para Mujeres." http://agendade lasmujeres.com.ar/notadesplegada.php?id=1078.

Chapman, Anne MacKaye. *Drama and Power in a Hunting Society: The Selknam of Tierra del Fuego,* Cambridge: Cambridge University Press, 1982.

Colmán, Narcizo. *Nuestros Antepasados (Ñande Ypy Kuéra).* http://www.bvp .org.py/biblio_htm/colman/indice.htm.

Cordeu, Edgardo Jorge. "The Religion of the Chamacoco (Ishir) Indians." In *Religions and Cultures of Central and South America: Anthropology of the Sacred*, ed. Lawrence Sullivan, 254–277. New York: Continuum, 2002.

Currie, Elizabeth. *Prehistory of the Southern Manabi Coast, Ecuador.* Oxford: BAR International, 1995.

Dashu, Max. "Female Divinity in South America." http://ww.suppressedhistories .net/goddess/fdivsa.html.

de Camaris, Zoe. "A Muiraquitã, o Talismã das Amazonas." *Mitologia Brasileira.* www.heramagica.com.br/zoe_muiraquitã.htm.

Escobar, Ticio. *The Curse of Nemur: In Search of the Art, Myth and Ritual of the Ishir.* Pittsburgh, PA: University of Pittsburgh Press, 2007.

Estrada, Emilio. *Las culturas pre-clasicas, formativas o arcaicas del Ecuador.* Pub. 5. Guayaquil: Museo Victor Emilio Estrada, 1958.

Grünberg, Friedl Paz. "Guarani (notas)." http://www.guarani.roguata.com/ articles/spa/gruenberg_notas_guarani_2004.pdf.

Halifax, Joan. *The Fruitful Darkness.* San Francisco: Harper, 1994.

Hill, Jonathan. "Shamanism, Colonialism, and the Wild Woman." In *Comparative Arawakan Histories: Rethinking Language Family and Culture Area in Amazonia,* 223–247. Urbana: University of Illinois Press, 2002.

Lowie, Robert. "Cosmogony and Cosmology (Mexican and South American)." In *Encyclopedia of Religion and Ethics,* 7:168–174. Whitefish, MT: Kessinger, 2003.

Martinez, Renilda. "Children of Rain and Earth: Respecting All That Lives." In *Woman of Power,* no. 23. Cambridge MA, 1992.

Mervin, Sabrina, and Carol Prunhuber. *Women Around the World and Through the Ages.* Wilmington, DE: Atomium, 1990.

Metraux, Alfred. "Indians of the Gran Chaco." In *Handbook of South American Indians,* vol. 1, *The Marginal Tribes,* ed. Julian Steward, 197–370. Washington, DC: Smithsonian Institution, 1950.

Monaghan, Patricia. *Goddesses and Heroines.* Santa Barbara, CA: Greenwood, 2009.

Montoya Sanchez, Javier. *Antología de creencias, mitos, teogónias, cosmogonías, leyendas y tradiciones de algunos grupos aborigines colombianos.* Bogotá: Concejo de Medellín, 1973.

Nimuendaju. "Kayapó (Horda Irãamráyre) Mitos coletados por Nimuendaju." http://www.terrabrasileira.net/indigena/index.html.

Ocampo Lopéz, Javier. *Mitos y leyendas latinoamericanos.* Bogotá, Colombia: Plaza y Janes Editores, 2006.

Olowaili, Antje. "Goldmother Created Her Children on Earth." Address, Second International Matriarchal Studies Congress, San Marcos, TX, September 29, 2005.

Palmatary, Helen Constance. "The Archaeology of the Lower Tapajos Valley, Brazil." *Transactions of the American Philosophical Society* 50, no. 3 (1960): 1–243.

Raleigh, Sir Walter. "The Discovery of . . . El Dorado." In *Voyages of the Elizabethan Seamen to America: Select Narratives,* ed. Edward John Payne, 163–272. Oxford: Clarendon, 1900.

Roth, Walter E. "An Inquiry into the Animism and Folk-Lore of the Guiana Indians." In *Thirtieth Annual Report of the Bureau of American Ethnology*, 1908–1909. Washington, DC, 1915. http://www.sacred-texts.com/nam/sa/aflg/aflg02.htm and aflg12.htm.

Saville, Marshall H. *The Antiquities of Manabi, Ecuador*. New York: Irving Press, 1907.

Schultz, Harald. "The Waurá: Brazilian Indians of the Hidden Xingu." *National Geographic* 129, no. 1 (1966): 130–152.

Southey, Robert. *History of Brazil*. Vol. 1. London: Longman, Hurst, Rees and Orme, 1810.

Spruce, Richard. *Notes of a Botanist on the Amazon and Andes*. London: Macmillan, 1908.

Sullivan, Lawrence E. "The World and Its End." In *Religions and Cultures of Central and South America: Anthropology of the Sacred*, ed. Lawrence Sullivan, 179–199. New York: Continuum, 2002.

Trimborn, Hermann. "South Central America and the Andean Civilizations." In *Pre-Columbian American Religions*, ed. Walter Krickenberg et al. New York: Holt, Rinehart and Winston, 1969.

van Heuvel, Jacob Adrien, and Sir Walter Raleigh. *El Dorado*. New York: J. Winchester, 1844.

Vizcaino, Eden E. *Sociologia del Derecho y la Cultura Wayúu*. Baranquilla, Colombia: Editorial Antillas, 1999.

Zerries, Otto. "Primitive South America and the West Indies." In *Pre-Columbian American Religions*, ed. Walter Krickenberg et al., 230–316. New York: Holt, Rinehart and Winston, 1969.

5

Earth and the Nahuas: The Goddess of Ancient Mexico

Sylvia Marcos

> My daughter. . . . Here in this world we walk along a very high, narrow and dangerous path like a very high hill with a narrow path along the top of it, and on both sides it is endlessly deep.
>
> *Florentine Codex*

Today the idea of the earth is informed by satellite photography: the astronomer's blue planet, lost in the dark immensity of space. By contrast, like all pedestrian peoples, Mesoamericans drew their worldview from embeddedness in the soil of their particular place. They regarded the layer of soil that supports all life on earth as itself alive. This view is in sharp contrast to the contemporary view of the earth in which that top life-supporting layer is subject to exploitation and destruction.

One day a gardener from a Nahuatl-speaking region, working in a garden, was instructed to throw the dirt from a planter into the garbage bin. He answered the request with a shocked but polite, "No, no, Señora, soil shouldn't be treated like garbage." Another time, an Indian woman heard another woman complaining about the dirt and dust blowing into the house. She chastised the speaker saying, "Señora, you shouldn't speak like that of dust, because it is soil and soil is our mother, *la madre tierra,* who nurtures us."

Figure 5.1 Goddess Xochiquetzal (Goddess of water/flowers) and several dualities of God-Goddess. (Author unknown, Codex Borgia fifteenth century.)

The implicit ecological dimensions associated with Mesoamerican views of the earth and soil are brought home by these comments. What these indigenous people were reacting to was an acquired contemporary concept of soil as inert matter that can be discarded like refuse or complained about like an intrusive pollutant.

In nearly all agrarian civilizations, Earth is sacred. Exactly how this sacredness is expressed and what forms it takes vary from one particular location to another. The unique features of the sacrificial sacredness of the Nahuas or Aztecs arise from their cosmovision. Many elements of the Mesoamerican concept of the cosmos were often expressed in metaphor, a prevalent mode of expression in Aztec culture.

Aztec Cosmovision

Mesoamerican concepts and understandings of the earth differ radically from standard modern perceptions. Primary sources speak of the earth as a disk floating on water, a rabbit, an iguana, or alligator (*Cipactli*) with a ridged back.[1]

Léon-Portilla writes:

> The surface of the earth is a great disk situated in the center of the
> universe and extending horizontally and vertically. Encircling the earth
> like a ring is an immense body of water (*teo-atl,* divine water), which
> makes the world *cem-a-nahuac,* "that-which-is-entirely-surrounded-by-
> water."[2]

In anthropomorphic representations, the earth was a body with eyes,
mouth, hair, and a navel. Earth itself is variously a womb, mouth, and
bowels. Body imagery was transferred to the multiple levels of the cosmos. The center of Earth was its navel, the trees and flowers its hair.
Grass was its skin. Wells, springs, and caves were its eyes. Rivers were
its mouth and its nose was the origin of mountains and valleys.[3]

Earth was also a devouring monster. According to Nahuatl cosmology,
Quetzalcoatl and Tezcatlipoca brought Tlaltecuhtli ("Lord of the Earth,"
also called Cipactli, "alligator") down from the heavens. Tlaltecuhtli was a
mythic male-female monster that snapped and bit like a savage beast. Two
gods divided Tlaltecuhtli, thus separating sky from earth.[4]

In ancient Mexico, horizontal space was emphasized much more than
vertical space, contrary to the vision of the 16th-century missionaries
with heaven above and hell below. Tlalocan was the "paradise" of Tlaloc,
the god of rain, and was located to the east rather than in the heavens.
In contemporary Nahuatl vision, Hell is a cave in the forest. These
examples indicate the strength of the horizontal metaphor in relation to
the vertical Christian one.[5]

The Mesoamerican universe is divided into four great quadrants of
space whose common point is the center or navel of the earth. From this
point the four quadrants extend out to the horizon, the meeting place of
the heavens and the surrounding celestial water (*ilhuica-atl*). Multilayered
symbolism is implicit in the concept of the four directions of the world.
Contemplating the passage of the sun, the Nahuas described the cosmic
quadrants from a position facing the West:

> There where it sets, there is its home, in the land of the red color.
> To thy left of the sun's path is the South, the direction of the blue
> color; opposite the region of the sun's house is the direction of
> light, fertility and life, symbolized by the color white; and finally, to
> the right of the sun's route, the black quadrant of the universe, the
> direction of the land of the dead, is to be seen.[6]

This is the Nahua image of horizontal space. Vertically, above and below the horizontal world (*cem-a-nahuac*) are thirteen heavens and nine underworlds. Above the upper worlds is the metaphysical beyond, the region of the gods. Ultimately above all is Omeyocan (the place of duality), the dwelling place of the dual supreme deity, the originator of the universe.

Rivers, lakes, waterholes, mountaintops, caves, forests, and deserts all had gods and goddesses who ruled over them and required rituals. Mountains had a particularly complex role in mythology. Rituals for mountain gods were celebrated throughout the annual cycle, as were those associated with *cenotes* (underground lakes). Contemporary Mesoamerican Indians have preserved some of the complexities of these rituals. Among the Cuicatec, for example, cave rituals, mountain ceremonies, and waterhole rituals are quite important. This has also been observed among Nahua communities of the state of Morelos near Mexico City.[7]

All deities that symbolized aspects of reproduction, birth, and death had earthly aspects. Symbols of vegetable or animal deities were earthly symbols because the earth was conceptualized as the primordial image of the generating and regenerating principles of life. Death was an integral part of these forces. The earth had both human and animal characteristics; it was both male and female, living and dead. Centuries of observing the world and its workings from the macrocosm to the microcosm of the body itself produced Nahuatl thought with its distinctive characteristics of duality, fluidity and balance.

Duality is ubiquitous in the Mesoamerican concept of the cosmos. Cipactli, the mythic monster who was Lord of the Earth, was male and female, singular and dual. Though opposites, these poles formed a complementary unit. Movement characterized the Mesoamerican universe, but fluidity was always in balance. The continuous seeking for balance gives duality a constant plasticity. The critical point of balance had to be found in continuous movement, redefined moment to moment. Change and flux of the entire cosmos had an impact on the way the earth was conceptualized. This concept of a dual fluid, shifting, yet balanced universe permeated the perception of beneficial and harmful actions as well as of good and evil forces, giving them a nonstatic, nonrigid quality.

The duality implicit in Mesoamerican cosmology gave its impulse to everything: divinities, people, objects, time, and space with its five directions.[8] "[F]rom the four pillars of the cosmos at the four corners came the heavenly waters and the beneficial and destructive winds."[9]

Metaphors for the Cosmovision

In the Nahuatl universe, everything was endowed with material, spiritual, temporal, and spatial qualities. Consequently, it was a metaphorically complex and allusorily sophisticated construction.[10] Léon-Portilla has called the Nahuatl culture a "philosophy and culture of metaphors."[11] Metaphorical language is found largely in prayers, rhetorical orations of the wise and old women and men (such as the *huehuetlatolli* and *ilamatlatolli*), songs (*cantares*), and incantations (*conjuros*). As the main means of transmission of an eminently oral tradition, they were memorized. The visual metaphors in the codices of all Mesoamerican cultures are pictorial, albeit codified, representations of their cosmos.

In the Nahuatl world, metaphors were cultivated as the highest and most valued means of expression. Through metaphors, the Nahuas expressed their vision of the earth and the divine forces that affected it. Immaterial, nonphenomenal things were not set off from the material world but were continuous with it, integrated into a single conception of reality. However, a tentative distinction can be made between "physical" and "ethical" metaphors: while there were special metaphors for the physical conception of the earth and for its position within the cosmos, other metaphors reveal the relationship the Nahuas maintained with the earth and life on it, such as, the moral perspective that guided them.

Moral Dimensions of the Nahua Earth and Metaphors for It

The Nahua perspective on the earth is a moral one. Earth is a "slippery" place and the moral prescription is that one must act very carefully in all circumstances.[12] One must live according to the guidelines established by the ancestors.[13] The earth is not a place of happiness. It is primarily a place of effort and strain. However, "so that we would not die of sadness, our lord gave us laughter, sleep and sustenance, our becoming strong, our growing up; and moreover, earthliness [sexuality], in order that people go on being planted."[14]

Earth is above all a perilous place. The word *tlalticpac* synthesized many of the physical and moral meanings of "earth" and "soil." It is formed by the substantive *tlalli* ("earth") and the suffix *icpac* ("on, above"). However, its meaning is not just "on earth," but rather "on the point or summit of the earth," referring to a point of equilibrium on its crest and suggesting a narrow path between abysses. One linked oneself with the earth by acts of *tlalticpacayol,* "earthliness" which included but was not restricted to sexual activity.[15]

Ancient chronicles are full of references to the relation between soil and "sexuality" as well as between soil and moral matters. For instance, the grandmothers in the discourses recorded by Fray Bernardino de Sahagún say "our bodies are like a deep abyss."[16] The *huehuetlatolli* and *ilamatlatolli,* moral precepts of the parents spoken to their children, refer to the danger of earthly existence in these words:

> Here in this world we walk along a very high, narrow and danger-
> ous path like a very high hill with a narrow path along the top of
> it, and on both sides it is endlessly deep. And if you swerve from
> this path to one side or the other, you fall into that abyss. So you
> have to go along this path very carefully.[17]

A father giving advice to his son would refer to the wisdom of the ancestors, whose bones are in the soil.[18]

> Indeed on a jagged edge we go, we live on earth. Here is down,
> over there is down. Wherever you go out of place to the side,
> wherever you take off to the side, there you will fall, there you will
> throw yourself over the precipice.[19]

As Burkhart says, "Tripping and stumbling, falling off precipices and into caves or torrents appear over and over again in the sources as metaphors for moral aberration and its result."[20] Opposing poles should not be avoided completely, but must be balanced against each other. Walking on the ridged back of Cipactli ("Earth") implied the moral duty of careful balancing the extremes to achieve a harmony of tensions. This shifting moral balance was expressed in people's careful and cautious pace on the narrow path everyone had to trace on the corrugated skin of Earth's surface. Undoubtedly, the mountainous geography of Mexico provided the ancient Nahuas with the metaphor of the earth as a giant iguana or alligator.

Aztec Concepts of the Divine

In Nahua religious thinking, gods depended as much on humans as humans depended on the gods. All had a shared interest in the maintenance of the universe. Yet, the Aztec world was an animated world that had little place for the concept of an inert physical world ruled by a *deus ex machina*. Nahua deities were "neither Aztec society writ large nor ethereal beings touching only tangentially on individual's lives."[21] A permanent interaction characterized the relations between the Nahuas and their divinities. The sacred domain was not distant; it was a presence that suffused every element of nature, every daily activity, every ceremonial action, and every physical being: flora and fauna, the sun, the moon and the stars, mountains, earth, water, fire were all divine presences. The Aztecs were so enmeshed in the "supernatural" and the "sacred" that the distinction between sacred and profane seems not to hold for them.

Sharing divine attributes with the god of duality were other forces, forces of nature that have been designated in popular thought as "innumerable gods." However, all these gods only embody the four powers that Ometeotl ("two-god") has produced. They are the four elements: earth, air, fire, and water.[22] Each one of them was conceptualized as a dual female-male couple.

Divine Earthly Forces and Earthly Deities

The gods were not "unique solutions" in that they did not have fixed unitary meanings.[23] One god could be conceived of as an aspect of another.[24] The religious representation of earth in the symbolism of ancient Mesoamericans embodies some of their most complicated and diversified ideas. Since Earth as a symbolic complex was coded and transformed into practically all other mythic and ritual codes, it is impossible to produce a complete list.[25]

Earth, like the images of the gods, manifested a fundamental ambivalence. This ambivalence can be understood as the expression of the duality that pervaded all Mesoamerican constructs. The earth was both loving and destructive, both nurturing mother and carnivorous monster. Reflecting ideas both complicated and disquieting, the earth was often represented as a demonic figure.[26] Thus the mythic earth deity Cipactli, or Tlaltecuhtli, was a monster with a ridged back like an iguana, a giant frog or an alligator, a metaphor for the mountains and the creviced valleys of the earth's surface.[27]

Tlazolli— Dirt, Mud, Foul Matter, Soil

The concept of dirt cannot be separated from soil. To the soil, living beings bequest excrement; bodies go back to the soil; to the soil is let fall what is no longer useful. In the Nahuatl language spoken by the Aztecs, one term covers a whole range of impurities used in moral discourse to connote negativity. It is the *tlazolli*, formed from the roots *tlalli* ("earth, soil") and *zoli* ("used, discarded"). In its most literal meaning, the word refers to something useless, used up, something that has lost its original order or structure and has been rendered "loose and undifferentiated matter." Broadly it denotes any sort of dirt, chaff, straw, twigs, bits of hair or fiber, excrement, muck. What one sweeps up with a broom is *tlazolli*.[28]

Yet, since most concepts were ambivalent, the word denoting "filth" also had multiple favorable connotations, for maize grows from mud, from the body of the earth deity, and one linked oneself with the earth by eating cultivated foods like maize. Besides, all acts of *tlalticpacayotl* (earthliness, often understood as sexual activity) put people metaphorically into contact with *tlazolli*. The *tlazolli* complex draws materials principally from the realms of excretion and decay to associate them, through the process of moral rhetoric, with less desirable activities. Manure used to fertilize crops is still called *tlazolli*.[29] Therefore some of these substances have a fertilizing, creative role. *Tlazolli* was also the realm of the deity Tlazolteotl, the goddess responsible for sex and connected to sexual transgressions.

Tlazolteotl, the Goddess of "Filth"

Tlazolteotl, the deity associated with the sensuous, was patroness of dust and filth, and of adulterers and promiscuous women. She had the power to provoke immoral activity as well as punish people for it. But she could also remove impurities. In that function she was called Tlaelcuani, "eater of foul things," because she cleansed those who submitted to the indigenous confession rite by absorbing their impurities. This rite, described in the *Florentine Codex,* was conducted by her diviners.

Tlazolteotl was closely related to the earth-deity complex.[30] As Thelma Sullivan puts it:

(Tlazolteotl-Ixcuina), in her quadruple aspect as the four sisters, is a metaphor for the generative and regenerative cycle of life. Her fourfold character represents the growth and decline of things. . . . She represents the Mother Goddess concept in its totality. This includes its negative as well as positive aspects.[31]

Earth's Womb: Caves and Earthquakes

Caves were metaphorically referred to as the earth's womb. Similarly, the *temazcal* ("sweat bath"), shaped like a cave, was symbolic of the womb of Mother Earth. Earthquakes were thought of in the same terms as uterine contractions: disorderly movements that could create but could also kill. The duality in the conception of a life-giving, life-destroying deity is evident here.

Tonantzin and Monantzin ("Our Mother" and "Your Mother" respectively) were titles of the Mother Goddess. Both names refer to the earth as the Great Womb. As one incantation says, "You (the seed) have been kept within Your/Our Mother."[32] Symbolism of the earth's interior, the mythical cave house-uterus, still persists among contemporary Mayas in Zinacantan, Chiapas.[33]

This overview of the ancient Nahua concepts of the earth and divinity, especially as expressed in metaphors and attitudes concerning morality, explains their distinct cosmovision. What bearing might it have on contemporary ecological concerns? Natural phenomena elicited awe in the Aztec mind. Physical beings were regarded as infused with the divine. Reciprocity with and understanding of other life forms is evident. This precludes abuse and exploitation of nature and natural resources. Their entire belief system fostered and sustained a measured, nonexploitative use of the earth's resources. Aztec creation myths and stories did not give them the role of dominating nature, nor were they created as the species that ruled over all life forms. Rather, they were interconnected not only with "nature" in the form of flora and fauna and with natural phenomena like wind and rain, but with the divinities that represented the entire natural domain.

This connectedness, however, could also prove fearful. The duality that pervades the Mesoamerican concept of the universe included both the positive and negative aspects of nature, the creative as well as the destructive, the nurturing and the annihilating forces. Metaphors for earth and nature were never romantic. It is difficult to conceive of the Nahuas—and this holds true for contemporary Indians—taking a stroll in nature. When they visit mountains and caves, it is to influence or placate the deities that live there. Because they have not lost their roots in nature, they still regard themselves as an integral part of earth. There is no sentimentality in their perception of the earth. Earth is a great nourishing deity and an unpredictable, fearsome monster: in all cases, it is necessary to move about on the earth with care.

In the moral domain, the *huehuetlatolli* and *ilamatlatolli* speak often of the extreme care to be used walking on Cipactli's slippery back with an abyss on each side. Behavior had to be such that balance was preserved, and this was a collective obligation. For Mesoamericans, appropriate behavior while living one's life and enjoying the pleasures of earth was necessary to maintain the cosmic order.

Notes

1. The main sources for this chapter are Fray Bernardino de Sahagún's interviews with Nahua elders as recorded in the *Florentine Codex: General History of the Things of New Spain*, translation of an original Nahuatl text by Arthur J. O. Anderson and Charles E. Dibble (Santa Fe, NM: School of American Research and University of Utah, 1950–1982); and also the work, attributed to Olmos, "Historia de 10s Mexicanos por sus pinturas," in *Teogonia e Historia de los Mexicanos*, ed. A. Garibay, Tres opúsculos del siglo 16. (Mexico City: Porrúa, 1973).

2. León-Portilla, *Aztec Thought and Culture* (Norman: University of Oklahoma Press, 1990).

3. Yototl Gonzalez Torres, *Diccionario de Mitologia y Religion de Mesoamerica* (Mexico City: Referencia Larousse, 1991).

4. Ibid.

5. Louise Burkhart, *The Slippery Earth: Nahua-Christian Moral Dialogue in 16th-Century Mexico* (Tucson: University of Arizona Press, 1989).

6. Leon-Portilla, *La Filosofía Náhuatl*.

7. These observations come from my own field data, corroborated by Eva Hunt, *The Transformation of the Hummingbird: Cultural Roots of a Zinacantecan Mythical Poem* (Ithaca, NY: Cornell University Press, 1977), 134–135.

8. S. Marcos, "Género y preceptos de moral en el antiguo Mexico," *Concilium* 238 (1991): 433–450.

9. A. López Austin, "Cosmovisión y Salud entre los Mexicas," in *Historia general de la Medicina en Mexico*, ed. A. López Austin and C. Víesca (Mexico City: UNAM, Facultad de Medicina, 1984), 101–114.

10. J. Richard Andrews and Ross Hassig, "Introduction," in Hernando Ruiz de Alarcon, *Treatise of the Heathen Superstitions That Today Live Among the Indians Native to This New Spain* (Norman: University of Oklahoma Press, 1984); originally published as *Tratado de los Naturales de esta Nueva Espana*, 1629.

11. Leon-Portilla has called the Nahuatl culture a "philosophy and culture of metaphors" (*La Filosofía Náhuatl*).

12. Burkhart, *The Slippery Earth*.

13. Marcos, "Género y preceptos de moral en el antiguo Mexico."

14. Sahagún, *Historia general de las cosas de Nueva España*, 2 vols., introduction, paleography, glossary, and notes by A. López Austin and J. García Quintana (Madrid: Alianza Editorial, 1988).

15. Burkhart, *The Slippery Earth*.

16. Marcos, "Género y preceptos de moral en el antiguo Mexico."

17. Sahagún, *Historia general de las cosas de Nueva España*.

18. Bones symbolized for the Nahuas not only death but life and fertility. Life and death are in a dialectical (dual) relationship. Earth was both a tomb and a uterus. López Austin reports the belief that semen originated in bone marrow (López Austin, "Cosmovisión y Salud entre los Mexicas"). Behaving

morally required following the guidelines of the ancestors. J. Knab, "Metaphors, Concepts, and Coherente in Aztec," in *Symbols and Meaning Beyond the Closed Community: Essays on Mesoamerican Ideas*, ed. G. H. Gossen (Albany: Institute for Mesoamerican Studies, SUNY, 1986).

19. Sahagún, *Historia general de las cosas de Nueva España*.

20. Burkhart, *The Slippery Earth*.

21. Andrews and Hassig, *Introduction to the Treatise of the Heathen Superstitions*.

22. Leon-Portilla, *La Filosofía Náhuatl*.

23. Hunt, *Transformation of the Hummingbird*.

24. Andrews and Hassig, *Introduction to the Treatise of the Heathen Superstitions*.

25. Hunt, *Transformation of the Hummingbird*.

26. Ibid.

27. Gonzalez Torres, *Diccionario de Mitologia*.

28. Burkhart, *The Slippery Earth*.

29. Ibid.

30. Sahagún, *Historia general de las cosas de Nueva España*.

31. T. Sullivan, "Tlazolteotl-Ixcuina," in *The Art and Iconography of Late Post-Classical Central Mexico*, ed. E. H. Boone (Washington, DC: Dumbarton Oaks, 1977).

32. Andrews and Hassig, "Introduction."

33. Hunt, *Transformation of the Hummingbird*.

Bibliography

Andrews, J. Richard, and Ross Hassig. "Introduction." In *Treatise of the Heathen Superstitions that Today Live Among the Indians Native to this New Spain*, by Hernando Ruiz de Alarcon. Norman: University of Oklahoma Press, 1984. Originally published as *Tratado de los Naturales de esta Nueva Espana*, 1629.

Burkhart, Louise. *The Slippery Earth: Nahua-Christian Moral Dialogue in 16th-Century Mexico*. Tucson: University of Arizona Press, 1989.

De la Serna, Jacinto. "Manual de Ministros de Indios (1650)." In *El Alma Encantada*, Mexico City: FCE-INI, 1987.

De Olmos, Fray Andres. "Historia de los Mexicanos por sus Pinturas." In *Teogonia e Historia de los Mexicanos,* ed. A. Garibay. Tres opúsculos del siglo 16. Mexico City: Porrúa, 1973.

Gonzalez Torres, Yototl. *Diccionario de Mitologia y Religion de Mesoamerica*. Mexico City: Referencia Larousse, 1991.

Hunt, Eva. *The Transformation of the Hummingbird: Cultural Roots of a Zinacantecan Mythical Poem*. Ithaca, NY: Cornell University Press, 1977.

Knab, J. "Metaphors, Concepts, and Coherente in Aztec." In *Symbols and Meaning Beyond the Closed Community: Essays in Mesoamerican Ideas*, ed. G. H. Gossen. Albany: Institute for Mesoamerican Studies, SUNY, 1986.

León-Portilla, Miguel. *Aztec Thought and Culture*. Norman: University of Oklahoma Press, 1990.

López Austin, A. "Cosmovisión y Salud entre los Mexicas." In *Historia general de la Medicina en Mexico*, ed. A. López Austin and C. Víesca. Mexico City: UNAM, Facultad de Medicina, 1980.

Marcos, S. "Género y preceptos de moral en el antiguo Mexico." *Concilium* 238 (1991): 433–450.

Ruiz de Alarcón, Herando. "Tratado de las supersticiones de los naturales de esta Nueva España." In P. Ponce and P. Sánchez Aguilar et al., *El Alma Encantada*. Mexico City: FCE-INI, 1987.

Sahagún, Bernardino de. *Florentine Codex: General History of the Things of New Spain*. Translation of an original Nahuatl text by Arthur J. O. Anderson and Charles E. Dibble. Santa Fe, NM: School of American Research and University of Utah, 1950–1982.

Sahagún, Bernardino de. *Historia general de las cosas de Nueva España*. 2 vols. Introduction, paleography, glossary, and notes by A. López Austin and J. García Quintana. Madrid: Alianza Editorial, 1988.

Sullivan, Therma. "Tlazolteotl-lxcuina." In *The Art and Iconography of Late Post-Classical Central Mexico*, ed. E. H. Boone. Washington, DC: Dumbarton Oaks, 1977.

6

Goddess Androgyne: Coatlicue of the Aztecs

Lanier Graham

Coatlicue was the great goddess of the Aztec people. Like great goddesses around the world, she was regarded as the origin of life, the mother of the gods and of all being. Because of her there are humans, animals, rocks, trees, the sun and moon and stars. She also was the one who devoured all that is at the end of its lifespan. In short, she was a typical great goddess who developed during a Stone Age context and remained very much alive among the Aztecs.

Images of her are considered among the most horrific ever made. A monumental stone statue of her in the National Museum in Mexico City is nine feet tall. It was found near the ceremonial center of the old Aztec capital (now Mexico City) in 1790 by Antonio Leon y Gama. Her head consists of a double-serpent, two rattlesnakes looking at each other. Although only her head can be seen, her entire body probably was visualized as a double-serpent.

Her hands and feet are claws. At her center is a large skull. Her skirt is made up of interwoven serpents, hence her name in the Nahuatl language means "she of the serpent skirt." Her necklace is made of human hearts and hands, apparently symbolic of life and death and life again. Her sagging breasts speak of having nourished millions of lives.

Many think this is one of the most hideous images ever carved. After the statue was excavated by the Spanish in the late 18th century, it was

Figure 6.1 Goddess Androgyne: Coatlicue of the Aztecs. (Copyright Hrana Janto.)

put back into the earth. Why was it reburied? Many have reported that it was because she is so ugly. That makes a good story, but a more rational answer is probably that the statue was reburied because the Christians feared her image would stir up the old faith. Indeed, when the statue was rediscovered in the 19th century and placed back in the main plaza, local people began to make offerings. It was quickly removed to a museum, and there it has remained.

She also was called Cihuacoatl, which means "Serpent Lady," and Toci, which means "our Grandmother." As Our Grandmother, she was the patron of women who died in childbirth. Among her many epithets is "Goddess of Life, Death, and Rebirth."

Many modern scholars often speak of Coatlicue only in connection with life and death. This is a narrow view of the subject and a dualistic way of thinking that overlooks the fact that continuous rebirth is what traditional metaphysics is all about. All great goddesses are involved with the eternal cycle of life, death, and rebirth, not just life and death.

"Serpent Lady" also was the mother of Feathered Serpent, who is pictured from time to time as Double-Serpent. It is difficult for modern minds to comprehend, but Feathered Serpent and Double-Serpent are interchangeable metaphors in this mythology. Mother and son were seen as aspects of each other, not as totally separate beings. She is a double-serpent and he is a double-serpent. They are reflections of each other.

Chronology of Coatlicue

When did the worship of Coatlicue begin? There is not enough evidence to form a detailed theory. However, she probably is as old as the Aztec people. How old are they? Their own legends say they entered the Valley of Mexico from somewhere to the northwest during the 1100s. That might mean the northwest of what is now Mexico or the southwest of what is now the United States where variations of the Uto-Aztecan language group are still spoken as far north as northern California and Nevada.

The Aztecs claim to have started their capital of Tenochititlan in 1325. That capital eventually became Mexico City. Their nomadic tribe learned a great deal about the "civilized arts" of writing and painting, as well as monumental art and architecture, from the Maya and the Toltec. By the 15th century the Aztecs had constructed a large empire that was conquered by the Spanish in 1519.

Elements of the Coatlicue legend suggest that some of her myth may have been borrowed from the Toltec people who were greatly admired by the Aztecs. Indeed, the Aztec traced their descent from the Toltecs, who were the most powerful empire in central Mexico until about 200 years before the Aztecs arrived. Little is known about them because the Aztecs destroyed most of the material culture of the Toltec capital at Tula, some fifty miles north of Tenochititlan, in order to construct their own capital. The Toltec origin is uncertain, but some think their ancestors came from Teotihuacán. Near Mexico City, Teotihuacán for many centuries was sacred to the Maya and the Aztec and most of Mesoamerica.

The monumental statues of Coatlicue now known are thought to be not earlier than about 1400–1500 CE, but they could be much older. Those large statues obviously were major public monuments. However, there is evidence that small statues of her were made for private use. A small stone example was exhibited at the University Art Gallery of California State University, East Bay, in 2008. As stone cannot be dated scientifically, there is no way to determine its age. However, it obviously has been well worn, that is to say intensely worshiped over a long period. It could be only a few centuries old, or it could be quite old, possibly older than 1500 CE.[1]

Her Mythology of Nonduality

A great deal can be learned about a society by looking at its creation myth where the core values of a society are reflected. For example, if a male deity and a female deity are regarded as co-creators, the gender named first in the myth usually is the gender held in higher regard by that society. In the typical mythology of the Oaleolithic world, the supreme being is the great goddess.

She is dominant in Old Stone Age societies around the world. She creates all. She does it alone, with no need for a male partner. This is one of the symbolic meanings of Coatlicue being visualized as a double-serpent. In the New Stone Age the typical great goddess usually gives birth to a great god who becomes her partner as co-creator of the universe. This could be Brother Sun and Sister Moon, but more often is Mother Earth and Father Sky.

In other words, in the Aztec world, the great Female and the great Male together constitute another way of understanding the great double-serpent. Male and female are one. In traditional mythological systems, at the highest level of understanding there is no duality. There is only one supreme reality that can be perceived from different perspectives. From lower levels of awareness, one is always perceiving dualities. From higher levels of awareness, there is only oneness.

A powerful image of the double-serpent being worshiped on an altar is an illustration of about 1500 CE in the Aztec-Mixtec book known as the *Codex Fejervary-Mayer*. The deity being visualized probably is Quetzalcoatl, god of civilization, learning, and the shamanic priesthood; but it also could be his mother Coatlicue. Why? Because they are aspects of each other—the "One which is not Two." Without further information, one cannot tell which aspect of divinity is being pictured, the male or the female.[2]

A related image of Quetzalcoatl is on a stone found in Veracruz, also dated to about 1500 CE.[3] His two hands are birds, while his two legs are serpents. In other words, this is a variation on the theme of Feathered Serpent—another striking image of nonduality. There is a certain degree of interchangeability among these symbols. Both Double-Serpent and Feathered Serpent are visual metaphors for the ultimate nonduality of Heaven and Earth.

The deep meaning of the bi-singular symbol is the ultimate nondualistic reality of oneness. The reference is not only to the nature of the gods and goddesses, but to the nature of human consciousness. In public myths, supreme qualities are associated with deities. In the secret teachings of the great wisdom paths, supreme qualities are associated with human beings who have moved beyond their self-centered ego to a transcendent truth. Once this level of understanding is gained, there is a new vision. Reason and intuition are one. Heart and Mind are one. Male and Female are one. Heaven and Earth are one. Humanity and God are one.

To realize the full truth of nonduality is to attain the full potential of our humanity. To know that fully is to have become an androgyne. This has nothing to do with sex or gender. The androgyne is a mythic metaphor. Androgyny is a quality of consciousness. Androgyny takes place when one has attained enlightenment, or the state of grace, or whatever words are used to describe that which cannot be described.

The Science of Nonduality

Modern brain science has revealed aspects of how the human mind perceives the world in ways that help explain types and qualities of consciousness. During the 1940s and 1950s, in an effort to relieve symptoms of severe epilepsy, surgeons cut that part of the brain that connects the two sides of the brain, the corpus callosum. This is the large bundle of nerves that connects the left hemisphere and the right hemisphere of the frontal cortex, the place where higher functions are processed. Those operations often relieved the worst symptoms.

A team of psychologists, including Roger Sperry at the California Institute of Technology, tested these patients to see what the effects of the surgery were. It was found that these two sides of the brain are pathways for two very different kinds of perception. The left brain processes linear information, for example, timelines, lines of writing, lines of math, individuated patterns, and other types of measurable, divisible realities. The right brain processes intuitive information, for example, feelings, colors, spaces, and synthetic patterns. Roger Sperry received a Nobel Prize for this discovery in 1981.

The left brain came to be known as the "male" brain, and the right brain came to be known as the "female" brain. The left brain also was commonly called the "dominant" brain. This naming followed the stereotype of men, who (it is said) usually think reason is more important than feeling. This naming also followed the gender stereotype of modern society as a whole that asserts males are naturally more "rational" than females, and females are naturally more "intuitive" than males.

This brain model entered popular culture during the 1970s and 1980s, bringing with it a great deal of superficial oversimplification among the trendy, and some interesting theorizing among the thoughtful. Individuals of different genders were said to be either "right-brain" or "left-brain" personalities.[4]

Clinical tests with EEG machines have tended to support this theory. Some people approach the world primarily in left-brain ways. Some people approach the world primarily in right-brain ways. Particular moments of perception literally "light up" on brain scans. For example, when just listening to music the right brain is active. When analyzing that music, the left brain goes to work.

Whole societies have been called "right brain" or "left brain" by widely respected theorists such as Gregory Bateson and Julian Jaynes.[5] Tribal societies are certainly more intuitive than modern societies. One study by Leonard Shlain strongly suggests that when tribal people learn to read and write, their theologies transform. When alphabetic reading and writing, which is linear and nonpictorial, replaces picture-writing, which is inherently intuitive, traditional goddess-oriented theologies are replaced by god-oriented theologies.[6]

Modern urban societies with education systems that stress "reading, writing, and arithmetic" clearly produce individuals who give special value to left-brain modes of perception and tend to think that left-brain types of reality are the most real type. Such people think rational reality is the only true reality. People so educated seem less able to recognize and deal with profoundly important intuitive realities such as art, love, and divinity. The traditional spiritual teachings argue for rational/intuitive balance.

As scientific testing continued during the 1980s and 1990s, females turned out to be naturally more balanced in their daily perceptions than males because their corpus callosums are larger. Less lateralization enables more equality of attention.

One very disturbing study of modern brain shapes as they have developed over the last century showed that the left brain is getting larger and larger while the right brain is getting smaller and smaller relative to each other. If this trend continues, the human race could become a very intelligent race with little or no capacity to feel.[7]

Some of the most interesting laboratory tests on unusual individuals, such as yogis, revealed that such people tend to have extremely high degrees of what is called by the scientists "interhemispheric phase coherence." In other words, the energy field generated by their right brain and the energy field generated by their left brain tend to be equal. This indicates that they are thinking and feeling with equal intensity and clarity. Such mental harmony is said to be typical of enlightened human beings.

This clinical finding is precisely what students of comparative religion would expect. The traditional wisdom paths tell us that to become whole we must bring heart and mind into harmony. The absolute balance of our capacity to be rational and our capacity to be intuitive is said to be the goal of the mystic quest.

In many religions, the psychological unification of both sides of consciousness is called the "sacred marriage." Visual metaphors for "sacred marriage" around the world include the Double-Serpent and the Androgyne. Coatlicue was both.

Her Legends

Many stories about Coatlicue have come down from Aztec times. How is it that she became the mother of the sun and moon and stars? There are many variations of the story but a general consistency. One story tells of how she became pregnant one day without realizing it. All she did was put into her skirt a little ball of blue hummingbird feathers that had fallen from the sky. After she had finished sweeping the temple, she looked for the feathered ball but it had disappeared.

The result was a "virgin birth"—a miraculous conception—"without sin." But her children did not believe and were sure she had dishonored the family by a sexual sin. So they planned to kill her. They gathered for the attack. She stood facing them on a high hill.

She was saved by the sudden birth of her son, who emerged fully grown and fully armed. He slew hundreds of the unbelieving children who were stars. The head of the sister who had led the attack was thrown into the sky, and that became the moon. Few stars survived the Battle of Serpent Hill.

Huitzilopochtli, the hummingbird who also was the Sun God, was her other famous son, along with Quetzalcoatl. Hummingbird was at the very center of public Aztec mythology. Feathered Serpent played a more esoteric role. Sometimes known by the shamanic name of "Hummingbird Wizard," Huitzilopochtli as a war god led the Aztecs into battle, and as the sun itself battled his way across the sky each day fighting the demons of darkness. At night he returned to his mother, the Earth, to be spiritually replenished. Physically, in order to live and to radiate life-giving light, he had to be nourished with human blood. Unless there was a sacrifice of a living human heart, the sun would not rise the next day.

Another creation myth has come down that many think is rooted in an even older level of Aztec mythology. It begins with Coatlicue as a strange-looking, frog-like creature swimming in the waters of chaos before there was an order in the universe. In other words, she was formless omnipotentiality. She had the capacity to take on any form. Then, it is said, Feathered Serpent and Tezcatlipoca ("Smoking Mirror") decided that there should be order in the universe. They turned themselves into serpents and divided Coatlicue so that her lower half became the earth and her upper half became the heavens.

That males are dividing up a female in this version of the story suggests it is a fairly late Stone Age or post–Stone Age rendering of the narrative with the distinctive element of patriarchy. In the original Old Stone Age version of the story, she probably divided herself by herself in order to be all that is.

In addition to daily blood sacrifices to feed her, there were two major public festivals devoted to Coatlicue. The spring festival was called Tozozontli. It took place at the start of the rainy season. As the goddess of agriculture, Coatlicue was offered the first fruits of the season. In the autumn, a hunting ritual was called Quecholli. This included a human sacrifice. The fact that as a fertility goddess she was associated with hunting and agriculture suggests she may have been worshiped since the prefarming era of the Old Stone Age.

Most scholarly discussions of Coatlicue, from the short ones on the Internet to the longer ones in books, usually stress her horrific aspects. Indeed, she often is compared with Kali, the fierce Hindu deity. A more balanced view would include how much she was loved as the everlasting bringer of the bounty. Here are some lines from an Aztec hymn:

Hail to our Mother
who causes the yellow flowers to blossom,
who scatters the seeds of the agave plants,
as She comes forth from Paradise. . . .

Hail to our Mother
who pours forth white flowers in abundance
who scatters the seeds of the agave plants,
as She comes forth from Paradise.

Hail to the Goddess
who shines in the thorn bush like a bright butterfly.

Ho! She is our Mother, Goddess of the Earth.
She supplies food in the desert to the wild beasts, and causes them to live.

Thus, she appears as an ever-fresh model of liberality toward all flesh.

And what the goddess of the earth does for the wild beasts, so does she also for the green herbs and the fishes.[8]

In the traditional mythology of the great goddess around the world, she is the material world, all of it. Her body is what makes up all that can be seen, touched, smelled, and tasted. All these are her gifts.

When the supreme reality is thought of as a couple, during and after the New Stone Age, she is matter and he is spirit. He activates; she manifests. He starts what is the intention of each moment with an impulse. She completes that invisible intention by bringing it into physical reality, the realm of space and time.

In earlier versions of traditional mythology, Old Stone Age versions, she is both matter and the spirit that animates matter. In short, she is the singular totality of doubleness. She is the cosmic androgyne.

Notes

1. Illustrated in Lanier Graham, *Global Vision: A Survey of World Art,* pt. 2, *Stone Age, Bronze Age, and the Americas* (Brentwood, CA: World Art Press, 2008), cat. no. 96.

2. This image may be found, with difficulty, in expensive facsimiles, and more easily online as External Links to the "Codex Fejervary-Mayer" article on Wikipedia. This contextual analysis of the image first appeared in Lanier Graham, *The Tribal Culture of Our Ancestors: An Overview of Shamanic Art from the Stone Age to the Iron Age* (San Francisco: World Art Press, 1976), and again in Lanier Graham, *Sacred Visions: A Survey of World Art and Architecture* (Antioch: World Art Press, 1991), 1:91. For a general overview of Mesoamerican codices of this type, see Elizabeth H. Boone, *Stories in Red and Black: Pictorial Histories of the Aztecs and the Mixtecs* (Austin: University of Texas Press, 2000).

3. Illustrated in Mary E. Miller and Karl A. Taube, *An Illustrated Dictionary of the Gods and Symbols of Ancient Mexico and the Maya* (New York: Thames and Hudson, 1997), 141.

4. The most widely read books on this aspect of modern brain science have been written by Robert Ornstein, a psychologist who has taught at the UC San Francisco Medical Center and Stanford University. His best-known books include *The Psychology of Consciousness* (1972), *The Evolution of Consciousness: The Origins of the Way We Think* (1992); and *The Right Mind: Making Sense of the Hemispheres* (1997).

5. Bateson's better-known books include *Steps to an Ecology of Mind* (1975), *Mind and Nature: A Necessary Unity* (1979), (with Mary Catherine Bateson) *Angels Fear: Towards an Epistemology of the Sacred* (1987), and *A Sacred Unity: Further Steps to an Ecology of Mind* (1991). From conversations I had with Bateson between 1975 and 1980 came a study guide to suggest research directions for students: "Bimodal Culture: The

Graham-Bateson Model, an Outline Summary" in *BOA: Bulletin of the Archives of the Art Information Center* 20 (1979). Our conversations were recorded in "Metalinguistic Mentations: Conversations with Gregory Bateson," in *Iconography of Infinity: Essays on Art and Philosophy* 4, no. 3 (1995). The projects we worked on together inspired *The Bimodal Brain: Parallel Structures in Art, Psychology, and Anthropology*, ed. Lanier Graham (1995). Jaynes, a research psychologist at Princeton University, is best known for his book, *The Origin of Consciousness in the Breakdown of the Bicameral Mind* (1977).

6. Leonard Shlain, *The Alphabet vs. The Goddess* (New York: Viking, 1998). Shlain also has written *Finding Balance: Reconciling the Masculine/Feminine in Contemporary Art and Culture* (2006).

7. Reported in Lanier Graham. "The Divine Androgyne in Sacred Art," a paper prepared for a conference of psychologists and anthropologists on "The Bicameral Mind" at the Esalen Institute, 1978. The finding reported is the relationship between the bicameral brain model and the sides of the traditional Androgyne image that are male and female. There was found to be a one-to-one relationship in Androgyne images from many parts of the world over thousands of years: Tribal America, Hindu India, Taoist China, the ancient Near East, and Judeo-Christian Europe. The proper right side of the Androgyne image, controlled by the left brain, is always male. The proper left side of the Androgyne image, controlled by the right brain, is always female. Androgyne images of this type, including those in the 1978 paper, are illustrated in Lanier Graham, *Duchamp and Androgyny: Art, Gender, and Metaphysics* (Berkeley: No-Thing Press, 2003).

8. This song is translated online in "Coatlicue," www.paganwiki.org/index .php?title=Coatlicue. The words are from "Hymn to the All Mother" translated in Daniel G. Brinton, *Rig Veda Americanus* (Philadelphia: Brinton, 1890). Brinton noted that Our Lady of Guadalupe first appeared on the site of an ancient Coatlicue temple. I have changed Brinton's past tense to present tense, and made other minor changes in the translation.

Bibliography

Alcina-Franch, J., and M. Leon-Portilla. *Âzteca-Mexica: Las Culturas del Mexico Antiquo.* Madrid: Lunweng Editores, 1992.

Boone, Elizabeth H. "The Coatlicues at the Templo Mayor." *Ancient Mesoamerica* 10 (1999): 189–206.

Boone, Elizabeth H. "Incarnations of the Aztec Supernatural: The Image of Huitzilopochtli in Mexico and Europe." *Transactions of the American Philosophical Society* 79, no. 2 (1989): 1–107.

Boone, Elizabeth H. *Stories in Red and Black: Pictorial Histories of the Aztecs and the Mixtecs.* Austin: University of Texas Press, 2000.

Brinton, Daniel G. *Rig Veda Americanus: Sacred Songs of the Ancient Mexicans.* Philadelphia: Brinton, 1890.

Bruhns, Karen Olsen, and Karen E. Stothert. *Women in Ancient America.* Norman: University of Oklahoma Press, 1999.

Cardoza y Aragon, Luis. *Apolo y Coatlicue: Ensayos Mexicanos de Espina y Flor.* [Mexico City]: Ediciones de La Serpiente Emplumada, 1944.

Dorafuhrer, C. "Quetzalcoatl and Coatlicue in Mexican Mythology." *Cuadernos Hispanoamericanos* 449 (1987): 6–28.

Fernandez, Justino. "An Aesthetic of Mexican Art: Ancient and Modern." *Journal of Aesthetics and Art Critics* 23, no. 1 (1964): 21–28.

Fernandez, Justino. *Coatlicue: Estetica del Arte Indigena Antiquo.* [Mexico City]: Centro de Estudios Filosoficos, 1954.

Gingerich, Willard. "Three Nahuatl Hymns on the Mother Archetype: An Interpretive Commentary." *Mexican Studies/Estudios Mexicanos* 4, no. 2 (1988): 191–244.

Graham, Lanier. *Global Vision: A Survey of World Art.* Vol. 2: *Stone Age, Bronze Age, and the Americas.* Brentwood, CA: World Art Press, 2008.

Graham, Lanier. *The Tribal Culture of Our Ancestors: An Overview of Shamanic Art from the Stone Age to the Iron Age.* San Francisco: World Art Press, 1976.

Graham, Lanier. *Sacred Visions: A Survey of World Art and Architecture.* Antioch, CA: World Art Press, 1991.

Granziera, Patrizia. "From Coatlique to Guadalupe: The Image of the Great Mother in Mexico." *Studies in World Christianity* 10, no. 2 (2005): 250–273.

Harrington, Patricia. "Mother of Death, Mother of Rebirth: The Mexican Virgin of Guadalupe." *Journal of the American Academy of Religion* 56, no. 1 (1988): 25–50.

Joyce, Rosemary A. *Gender and Power in Prehispanic Mesoamerica.* Austin: University of Texas Press, 2001.

Keen, Benjamin. *The Aztec Image in Western Thought.* New Brunswick, NJ: Rutgers University Press, 1971.

Kehoe, Alice B. "The Sacred Heart: A Case for Cultural Diffusion." *American Ethnologist* 6, no. 4 (1979): 763–771.

Klein, Cecelia F. "A New Interpretation of the Aztec Statue called Coatlicue, 'Snakes-her-Skirt.'" *Bulletin of the Ohio Valley Historic Indian Conference* 55, no. 2 (2008): 229.

Kubler, George. "The Circle of Life and Death in Metropolitan Aztec Sculpture." In *Studies in Ancient American and European Art: The Collected Essays of George Kubler,* 219–224. New Haven, CT: Yale University Press, 1985.

Leon y Gama, Antonio. *Descripcion Historica y Chronologica de las Dos Piedras.* 1792.

Leon-Portilla, Miguel. *Aztec Thought and Culture,* Norman: University of Oklahoma Press, 1963.

Miller, Mary E. *The Art of Mesoamerica, from Olmec to Aztec.* London: Thames and Hudson, 1996.

Miller, Mary E., and Karl A. Taube. *An Illustrated Dictionary of the Gods and Symbols of Ancient Mexico and the Maya.* New York: Thames and Hudson, 1997.

Moctezuma, Eduardo Matos. "Archeology and Symbolism in Aztec Mexico: The Templo Mayor of Tenochitilan." *Journal of the American Academy of Religion* 53, no. 4 (1985): 797–813.

Moctezuma, Eduardo Matos. *Las Piedras Negadas: De la Coatlicue al Templo Mayor.* [Mexico City]: Consejo Nacional para la Cultura y las Artes, 1998.

Nuno, Ruben Bonifaz. *Art in the Great Temple.*[Mexico City]: Instituto Nacional de Anthropologia e Historia, 1981.

Nuno, Ruben Bonifaz. *Escultura Azteca en el Museo Nacional de Antropologia.* [Mexico City]: Universidad Nacional Autonoma de Mexico, 1989.

Pasztory, Esther. *Aztec Art.* Norman: University of Oklahoma Press, 2000.

Paz, Octavio. *Essays on Mexican Art.* New York: Harcourt Brace, 1993.

Pimentel, Luz A. "Ekphrasis and Cultural Discourse: Coatlicue in Descriptive and Analytical Texts." *Neohelicon* 30, no. 1 (2003): 61–75.

Read, Kay Almere. *Time and Space in the Aztec Cosmos.* Bloomington: Indiana University Press, 1998.

Read, Kay Almere, and Jason J. Gonzalez. *Mesoamerican Mythology.* Oxford: Oxford University Press, 2002.

Serna, Enrique. "La Coatlicue de Saks." *Letras Libres,* July 31, 2005.

7

Xochiquetzal: Goddess of Flowers and Love

Patrizia Granziera

Xochiquetzal ("flower feather" or "precious flower") was the goddess of flowers and love in ancient Mexico. Originally, she was a goddess of the Tlahuicas, a Nahuatl-speaking people who inhabited the southern half of the present state of Morelos—a region that was, and still is, renowned for its luxuriant vegetation and flowering trees. She was adopted into the Aztec pantheon when the cotton-producing area of southern Morelos was incorporated into the Aztec empire.

Xochiquetzal was the patron of the thirteen-day period of Aztec calendar that started with the day *ce xochitl* ("one flower"). The name Xochiquetzal, from *xochitl* ("flower" in Nahuatl), was related to femininity and thus to fertility. In the *Codex Magliabecchiano* it is reported that all flowers were the product of Xochiquetzal's genitals. It is said that one day, while he was bathing, Quetzalcoatl masturbated and his sperm fell upon a rock and was transformed into a bat. The gods sent the animal to Xochiquetzal's house, where it bit off a piece of her vagina while she slept. From this flesh all sweet-smelling flowers originated.[1]

Flowers were given considerable importance in Nahua world. "They were offered to the gods and given to leaders to strengthen them for their tasks and to affiliate them more closely with divine powers. Their fragrance was thought to be derived from gods and was equated with leadership." Sweet-smelling flowers like *yolloxochitl* (*Talauma mexicana* or Mexican magnolia), *izquixochitl* (*Bourreria huanita* or little strongbark), *cacaloxochitl* (*Plumeria acutifolia* or fragipani tree), and *tlilxochitl* (*Vanilla planifolia*, the plant from

Figure 7.1 The Aztec goddess of flowers and love, Xochiquetzal was also connected to magic and spiritual transformation. (Copyright Hrana Janto.)

which vanilla flavoring is derived) were considered luxuries and therefore were connected with the ruling class. In addition, many plants "were used for shamanic reasons, serving as a means of communication between man and gods and many of them were considered gods themselves."[2]

Xochiquetzal was especially associated with the izquixochitl, a flower that "was very much appreciated for its fragrant smell and curative properties. It was mixed with cacao to make chocolatl. In Nahuatl *izquixochitl* means "toasted maize," because its seeds pop out like toasted corn. The flower was a metaphor for maize, a basic plant in Mesoamerican alimentation. Most probably its association with Xochiquetzal could derive from a myth recounted in *Historia de los Mexicanos por sus pinturas*, which indicates that Xochiquetzal's union with the solar god Pilzintecuhtli resulted in the birth of the maize god Cinteotl. This makes her the mother of maize, a position she shares with other Aztec goddesses like Teteoinnan Toci.[3]

The Locus of Creation

Being a goddess of fertility and vegetation, Xochiquetzal was also associated with Tamoanchan, a place of luxuriant vegetation, the mythological locus associated with the creation of both the gods and humankind. Thus Tamoanchan had both celestial and terrestrial features of the "paradise of origins." In the codices of central Mexico, Tamoanchan was often represented by an anthropomorphic tree, sometimes bearing fruits and flowers, sometimes broken. In the *Cantares Mexicanos*, a series of poems in Nahuatl, the location is often referred to as a blossoming tree:

> The Blossoming Tree erect is in Tamoanchan
> There you were created, there we were given the law;
> With royal words it made us turn;
> This god of ours for whom everything lives.
> Which gold do I cast, which jade do I carve
> Our brotherly song;
> Like a turquoise for four times
> He makes us turn four times in Tamoanchan,
> Tamoanchan, home of the giver of life.[4]

Tamoanchan has been identified with the cosmic tree, the *axis mundi*, center of the world and place of origin, with its roots in the underworld and its branches in the sky.[5] "Trees, both real and symbolic, acted as important cosmic metaphors in Mesoamerica. In Mesoamerican mythology, the world was imagined as floating in a large lake and as having at its center a mountain or large tree that connects sky, earth, and underworld. While the most important and sacred tree is this central tree, Mesoamerican belief also includes references to four other trees at the earth's four corners that help support the sky. These large trees are generally depicted in pre-Hispanic codexes with their roots growing out from the body of an earth goddess, with fruit flowers growing on them and birds or insects in their branches."[6] Thus the tree as cosmic symbol of life was related to the feminine in pre-Hispanic worldview.

Celebrations in the Goddess's Honor

A feast celebrated to honor Xochiquetzal, reported by Fray Diego Duran in his chronicle *History of the Indies of New Spain 1581*, seems to illustrate this relation.[7] Xochiquetzal, as goddess of flowers, was celebrated in the festival of Atamalqualiztli, which took place every eight years. During this festival the temple of the god Huitzilopochtli was decorated with sweet-smelling flowers intertwined near trees, and a Xochiquetzal impersonator sat with a loom near the central tree. She wove with her loom hanging from the tree covered with flowers and beautiful birds. The blossoming tree in the center recalls the tree of Tamoanchan, and Xochiquetzal weaving near it may represent the Earth Mother as World Tree, weaving the threads of life in the paradise of origin.

Young people dressed as hummingbirds and butterflies danced and jumped from branch to branch pretending to suck the dewdrops of the flowers. Then people dressed like various gods of the Aztec pantheon would chase the birds and butterflies. Xochiquetzal would receive the gods with honor, offering flowers to them, and everybody would then dance. This was the most important dance ritual performed by the Mexica. Most probably it was a fertility celebration where the sexual act was represented by the hummingbirds and butterflies penetrating the flowers. It is not a coincidence that this festival took place during harvest time to secure the renewal of vegetation.[8]

The connection of Xochiquetzal with the paradise of origin is attested by sources that describe her as the lover of the god Pilzintecuhtli. The myth said that at the beginning of time, in Tamoanchan, all of the gods went down to a cave in which the god Pilzintecuhtli, "the Venerable Lord prince," was "in bed" with Xochiquetzal, who gave birth to Cinteotl the "Maize God."[9] This myth is corroborated by a *nahua* song dedicated to Xochiquetzal, as reported by the chronicler Fray Bernardino de Sahagún in his *Florentine Codex*:

> From watery mistland
> From near there came I?
> I Xochiquetzal?
> Not as yet
> It's the house at the brink
> And in Tamoanchan
> You have wept until now
> Wind priest Piltzintecuhtli
> He seeks Xochiquetzal
> To mist lands of turquoise
> For our sake he goes[10]

Goddess of Beauty and Love

Xochiquetzal was not only a vegetation goddess. She was the Aztec goddess of beauty and love. She epitomized young feminine sexual power and was associated with licentiousness. She is the Aztec goddess who best represents the archetype of the young maiden goddess. In pre-Hispanic and colonial codexes she is always depicted in a luxuriously embroidered dress with flower decorations and wears a quetzal feathers headdress.

Quetzals birds were considered divine by pre-Columbian Central American civilizations and the term *quetzal* in some Mesoamerican languages meant "precious" or "sacred." Their iridescent-green tail feathers, symbols for spring plant growth and maize, were venerated by the ancient Mayas and Aztecs, who sometimes valued them more than gold. Mesoamerican rulers and nobility of other ranks wore headdresses made from quetzal feathers. The name of the goddess is sometimes translated as "most precious flower" indicating that the meaning of *quetzal* is not simply feather.[11]

As a goddess of pleasure and beauty, Xochiquetzal was associated with both *ahuianimes/ahuiateteos* ("prostitutes") and *maqui* ("ritual priestesses") who accompanied unmarried young warriors. The *maqui* would risk their life going to war with these young men. Xochiquetzal also had a reputation as a harlot, a goddess with multiple sexual partners.[12]

Complications in the Goddess's Story

Mythological accounts give confusing descriptions of Xochiquetzal. Some historians report that she was the goddess involved in the first sexual transgression. In Tamoanchan, the Aztec paradise of origins, she was seduced by the god Tezcatlipoca ("smoking mirror") disguised as a royal vulture or a coyote. Xochiquetzal was the wife of Tlaloc, the Rain God, but Tezcatlipoca took her.[13] According to other sources, Xochiquetzal was also the lover of the god Pilzintecuhtli ("lord prince"). Because of these myths, the Aztecs associated the goddess with licentiousness and venereal diseases, which she could provoke but also cure.

She was also associated with weaving and embroidery as she invented these arts. Girls who were born on the day *xochitl*, of which she was a patroness, had the potential to become good embroiders—or debauched whores.[14] Xochiquetzal was the patroness of painters, silversmiths, sculptors, and all artisans involved in the manufacture of luxury items. Her relation to productivity extended into the domain of fertility, for women made offerings to her for help during childbirth. Xochiquetzal was the essential creative force and those who participated in creative acts—transforming nature into art—paid homage to her.[15]

Command of Magic

Xochiquetzal's domain also included magic. Nahua magical practitioners often invoked her. Her name appears many times on the treatise written in 1629 by Hernando Ruiz de Alarcón as an aid to Roman Catholic churchmen in their efforts to root out the vestiges of Aztec religious beliefs and practices. With great care and attention to detail, Ruiz de Alarcón collected and recorded Aztec religious practices and incantations that had survived a century of Spanish domination. He wrote down the incantations in Nahuatl and translated them into Spanish. The name of the goddess appears in spells that induced a person to sleep or into a kind of hypnosis. This incantation, states Alarcón, was especially employed to favor adultery and robbery. As goddess of love and the representative of human desire and pleasure, Xochiquetzal was especially invoked in spells used to attract and seduce a lover.[16]

Alarcón recorded rites and incantations for hunting and fishing where the goddess was invoked for protection and success in these activities. At the end of his book, Alarcón affirms that the only cure indigenous people used for scorpions stings was a spell that alluded to a mythical legend. In this legend, the hermit Yappan was transformed into a scorpion after being seduced by Xochiquetzal. From that time onwards, healers called upon the goddess to help counteract the venom of a scorpion's sting while referring to the legend of Yapan.[17]

From all this, it appears that Xochiquetzal was the ruler of those who employed charms to work magic and spiritual transformations. She epitomized the transformation of life from death, as shown by the symbolic use of butterfly motifs worn as a golden nose ornament (*yacapapalotl*). The transformation of caterpillar into butterfly is a natural example of the principle of metamorphosis. Thus Xochiquetzal was not only the embodiment of female ideals of sexuality and fertility, she was also the shape-changer, the witch, which connects her figure to chthonic power. In the Aztec cosmovision, sorcery and magic were the domain of the divine feminine.

The Aztecs believed divination and medicine were decreed to be women's activities by the primordial gods at the beginning of the world. In mythological creation accounts, the gods gave to women certain grains of maize so they could use them for curing and divinization activities.[18] These women healers, like the Nahua magical practitioners, reportedly ground up insects and other poisonous creatures, together with seeds of the indigenous plants to create a powerful, hallucinogenic ointment used for medicinal purposes and/or magic spells.

Connection of Xochiquetzal and War

Although Xochiquetzal was personified as young and attractive, being the essence of sensual femininity, in some codexes she is depicted with shield and arrows while holding spindles. According to one myth, she was the first mortal to die in war, making her the first woman warrior and the first goddess to be sacrificed.[19] She was recognized as the first woman to die in childbirth, before the birth of the god of maize Cinteotl, which relates her to the earth goddess Tlaltecuhtli, who was sacrificed to create the earth.

In Mexico, many goddesses, despite their maternal associations, appear terrifying and ominous, sometimes wearing weapons of death and destruction. This was in part because motherhood was a dangerous undertaking, and women who died in childbirth were compared to warriors who died in battle. A woman in childbirth was a woman going to battle; if she survived the battle her prize was the child, the captive she had valiantly taken. However, if a woman did not survive the battle of childbirth she joined the Cihuateteo, demonic women who were deified and transformed into warriors to accompany the sun from zenith to its disappearance at the western horizon. War was important for the Mexica not only because it implied a territorial expansion and the security of new tributes, but also because it assured the capture of prisoners for the sacrifices to honor the gods during their festivities.

The dualism of Xochiquetzal as creative force and warrior was a common aspect of the majority of earth and fertility goddesses who were equally associated with life and death, just as the earth was seen as both the womb and tomb of life. Like Xochiquetzal, female deities in the Aztec preconquest time were a blend of positive and negative qualities capable of causing illness and curing it as well.

The Goddess's Ritual

Xochiquetzal was patron of the thirteen-day period that started with the day *ce xochitl* ("one flower"). She was celebrated during the thirteenth *veintena* (month) of *Tepeilhuitl* ("feast of mountains"). The image of the goddess was venerated in a small temple near the one of Huitzilopochtli, the Mexica god of war. Priestesses started the celebration by making maize dough that they put inside the temple of the goddess. Then they waited until they could see in the dough a child's footprint and two hairs of his mother as a sign of Cinteotl's birth.

When this occurred everyone would perform a penitence, piercing their tongues and ears. Twenty days later, on the last day of this month's celebration, two young girls of the royal family represented the goddess. Dancers and priests escorted them to the Cuauhxicalli (sacrificial stone). Here an important agricultural ceremony took place. Four priests entered carrying four small cups full of different kinds of corn. The two girls pretended to sow, throwing the black maize to the North, the white maize to the west, the yellow maize to the East and the violet maize to the South. People fought to get the grains, which were considered as amulets of good luck and fertility. Later in the season they were mixed with the seeds that were going to be sown that year.

At the end of the ceremony the two girls were sacrificed. Their hearts were torn from their bodies and offered to Xochiquetzal. The bodies were then thrown down from the pyramid. Later the same day another woman dressed with the attributes of Xochiquetzal was beheaded and skinned. A priest wearing the skin of the victim and representing the goddess knelt near the steps of the temple and pretended to weave. All the artisans whose patron was Xochiquetzal—silversmiths, painters, sculptors, embroiders, and weavers—danced around him holding the utensils of their trade.

Then at dawn people took ritual baths in rivulets and streams. It was said that those who did not wash themselves would be punished with venereal diseases or leprosy. During this same festival an important confession ritual took place. People pierced their tongues in front of the image of the goddess inside the temple as many times as they had sins. Then a priest collected all the thorns used in the penitence ritual and threw them into a fire. The penitents then took a ritual bath and ate *tzoalli* (maize dough with maguey honey), which represented the body of the goddess.

The existence of a confession ceremony similar to the Catholic one was soon noted by the friars who explained in detail the differences in their rituals.[20] At the same time this similarity certainly helped in explaining the Catholic sacrament and contributed to a religious syncretism. It appears that in the Aztec religion the act of confession was done in front of only two goddesses, Xochiquetzal and Tlazolteotl. Moreover, the confession in front of Tlazolteotl seems to have had a deeper meaning, as it was to be performed only once in a lifetime and at an old age.

Image and Symbolism

Both pre-Hispanic and colonial pictorial representation of this goddess still exist. In both the pre-Hispanic and colonial codexes, she wears her quetzal headdress and a *yacapapalotl* (butterfly-shaped nose adornment) made of turquoise stone. Her dress is always luxurious and colorful. She usually wears a *quechquemitl* (triangular cape), and her skirt is elaborately decorated with embroidered and woven designs, probably in reference to her role as patroness of the textile arts. She is frequently shown partially nude with her breasts bare beneath the quechquemitl, sometimes feeding a baby, possibly to emphasize her role as voluptuous goddess of sexuality and reproduction. In other depictions, Xochiquetzal is represented in front of a flowering tree, probably a reference to Tamoanchan and the creation myths related to her.

In one of the best colonial representations of Xochiquetzal, she wears a headdress of a white ribbon made of paper and green quetzal feather tufts. The head of a quetzal bird with open beak frames her head. Several colorful feathers drop from her shoulders. The upper part of her face is painted yellow and the lower part blue with a band of circular "jewels" across the cheeks to the nose. A *tecpatl* (flint) and two flowers protrude from her mouth. Flints were symbols of human sacrifice and the debt owed by humanity to the gods.

Her pectoral garb is blue with golden beads. She wears a colorful quechquemitl with red, yellow, and blue stripes, decorated with white beads at the edge. Her *cueitl* (skirt) is red with a wide blue stripe and decorated with white circles or jewels. She wears white *cactli* (sandals) with a red cord. She wears blue bracelets with a red stripe with golden beads on the edge. Xochiquetzal is sitting on an *icpalli* (a seat used by aristocrats, governors, and powerful people) with a cushion made of jaguar skin. The jaguar represents the night and it was the *nahual* (mascot) of shamans and powerful people.[21] From her feet extends a serpent. In Mesoamerica the snake is always related to the powers of fertility and regeneration, becoming a typical attribute of the goddess.

Around Xochiquetzal are symbolic objects. Above her can be seen a stone, a white-and-black square, a beheaded man (symbol of sacrifice), the ball game, (Xochiquetzal was also the goddess of games and dance), and a couple under the bedcovers (representing the sexual act). To the right are drawn a white container with a serpent, the figure of Tezcatlipoca—the god who, disguised as an animal, seduced her in Tamoanchan—dressed with a quetzal headdress like that of the goddess. Other objects include a maguey spike used for sacrifice, a spider, a flint, and a container with a flower and a piece of unspun cotton. At the bottom is a container for offerings with a serpent and near it a skull in the night and, below the goddess, a yellow centipede and flowers. In Mesoamerica spiders and tarantulas were related to weaving and magical powers.

Durán's description and pictorial representation of the goddess give additional information about her iconography.

The image of the divinity Xochiquetzal was of wood in the form of a young woman, with a man's queue hanging to the shoulders and bangs over the forehead. She wore golden earplugs and in her nose a golden ornament which hung over her mouth. She was crowned with a garland of red leather woven like a braid. From its sides emerged splendid green feather ornaments that were round and looked like horns. She wore a finely worked blue tunic decorated with beautifully woven flowers formed of feathers with many little plaques of gold pendants all over them. She was represented with her arms open like a woman who is dancing.[22]

The image of Xochiquetzal summarizes the main attributes of this important goddess. Her luxurious attire and gold ornaments are a reference to her role as patroness of pleasure, love and the arts. Her quetzal headdress, the snake, and the flowering tree are symbols of her power as a fertility goddess while spiders and the butterfly nose ornament refer to her magical powers.

Notes

1. *Codex Magliabecchiano,* manuscrit mexicain post-colombien de la Bibliotheque Nationale de Florence, ed. Duc Loubat (Rome: Danesi, 1902), 61.

2. Patrizia Granziera, "Huaxtepec: The Sacred Garden of an Aztec Emperor," *Landscape Research* 30, no. 1 (2005): 81–107.

3. Francisco Hernández, *Historia Natural de la Nueva España: Obras Completas,* 2 vols. (1651; Mexico City: Universidad Nacional de Mexico, 1976), 389; Angel María Garibay, *Veinte Himnos Sacros de los Nahuas: Fuentes Indígenas de la Cultura Náhuatl* (Mexico City: Universidad Nacional Autonoma de Mexico, 1958), 165; Edouard de Jonghe, ed., "Histoyre du Mechique: Manuscript Francais inédit du XVIe siècle," *Journal de la Société des Américanistes de Paris,* n.s., vol. 2 (1905): 41; "Historia de los Mexicanos por sus pinturas," in *Teogonía e historia de los mexicanos,* tres opúscolos del siglo XVI, ed. Angel María Garibay (Mexico City: Editorial Porrúa, 1965), 27, 33.

4. Angel María Garibay, *Poesia Nahuatl,* 3 vols. (Mexico City: Universidad Nacional Autonoma de Mexico, 1963), 2:139.

5. Alfredo López Austin, *Tamoanchan and Tlaloacan* (Mexico City: Fondo de Cultura Economico, 1994), 226–229.

6. Granziera. "Huaxtepec," 81–107.

7. Fray Diego Dúran, *Book of the Gods and Rites and the Ancient Calendar,* trans. and ed. Fernando Horcasitas and Doris Heyden (Norman: University of Oklahoma Press, 1971), 246–247.

8. Ibid.

9. de Jonghe, "Histoyre du Mechique," 41.

10. Bernardino de Sahagún, *Florentine Codex: General History of the Things of New Spain,* 13 parts, 2nd ed., revised, translated with notes and illustrations by

Arthur J. O. Anderson and Charles E. Dibble (Santa Fe, NM: School of American Research and University of Utah, 1950–1982), bk. 2, appendix, 232.

11. In Nahuatl, the term *Quetzalli* usually refers to the *quetzal* feather and *quetzaltototl* to the bird.

12. Juan de Torquemada, *Monarquía Indiana*, ed. Miguel Leon-Portilla, 3 vols. (Mexico: Editorial Porrúa, 1969), 2:299; Dúran, *Book of the Gods*, 68.

13. Muñoz Camargo Diego, *Historia de Tlaxcala* (Mexico: Oficina Tipografica de la Secretería de Fomento, 1892), 155.

14. *Codex Telleriano-Remensis: Ritual, Divination, and History in a Pictorial Aztec Manuscript*, ed. Eloise Quiñones Keber (Austin: University of Texas Press, 1995), 48 (folio 22v), 187–188.

15. Dúran, *Book of the Gods*, 68.

16. Hernando D. Ruiz de Alarcón, *Tratado de las Supersticiones y Costumbres Gentílica que aún se encuentran entre los Indios de la Nueva España* (Mexico: Ediciones Fuente Cultural, 1953), 63, 109–110.

17. Ibid., 76–79, 85–86, 93–95, 176–179; "Historia de los Mexicanos por sus pinturas," in *Anales del Museo Nacional* (Mexico City: Imprenta Ignacio Escalante, 1882), 2:86.

18. "Historia de los Mexicanos por sus pinturas," in *Nueva Colección de documentos para la historia de Mexico*, ed. Joaquín García Icazbalceta (Mexico City: Salvador Chavez Hayhoe, 1941), 215–216.

19. Dúran, *Book of the Gods*, 238–246.

20. Carmen Aguilera, *Flora y Fauna Mexicana: Mitología y Tradiciones* (Mexico City: Editorial Everest Mexicana, 1985), 15.

21. Ibid., 96.

22. Dúran, *Book of the Gods*, 239.

Bibliography

Aguilera, Carmen. *Flora y Fauna Mexicana: Mitología y Tradiciones*. Mexico City: Editorial Everest Mexicana, 1985.

Camargo Diego, Muñoz. *Historia de Tlaxcala*. Mexico City: Oficina Tipografica de la Secretería de Fomento, 1892.

Codex Borbonicus. Mexico City: Siglo Veintiuno Editores, 1979.

Codex Magliabecchiano. Manuscrit mexicain post-colombien de la Bibliotheque Nationale de Florence, ed. Duc Loubat. Rome: Danesi, 1902.

Codex Telleriano-Remensis: Ritual, Divination, and History in a Pictorial Aztec Manuscript, ed. Eloise Quiñones Keber. Austin: University of Texas Press, 1995.

de Jonghe, Edouard, ed. "Histoyre du Mechique: Manuscript Francais inédit du XVIe siècle." *Journal de la Société des Américanistes de Paris*, n.s., vol. 2 (1905).

Díaz, Gisela, and Alan Rodgers. *The Codex Borgia: A Full-Color Restoration of the Ancient Mexican Manuscript*. New York: Dover Publications, 1993.

Dúran, Fray Diego. *Book of the Gods and Rites and the Ancient Calendar*, trans. and ed. Fernando Horcasitas and Doris Heyden. Norman: University of Oklahoma Press, 1971.

Dúran, Fray Diego. *The History of the Indies of New Spain*, translated, annotated, and with an introduction by Doris Heyden. Norman: University of Oklahoma Press, 1994.

Garibay, Angel María. *Poesia Nahuatl.* 3 vols. Mexico City: Universidad Nacional Autonoma de Mexico, 1963.

Garibay, Angel María. *Veinte Himnos Sacros de los Nahuas: Fuentes Indígenas de la Cultura Náhuatl.* Mexico City: Universidad Nacional Autonoma de Mexico, 1958.

Granziera, Patrizia. "Huaxtepec: The Sacred Garden of an Aztec Emperor." *Landscape Research* 30, no. 1 (2005): 81–107.

Hernández, Francisco. *Historia Natural de la Nueva España: Obras Completas.* 2 vols. Mexico City: Universidad Nacional de Mexico, 1976.

"Historia de los Mexicanos por sus pinturas." In *Anales del Museo Nacional.* Mexico City: Imprenta Ignacio Escalante, 1882.

"Historia de los Mexicanos por sus pinturas." In *Colección de documentos para la historia de Mexico*, ed. Joaquín García Icazbalceta, 3:209–240. Mexico City: Salvador Chavez Hayhoe, 1941.

"Historia de los Mexicanos por sus pinturas." In *Teogonía e historia de los mexicanos,* tres opúsculos del siglo XVI, ed. Angel María Garibay. Mexico City: Editorial Porrúa, 1965.

López Austin, Alfredo. *Tamoanchan and Tlaloacan.* Mexico City: Fondo de Cultura Economico, 1994.

Ruiz de Alarcón, Hernando D., *Tratado de las Supersticiones y Costumbres Gentílica que aún se encuentran entre los Indios de la Nueva España.* Mexico City: Ediciones Fuente Cultural, 1953.

Sahagún, Bernardino de. *Florentine Codex: General History of the Things of New Spain.* 13 parts. 2nd ed., revised, translated with notes and illustrations by Arthur J. O. Anderson and Charles E. Dibble. Santa Fe, NM: School of American Research and University of Utah, 1950–1982.

Torquemada, Juan de. *Monarquía Indiana*, ed. Miguel Leon-Portilla. 3 vols. Mexico City: Editorial Porrúa, 1969.

8

Our Lady of Guadalupe: Mother of a New Race

Barbara Flaherty

José María Morelos, the revolutionary rebel leader who led the Mexican War of Independence movement from 1811 until his capture and execution in 1815, declared that "New Spain [Mexico] puts less faith in its own efforts than in the power of God and the intercession of its Blessed Mother, who appeared within the precincts of Tepeyac as the miraculous image of Guadalupe that had come to comfort us, defend us, visibly be our protection."[1] The Virgin of Guadalupe's image, displayed in most Mexican homes today, is so central to Mexican identity it has been carried on flags, banners, and uniforms not only in the revolution of independence from Spain, but in subsequent political uprisings that have occurred on behalf of the poor. She is the protectress of the needy and the mother of Mexico itself.

December 12 is the feast of Our Lady of Guadalupe, who bears the titles Queen of Mexico and Empress of the Americas. On that day, millions of pilgrims flock to her shrine in Mexico City, which is located on Tepeyac Hill, the sacred site of the Mexica-Aztec earth goddess Tonantzin. Holding lighted candles, these faithful process through the streets to the new Basilica, built in 1976 to replace the sinking structure of the original Basilica which was the first to be built in the New World and whose construction spanned the years 1531–1709. In this modern building an almost 500-year-old image hangs: *La Morenita*, the Brown Skinned Virgin. This controversial icon in which the indigenous Aztec and Christian sacred persons and cosmologies meet has ignited the contemplation, faith, and imagination of generations.

Throughout Mexico and the Americas smaller services celebrate her feast day with communal prayer, litanies, and feasts like the following litany of the Virgin of Guadalupe led annually at the United States/Mexican Border in Columbus, New Mexico, and Palomas, Chihuahua.

> Who is she that comes forth arrayed with the sun, and the moon under
>   her feet, and upon her head a crown of twelve stars?
> Our Lady of Tepeyac, la Santa Patrona de los Mexicanos,
> Earth keeper, ancient giver of sustenance, honored grandmother,
> Woman of flowers and precious stone, mother of corn, sister of rain,
> Renewer of Life, roaring warrior for Life, Empress of the Americas.
> Boundary-crossing mestiza, your warm beauty dazes our senses,
> Mother of the son of God, Mother of the sons and daughters of God . . .
> you came to us pregnant with a new race of people.[2]

The Encounter of Two Cultures

Beneath the Virgin's icon in a story of bloody devastation of apocalyptic proportions, a profound divine tenderness and surprising possibility announces itself when a poor Aztec man walking on Tepeyac Hill meets a woman radiant as the sun.

Although the threads of the story appear as humble as the man's roughly woven *tilma*, a garment used as both cloak and apron, they are as evocative as the ancient prophecies of two great civilizations, as destructive as the history of colonial empire and greed, as archetypally creative as the great goddess, nurturing as a mother's womb and as powerful as her loving touch.

The history surrounding the Virgin's appearance is recorded in *The Florentine Codex,* compiled between 1540 and 1585.[3] The codex, written in the Aztec Nahuatl language, purports to be derived from primary sources and interviews. Consisting of twelve books with over 1000 illustrations by Aztec artists of Aztec life before the conquest, its composition was supervised by the Franciscan priest Bernardino de Sahagún. Although some modern ethnohistorians question the veracity of this postconquest document, it remains a major source material for the events of the last days of the Aztec empire, and its words have clearly influenced the spiritual imaginations of Aztecs, Christians, and their descendants.

In 1519, twenty-seven years after the arrival of Columbus in the Americas, the conquistador Hernán Cortés landed in the area now known as Mexico in search of riches and conquest. The Aztec, whose complicated mythologies incorporated the gods and legends of other Mezoamerican peoples, were approaching the end of a sacred era on their calendar. To ensure the new era's dawn, the sun's strength needed to be maintained through human sacrifices. Cortés found the various regional indigenous tribes immersed in a series of "flower wars" against the powerful Aztec empire, which sought to gain captives for sacrifices. From these tribes Cortés amassed an army of over 200,000 warriors that would defeat the Aztecs in two short but bloody years.

The codex describes the initial meetings of Cortés and the Aztec emperor, Montezuma II, at Tenochtitlan, the island capital of the Mexica-Aztec people. Tenochtitlan was reported to rival European cities in culture, beauty, population, and architectural complexity, with its system of aqueducts and great pyramids. The codex presents Montezuma as a man deeply aware that his reign is the last of an era, a man under the influence of the Mexica prophecies, awaiting the return of the Toltec god Quetzalcoatl. According to the account of the November 8, 1519, meeting with Cortés, Montezuma invoked the mythological and spiritual realms of his people by gifting Cortés with a golden Aztec calendar and crowning him with the headdress of Quetzalcoatl.

Quetzalcoatl, mythically and historically combined in the sacred stories, is both a god and the last ruler of the Toltecs. In *The Anales de Cuauhtitlan* found in *Codex Chimalpopoca* he contains in his person the three shamanic worlds.[4] Born of the snake goddess in union with the mineral depths of the earth, his being is of the underworld. Dressed in the feathers of the *quetzal* bird, he is the messenger of the upperworld. As emperor of the Toltecs, he is the intersection of both of upper and lower in the realm of middle world, ordinary reality.

> Quetzalcoatl is the promised god who will return. He is said to have created human life and refused to offer human sacrifices but offered instead the animals of transformation, snakes, birds, butterflies, and his own blood. In his death as he entered flames, his soul was seen resurrecting from the ashes surrounded by rare and precious singing birds. As patron of the priesthood, learning, arts, and knowledge Quetzalcoatl bestowed many gifts: maize for physical sustenance, the calendar for understanding cosmic events, and written language itself. He is the feathered serpent, symbol of death and resurrection, and the god to whom Montezuma spoke when presenting the headdress.

The Spanish stayed at Tenochtitlan for months. Montezuma's authority eroded until he became a hostage in his own city. Realizing their mistake, the Aztecs through a series of diplomatic exchanges sought the removal of Spaniards and their allies. When the Spanish massacred Aztec nobility at the main temple during a ritual, full hostilities opened up and the Spanish were driven from Tenochtitlan, but Montezuma, the last great Aztec emperor, was killed. Accounts of his death vary. Spanish records report Montezuma was stoned by his own people, but the British Museum has recently unearthed two manuscripts that indicate he was killed by the Spanish.[5] After the Aztec victory Montezuma's brother took his place, but died quickly from the smallpox that was devastating the chain of command. Montezuma's nephew, Cuauhtémoc, assumed the emperor's responsibilities and eventually presided over the Aztecs' final defeat.

With only Tenochtitlan and Tlatelolco, its neighboring island and site of the temples and the Great Pyramid, remaining unconquered, Cortés sealed the conquest of Mexico in a fierce three-month siege of Tenochtitlan, using a large Tlaxcalan army from old Aztec enemies. The city was also ravaged by smallpox, estimated to have killed 25 percent of the Aztec population. War, disease, and famine left thousands of corpses rotted in piles in the streets, yet records indicate a fierce resistance. At Tlatelolco the intense fighting devastated and left in ruin the temples and pyramid.

In August 1521, less then two years after Cortés' arrival in Mexico, Tenochtitlan surrendered, with an estimated 240,000 Aztecs dead.[6] The Aztec emperor, Cuauhtémoc, was taken hostage, personally tortured by Cortés, and finally executed. In a moving account from the oral tradition of the Aztec Supreme Council's decision to surrender, translated by Ignacio Vejar and Mariano Leyva, Cuauhtémoc speaks to those assembled:

> Our Sun has hidden itself
> Our Sun is lost
> and has left us
> complete darkness
> but we know that it will return another time
> that it will come out at another time
> to light our way once again.
> But while it is there in the Mansion of Silence
> very soon let us meet, let us come together,
> and in the center of our Being let us hide
> all that our heart loves, that which is our great treasure. . . .
> Teach the children and the youth
> how our Beloved Mother, Tonantzin Anahuak,
> was and will be great
> and how the destinies of our people will be realized.[7]

Tenochtitlan, the great temple city and seat of an empire, was practically leveled by cannons during the siege. Its ruins became the foundation for Mexico City, the capital of New Spain. Within two brief years, an era had ended in war, famine, pestilence, and cultural collapse. A new epoch was about to rise out of the ashes of the clash of two civilizations.

In August 1523 the first Franciscan missionaries arrived in Mexico to begin the conversion of the remaining Mexica-Aztec populations. Under the influence of their own Christian millennial spirituality of the returning Christ in the Book of Revelations, they embraced the apocryphal history of the Mexica-Aztec with its god-man who offers his own blood in sacrifice in a story of death and resurrection, and they incorporated it into their missionary zeal and their own historical accounts. In 1524 the Spanish built the church of Santiago Tlatelolco at the site of the Great Pyramid.

Contemporary ethnohistorians acknowledge the bias of these early Franciscans, such as Bernardino de Sahagún of the *Florentine Codex* and historian Gerónimo de Mendietaare. These same ethnohistorians acknowledge that the reports of the events of the conquest in the postconquest by the Aztec informants of these historians are also influenced by an attempt to spiritually understand devastating events that occurred within the span of two years. Objective truth may, as a result, never be known, but the accounts of both peoples show that what followed for each was a deep spiritual and physical contemplation—a divine revelation embodied in the Virgin of Guadalupe.

The Apparition to Juan Diego

Ten years after these horrific events, in early December 1531, a humble Aztec man, Cuauhtlatoa ("Eagle Speaks"), with the baptismal name of Juan Diego Cuauhtlatoatzin, was making his way to Mass. He was walking upon Tepeyac Hill, the sacred site of the Aztec earth goddess, Tonantzin, called Our Beloved Mother.

Suddenly he heard the singing of rare and precious birds. The *Nican Mopohu* records his confusion:

Perhaps I am only dreaming it? Perhaps I'm only dozing? Where am I? Where do I find myself? Is it possible that I am in the place our ancient ancestors, our grandparents, told about, in the land of the flowers, in the land of corn, of our flesh, of our sustenance, possibly in the land of heaven?[8]

Just as the singing ceased, a woman's voice called to him by name. He made his way toward the voice at the hilltop and saw a woman radiant as the sun, shining like precious stones, waves of light flowing from her, the entire natural world around her exuding a radiance.

The *Nican Mopohua*, composed in 1560 in the Nahuatl language, is the first written account of these events. Its disputed authorship is most commonly attributed to Antonio Valeriano (1531–1605). Its first lines are direct and straightforward.

> Here it is told, and set down in order, how a short time ago the Perfect Virgin Holy Mary Mother of God, our Queen, miraculously appeared out at Tepeyac, widely known as Guadalupe.

Juan Diego is described as:

> a humble but respected Indian, a poor man of the people; his name was Juan Diego; he lived in Cuauhtitlán, as they say. And in all the things of God, he belonged to Tlaltilolco [Tlatelolco].

In this one sentence, "In all things of God, he belonged to Tlaltilolco"—Tlaltilolco, the heart of Aztec culture, the site of its holy temples—the author shows there are two traditions in this story, and neither will be denied.

The woman spoke most tenderly to the man in his native language.

> Know, be sure, my dearest-and-youngest son, that I am the Perfect Ever Virgin Holy Mary, mother of the one great God of truth. . . . I want very much that they build my sacred little house here, in which I will show him, I will exalt him on making him manifest; I will give him to the people in all my personal love, in my compassionate gaze, in my help, in my salvation, because I am truly your compassionate mother, yours and of all the people who live together in this land, and of all the other people of different ancestries, those who love me, those who cry to me, those who seek me, those who trust in me, because there I will listen to their weeping, their sadness, to remedy, to cleanse and nurse all their different troubles, their miseries, their suffering.

She instructed Juan Diego to go to the home of the bishop and report what he had witnessed. He did as he was asked and went to the residence of the bishop Don Fray Juan de Zumárraga, a Franciscan priest who had recently arrived in New Spain. The bishop listened to the poor Indian man and sent him away. Juan Diego returned to beg the Virgin to choose another.

I beg you, my Lady, Queen, my Beloved Maiden, to have one of the nobles who are held in esteem, one who is known, respected, honored, (have him) carry, take your dear breath, your dear word, so that he will be believed. Because I am really (just) a man from the country, I am a (porter's) rope, I am a back-frame, a tail, a wing, a man of no importance.

The Virgin affirmed that he was her chosen one and that it was important that he do this task. He agreed and once again the bishop dismissed him, telling him that his word was not good enough, that he must bring a sign. Juan visited the Lady again, and she told him to return the next day when she would give him a sign. But he did not return the next day because his uncle, Juan Bernadino, was gravely ill. At midnight his uncle felt death and called for a priest. Juan set out to Tlatelolco for a priest for his dying uncle, trying to sneak by Tepeyac Hill early in the night. The *Nican Mopohua* wryly comments,

He thinks that where he made the turn, the one who is looking everywhere perfectly won't be able to see him. But the voice of the Lady is upon him, "Where are you going, my youngest-and-dearest son? Where are you headed for?"

Juan Diego was a man caught in a cosmic trap, a mere mortal in the lands of the gods, and he knew it. Embarrassed, he promised to return the next day. The tenderness of the Virgin's reply is perhaps more powerful to those who seek her aid then the miracles that follow.

Am I not here, I, who am your mother? Are you not under my shadow and protection? Am I not the source of your joy? Are you not in the hollow of my mantle, in the crossing of my arms? Do you need something more? Let nothing else worry you, disturb you. Do not let your uncle's illness pressure you with grief, because he will not die of it now. You may be certain that he is already well.

The Lady sent him on a cold December night to pick flowers at the top of Tepeyac, a craggy summit with only "rocks, thorns, spines, prickly pears and mesquite trees" growing. To his amazement a field of various flowers in full bloom awaited him. He gathered them in his tilma and carried them to the Lady who blessed them and replaces them in the tilma. Her instructions were clear: take the flowers to the bishop.

So Juan Diego brought himself before the bishop. Standing directly in front of him he let go of his tilma and poured out its contents, flashing many colored Castilian roses. The bishop, awed at Spanish roses blooming in Mexico in December, fell to his knees and began to weep, his eyes riveted on the tilma itself. There the image of the Virgin Mary appeared, clothed in the sun. The bishop's understanding of this experience is predicated within his own tradition on the history of Marian apparitions whose honorific is the Mystical Rose.

They proceeded to the site on Tepeyac Hill where Juan Diego showed the bishop the plain where La Virgen desired her temple. Then, when Juan Diego returned to his uncle he found a vital and well man who recounted a miraculous visitation by the Lady of Heaven who healed him and revealed to him the name of her beautiful image, Holy Mary of Guadalupe.

Source of the Virgin's Name

Why would a woman speaking in Nahuatl call herself "*de Guadalupe*" after the Virgin of Guadalupe, a black Madonna whose image is honored near the Guadalupe River in Spain? Guadalupe itself is Arabic, from *Wad(i)-al-hub* ("river valley of love"). More likely, the bishop's mistake is easily understood in light the similarity of the dark-skinned Virgin and of the sound patterns in the two languages. The Nahuatl word that is homophonic with Guadalupe is *Tlecuauhtlapcupeuh* ("She who emerges from the region of light like the Eagle from fire").

If the recorded story in the *Nican Mopohua* speaks a cosmic tenderness through the Virgin Mother's words, her choice of place for her shrine, the plain at the foot of the hill of the goddess Tonantzin, and the image of her on Juan Diego's tilma speak the language of symbol that reverberates in the human consciousness. The message of the Virgin does not rest in any isolated aspect of this story. Like the tilma of Juan Diego, it is woven of many threads. Depth of meaning arises in the interplay of all the elements, the relationship of apparent diversity to the whole. On the hard road of postconquest the Lady holds in her person the dynamic prophesy, the road to something unforeseen. In the apparent cacophony of disparate worldviews, in the paradox of her person, her presence radiates a promise of beauty, flowers in the harsh winter, a living unity giving birth on the hill of the Aztec mother goddess.

Tonantzin's titles reflect her status as earth goddess: Ancient Giver of Sustenance, Honored Grandmother, Protectress of the Birthing Time, Renewer of Life, Snake Woman of Transformations, Bringer of Maize, Mother of Corn, Sister of Rain, Woman of the Seven Flowers. As earth and mother goddess she was honored in a top room of Tenochtitlan's Great

Pyramid; and at the festival of Xochilhuitl, the "feast of the flowers" (see Patrizia Granziera's chapter in this volume). The *Florentine Codex* describes how all at the festival were "adorned with flowers" as they celebrated with games, drama, dance, poetry, and "flower songs."

The Aztec flower song is a specific genre whose themes of ecstasy and sorrow vary from a celebration of love and pleasure to contemplations of the meaning of life and death. The people reveled in these songs and knew them well. The following excerpt is translated from Nahuatl.[9]

> Let us have friends here!
> It is the time to know our faces.
> Only with flowers
> can our song enrapture.
> We will have gone to His house,
> but our word
> shall live on here on earth.
> We will go, leaving behind
> our grief, our song.
> For this will be known,
> the song shall remain real.
> We will have gone to His house,
> but our word
> shall live here on earth.

When the radiant Lady offered the sign of flowers from Tepeyac, Tonantzin's sacred hill, she was speaking in two languages to two interpreting communities. Marian apparitions historically are revealed to the poor, the outcast, and children, often occurring before disaster or on its heels. Her concerns are the prophet's concerns: a restoration of spiritual commitment, compassion, and justice. In her apparitions she frequently institutes practices to attain restoration: formal prayers, use of sacramentals, devotions, the building of a church. Veneration of Mary in the Catholic Church is called "hyperdulia," greater then the "dulia" veneration given to the saints, and less than the "latria," worship offered only to God.

In 1648 Miguel Sanchez described the Virgin of Guadalupe's image as the Woman of the Apocalypse from the Book of Revelations 12:1: "arrayed with the sun, and the moon under her feet, and upon her head a crown of twelve stars."[10] The Virgin, mother of Christ, functions both as prophet and coredemptrix. Her voice has authority. Thus Mary, as Virgin of Guadalupe, can be seen as a prophetic force. Rabbi Abraham Heschel states, "Prophecy is the voice that God has lent to the silent agony, a voice to the plundered poor, to the profane riches of the world. It is a form of living, a crossing point of God and man."[11] A prophet uses word or symbol to name the imbalance, calls people to repentance, gives hope in dire times, and offers a way to proceed.

The New Testament relates that Mary was a young Jewish woman who was visited by the angel Gabriel and conceived Jesus miraculously. Thus Mary not only speaks the word, she embodies it and gives it body. Although a single authoritative voice of the Virgin speaks out of the Mexican narrative, she can be heard to be "speaking in tongues," in a plurality of voices and points of view to two interpretive communities, Mesoamerican and European, each with its own symbologies, values, and interpretive assumptions. In the interplay of symbols no one worldview is denied or speaks louder than the other.

How the Tilma Speaks

If the medium is the message, Juan Diego's tilma, which should have disintegrated centuries ago, holds a visual alphabet of meaning. On it a woman with Native American features and skin coloring stands upon a crescent moon upheld by an angel; from behind her the sun's rays illuminate her presence. Her head is tilted and bowed, her hands clasped, one knee is bent, as if she is in motion or about to begin a magnificent dance.

Her mantle is the blue-green of the Aztec gods. Upon it are the constellations. Some postulate that the northern hemisphere is portrayed on her right side, the southern on her left in star patterns that would be seen from Tepeyac Hill in December. Above the angel's hand at the Virgin's foot is a leaf of the "Flower of Flesh," the Aztec name for the poinsettia leaf, appropriate to the Virgin who brings the word into flesh. The woman is supported by a divinely charged universe; her embodied presence with its message is of cosmic import.

The Lady's star-patterned mantle drapes over her hair in the style of the eastern Mediterranean at the time of Christ's birth. Her dress is the color of a rose covered with Aztec flower patterns, a flower song of endings and beginnings, sacrifice and rebirth; the *Nahui Ollin*, the single four-petaled flower, like the shape of a cross, which signifies the world navel and the cardinal points around it, is placed over her womb. Nine large triangular Mexican magnolia flowers, one on each sleeve, one over her heart, and six below her heart represent the nine underworlds—a complete Aztec spiritual cosmology, a visual flower song. Around the dress she wears an Aztec maternity belt, making this the only recorded pregnant apparition of the Virgin Mary.

Historically the European and Native American communities interpenetrated their own interpretations through the mythos of the other. Quetzalcoatl, the god who did not require human sacrifice, returned, but not in the person of Cortés. Instead, he appeared as Christ, born of La Morenita, the first mestiza, mother of a new race of people. The Virgin stands on top of the moon, in front of the sun eclipsing in the new era the old sun and moon mythos and the former gods whose reign has now ended. Christ, the sacrifice that ends all sacrifice, is born out of the ruins.

The fabric and paint of the tilma have been examined scientifically and declared both inexplicable and a hoax. Early "proof" of the apparition was found of the reflected image of the bishop in the eyes of the Virgin—the bishop who in later life expressed serious concern that the people were praying not to Mary, but to the Aztec goddess. Modern historians, who acknowledge the bias in the lens of each community, speculate the icon's syncretic representation of the Virgin Mary and the goddess Tonantzin provided a way for 16th-century Spaniards to gain converts among the indigenous population. It also provided a way for 16th-century indigenous Mexicans to covertly practice their native religion.

For the individual or interpretive communities approaching the image, the iconographic layers of sign and symbol are read as a coded message, carrying within them the historical assumptions and previous interpretations of the community. The multiple symbolic layers within the image have the iconic power to draw the interpreting communities into deeper areas of resonance and revelations. In the icon the range of signified meanings is not static or flat but varies and modifies itself as the interpretive communities' values and assumptions change over the course of time, as today in the litany done at the United States/Mexican border.

> Mother Who Never Turns Her Back, tear down the fences that divide
> us from one another,
> Sister in Suffering, comfort those who live in the cold, who have
> no food, who cry for basic human needs,
> Subversive Virgin, teach us to be community beyond nation states,
> Undocumented Virgin, enfold in your arms the undocumented
> immigrants in the desert's wilds.
> Mother Most Vulnerable, fleeing violence and the injustice of rulers,
> fleeing through the desert, help us to become justice. . . .
> Mother who comforts our sorrows, be with us in our grief and fear.[12]

Who Is Guadalupe?

In 1531, when Mexico was born through the image of the pregnant Virgin Guadalupe, a way was found to move forward after devastation. After she appeared with her proclamation of a new era of identity, compassion, and justice, millions converted to Christianity, just as tens of millions annually visit her shrine today. Throughout the centuries her image in revolution and in peace added definition and depth to new identities and values. Her very being spoke a prophetic call to the Americas, beginning with Mexico; she became the mother of new races of people. The Mexican identity of mixed European and indigenous American people was blessed and sanctioned in her as the divine will itself, and as an extension to all those of the Americas of differing descents and their children.

Her teaching is powerfully portrayed at La Plaza de las Tres Culturas ("Plaza of the Three Cultures") located at Tlatelolco, the site of the Aztec temples and great pyramid where the Church of Santiago de Tlatelolco was built on the ruins, where Juan Diego was reported baptized in 1524. There today amid both pre-Columbian and colonial Spanish buildings is a monument with this inscription:

> On 13 August 1521 Tlatelolco, so heroically defended by Cuauhtémoc, finally fell into the hands of Hernán Cortés. It was neither a triumph nor a defeat; it was the painful moment of birth of the Mexico of today, of a race of mestizos.

The language of symbol silences the reasonable tongues. La Morenita, fierce and loving, redefines identities. She confronts acts of injustice, violence from the greedy, the bribed, and the lawless. Her fierce and tender ways come to defend the needy. La Morenita's continued energies of blessing are of significant importance not only to the Mexican people, but to all the Americas, perhaps even the global village. She announces a unity beyond tribal gods.

Notes

1. Enrique Krauze, *Mexico, Biography of Power: A History of Modern Mexico, 1810–1996* (New York: HarperCollins, 1997).

2. Barbara Flaherty, *La Morenita, Litany of Our Lady of Guadalupe* (Columbus, NM: Our Lady of Las Palomas Interfaith Retreat Center, 2007). Elements of this liturgy are indebted to Robert Orsi, "Goddess of the Americas: Writings on the Virgin of Guadalupe," *Commonweal*, March 14, 1997.

3. Bernardino de Sahagún, *Florentine Codex: General History of the Things of New Spain,* trans. Arthur J. O. Anderson and Charles E. Dibble (Santa Fe, NM: School of American Research and University of Utah, 1969).

4. David K. Jordan, trans., "The Death of Quetzalcöätl," *Anales de Cuauhtitlan* (*Codex Chimalpopoca*), secs. 5–8, http://weber.ucsd.edu/~dkjordan/nahuatl/ReadingQuetzalcoatl.html.

5. Bernal Díaz del Castillo, *The Conquest of New Spain*, trans. J. M. Cohen (New York: Penguin, 1963); Maev Kennedy, "Murder Most Foul: British Museum Unmasks Who Really Killed Aztec Leader," *The Guardian*, April 8, 2009.

6. Ross Hassig, *Mexico and the Spanish Conquest* (New York: Longman, 1994).

7. Elissa Rashkin (English translator), from Nahuatl to Spanish, written transcription from the oral tradition; Ignacio Vejar and Mariano Leyva (translators), "The Conquest of Mexico—The Heroic Defense of Mexiko-Tenochtitlan from the Oral Tradition," *The Dagger Journal*, http://www.thedagger.com/archive/conquest/conquest1.html. Reprinted with permission.

8. David K. Jordan, trans., *Nican Mopohua: Here It Is Told*, http://weber.ucsd.edu/~dkjordan/nahuatl/nican/NicanMopohua.html.

9. Excerpts from Miguel León-Portilla, ed., *Native Meso-American Spirituality: Ancient Myths, Discourses, Stories, Doctrines, Hymns, Poems from the Aztec, Yucatec, Wuiche-Maya, and Other Sacred Traditions*, trans. Miguel Leon Portilla, J. O. Arthur Anderson, Charles E. Dibble, and Munro S. Edmondson (Mahwah, NJ: Paulist Press, 1980). Copyright © 1980 by the Missionary Society of St. Paul the Apostle in the State of New York. Paulist Press, Inc., New York/Mahwah, NJ. Reprinted by permission of Paulist Press, Inc., www.paulistpress.com.

10. Timothy Matovina, "Guadalupe at Calvary: Patristic Theology in Miguel Sanchez's Imagen de la Virgen Maria," *Theological Studies* 64, no. 4 (2003): 795ff.

11. Abraham J. Heschel, *The Prophets*, Harper Perennial Modern Classics (New York: HarperCollins, 2001).

12. Flaherty, *La Morenita*.

Bibliography

del Castillo, Bernal Díaz. *The Conquest of New Spain*. Translated by J. M. Cohen. New York: Penguin, 1963.

Flaherty, Barbara. *La Morenita, Litany of Our Lady of Guadalupe*. Columbus, NM: Our Lady of Las Palomas Interfaith Retreat Center, 2007.

Hassig, Ross. *Mexico and the Spanish Conquest*. New York: Longman, 1994.

Heschel, Abraham J. *The Prophets*. Harper Perennial Modern Classics. New York: HarperCollins, 2001.

Jordan, David K., trans. "The Death of Quetzalcöätl." *Anales de Cuauhtitlan* (*Codex Chimalpopoca*), secs. 5–8, http://weber.ucsd.edu/~dkjordan/nahuatl/ReadingQuetzalcoatl.html.

Jordan, David K., trans. *Nican Mopohua: Here It Is Told*. http://weber.ucsd.edu/~dkjordan/nahuatl/nican/NicanMopohua.html.

Kennedy, Maev. "Murder Most Foul: British Museum Unmasks Who Really Killed Aztec Leader." *The Guardian*, April 8, 2009.

Krauze, Enrique. *Mexico, Biography of Power: A History of Modern Mexico, 1810–1996*. New York: HarperCollins, 1997.

León-Portilla, Miguel, ed. *Native Meso-American Spirituality: Ancient Myths, Discourses, Stories, Doctrines, Hymns, Poems from the Aztec, Yucatec, Wuiche-Maya, and Other Sacred Traditions*, trans. Miguel Leon Portilla, J. O. Arthur Anderson, Charles E. Dibble, and Munro S. Edmondson. Mahwah, NJ: Paulist Press, 1980.

Matovina, Timothy. "Guadalupe at Calvary: Patristic Theology in Miguel Sanchez's Imagen de la Virgen Maria." *Theological Studies* 64, no. 4 (2003): 795ff.

Orsi, Robert. "Goddess of the Americas: Writings on the Virgin of Guadalupe." *Commonweal*, March 14, 1997.

Sahagún, Bernardino de. *Florentine Codex: General History of the Things of New Spain*, trans. Arthur J. O. Anderson and Charles E. Dibble. Santa Fe, NM: School of American Research and University of Utah, 1950–1982.

Vejar, Ignacio, and Mariano Leyva, trans. "The Conquest of Mexico—The Heroic Defense of Mexiko-Tenochtitlan from the Oral Tradition." *The Dagger Journal*, http://www.thedagger.com/archive/conquest/conquest1.html.

9

La Virgen de la Caridad del Cobre: Cuba's Virgin of Charity

Karen Dillon

The different names given to Cuba's Virgin of Charity each represent a particular aspect of her complex and unique character. Known formally as Our Lady of Charity, she is part of the Catholic veneration of the Virgin Mary and is the official patroness of Cuba. A mixture of folk and religious traditions, *la Virgen de la Caridad del Cobre*, affectionately known as Cachita ("little Charity"), is a synthesis of the Yoruba (Nigerian) goddess Òsun and the Catholic virgin mother in the Afro-Cuban religion of Santería. Giving her the honorable title of *la Virgen mambisa* ("the rebel Virgin"), Cuban soldiers called upon her to protect and sanction them during the Cuban wars of independence in the latter half of the 19th century, the revolution of 1959, and the subsequent Cuban diaspora in the United States, symbolizing the varied sentiments of Cuban nationality at different moments in Cuba's history. Finally, as *Gran Madre mulata* ("the mixed-race grandmother"), the Virgin of Charity cannot be separated from Cuba's cult of the mulata, a cultural and literary tradition that places racial mixture at the center of Cuban national discourse. In the many facets of her character, the Virgin of Charity embodies the very essence of cultural and religious syncretism, one of many examples of such synthesis in the Caribbean.

Although she is celebrated outside of Cuba—in Puerto Rico, for example—the Virgin of Charity's multifaceted character narrates Cuban history itself.

By looking closely at the mulata Virgin, "we should be able to detect in the color of her skin or in her attributes the different cultures and elements from which she derives"—Spanish, Indian (Taínos), African, and Creole.[1] As such, the story of the Virgin of Charity must be told through the particular social and political conditions in the history of Cuba.

Historical Narrative of the Virgin of Charity

El Cobre, the home of the Virgin of Charity and the oldest colonial settlement in Cuba founded in the early 16th century, is a copper-mining town in the mountains of Sierra del Cobre in Oriente Province, the southernmost region of Cuba about ten miles outside the capital city of Santiago de Cuba. The Virgin first appeared in El Cobre in the early 17th century during a time defined by the exploitation of indigenous Indians, the enslavement of Africans, and Spanish Catholic colonialism. The definitive narrative of the Virgin of Charity comes from the eyewitness testimony of Juan Moreno, who as a young boy was present when the Virgin first appeared. The oral legend and the visual representations of the Virgin of Charity are based on Moreno's testimony, which was given in Santiago del Prado, present-day El Cobre, in 1687, and notarized by the Catholic Church.[2]

Secondary sources disagree as to the precise year the Virgin of Charity appeared; depending on the interpretation of Juan Moreno's testimony given as witness, the year falls somewhere between 1604 and 1612. The narrative begins with two native Indian (Taíno) brothers, Rodrigo and Juan de Hoyos, and ten-year-old black slave Juan Moreno in a canoe in the Bay of Nipe looking for salt mines needed to preserve the meat of the slaughterhouse in Barajagua, a small settlement near El Cobre. Some variances to the story represent the three witnesses specifically as fishermen or as workers in the El Cobre copper mines. While they were searching for or coming back from the salt mines, depending on the version, a violent storm brewed in the Bay of Nipe and caused the brothers and the boy to pray for help.

During the calm that followed the storm, they saw something floating in the distance, which at first they mistook for a bird, but soon saw that it was a statue of the Virgin Mary floating on a wooden plank. The Virgin was holding the infant Jesus in one arm and a gold cross in the other, and inscribed on the wooden plank were the words "*Yo soy la Virgen de la Caridad*" ("I am the Virgin of Charity"). Despite the storm and the fact that it was floating on the water, the statue of the Virgin was not wet. The statue, which still can be seen, is about sixteen inches high, and the Virgin, wearing a cloak that gives the statue a triangular shape, rests her feet on a crescent moon.

Sensing the miraculous nature of the Virgin's appearance, the de Hoyos brothers and Juan Moreno took the statue back to the overseer of the cattle ranch in Barajagua, who then took it to Captain Don Francisco Sanchez de Moya, administrator of the El Cobre copper mines. De Moya ordered a small palm-thatched shrine built for the Virgin in the pasture land of Barajagua on the outskirts of the mines. Although the Virgin continued to perform small miracles, the statue disappeared each night from the palm-thatched shrine built for her, only to appear in the morning on top of a nearby hill overlooking the copper mines. A hermitage was then built for her on top of the hill overlooking the copper mines, but again she disappeared each night only to return in the morning. Thinking that the Virgin of Charity wanted to be closer to the copper mines of El Cobre to preside over the safety of the slaves who worked there, the statue was taken and placed on the main altar in the parish of El Cobre.[3] It was through the Virgin of Charity's "metonymical association with the mines that she became, at least in Moreno's implicit text, the protector of the mines and its slaves."[4]

Juan and Rodrigo de Hoyos and Juan Moreno became known collectively as "Los Tres Juanitos," the three Juans: Juan Criollo, a term from Spanish colonial times for a person born in the colonies with pure European bloodlines, Juan Indio, and Juan Esclavo, representing the three primary racial categories of Cuba (Spanish European, native Indian or Taínos, and Black African). The Juans' "non-Spanish ethnic backgrounds are a touchstone for the complexity of the image of La Caridad del Cobre," whose mulata complexion makes her "a figure of the inalterable mixture of identities in a creole society. She is herself a creole, born out of the stormy waters of the Atlantic."[5] The Virgin of Charity's appearance to two indigenous Indians and an African (Creole) slave in the Bay of Nipe fits with the traditional master narrative of the Virgin Mother appearing to society's most disempowered.[6] However, Moreno's testimony was given within the confines of the Catholic Church and the Spanish crown, thereby dogmatizing the narrative of the Virgin of Charity and possibly eclipsing her pre-Spanish, pre-Catholic roots.

Alternative Versions of the Virgin of Charity's Origins

Though the appearance of the Virgin of Charity in the Bay of Nipe is considered the definitive narrative of her origin, there are other possibilities for how she could have arrived in Cuba. As María Elena Díaz points out, "it is impossible to know what other versions less 'supervised' by the church coexisted with this particular foundational story," and just because the Christian Marian narrative serves as the foundational narrative for the

Virgin of Charity does not mean that indigenous or hybrid versions of her character did not exist prior to the beginning of the Cuban cult of the Virgin of Charity.[7]

According to Anthony Stevens-Arroyo, the society of the Taínos Indians, native inhabitants of Cuba before Spanish colonialism, disappeared by the middle of the 16th century due to the Spanish colonial invasion, but elements of the Taínos's religious beliefs match up with that of the Virgin of Charity. Juan Indio, one of the three witnesses to whom the Virgin appeared in the Bay of Nipe, was supposedly a Christianized Taíno. The Virgin of Charity's association with the copper mines at El Cobre also links her to the Taínos because they were devoted to copper's brilliance and held it as a sacred metal.[8] Atabey, the mother goddess of the Taínos Indians to whom women prayed for successful childbirth, is thought to be a precursor to the Virgin of Charity.[9] Furthermore, the statue of the Virgin of Charity in the church at Illescas in Spain shows her standing on a crescent moon with the tips pointing upward, a classic European Catholic image. Cuban representations of the Virgin often show the moon with the crescents pointing downward "in accord with the Taíno perception, rather than in imitation of the Spanish statue."[10] Even after the Spanish settled in Cuba, the Virgin of Charity's image could have been brought by a Spanish colonist or sailor as far back as Columbus because "a Madonna named Our Lady of Charity was popular in certain regions of Spain during the second half of the 16th century and the early years of the 17th century."[11] Regardless of the many possibilities for the formulation of her identity, the Virgin of Charity became a distinctive Cuban figure within the Marian cult with the narrative of the Virgin's finding in the Bay of Nipe.

Historical Invocations for Religious and National Purposes

As a local deity, the Virgin of Charity became the protector of the copper mines of El Cobre and of the slaves who worked them. Her worship spread locally among the slaves and then regionally and ultimately nationally during the Cuban wars for independence from Spain during the latter half of the 19th century. During the wars, revolutionary leader Carlos Manuel Céspedes pledged himself and his majority black army at the shrine of the Virgin and in 1895 Cuban soldiers had images of the Virgin sewn onto their uniforms during the second war of independence.[12] Calixto García, the general who finally led Cuban troops to victory in the 1898 War of Independence, supposedly knelt in gratitude before the Virgin of Charity after achieving independence from Spain.[13]

With the Spanish defeated in 1898 and the Cuban republic established in 1902, the Virgin of Charity became known as *la Virgen mambisa* ("the rebel Virgin") named after the victorious Cuban soldiers known as *mambises*.[14] At the request of the veterans of the War of Independence, Pope Benedict XV crowned the Virgin of Charity "Our Lady of Charity," patroness of Cuba, in 1916, and a national shrine was dedicated in El Cobre on her feast day, September 8, in 1927. Pope Paul VI raised her sanctuary to the category of Basilica in 1977.

Almost half a century after the Virgin of Charity was declared patroness of Cuba and ultimate symbol of Cuban nationality and unity, Fidel Castro and his soldiers celebrated their socialist victory during the revolution in 1959 at a mass in Havana. At the mass, Castro wore a medal of the Virgin of Charity on his chest, embracing the Virgin "as a symbol of the new revolutionary government."[15] Anti-Castro Catholics fled Cuba after the revolution of 1959, principally to Miami, Florida, a major location of the Cuban diaspora. The Shrine of Our Lady of Charity in Biscayne Bay, Miami, is the cornerstone of the Cuban Catholic exile community there, and by the 1990s the shrine became the sixth largest Catholic pilgrimage site in the United States.[16] For Cubans living at home and abroad, the Virgin of Charity has represented an essential part of Cuban identity. As patron saint of Cuba and the rebel Virgin, she "supports the beliefs and practices of the Roman Catholic Church and, at the same time, legitimates the nationalistic values of the Cuban nation state."[17] No matter what political conditions dictated the relationship between Cubans and the nation, the Virgin of Charity played an integral role in how Cubans imagined that relationship.

The Virgin of Charity and the Royal Slaves of El Cobre

The tradition of the Virgin of Charity emerged and was transmitted into written text at a particular historical moment in Cuba when slaves struggled to define their identity and place within the Spanish imperial colony. Before the Virgin of Charity embodied the story of Cuba as a national symbol, she first represented the story of a group of slaves who had to negotiate their freedom within the confines of Catholic Spanish imperialism, and the slaves' relationship with the Virgin became an important part of that negotiation.[18] For the royal slaves of El Cobre, the Virgin of Charity became a means of establishing their independent identity and importance by showing themselves to be the Virgin's chosen people. According to Juan Moreno's testimony given as an old man and as a royal slave of El Cobre, the Virgin's appearance to two Indians and an African slave reveals who her chosen people were.

More than sixty years after the Virgin of Charity was placed on the altar in the parish of El Cobre to preside over the copper mines, the Spanish crown confiscated the copper mines and slaves of El Cobre in 1670, and about 271 creole slaves became royal slaves—the king's slaves. The private mining slaves were reconstituted into a pueblo, a village community of royal slaves and free people of color with a limited local self-government.[19] At the same time the royal slaves of the copper mines were being placed into pueblo communities, the local shrine of El Cobre was growing in following and became a major center of religious worship. By the mid-18th century, the hermitage of the Virgin of Charity in El Cobre had grown from a local to a regional to a national shrine as "the richest sanctuary on the island." Since the late 17th century, after the slaves of the copper mines became royal slaves, the tradition of ex-votos, votive offerings, had been a large part of worship at the El Cobre shrine. Testimonies and gifts left behind attested to the miraculous powers of the Virgin and helped to spread word of her healing power. As the Virgin of Charity's worship grew, "the royal slaves played a central role in shaping the contours of this tradition, particularly as they claimed this Virgin patroness and protectress of their budding community."[20] For the royal slaves of El Cobre, the Virgin of Charity's shrine was an essential part of who they were as a distinctive community in the Spanish colony.

Knowing that the figure of the Virgin was a political and religious trope through which they could negotiate both their identity and their freedom, in the years following their appropriation by the Spanish crown the El Cobre royal slaves invoked the Virgin when they "litigated for their freedom all the way to Madrid."[21] In a petition for their freedom in 1779, one of the slaves' main bargaining tools was a promise to build a new sanctuary for the Virgin of Charity.[22] The royal slaves were finally granted their freedom in 1800. Juan Moreno was a royal slave of El Cobre when he testified before the Catholic Church in 1687 about finding the statue of the Virgin of Charity, and this fact, along with "the development of the island's major 18th-century shrine in an Afro-Cuban *pueblo*," constitutes "remarkable (yet all too often unremarked) historical aspects in the making of the 'Cuban' Marian tradition" of the Virgin of Charity.[23]

From Copper Mines to Sugar Plantation: The Virgin of Charity and Santería

Native Taíno Indians were the first to work the copper mines when they were discovered in El Cobre in 1530, but by the middle of the 16th century the Spanish imported African slaves whom they felt were more resistant to the diseases of colonialism.[24] It was toward the end of the 18th century that large numbers of African slaves, primarily the Yoruba from Nigeria in West Africa, were brought to Cuba to work the sugar plantations. Cuba's sugar industry, the largest sugar producer by the middle of the 19th century, "heralded the transformation of all Cuba": geographically, technologically, culturally, but, most significantly, racially.[25] In 1840 the black population officially became the majority in Cuba, and it was on the sugar plantation that the Virgin of Charity became meaningful to Cuba's black population as a sister goddess to an African one in the Afro-Cuban religion of Santería.

Because Cuba had such a large African population under Spanish colonial rule, Spain tried to create a unifying ideology by imposing Roman Catholicism as a state religion. To promote Catholicism, beginning in the 17th century the Spanish church sponsored *cabildos*, religious communities that indoctrinated indigenous Indians and African slaves to Catholic principles, including veneration of specific saints. This allowed followers the opportunity to see parallels between Catholic saints and African deities, or *orishas*.[26] In the cabildos, slaves adapted their own religious customs of Orisha (deity) worship to the Catholic Church's worship. The cabildos were "ostensibly devoted to the cultivation of Catholic virtues, where Yoruba music, dance, and religion were celebrated."[27] Thus, the Afro-Cuban religion Santería mixes attributes of Catholic saints with Yoruban deities.

Cuba's Virgin of Charity became syncretized in Santería with the Yoruba goddess Òsun, goddess of love, becoming the Afro-Cuban goddess Oshún, goddess of rivers and streams and representing fertility and love. According to Raul Canizares, Oshún traveled to Cuba to be with her children (slaves) who were taken away, and she asked a sister goddess to make her hair straighter and her skin lighter "so that all Cubans can see a bit of themselves in me."[28] Santería goddess Oshún, also known as "Cachita," represents *Caridad del Cobre*, the folk name of the mulata Virgin of Charity. The Yoruba slaves found in the image of the Virgin of Charity "a crowned female divinity, who miraculously appeared from the waters to save humble people of color from the storm. She herself is 'of color,' and [a] warrior patroness . . . a compassionate mother who lovingly holds her child and fiercely protects her children."[29] Intertwined in the Santería variation of the Virgin of Charity are the threads of the Taíno mother goddess Atabey, protector of childbirth, the African goddess Òsun, goddess of love, and the Catholic Virgin of Charity, found in the waters of the Bay of Nipe and protector of the "children" (slaves) of the copper mines.

The Virgin of Charity as a National and Cultural Tradition

Racial and cultural diversity and mixture define, in part, Cuba's national history, and the figure of the mulata has been the "principal signifier of Cuba's national cultural identity" both politically and in literature since the 19th century. According to Vera Kutzinski, Cuba "encodes its national identity in the iconic figure of a *mulata*—that of the *Virgen de la Caridad del Cobre*, the coppery Virgin of Charity who is Cuba's patron saint." Not only is the mulata the national symbol and primary deity of Cuba, but the mulata Cecilia Valdés, title character of Cirilo Villaverde's *Cecilia Valdés*, an 1837 short story that turned into the 1882 abolitionist novel, officially introduced the mulata into Cuban literary history as "Cuba's greatest cultural heroine" and arguably the figure responsible for "the construction of Cuban national identity" through literature. The mulata Virgin of Charity and the figure of the mulata as represented by *Cecilia Valdés* become conflated because of their roles as signifiers of Cuba's colonial history, and together they form the Cuban cult of the mulata often invoked in Cuban literature and culture.[30]

The figure of the mulata is the ultimate symbol of the ideal of racial and national unity because her body is a literal synthesis of different races and cultures; the mulata is "a symbolic container" for all the questions of race, gender, and sexuality that are part of colonial and postcolonial Cuba.[31] Typically, the mulata is an exotic figure of desire, but her conflation with Cuba's cult of the Virgin, the mulata patroness, puts a unique spin on the Virgin of Charity in that she is both a holy mother and a woman characterized as a sexual being. The mulata Virgin embodies a duality of existence in that her identity harkens to both the sexual and the spiritual. Cuban literature in the tradition of *Cecilia Valdés* offers Cuba a national myth in the cult of the mulata that celebrates contact between cultures rather than a history that marginalizes racial mixture. The Cuban literary tradition from *poesía mulata* to contemporary Cuban novelists such as Oscar Hijuelos and Christina García invoke the cult of the mulata, and thus the Virgin of Charity, to portray the complex intercultural relations of Cuban history and the construction of Cuban conceptions of race and gender.

Cuba's Virgin of Charity has taken on mythic proportions due to narratives of creolization and religious syncretism, and as a figure who has her origin in three cultures—European, Indian, and African—she is not only a cultural and historical symbol of Cuba, but of the Caribbean itself. For Antonio Benitez-Rojo, the mulata Virgin of Charity illustrates the unending origins of cultural syncretism, as "a meeting or confluence of marine flowings that connects the Niger with the Mississippi, the

China Sea with the Orinoco, the Parthenon with a fried food stand in an alley in Paramaribo."[32] In the figure of the Virgin of Charity, then, lies the history of a place where cultures from around the world meet and exchange, and in whom the various communities of Cuba have been able to define their national and cultural identity.

Notes

1. Silvia Spitta, "Transculturation, the Caribbean, and the Afro-Cuban Imaginary," in *Tropicalizations: Transcultural Representations of Latinidad*, ed. Frances R. Aparicio and Susana Chávez-Silverman (Hanover, NH: University Press of New England, 1997), 170.

2. María Elena Díaz, "Rethinking Tradition and Identity: The Virgin of Charity of El Cobre," in *Cuba, the Elusive Nation: Interpretations of National Identity*, ed. Damián J. Fernández and Madeline Cámara Betancourt (Gainesville: University Press of Florida, 2000), 58 n.13.

3. María Elena Díaz, *The Virgin, the King, and the Royal Slaves of El Cobre: Negotiating Freedom in Colonial Cuba, 1670–1780* (Stanford, CA: Stanford University Press, 2000), 99–100.

4. Díaz, "Rethinking Tradition and Identity," 52.

5. Joseph M. Murphy and Mei-Mei Sanford, *Òsun Across the Waters: Yoruba Goddess in Africa and the Americas* (Bloomington: Indiana University Press, 2001), 88.

6. Díaz, "Rethinking Tradition and Identity," 50.

7. Ibid., 56.

8. Anthony M. Stevens-Arroyo, "The Persistence of Religious Cosmovision in an Alien World," in *Enigmatic Powers: Syncretism with African and Indigenous Peoples' Religions Among Latinos*, ed. Anthony M. Stevens-Arroyo and Andres I. Perez y Mena (New York: Bildner Center Books, 1995), 114, 125.

9. Thomas A. Tweed, *Our Lady of the Exile: Diasporic Religion at a Cuban Catholic Shrine in Miami* (New York: Oxford University Press, 1997), 113.

10. Stevens-Arroyo, "Persistence of Religious Cosmovision," 126.

11. Tweed, *Our Lady of the Exile*, 20.

12. Murphy, *Òsun Across the Waters*, 90.

13. Harry G. Lefever, "The Virgin of Charity of Cuba: Both Patron Saint and Outsider," *Southeastern Latin Americanist* 43, no. 2 (2000): 85.

14. Murphy, *Òsun Across the Waters*, 90.

15. Lefever, "The Virgin of Charity of Cuba," 85.

16. Tweed, *Our Lady of Exile*, 3.

17. Lefever, "The Virgin of Charity of Cuba," 83.

18. Díaz, *The Virgin, the King, and the Royal Slaves of El Cobre*.

19. Díaz, "Rethinking Tradition and Identity," 48, 49.

20. Díaz, *The Virgin, the King, and the Royal Slaves of El Cobre*, 95, 116, 139–140.

21. Díaz, "Rethinking Tradition," 49.

22. Murphy, *Òsun Across the Waters*, 90.

23. Díaz, "Rethinking Tradition," 55.

24. Murphy, *Òsun Across the Waters*, 88.

25. Louis A. Pérez Jr., *Cuba: Between Reform and Revolution* (New York: Oxford University Press, 1988), 76.

26. George Brandon, *Santeria from Africa to the New World* (Bloomington: Indiana University Press, 1993).

27. Murphy, *Òsun Across the Waters*, 91.

28. Raul Canizares, *Walking with the Night: The Afro-Cuban World of Santeria* (Rochester, VT: Destiny Books, 1993), 65–66.

29. Murphy, *Òsun Across the Waters*, 91.

30. Vera Kutzinski, *Sugar's Secrets: Race and the Erotics of Cuban Nationalism* (Charlottesville: University Press of Virginia, 1993), 5, 7.

31. Ibid.

32. Antonio Benitez-Rojo, *The Repeating Island: The Caribbean and the Postmodern Perspective* (Durham, NC: Duke University Press, 1996), 16.

Bibliography

Benitez-Rojo, Antonio. *The Repeating Island: The Caribbean and the Postmodern Perspective* 2nd ed. Durham, NC: Duke University Press, 1996.

Brandon, George. *Santeria from Africa to the New World.* Bloomington: Indiana University Press, 1993.

Canizares, Raul. *Walking with the Night: The Afro-Cuban World of Santeria.* Rochester, VT: Destiny Books, 1993.

Díaz, María Elena. "Rethinking Tradition and Identity: The Virgin of Charity of El Cobre." In *Cuba, the Elusive Nation: Interpretations of National Identity,* ed. Damián J. Fernández and Madeline Cámara Betancourt, 43–59. Gainesville: University Press of Florida, 2000.

Díaz, María Elena. *The Virgin, the King, and the Royal Slaves of El Cobre: Negotiating Freedom in Colonial Cuba, 1670–1780.* Stanford, CA: Stanford University Press, 2000.

Kutzinski, Vera. *Sugar's Secrets: Race and the Erotics of Cuban Nationalism.* Charlottesville: University Press of Virginia, 1993.

Lefever, Harry G. "The Virgin of Charity of Cuba: Both Patron Saint and Outsider." *Southeastern Latin Americanist* 43, no. 2 (2000): 82–95.

Murphy, Joseph M., and Mei-Mei Sanford. *Òsun Across the Waters: A Yoruba Goddess in Africa and the Americas.* Bloomington: Indiana University Press, 2001.

Pérez, Louis A., Jr. *Cuba: Between Reform and Revolution.* New York: Oxford University Press, 1988.

Spitta, Silvia. "Transculturation, the Caribbean, and the Cuban-American Imaginary." In *Tropicalizations: Transcultural Representations of Latinidad*, ed. Frances R. Aparicio and Susana Chávez-Silverman, 160–180. Hanover, NH: University Press of New England, 1997.

Stevens-Arroyo, Anthony M. "The Persistence of Religious Cosmovision in an Alien World." In *Enigmatic Powers: Syncretism with African and Indigenous Peoples' Religions Among Latinos*, ed. Anthony M. Stevens-Arroyo and Andres I. Perez y Mena, 113–135. New York: Bildner Center Books, 1995.

Tweed, Thomas A. *Our Lady of the Exile: Diasporic Religion at a Cuban Catholic Shrine in Miami*. New York: Oxford University Press, 1997.

10

Gran Brijit: Haitian Vodou Guardian of the Cemetery

Kerry Noonan

Gran Brijit is a Haitian Vodou *lwa*, or intermediary divine spirit, also known as Grande Brigitte, Maman Brigitte, and Gran Boujitte. Gran Brijit is believed to rule over the dead in cemeteries, along with her husband, Bawon Samdi.[1] She is both an old, asexual woman who, when she comes in possession in ritual, is mute and attired like a corpse, but she is also a sexual being, a former prostitute who had numerous children with her husband the Bawon. Images of Gran Brijit found in works of art or on the sequined flags used in Vodou rituals can range from a stately woman in purple, to a lamia-like figure with a split tail, to a provocatively posed young woman with her legs open. Food offerings for Gran Brijit include potatoes, plantains, salted herring and dried cod, corn and grilled pistachios, cane syrup, and white rum. Black pullets are sacrificed to her. Her special days are Monday and Friday, and her color is black.[2] Gran Brijit can trace her roots to the Yoruba orisa Oya and the Irish Catholic saint Brigit of Kildare, popular in both Ireland and Brittany; in some of Gran Brijit's attributes an "echo" can be discerned of those enigmatic carvings found in churches all over Ireland and in parts of England, the Sheela na gig (see Starr Goode's chapter in volume 2). While there are no full narratives about her, she is present in the art, lore, and rituals of Vodou.

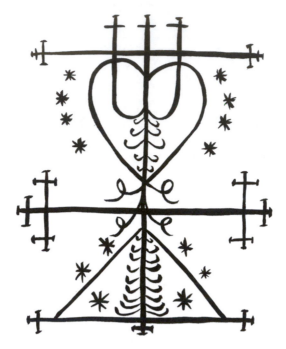

Figure 10.1 Ruler of cemeteries in Haitian Vodou, Gran Brijit is a fascinating amalgam of indigenous, African, and Irish mythic figures. (Copyright Hrana Janto.)

Vodou: An Afro-Caribbean Religion

Haitian Vodou is made up of elements of the religions of the various West
African peoples brought to Haiti in slavery, combined with folk Catholicism.
This combination of disparate religious systems with underlying structural similarities is called "syncretism." As an Afro-Caribbean religion, Vodou follows a
cosmological model found in many West African religions, with a *deus otiosus* (a
creator who creates the world and then is distant, not directly concerned with
the daily lives of mortals) and a coterie of divine intermediary spirits who over-
see and control the natural world and all its inhabitants. African slaves in the
Caribbean recognized this familiar model (a creator aided by lesser sacred
beings with specific duties, who are more accessible to human beings) in
the Catholic system of God and the saints, which was introduced to them in
the New World. They creatively combined their own divine spirits with these
saints, resulting in the complex and compelling religions created to meet the
pressing needs of horrific conditions on the plantations: Vodou in Haiti, Santería in Cuba, and Candomblé in Brazil, among others. Like the Catholic saints
with whom they are identified, the lwa each rule over a particular area of life,
and have their own sacred colors, symbols, images, and appropriate offerings.

Although Vodou is often looked down upon by the Haitian elite and by the Catholic Church, it is an important part of ordinary Haitians' lives, and legend has it that the Haitian revolution—the only successful slave revolution in history—was begun at a Vodou ritual. People in the United States often have distorted ideas about Vodou, equating "voodoo" with everything from Satanism to evil magic, and even using it as a way to disparage political rivals' economic systems, as when the first President Bush famously called Ronald Reagan's ideas "voodoo economics." Despite efforts to stamp out the practice of Vodou by the Catholic Church, by the Haitian government at various times, and by Protestant missionaries, Vodou remains the spiritual system most Haitians turn to as they negotiate the often harsh realities of their daily lives.

Vodou has no sacred text, no official hierarchy, and no required dogma, so information about any of its myriad lwa and spirits must come from the practices of Haitian people as recorded by ethnographers, historians, missionaries, and practitioners themselves. Without official doctrine or a holy book, the two most important sources for Vodou are oral tradition, passed on by priestesses and priests (*manbos* and *oungans*), and direct contact with the divine beings through possession, divination, or dreams. Initiated priestesses or priests receive the lwa in possession trances within Vodou ceremonies; each lwa has its own special signs, symbols, drum rhythms, and songs with which they are called, and when a lwa appears and "mounts" a *manbo* or *oungan*, the appropriate attire must be given the human "horse" who is being "ridden" by the lwa, and the proper offerings should be brought. The beauty of Vodou is that the lwa come into the body of a human and speak directly to those gathered at the ritual, giving personal attention and advice to the mortals who honor them.

Who Is Gran Brijit?

When discussing Bawon Samdi, most works on Haitian Vodou mention that he has a wife, known variously as Gran Brijit or Maman Brijit. However, this mention is usually no more than a line or two; almost no scholarship exists on this shadowy figure. She is important enough to be included in the lists of lwa by eminent writers on Vodou like Maya Deren, Alfred Metraux, and others, and so she must have devotées among those who serve the lwa, whether in Haiti or in the United States. Either scholars of Vodou have never found many informants who were dedicated to her, or she is always considered a secondary figure, a member of the usually large retinue of spirits who are associated with the Bawon or the other Gedes. Gede is both a lwa himself and also a "family" of similar lwa, like the Bawon, all of whom are connected with death and sex; Gede is the stark reality of death as well as the life-affirming powers of sex, and as the lord of these two realms which all mortals must face, he is a humorous yet confronting spirit that peels away the veneer of civilized manners and hypocrisy.

Bawon Samdi is one aspect of Gede and is most associated with death and the dead. The large central cross found in every Haitian cemetery, symbol of the intersection of this world and the next, is sacred to him, and the first male buried in every cemetery is dedicated to him. People who "serve the spirits," as practitioners call the practice of Vodou, often make offerings to the Bawon at the central cross. If the first person buried in the cemetery is a female, then she is dedicated to Gran Brijit, the Bawon's wife. Maya Deren, in *Divine Horsemen*, her influential work on Vodou, says that "the graves that are under the special protection of [Bawon Samdi's] female counterpart, Maman Brigitte, are marked by a mound of stones."[3] Alfred Metraux confirms that "Baron's wife, Big Brigitte, Maman or Mademoiselle Brigitte, also has authority over cemeteries, particularly those in which the first person buried was a woman."[4] Karen McCarthy Brown, usually such a rich source for information on the female lwa and on women's relationship to them, does not say much more about Maman Brijit:

> The Gede persona and the cemetery rituals that fall within his domain reflect a somewhat anachronistic but still powerful patriarchal ideology. Papa Gede . . . has a wife. But . . . Gede's wife, Brijit, is clearly his inferior. Haitians pay special attention to the grave of the first female buried in every cemetery, calling it the Brijit grave. But the ritual attention to Brijit is only a small and perfunctory part of rites intended mainly for Baron. Brijit is not Gede's female counterpart outside the cemetery, either. Possessions by her are infrequent; I have never seen her ride Alourdes. In other contexts, she comes as an ancient, hobbled woman who can barely talk or walk. Gran Brijit (Grandmother Brijit), as she is usually called, is an old woman who no longer has sexual power. Papa Gede's enlivening sexual energy, his infectious humor and telling satire, his childlike disregard for social control have no parallel in Gran Brijit.[5]

In this description, Brown not only refutes Deren's claim that Brijit is a female Gede, but she also criticizes what Deren does know of Brijit; this is a preface for her own claim that a female version of Gede, called Gedelia, has begun to manifest in possession. This new Gedelia has a female form of

Gede's sexual energy and humor, whereas Brijit is old and nonsexual. Contrary to Brown's assertion that Brijit has no sexual power, Michel S. Laguerre describes her in highly sexual terms: "Gran-n Brigit, [the Baron's] wife, was formerly a ritual prostitute and used to execute sensuous dances for Baron Samedi. From their union were born all the other Guédés, their children."[6] He also includes a photo of two women possessed by Gran Brijit who are dancing the *banda*, the lascivious dance usually performed by Gede when he possesses someone. The Gedes wear dark or purple clothes, according to Laguerre, and presumably this includes Brijit, whom he names as one of the most important members of the Gede family. "Usually the Guédés have a heavy layer of powder on their faces and white cotton in their ears and noses"[7] Although cotton is used in this way to stop the orifices of corpses, Laguerre shows a dancing, sexual Brijit, who has more in common with Gede's combination of the obscene, fertility, and death than with an asexual or old or corpse-like figure other scholars describe.

In the comprehensive and opulent catalog *Sacred Arts of Haitian Vodou*, Gran Brijit is the smallest of bit players, showing up only twice. She appears in a painting by André Pierre, dark skinned, wearing a purple and black outfit (the colors of mourning) with a skirt wrapped in a very snake-like way around the lower half of her body. She is not particularly old; her hair is black and flowing, done up in an elaborate coiffure rising above her head. She holds what appears to be Veronica's veil, with the bleeding head of Christ crowned with thorns on it. She stands to the Bawon's right, and behind the top of her hairdo are flames or flame-like foliage.[8] This rendering of Brijit is very similar to one made by Pierre Joseph Valcin.

The Valcin version shows Brijit attired in a purple dress with a black decorated cloth over her shoulders. The skirt of the dress is extremely snakelike in this painting. She holds a handkerchief in one hand and has a cross within a heart emblazoned on her breast. Her hair is black and flowing in this version also, but in place of the high hairdo she wears a tall, conical purple hat. It seems that a purple and black dress with sinuous, snaky coils is part of a recognizable depiction of Brijit, as well as long, flowing black hair. This does not jibe with the above descriptions of Brijit as ancient and nonsexual. In these paintings she may not be a ravishing beauty, but she is not a withered hag either. She has a dignity appropriate to her state.

Donald Cosentino offers only two brief, intriguing mentions of Brijit. A paraphrase from Michel Laguerre alludes to her past as a ritual prostitute, although the "ritual" aspect of this vocation is never explained. Another description from André Pierre, the painter, reads: "Bawon Samdi is Adam.

Guardian of the cemetery. Guardian of all the dead. Everyone's father. And Gran Brijit is Eve."[9] If Brijit is Eve, then she is the mother of all the living and the dead. Eve is also associated with temptation, particularly of a sexual nature, and so Pierre also refers to the sexual component of Brijit. And this reference to Eve gives the snakelike attributes of the images just described even more interesting resonances.

Connection with St. Brigit of Ireland

The longest reference to Brijit is found in the work of Milo Marcelin.[10] Marcelin agrees that Brijit is very old, but says she is as powerful as her husband and declares her identification with St. Brigit of Ireland. Although he claims cases of possession are rare, he describes how Brijit manifests herself. She lies like a dead person, and the others bind her jaw with a black scarf, sealing her ears and nose with cotton, and covering her with a white cloth while spraying white rum upon her. Brijit never speaks. When Bawon and Brijit appear together, he, too, is treated like a corpse, with a shroud over him and cotton in his nose and ears. He lies on the bed where Brijit is laid out. Marcelin implies that Brijit lies still and is silent when she comes in possession. In the song he quotes, the lyrics seem to imply there is some question as to whether Brijit is dead or sleeping.

You say Maman Brijitte is in bed
'And that she sleeps!
You say Maman Brijitte is in bed
'And that she sleeps!
When she awakens
The last *hounsi* [initiated ritual attendant] will curtsey!
'There is water in Maman Brijitte's eyes!
When she awakens
The last hounsi will curtsy!

The salted herring, dried cod, and white rum Marcelin lists as the proper offerings for Brijit all evoke European (perhaps Irish?) sailors' rations. And of course, potato dishes play a part in the foodways of the Irish feast of St. Brigit.

Irish and Breton Roots

There is historical evidence of Irish presence in the Caribbean from the 17th to the 19th century. Large numbers of Irish people were sold as indentured servants to America and the West Indies in the mid-1600s, as part of Cromwell's punitive treatment of Ireland following the British civil war.[11] Other Irish were making their way to the Caribbean as members of various European navies. Irish sailors and soldiers fought on both sides of the Napoleonic wars, including the sea battles fought in the Caribbean by France and England.[12] Priests from Brittany, the Celtic province of France, were present in Haiti both before its independence in 1804–1805, and also since 1860, when Catholic priests again came to the country, for the Church had withdrawn its presence in Haiti in protest against the revolution. Catholics in both Ireland and Brittany are devoted to the Irish St. Brigit of Kildare, and many churches are dedicated to her in both areas. The influence of Irish settlers and sailors and Breton priests in spreading knowledge of St. Brigit in Haiti cannot be overstated.

St. Brigit of Kildare, the most important female saint in Ireland—called "the Foster Mother of Christ"—was a fifth-century Christian nun whose holiness so blinded the man who was ordaining her as a nun that he created her a bishop instead, according to the legendary accounts of her life and deeds.[13] The medieval tales told about her include such miracles as causing cows to give three times as much milk to accommodate unexpected guests, changing water to ale, and in various ways blessing and increasing food products and food production.[14] She famously hung her cloak on a sunbeam and along with nineteen other nuns tended a perpetual flame at her convent. St. Brigit inherited the attributes and popular devotions of a pre-Christian goddess who ruled over poets, smithcraft, and healing, and medieval writers made reference to her pagan past.[15]

St. Brigit's feast on February 1 was marked with many customs having to do with food, animal blessing, prayers, dramatic enactments of Brigit's entry into the house and feasting with the family, and the making of certain material objects.[16] Of the latter, the *brídeog* and the St. Brigit's cross are the most relevant. The brídeog was the poppet made and carried by the costumed young men and women of the district, who went from house to house on St. Brigit's night performing music, songs, and rhymes and bestowing luck and blessings in return for food and drink; the maskers themselves were also known as brídeogs, or "Biddies" in English. The doll image of Brigit, also called a bride, could be made out of many things: a turnip with a stick in it, draped as if for a christening; a churn dash with clothes on it; or a sheaf of corn. Ó Catháin discusses "Brigit 'the Speechless'": "The brídeog is often adverted to in the rhymes recited by the [Biddies] in terms of her inability to speak. . . . The folk prayer, Teagasc Bríde, would also seem to contain a reference to her speechlessness." Special foods for the eve of feast always included butter due to Brigit's association with dairy products but also included potatoes. A dish called "poundies," made with potatoes and butter, was customarily served. Other customs involve smoothing ashes around the hearth the night before the festival, which should show traces of the saint's presence the following morning. If the traces are there, the family knows it will have prosperity in the coming year. If traces are not found, St. Brigit is offended and must be placated with a cockerel or a pullet buried alive near the joining of three streams, and with incense burnt on the hearth at night.[17] This ceremony is very Vodou-like, and the potatoes and pullets sound familiar after reading Laguerre's description of offerings for Gran Brijit.

St. Brigit is a saint strongly associated in folk tradition and custom with crosses, with the fertility of humans and the natural world, with protection from fire and wind, with dolls called "brides" which may also be "hags," the latter term referring to sheaves left over from the previous harvest. On her feast she is described as speechless and is offered potatoes; if she seems to be offended, she is given a chicken as a sacrifice. Although there are few images of St. Brigit, those that do exist show her clad in a black nun's habit and holding a cross and a bishop's crozier. While sailors and indentured servants might not bring religious images with them, they would be likely to bring customs, and perhaps straw crosses, honoring the second most popular saint in Ireland. The connections to Gran Brijit should be getting clearer.

West African Roots

Leaving St. Brigit for the moment, consider the Yoruba *orisa* Oya. Orisa are the intermediary divine spirits in the Yoruba pantheon, located cosmologically between the creator deity and human beings; they each rule over a specific area of life and nature. While Oya persists in the New World African-derived Santería and the Afro-Brazilian religions, she is not present in Haiti. The Yoruba tradition is not as strong in Haiti as it is in Cuba or Brazil, for historic reasons of the makeup of slave populations, and the lack of new infusions of people from Africa during the 19th century.

Oya is a goddess associated with the marketplace, female trading, storm winds, lightning, and the Oya River, better known as the Niger. She is the gatekeeper of the cemetery and a masquerader, and she oversees rituals for the dead.[18] She is usually said to be married to Shango and to be his most loyal wife, although in some myths she was first married to Ogun, the orisa of iron, smithcraft, and war. In one tale she engages in a competition with her rival, the orisa Oshún, and reveals her sexual power in the form of sixteen smoking vaginas; she loses the contest, but that is beside the point.[19] Her feast day is Candlemas, February 2. Oya is associated with the dead, with cemeteries, and with sexuality, as is Gran Brijit. Oya is also associated with winds and fire, and with masking/costuming customs, and her feast day is the day after St. Brigit's. The family resemblance is taking shape.

Sheela Na Gig: The Last Piece of the Puzzle

Patrick A. Polk has in his collection a slide he took in Haiti of a vodou flag for Gran Brijit. The flagmaker identified it as Brijit, yet it seems to be a young aspect of the lwa called Belle Caresse. This Brijit was not only young, she was beautiful and definitely sexual: she had her legs open and her hand on her vulva, posed like a centerfold. This calls to mind Laguerre's assertion that Brijit had been a prostitute, as well as Oya's "16 smoking vaginas." In addition, it was very reminiscent of an Irish figure carved on churches, cemetery gates, and castles in the early medieval period, the Sheela na gig. This figure is a female, usually old and emaciated, with her legs spread, holding open her vagina. Patrick Ford has even documented one such figure placed atop a pointed stone arch leading into a cemetery, in his collection of Sheela na gig photos in the UCLA folklore archives; to pass through the opening, which is very vaginal in shape, one is supposed to touch the Sheela na gig for luck.

New World Hybrid Divinity

Roger Bastide has said that African culture only survives if there is a niche in the new culture into which it fits.[20] This may also be true of non-African cultures, if the right conditions are present. If Irish servants, soldiers, and sailors, and Breton sailors and priests, were present in Haiti, St. Brigit would have been introduced to the African slaves and freedmen through customary observances, prayers, and material objects. Her attributes would have reminded some of the slaves of the Yoruba Oya, with almost the same feast day, associated with fire and wind, with a body of water, and with smithcraft. Oya in turn may have reminded some Irish folks of the Sheela na gigs of their homeland. Gran Brijit is a cultural assemblage, created by people in Haiti under the conditions of cultural contact, slavery, oppression, creativity, freedom from the Catholic Church for over fifty years, and a spiritual aesthetic that valued the incorporation of new elements. The religious practices of Ireland in the 16th to the 19th centuries may not have been as foreign to an African worldview as it might appear, and the blending of traditions that created Gran Brijit may not have been such a difficult chore. The meeting of Oya and St. Brigit was the birth of Gran Brijit, who then took on a life of her own, as deities—especially those who appear in possession—usually do.

Notes

1. I use modern Haitian Kreyol spellings except in quotations from other authors.

2. Milo Marcelin, *Mythologie Vodou (Rite Arada)* (Pétionville, Haiti: Editions Canapé-Vert, 1950).

3. Ibid.

4. Maya Deren, *Divine Horsemen: The Living Gods of Haiti* (New York: McPherson and Company, 1953), 103.

5. Alfred Metreux, *Voodoo in Haiti* (Oxford: Oxford University Press, 1959), 114.

6. Karen McCarthy Brown, *Mama Lola: A Vodou Priestess in Brooklyn* (Berkeley: University of California Press, 1991), 380.

7. Michel S. Laguerre, *Voodoo Heritage* (Beverly Hills, CA: Sage Publications, 1980), 95.

8. Donald J. Cosentino, ed., *Sacred Arts of Haitian Vodou* (Hong Kong: South Sea International Press, 1995), xxi.

9. Ibid., 407.

10. Milo Marcelin, *Mythologie Vodou (Rite Arada)* (Pétionville, Haiti: Editions Canapé-Vert, 1950). The translation of the song is the author's own.

11. Seamus MacManus, *Story of the Irish Race: A Popular History of Ireland* (Old Greenwich, CT: Devin-Adair Company, 1921), 429.

12. John de Courcy Ireland, *Ireland and the Irish in Maritime History* (Dun Laoghaire: The Glendale Press, 1986), 158–161.

13. Sean Connolly, "Vita Prima Sanctae Brigitae: Background and Historical Value," *Journal of the Royal Society of Antiquaries* 119 (1987): 5–49.

14. Kerry Noonan, "Got Milk? The Food Miracles of St. Brigit of Kildare," unpublished paper presented at the 19th Annual UC Celtic Colloquium in Berkeley, CA, March 1997.

15. Séamas O Catháin, *The Festival of Brigit: Celtic Goddess and Holy Woman* (Dublin: DBA Publications, 1995), ix.

16. Kevin Danaher, *The Year in Ireland* (Cork: The Mercier Press, 1972).

17. Séamas O Catháin, *The Festival of Brigit: Celtic Goddess and Holy Woman* (Dublin: DBA Publications, 1995), 10–13, 24n124, 54, 68–69.

18. Ysamur Flores-Peña and Roberta J. Evanchuk, *Speaking without a Voice: Santería Garments and Altars* (Jackson: University of Mississippi Press, 1994), 10.

19. William Bascom, *African Folktales in the New World* (Bloomington: Indiana University Press, 1992), 7–11.

20. Roger Bastide, *The African Religions of Brazil: Toward a Sociology of the Inter-penetration of Civilizations*, trans. H. Sebba (Baltimore: Johns Hopkins University Press, 1978), 160.

Bibliography

Bascom, William. *African Folktales in the New World*. Bloomington: Indiana University Press, 1992.

Bastide, Roger. *The African Religions of Brazil: Toward a Sociology of the Interpenetration of Civilizations*. Translated by H. Sebba. Baltimore: Johns Hopkins University Press, 1978.

Brown, Karen McCarthy. *Mama Lola: A Vodou Priestess in Brooklyn*. Berkeley: University of California Press, 1991.

Connolly, Sean. "Vita Prima Sanctae Brigitae: Background and Historical Value." *Journal of the Royal Society of Antiquaries* 119 (1987): 5–49.

Cosentino, Donald J., ed. *Sacred Arts of Haitian Vodou*. Hong Kong: South Sea International Press, 1995.

Danaher, Kevin. *The Year in Ireland*. Cork: Mercier Press, 1972.

Deren, Maya. *Divine Horsemen: The Living Gods of Haiti*. New York: McPherson and Company, 1953.

Flores-Peña, Ysamur, and Roberta J. Evanchuk. *Speaking without a Voice: Santería Garments and Altars*. Jackson: University of Mississippi Press, 1994.

Gleason, Judith. *Oya: In Praise of the Goddess*. Boston: Shambhala, 1987.

Ireland, John de Courcy. *Ireland and the Irish in Maritime History*. Dun Laoghaire: Glendale Press, 1986.

Laguerre, Michel S. *Voodoo Heritage*. Beverly Hills, CA: Sage Publications, 1980.

MacManus, Seamus. *Story of the Irish Race: A Popular History of Ireland*. Old Greenwich, CT: Devin-Adair Company, 1921.

Marcelin, Milo. *Mythologie Vodou (Rite Arada)*. Pétionville, Haiti: Editions Canapé-Vert, 1950.

Metreux, Alfred. *Voodoo in Haiti*. Oxford: Oxford University Press, 1959.

Noonan, Kerry. "Got Milk? The Food Miracles of St. Brigit of Kildare." Unpublished paper presented at the 19th Annual UC Celtic Colloquium in Berkeley, CA, March 1997.

O Catháin, Séamas. *The Festival of Brigit: Celtic Goddess and Holy Woman*. Dublin: DBA Publications, 1995.

11

Corn Mother in North America: Life-Bringer and Culture-Bearer

Dave Aftandilian

For many indigenous peoples of the Americas, corn is the most important staple food in their diet. Among the Nahua of Mesoamerica, for instance, "No meal is complete without corn and regardless of how much rich food a person has eaten, he or she will complain of hunger if the dish lacks a corn component."[1] But corn is seen as much more than just a food; because of its crucial sustaining role in their lives, Pueblo peoples of the Southwest all say that "corn is our mother."[2] Similar views of corn as a mother are shared throughout North America and are also found in parts of Mesoamerica and South America.[3]

Although not every tribe knows Mother Corn, generally speaking, wherever corn is grown, there are stories and rituals and images of her, and there probably have been for hundreds to thousands of years. The more important corn is in the diet and the more effort people devote to growing this crop, the more native peoples describe corn as a mother. Hence the Corn Mother appears frequently in the sacred stories or myths of the agricultural peoples of the Northeast, Southeast, Plains, and Southwestern Pueblos, but much less frequently, if at all, in the stories of hunting/fishing peoples of the Great Lakes, Plains, Northwest Coast, and far North. The Cherokee call her Selu; the Pawnee, Atira; the Yuchi, Tso; and the Keresan-speaking peoples of the Eastern Pueblos know her variously as Iemaparu,

Iyatiku, Uretsete, Utset, and Utshtsiti.[4] In Illinois, blood-red carved stone figurines of a mythic woman associated with corn, bottle gourds, and/or other agricultural products have been found dating back to at least 850 years ago, which suggests that the concept of a Corn Mother, by whatever name she is known, is an ancient one in North America.[5]

This chapter explores the different roles of the Corn Mother among Native North American tribes, drawing primarily on stories told about her. It begins by discussing why corn is seen as a mother, then considers how the Corn Mother brings corn to various tribes. Tracing the Corn Mother's connections with animals, especially snakes and birds, will allow reflection on what those connections say about her place in Native American cosmologies. The Corn Mother's many roles in Native American cultures is then considered, not just as a bringer of corn and agricultural fertility, but as a creator, leader of tribal migrations, protector, healer, and culture-bringer/teacher. Finally, we examine stories of the Corn Mother for lessons about proper relations between women and men and between humans and nature.

Geographical Note

Before diving into the stories of the Corn Mother, however, it might be helpful for the reader to first have a brief introduction to the many tribes whose stories will be discussed, and to where these peoples have traditionally lived in North America. This brief geographic survey will begin in the Southwest, move through the Plains, then on to the Southeast, and finally conclude with the Northeast.[6]

At least two groups of Pueblo peoples are traditionally recognized in the Southwest: the Western Pueblos, which include the Hopi of northeastern Arizona and the Zuni who live on the border between Arizona and New Mexico, and the Eastern Pueblos of New Mexico, which include the Cochiti, San Juan, Sia, and Tewa.

Peoples of the central Plains include the Pawnee of Nebraska; their close relatives, the Arikara, however, live on the northern Plains, in northern South Dakota. The Oglala Lakota (Teton Sioux) live just south of the Arikara in South Dakota, and the Mandan and Hidatsa live just north of the Arikara, in southern North Dakota.

The Caddo traditionally lived on the border between the southern Plains and the Southeast, in the area now known as southeastern Oklahoma, southwestern Arkansas, and northeastern Texas. The Natchez come from the border between Louisiana and Mississippi, and the Choctaw are from southern Mississippi. In eastern Alabama, both the Koasati and the Creeks live; the Creeks also traditionally occupied much of northern Georgia. The Yuchi lived in northeastern Tennessee, close to the Cherokee, who also live throughout Western North Carolina. The Tuscarora also come from North Carolina, while the Tutelo come from Virginia.

Finally, the Abenaki and Penobscot live in Maine, and the Seneca, one of the tribes of the Iroquois Confederacy, live in western New York State.

Why Corn Is Seen as a Mother

Many of the native peoples of North America see corn as a mother first and foremost because she sustains people; the people draw their life from her, just as babies draw life from their mothers. For instance, in the Seneca creation story, after the Corn Mother dies, her mother, Sky Woman, tells the people that "the corn shall be your milk and sustain you. You shall make the corn grow in hills like breasts, for from the corn shall flow our living."[7] Similarly, a Hopi man once observed, "Do we not live on corn, just as the child draws life from the mother?"[8] And the Pawnee say that "[t]he ear of corn represents the supernatural power that dwells in H'Uraru, the earth, which brings forth the food that sustains life; so we speak of the ear of corn as H'Atira, mother breathing forth life."[9]

But corn is also seen as a mother because it has many physical similarities to human women. The Seneca quotation above, for instance, mentions that both corn and women produce liquid milk, which sustains their children; anyone who has bitten into a corn kernel and seen the milky white liquid seep out from inside it knows this to be true. Because corn is traditionally grown in low hills, which have a certain visual similarity to human breasts, corn's milk can also be seen as coming from a breast, just like a woman's milk. The Abenaki, among other tribes, also see an analogy between the long silk on ears of corn and a woman's long hair.[10] And both the Choctaw and the Tuscarora speak of the Corn Mother as plaintively singing, like the sound of the lonely wind sighing through the leaves of corn plants.[11]

How the Corn Mother Brings Corn

The Corn Mother can bring the sustaining gift of corn to her people in a variety of ways, either as a living woman or as a fertile corpse. As a living woman, the Corn Mother of the Seneca came to the tribe when they were starving and told them to remove the tops from the corn-storage barrels and cover their faces; they heard a sound like corn raining into the barrels, and when they opened their eyes, they found the barrels filled with corn. Similarly, during a drought year, the Corn Mother of the Arikara passed by the women's empty corn-storage pits one morning, and after four days, the women found their pits were full of corn. And among the Caddo, the Corn Mother, whom they know as the Snake-Woman, gave six seeds of every kind of agricultural plant to each member of the tribe with the help of her two sons.[12]

But the most common way in which the living Corn Mother provides food to her people is by shaking or rubbing or scraping it directly from her body. For instance, a story of "The Origin of Corn" among the Creek tribe relates how the Corn Mother washed her feet in water and rubbed them to produce a corn stew (*sofki*) for her people. And the Koasati describe how the ugly old Corn Mother was covered with sores, and was spurned by everyone but some orphan children, who asked her to stay with them; "she rubbed herself as one rubs roasting ears [to dislodge the kernels] and made food of what came off, which they continued to eat."[13]

In many other stories, the Corn Mother is described as feeding the people secretly with corn made from her body. When the people discover the way in which she produced their food, they consider it disgusting or sorcerous and refuse to eat; then the Corn Mother is killed so that people can eat corn cultivated from the fertile soil above her grave. Perhaps the most famous of these stories is the Cherokee tale of "Kanati and Selu: Origin of Game and Corn." In this story, twin boys spied on their mother, Selu the Corn Woman, and discovered that she rubbed her stomach to produce corn and her armpits to produce beans, which she then fed to them. They decided Selu was a witch and was trying to poison them, and so they resolved to kill her. Selu knew their intentions, and before they murdered her, she told them to clear a patch of ground in front of their house, drag her dead body around it seven times and across it seven times, stay up all night and watch, and in the morning they would have plenty of corn. Other southeastern tribes, including the Creek and the Natchez, tell similar stories. And in the Seneca creation story, the Corn Mother was killed by the birth of one of her twin sons; the other son tended her grave and saw first grass grow, then stringed-potatoes above her feet, beans above her fingers, squash from her abdomen, corn from her breasts, and tobacco from her forehead.[14]

The Pawnee of the Plains also used to link agricultural fertility with the death of the Corn Mother. Until the late 19th century, the Pawnee occasionally captured a young girl from another tribe in the fall, cared for her tenderly for a while, and then sacrificed her in the spring to the Morning Star, symbolizing the death of the Corn Mother. They then cut her body up into small pieces, which they carried to their fields in the same type of baskets they used to gather corn ears and squeezed a few drops of blood from the flesh onto each corn hill to fertilize it.[15]

When corn is given by a living Corn Mother, she most often provides it to the needy—to people who are starving, or to orphans—and especially to those who treat her kindly and generously. In the Choctaw tale of the "The Origin of Corn," for instance, two hunters had been out all day trying to find food for their starving families, but caught nothing but a black hawk. They heard a young woman crying plaintively that night, and they found her nearby, standing on a low mound. She said she was hungry and wanted food, and immediately they offered her the black hawk they had caught, the only food they or their families had. She ate a little of the hawk, and thanked them for their kindness; she told them to come back a month later, on the night of the full moon, which they did, and found corn growing on the mound where she had been standing.[16]

Birds and the Corn Mother

In the Choctaw story just discussed, the Corn Mother was given a black hawk to eat by two hunters. Several other tribes also connect the Corn Mother with birds—specifically, with black birds (crows, ravens, blackbirds) and with waterbirds.

Because crows, ravens, and blackbirds are only too happy to steal their share of the Corn Mother's produce from the fields today, it is not surprising that some Native American peoples have told stories that link black birds with the origin of corn and the Corn Mother. However, where many Americans take a dim view of these avian corn thieves, native peoples often take more of a "live and let live" approach, opting to try to coexist with the blackbirds, rather than just demonizing them. For example, the Creek story of "The Orphan and the Origin of Corn" tells how the Corn Mother provided corn, which an orphan boy gathered into a storehouse. A hawk later broke open the storehouse, and all kinds of birds came to eat up the corn kernels. However, the orphan watched some crows flying and fighting in the air, and then picked up and planted the corn kernels they dropped, ensuring a plentiful supply of corn for the future.[17]

Hidatsa stories of the Corn Mother from the northern Plains say that red kernels of corn are actually the spirits of blackbirds, who help the Corn Mother care for her gardens.[18] And Freeman Owle's contemporary Cherokee story about "Corn Woman Spirit" describes how the evil spirit Hunger once imprisoned the Corn Mother in a deep, dark cave; a multitude of ravens, black and clever, hid themselves in the cave, and then at a signal they all attacked Hunger at once, frightening him into the daylight, which melted him. This is why the Cherokee don't kill crows and ravens or frighten them out of their cornfields; they figure that since the ravens saved the Corn Mother, they have a right to steal some corn from fields today—and in return, the crows and ravens pitch a fit if other animals come into the fields, alerting the Cherokee so that they can come and chase the other animals away.[19]

The Mandan, Hidatsa, and Zuni also link the Corn Mother with waterbirds. Among the Mandan and Hidatsa, the Corn Mother is known as Old Woman Who Never Dies. All the agricultural plants that feed the people have their origin in her gardens. Once she lived close to the people on the northern Plains, but eventually she grew tired of them continually pestering her for food, and so she moved to an island in the ocean at the mouth of the Mississippi River. During the fall, the corn spirits fly south to Old Woman's home along with the migratory waterbirds such as the ducks, geese, and swans; once they arrive, they turn into ears of seed corn, and she cares for them over the winter. In the spring, the corn spirits return with the waterbirds to the northern Plains, where they spiritually fertilize the women's cornfields.[20] Like the Mandan and Hidatsa, the Zuni of the Southwestern Pueblos also link the Corn Mother, in the form of multiple Corn Maidens, with waterbirds; for example, when the Corn Maidens were hiding from the twin War Gods, who wanted to have sex with them, they first took shelter in the ocean under the wings of a duck, and later hid in the house of two white swans.[21]

Snakes and the Corn Mother

Interestingly, the Corn Mother is also connected with snakes, for both practical and cosmological reasons. In practical terms, this link makes logical and ecological sense—rodents and small birds visit the Corn Mother's fields to eat her grain, and the snakes then come to eat them. This makes snakes friends of traditional farmers, so long as one knows to watch out for them while working in the fields. In terms of cosmology, snakes are viewed by Native Americans as spiritually associated with the Under World; the Under World, in turn, is associated with water and agricultural fertility.[22] Therefore, snakes can be seen as helping spiritually fertilize the Corn Mother's fields, as well as keep them free of rodent vermin.

Some of the earliest and most direct connections of the Corn Mother with snakes date from about 850 years ago. At about that time the ancient native peoples of Illinois, the Mississippians, made blood-red stone figurines show-ing a woman, most likely the Corn Mother, interacting directly with serpents. For example, the Birger Figurine, which was excavated from the BBB Motor Site in southwestern Illinois, depicts a kneeling woman with bared teeth hoe-ing the back of a monstrous feline-headed serpent. Behind where the wom-an's hoe has struck the serpent, its body splits into two vines, which twine around her and bear bottle gourds, which were one of the first domesticated crops in Illinois. As several scholars have persuasively argued, this figurine is almost certainly an early depiction of the Corn Mother (here the Gourd Mother) associated with a mythic serpent. Several figurines from the nearby Sponemann site also seem to depict the Corn Mother, and one of them, the West figurine, shows several rattlesnakes wrapped around the head and back and held in the hand of a human figure that may be the Corn Mother.[23]

In more recent times, the Caddo of the southern Plains have known the Corn Woman as the Snake Woman; with the help of her two sons, she dis-tributed the seeds of all the agricultural crops, and taught the people how to plant them. Until the fruits of these crops are ripe, they belong to the Snake Woman, and if anyone harvests them too early, she will send a poisonous snake to bite him or her.[24]

A story told by the Oglala Lakota describes the leaves of corn plants as snakes. In this story, the White Buffalo Cow is also the Corn Mother, and brings the Lakota both buffalo and corn to eat.[25] Snakes twined around the White Buffalo Cow's waist and ankles were actually the leaves of corn plants.[26]

Most frequently, though, Native American stories describe the Corn Mother as married to, or at least having sexual relations with, a serpent. For example, in the Penobscot tale of "The Origin of Corn and Tobacco" from the Northeast, the Corn Mother came to the people as a beautiful young maiden when they were starving, and married a young man from the tribe. However, she eventually became sad, and started stealing away to a secret place; her husband followed her and found out that she was meeting a snake, her lover.[27] The Mandan and Hidatsa of the northern Plains both tell stories of their Corn Mother, Old Woman Who Never Dies, that say she was married to a monstrous serpent, who was later put into the Short Mis-souri River and regulated its water flow; four horned water serpents also guard the island on which she lives.[28]

Other Roles of the Corn Mother

While the Corn Mother's main purpose among the native peoples of North America is to provide them with corn and agricultural fertility, she also plays a number of other roles in various tribes. Specifically, some native peoples see her as a creator, leader of the tribe's migrations, protector, healer, and culture-bringer/teacher.

Among the Keresan-speaking peoples of the Eastern Pueblos, the Corn Mother, Uretsete, is not just the mother of corn, but also of the Pueblo peoples themselves. Along with her sister, Naotsete, she finishes the work of creation that Thought Woman began. The Corn Mother and her sister create by singing to seeds or images of animals, natural features, and so on in their baskets, thereby bringing them to life.[29]

Many agricultural tribes of North America say that their people originated underground, like seeds, and only arrived at the places where they live now after long migrations. Both the Keresan peoples of the Eastern Pueblos and the Arikara of the southern Plains describe the Corn Mother as their people's leader during the emergence and subsequent migrations.[30]

The Pawnee, Arikara, and Pueblo tribes also see the Corn Mother as a protector of people. This protective function begins at birth. For instance, in the Zuni, Cochiti, Sia, San Juan, and Tewa Pueblos, perfect ears of corn symbolizing the Corn Mother are placed on either side of an infant's cradleboard to protect the infant during the early days of his or her life.[31] Arikara midwives also sing a lullaby for newborn infants, asking the Corn Mother to protect them.[32]

The Corn Mother also protects children and even adults. For example, a Cochiti Pueblo story tells how the Corn Mother rescued two lost children, protected them, and finally led them back to their parents. Likely this protective function explains why perfect ears of corn, representing the Corn Mother, are given to children and adults during naming ceremonies and initiations into the kachina and other religious societies in all the Pueblos. And among the Pawnee of the Plains, sacred ears of corn are carried by leaders of war parties, peace delegations, and doctors, and are present in almost every ritual to ask for the protection and favor of the Corn Mother.[33]

Pawnee doctors do not just carry ears of corn to represent the Corn Mother; they also use them to ask the Corn Mother's help in healing people during their annual Thirty Day Ceremony. Selu, the Cherokee Corn Mother, also helps heal people during private rituals.[34]

But the Corn Mother doesn't just help heal people; she also teaches them how to farm and how to do ceremonies, rituals, and dances. For example, in the Abenaki story of "The Origin of Maize," the Corn Mother taught a man how to make a fire and burn the grass to provide fertilizer for the corn. Among the Seneca and Tutelo, the Corn Mother taught women certain rituals, dances, and songs related to agriculture. She brought laws and rules to govern behavior from the Creator to the Arikara tribe, and the office of the chief to enforce them; she also gave them the first medicine bundles to use in their ceremonies, the songs to sing to activate the spiritual powers of the bundles, and medicine men to be the keepers of the bundles and the songs.[35]

Lessons of the Corn Mother

The prominence of stories of the Corn Mother in native North American cultures shows the importance of women in general in those cultures. But stories about the Corn Mother also tell about the proper roles for both women *and* men in traditional cultures. For example, in the Cherokee story of "Kanati and Selu: Origin of Game and Corn," Kanati brought animal meat from hunting, and Selu the Corn Mother provided corn and beans from her body. Similarly, in many Tewa stories from the Southwest, a male deer hunter and a female Corn Maiden are paired. Such stories teach the importance of harmony and balance in gender roles—neither women nor men should be placed above the other, since neither alone can provide all the food the people need; the work of both is crucial to the tribe's survival.[36]

But as in life, all is not sweetness and light in the stories of the Corn Mother. As discussed above, the Corn Mother is often brutally killed so that the people can eat corn. For example, in the Penobscot story of "The Origin of Corn and Tobacco," the Corn Mother's human husband, after finding out she had a snake lover, killed her with a stone axe, dragged her body seven times among the stumps of a clearing in the forest until the flesh was stripped from the bones, and finally buried the bones in the center of the clearing.[37] Such stories acknowledge the real violence of agriculture, which necessitates a painful tearing or penetrating of the Earth Mother's body so that humans can raise crops from her fertile soil. And since the person doing the killing is most often male, these stories also suggest a deep tension and discomfort between men and women, which again is true to life.

But as Marilou Awiakta points out, stories of the death of the Corn Mother teaches another, more important lesson. Awiakta focuses on a different Cherokee story of the Corn Mother from the one about Kanati and Selu retold above. In this other story, the Corn Mother falls ill and dies, rather than being killed, after her two grandsons had found out that she got corn for them by striking it off from both sides of her body, and then decided the food was "unsavory" and refused to eat it.[38] Awiakta reads this story as meaning that the Corn Mother had to leave the boys (die) because of a law the creator put into Mother Earth: that if you take from her, you have to give back respect and thoughtfulness. Since the boys did not do this, the Corn Mother had to leave them. But she gave them a second chance by coming back as the corn plant; since the boys had learned their lesson and cared for the corn as they would for a beloved relative, humanity still has corn to eat today.[39] This story suggests that if humanity want to enjoy the fruits of Mother Earth, such as corn, on a long-term basis, she must be treated with respect and kindness. Following this sacred law of reciprocity means that the Corn Mother will continue to sustain humanity for generations to come.

Notes

1. Alan R. Sandstrom, *Corn Is Our Blood: Culture and Ethnic Identity in a Contemporary Aztec Indian Village* (Norman: University of Oklahoma Press, 1991), 132.

2. Richard I. Ford, "Corn Is Our Mother," in *Corn and Culture in the Prehistoric New World*, ed. Sissel Johannessen and Christine A. Hastorf (Boulder, CO: Westview Press, 1994), 513.

3. Concepts of a Rice Mother, Yams Mother, and so on are common in Indonesia, New Guinea, Melanesia, and New Zealand; see Gudmund Hatt, "The Corn Mother in America and in Indonesia," *Anthropos* 46 (1951): 853–914.

4. Marilou Awiakta, *Selu: Seeking the Corn-Mother's Wisdom* (Golden, CO: Fulcrum, 1993); James Mooney, *Myths of the Cherokee* (1900; rpt., New York: Dover, 1995), 242–249, 323–324; James R. Murie, *Ceremonies of the Pawnee*, ed. Douglas R. Parks (1981; rpt., Lincoln: University of Nebraska Press, 1989), 45; Patricia Monaghan, *The Encyclopedia of Goddesses and Heroines* (Santa Barbara, CA: Greenwood, 2009); Hatt, "Corn Mother," 858; Elsie Clews Parsons, *Pueblo Indian Religion*, vol. 1 (1939; rpt., Lincoln: University of Nebraska Press, 1996), 243–245.

5. Thomas E. Emerson, "Exotic Artifacts" and "Overview of the Stirling Phase Component," both in *The BBB Motor Site*, ed. Thomas E. Emerson and Douglas K. Jackson (Urbana: University of Illinois Press, 1984), 254–261 and 338–339, respectively; Andrew C. Fortier, "Stone Figurines" and "Radiocarbon Dates," both in *The Sponemann Site 2: The Mississippian and Oneota Occupations*, ed. Douglas K. Jackson, Andrew C. Fortier, and Joyce A. Williams Jackson (Urbana: University of Illinois Press, 1992), 277–303 and 335–337, respectively.

6. For helpful maps of these and other tribes' traditional homelands in North America, see Carl Waldman, *Atlas of the North American Indian*, rev. ed. (New York: Checkmark Books, 2000), 33–49. For more detailed information on the geographic locations of various tribes at and since the time of first contact with Euro-Americans, see John R. Swanton, *The Indian Tribes of North America* (1952; rpt., Washington, DC: Smithsonian Institution Press, 1969). I have relied primarily on this latter source for the information in this section.

7. Arthur C. Parker, *Seneca Myths and Folk Tales* (1923; rpt., Lincoln: University of Nebraska Press, 1989), 64.

8. Parsons, *Pueblo Indian Religion,* 21. See also Dennis Wall and Virgil Masayesva, "People of the Corn: Teachings in Hopi Traditional Agriculture, Spirituality, and Sustainability," *American Indian Quarterly* 28, nos. 3–4 (Summer–Fall 2004): 435–453.

9. Alice C. Fletcher and James R. Murie, *The Hako: Song, Pipe, and Unity in a Pawnee Calumet Ceremony* (1904; rpt., Lincoln: University of Nebraska Press, 1996), 44.

10. George E. Lankford, ed., *Native American Legends, Southeastern Legends: Tales from the Natchez, Caddo, Biloxi, Chickasaw, and Other Nations* (Little Rock, AR: August House, 1987), 156–157.

11. Hatt, "Corn Mother," 858; John R. Swanton, *Source Material for the Social and Ceremonial Life of the Choctaw Indians* (1931; rpt., Tuscaloosa: University of Alabama Press, 2001), 208–210.

12. Parker, *Seneca Myths,* 205–207; Douglas R. Parks, ed., *Myths and Traditions of the Arikara Indians* (Lincoln: University of Nebraska Press, 1996), 154–159; George A. Dorsey, *Traditions of the Caddo* (1905; rpt., Lincoln: University of Nebraska Press, 1997), 18.

13. John R. Swanton, *Myths and Tales of the Southeastern Indians* (1929; rpt., Norman: University of Oklahoma Press, 1995), 9–10, 168.

14. Mooney, *Myths of the Cherokee,* 242–249; Swanton, *Myths and Tales,* 10–15, 230; Parker, *Seneca Myths,* 63–64.

15. Vorsila L. Bohrer, "Maize in Middle American and Southwestern United States Agricultural Traditions," in *Corn and Culture in the Prehistoric New World,* ed. Sissel Johannessen and Christine A. Hastorf (Boulder, CO: Westview Press, 1994), 505; Hatt, "Corn Mother," 864.

16. Tom Mould, ed., *Choctaw Tales* (Jackson: University Press of Mississippi, 2004), 77; Swanton, *Source Material,* 208–210.

17. Swanton, *Myths and Tales,* 15–17.

18. Alfred W. Bowers, *Hidatsa Social and Ceremonial Organization* (1963; rpt., Lincoln: University of Nebraska Press, 1992), 334.

19. Barbara R. Duncan, ed., *Living Stories of the Cherokee* (Chapel Hill: University of North Carolina Press, 1998), 228–231.

20. Alfred W. Bowers, *Mandan Social and Ceremonial Organization* (1950; rpt., Lincoln: University of Nebraska Press, 2004), 197–205.

21. Elsie Clews Parsons, "The Zuñi Molawia," *Journal of American Folklore* 29, no. 113 (July–September 1916): 392–394.

22. Thomas E. Emerson, "Water, Serpents, and the Underworld: An Exploration into Cahokian Symbolism," in *The Southeastern Ceremonial Complex: Artifacts and Analysis,* ed. Patricia Galloway (Lincoln: University of Nebraska Press, 1989), 58–59; Charles Hudson, *The Southeastern Indians* (Knoxville: University of Tennessee Press, 1976), 122–132.

23. Emerson, "Exotic Artifacts," 254–261; Thomas E. Emerson, *Cahokia and the Archaeology of Power* (Tuscaloosa: University of Alabama Press, 1997), 207–212; Guy Prentice, "An Analysis of the Symbolism Expressed by the

Birger Figurine," *American Antiquity* 51, no. 2 (1986): 239–266; Fortier, "Stone Figurines," 277–303.

24. Dorsey, *Traditions of the Caddo,* 18.

25. Tribes that practice a mix of hunting and farming often tell stories that link the origin of the major hunted animals and farmed crops. For example, the Cherokee story of "Kanati and Selu" explicitly links the origin of both game animals and corn (see Mooney, *Myths of the Cherokee,* 242–249), as does the Arikara story of "Corn Woman and Buffalo Woman" (see Parks, ed., *Myths of the Arikara,* 153–159).

26. W. M. Beauchamp, "Indian Corn Stories and Customs," *Journal of American Folklore* 11, no. 42 (July–September 1898): 195–202.

27. Frank G. Speck, "Penobscot Tales and Religious Beliefs," *Journal of American Folklore* 48, no. 187 (1935): 75.

28. Bowers, *Mandan Organization,* 197–205; Bowers, *Hidatsa Organization,* 335, 359, 372.

29. Parsons, *Pueblo Indian Religion,* 243–245.

30. George A. Dorsey, *Traditions of the Arikara* (1904; rpt., Whitefish, MT: Kessinger, 2004), 12–17, 26–30; Parsons, *Pueblo Indian Religion,* 243–245.

31. Alfonso Ortiz, "Some Cultural Meanings of Corn in Aboriginal North America," in *Corn and Culture in the Prehistoric New World,* ed. Sissel Johannessen and Christine A. Hastorf (Boulder, CO: Westview Press, 1994), 529; Parsons, *Pueblo Indian Religion,* 321; Wall and Masayesva, "People of the Corn," 451.

32. Parks, ed., *Myths of the Arikara,* 117–119.

33. Hatt, "Corn Mother," 859; Ortiz, "Cultural Meanings of Corn," 532; Parsons, *Pueblo Indian Religion,* 321–323; Wall and Masayesva, "People of the Corn," 452; Fletcher and Murie, *The Hako,* 156; Murie, *Ceremonies of the Pawnee,* 52; Gene Weltfish, *The Lost Universe: Pawnee Life and Culture* (1965; rpt., Lincoln: University of Nebraska Press, 1977), 254.

34. Murie, *Ceremonies of the Pawnee,* 174–175; Awiakta, *Selu,* 320.

35. Lankford, ed., *Southeastern Legends,* 156–157; Hatt, "Corn Mother," 858; Dorsey, *Traditions of the Arikara,* 12–30.

36. Awiakta, *Selu,* 120; Mooney, *Myths of the Cherokee,* 242–249; Ortiz, "Cultural Meanings of Corn," 530.

37. Speck, "Penobscot Tales," 75.

38. Jack F. Kilpatrick and Anna G. Kilpatrick, *Friends of Thunder: Folktales of the Oklahoma Cherokees* (1964; rpt., Norman: University of Oklahoma Press, 1995), 129–134.

39. Awiakta, *Selu,* 15.

Bibliography

Awiakta, Marilou. *Selu: Seeking the Corn-Mother's Wisdom.* Golden, CO: Fulcrum, 1993.

Beauchamp, W. M. "Indian Corn Stories and Customs." *Journal of American Folklore* 11, no. 42 (July–September 1898): 195–202.

Bohrer, Vorsila L. "Maize in Middle American and Southwestern United States Agricultural Traditions." In *Corn and Culture in the Prehistoric New World,* ed. Sissel Johannessen and Christine A. Hastorf, 469–512. Boulder, CO: Westview Press, 1994.

Bowers, Alfred W. *Hidatsa Social and Ceremonial Organization.* Lincoln: University of Nebraska Press, 1992.

Bowers, Alfred W. *Mandan Social and Ceremonial Organization.* 1950; rpt., Lincoln: University of Nebraska Press, 2004.

Dorsey, George A. *Traditions of the Arikara.* 1904; rpt., Whitefish, MT: Kessinger, 2004.

Dorsey, George A. *Traditions of the Caddo.* 1905; rpt., Lincoln: University of Nebraska Press, 1997.

Duncan, Barbara R., ed. *Living Stories of the Cherokee.* Chapel Hill: University of North Carolina Press, 1998.

Emerson, Thomas E. *Cahokia and the Archaeology of Power.* Tuscaloosa: University of Alabama Press, 1997.

Emerson, Thomas E. "Exotic Artifacts." In *The BBB Motor Site,* ed. Thomas E. Emerson and Douglas K. Jackson, 254–261. Urbana: University of Illinois Press, 1984.

Emerson, Thomas E. "Overview of the Stirling Phase Component." In *The BBB Motor Site,* ed. Thomas E. Emerson and Douglas K. Jackson, 338–342. Urbana: University of Illinois Press, 1984.

Emerson, Thomas E. "Water, Serpents, and the Underworld: An Exploration into Cahokian Symbolism." In *The Southeastern Ceremonial Complex: Artifacts and Analysis,* ed. Patricia Galloway, 45–92. Lincoln: University of Nebraska Press, 1989.

Fletcher, Alice C., and James R. Murie. *The Hako: Song, Pipe, and Unity in a Pawnee Calumet Ceremony.* 1904; rpt., Lincoln: University of Nebraska Press, 1996.

Ford, Richard I. "Corn Is Our Mother." In *Corn and Culture in the Prehistoric New World,* ed. Sissel Johannessen and Christine A. Hastorf, 513–525. Boulder, CO: Westview Press, 1994.

Fortier, Andrew C. "Radiocarbon Dates." In *The Sponemann Site 2: The Mississippian and Oneota Occupations,* ed. Douglas K. Jackson, Andrew C. Fortier, and Joyce A. Williams Jackson, 335–337. Urbana: University of Illinois Press, 1992.

Fortier, Andrew C. "Stone Figurines." In *The Sponemann Site 2: The Mississippian and Oneota Occupations,* ed. Douglas K. Jackson, Andrew C. Fortier, and Joyce A. Williams Jackson, 277–303. Urbana: University of Illinois Press, 1992.

Hatt, Gudmund. "The Corn Mother in America and in Indonesia." *Anthropos* 46 (1951): 853–914.

Hudson, Charles. *The Southeastern Indians.* Knoxville: University of Tennessee Press, 1976.

Kilpatrick, Jack F., and Anna G. Kilpatrick. *Friends of Thunder: Folktales of the Oklahoma Cherokees.* 1964; rpt., Norman: University of Oklahoma Press, 1995.

Lankford, George E., ed. *Native American Legends, Southeastern Legends: Tales from the Natchez, Caddo, Biloxi, Chickasaw, and Other Nations.* Little Rock, AR: August House, 1987.

Monaghan, Patricia. *The Encyclopedia of Goddesses and Heroines.* Santa Barbara, CA: Greenwood, 2009.

Mooney, James. *Myths of the Cherokee.* 1900; rpt., New York: Dover, 1995.

Mould, Tom, ed. *Choctaw Tales.* Jackson: University Press of Mississippi, 2004.

Murie, James R. *Ceremonies of the Pawnee.* Edited by Douglas R. Parks. 1981; rpt., Lincoln: University of Nebraska Press, 1989.

Ortiz, Alfonso. "Some Cultural Meanings of Corn in Aboriginal North America." In *Corn and Culture in the Prehistoric New World,* ed. Sissel Johannessen and Christine A. Hastorf, 527–544. Boulder, CO: Westview Press, 1994.

Parker, Arthur C. *Seneca Myths and Folk Tales.* 1923; rpt., Lincoln: University of Nebraska Press, 1989.

Parks, Douglas R., ed. *Myths and Traditions of the Arikara Indians.* Lincoln: University of Nebraska Press, 1996.

Parsons, Elsie Clews. *Pueblo Indian Religion.* Vol. 1. 1939; rpt., Lincoln: University of Nebraska Press, 1996.

Parsons, Elsie Clews. "The Zuñi Molawia." *Journal of American Folklore* 29, no. 113 (July–September 1916): 392–399.

Prentice, Guy. "An Analysis of the Symbolism Expressed by the Birger Figurine." *American Antiquity* 51, no. 2 (1986): 239–266.

Sandstrom, Alan R. *Corn Is Our Blood: Culture and Ethnic Identity in a Contemporary Aztec Indian Village.* Norman: University of Oklahoma Press, 1991.

Speck, Frank G. "Penobscot Tales and Religious Beliefs." *Journal of American Folklore* 48, no. 187 (1935): 1–107.

Swanton, John R. *The Indian Tribes of North America.* 1952; rpt., Washington, DC: Smithsonian Institution Press, 1969.

Swanton, John R. *Myths and Tales of the Southeastern Indians.* 1929; rpt., Norman: University of Oklahoma Press, 1995.

Swanton, John R. *Source Material for the Social and Ceremonial Life of the Choctaw Indians.* 1931; rpt., Tuscaloosa: University of Alabama Press, 2001.

Waldman, Carl. *Atlas of the North American Indian.* Rev. ed. New York: Checkmark Books, 2000.

Wall, Dennis, and Virgil Masayesva. "People of the Corn: Teachings in Hopi Traditional Agriculture, Spirituality, and Sustainability." *American Indian Quarterly* 28, nos. 3–4 (Summer–Fall 2004): 435–453.

Weltfish, Gene. *The Lost Universe: Pawnee Life and Culture.* 1965; rpt., Lincoln: University of Nebraska Press, 1977.

12

Nookomis and Mindemoya: Grandmother Moon and the Old Woman of the Mists

Ann Megisikwe Filemyr

Grandmother Moon (Nookomis Tibik Giizis) and the Old Woman of the Mists (Mindemoya) are two sacred female beings whose stories are told among the Anishinaabeg of the northwoods in the Great Lakes region.[1] Nookomis literally means "my grandmother," and Mindemoya (also spelled "Mindimooyenh") can be translated as "old woman." These are not your ordinary old ladies.[2]

The Meaning of Nookomis

Nookomis ("Grandmother") is a term of profound respect. A plant, animal, mineral, specific geologic feature, or celestial body may be honored with this kinship term. Grandmother is the source of life and female wisdom. The term does not strictly refer to a woman who has given birth to a child who has then had a child of his or her own. It is used respectfully to mean any elder female. And "elder" in this context does not simply denote age, but refers to one who has lived well and has learned the knowledge necessary to become a full human being. This knowledge may include, among other things, the telling of elaborate cultural stories, the singing of song-prayers, and the administering of herbs for healing. It means one has entered old age in good health, for one has learned how to keep one's inner balance.

This inner balance is best expressed by a peaceful, joyful heart. To be around such a grandmother is to experience warmth, understanding, and forgiveness. She may give you a light touch or a quiet look, and your heavy burden of responsibility or grief becomes less heavy. Young women may seek to be near such a grandmother for she embodies the principles of generosity, patience, kindness, and courage. By her steady loving presence a grandmother may help a younger woman learn to keep her own inner balance.

This quality of being in balance is prized among the traditional Anishinaabeg as the source of health and well-being. To be out of balance is dangerous to oneself and others. To be out of balance is to be physically, mentally, emotionally, or spiritually sick. Symptoms of the loss of balance include anger, violence, grief, selfishness, hoarding, addiction, joylessness, chronic pain, inability to contribute to the community or express oneself, withdrawal from human company, and so on. To maintain balance is not a simple act, for life's journey is full of unseen twists and turns. Along the way people may experience tragedy and loss, betrayal and heartbreak. Some may grow weak and weary. The act of keeping balance amid human suffering requires an abiding relationship with spirit. The grandmother who has walked her journey well exemplifies this ability to maintain balance. She has kept faith with the spirits and has not lost her love for humanity. She may have suffered, but she has not given in to despair or bitterness. This elder can assist the younger ones who are encountering loss or suffering for the first time. Grandmother stands ahead, reaching back to help others find the way.

Nookomis Tibik Giizis: Grandmother Moon

Grandmother Moon, Nookomis Tibik Giizis, is pre-eminent among the grandmothers. She is the symbol of grandmotherness itself. It is said of Nookomis that she has a special relationship to women. She teaches by her action of waxing and waning that all things come in the cycle of time. There is a time to blossom (expand) and a time to wither (contract), a time to celebrate, a time to mourn.

Flowers are sacred to her. She blesses both the seed and the harvest. Nookomis is the chief woman who resides in the sky watching with open eyes all that her grandchildren do. She loves her grandchildren and her light is her love. To be bathed in her moonlight is to be fully blessed. Moonlight is precious. It is required in certain healing ceremonies, and some ceremonies may be timed according to the phases of the moon. Certain sacred objects or beings used by the healer are set out in the moonlight to receive "grandmother power."

Nookomis Tibik Giizis is the rhythm of tides and the fertility of women. Menses is referred to as the moontime and in the old days women retreated to the moon lodge where together they sang and danced, honoring their grandmother (some communities are reviving this ancient practice). The pattern of her lunar phases guides the physical cycle of menses. When electric light did not trick the female body, women bled together and ovulated at the same time. Individual cycles were triggered by the light of the moon. In this way, Nookomis connected all women as sisters.

Far away from the busyness of village life, in the moon lodge, a place of communal retreat, the women were able to rest and share knowledge of the sacred womb. Nookomis is understood to be the keeper of this knowledge. She oversees conception, pregnancy, and birth. She oversees the important ceremonies for the girl-becoming-woman and the woman-becoming-elder. Nookomis is associated with all activities of growing food and gardening, especially with the three sisters: squash, corn, and beans. The sacred womb of Mother Earth (N'gah Wegemund Aukeeg) is understood to be like the wombs of individual women. Nookomis blesses both.

It is said that Nookomis Tibik Giizis carries her moon shield as she dances across the night sky. If you listen, you can hear her sing. Nookomis sings, "*Inowendewin, Inowedewin, Ni mino Inowendewin.*" One translation for this is: "Peace and Harmony, Peace and Harmony, Peace and Harmony Among All Beings is the Greatest state of Harmony."[3]

The song is her instruction to never make an enemy of another human being. She teaches that every child is the child of a mother, and no mother births the enemy. Nookomis reminds us that every man and every woman are her grandchildren. All belong to her as one human family. She counsels against violence or the misuse of anger. She warns against weapons and defensive behavior. She asks her children to pay attention to their hearts and not hurt one another. She sees the root of war like a shadow in each heart. She knows hurt can erupt, causing violence, jealousy, rivalry, betrayal, revenge, war. She calls down "Peace and harmony! Peace and harmony!" She calls out to soothe and heal each broken heart, to maintain inner balance and so not choose to hurt another.

Nookomis Tibik Giizis dances with the stars, the ancestors, in the place of forever. She never dies. She lives on and on among the ancestors. She shines with the light of her love. She is unambiguous in her love. Her love is for everyone and everything. When feeling unloved, gaze upon her face. She radiates joy.

Nookomis and the Dance of Time

Tibik Giizis can be literally translated as "night sun." Together the solar and lunar cycles serve as an easily observable recorder of time's movement. The interplay of Grandfather Sun and Grandmother Moon was understood as a beautiful dance between powerful partners. The male/female of sun/moon was seen as another expression of the dynamic balance of life. Elder and traditional teacher Eddie Benton-Banai explains it this way: "The Earth was arranged in the Universe so that Gee'sis [sun] and Ne-ba-gee'-sis [night sun or moon] would alternate walking in the sky keeping watch over the Creation. . . . It is this movement of the Sun and Moon that we imitate in ceremonies today."[4]

Nookomis lives in the realm beyond time and sets time in motion. In this way she is the keeper of rhythm and male drummers often honor her. The round, light-colored drumhead may be seen as a moon face. Nookomis sings and her song sets in motion the growth of plants, the migration of birds, the hibernation of bears, the tides, and all female fertility cycles. All are her grandchildren.

The calendar of the year is a rhythmic cycle counted in moons. Unlike the pre-Roman Celtic calendar, counted from new moon to new moon, the Anishinaabeg calendar is counted from full moon to full moon. Perhaps this is because whenever Nookomis Tibik Giizis turned her full face to watch her grandchildren, they looked up and noted another cycle beginning. The names for the procession of the moons throughout the seasons of the year vary from region to region. These names indicate specific seasonal occurrences. Four examples in Anishinaabemowin include Nin Autig Giizis (literally "Our Tree," refers to the Sugar Maple, also translated as the Moon of the Maple Sap Rising; March); Miskwimini Giizis (the Raspberry Moon; July); Manoominiki Giizis (the Ricing Moon, the time of the wild rice harvest; September); Manitou Giizisoons (Little Spirit Moon; January).[5]

As the keeper of time, Nookomis Tibik Giizis shows that time is motion, and within it all things move. For this reason, dance is sacred to her. To move in harmony with others is to dance. This brings Nookomis joy. Woman's moon dances are held beneath her glowing light as a way to honor her. To move joyfully together is to keep peaceful relations. Those who fail to keep peace in all relationships endanger themselves and others, and fall from balance. Her ceremonies are aimed at the restoration of peaceful relationships between people, between families, between tribes and nations. Peaceful relationships are right relationships and the keeping of right relations is necessary to maintain inner balance. Nookomis teaches the appropriateness of living within the cycles of time, neither forcing things to happen nor neglecting the rightful moment for them to happen. She stresses that all good things come in their own time. She teaches acceptance. Through her own cycle of changing, Nookomis teaches that change is the only constant. To keep balance amid this dynamic changing world of relationships is the challenge of the dancer engaged in the dance of life. Dancing with others in ceremony or in the pow-wow circle is an expression of dance as a way to maintain good relations. Dancing with other women in the moonlight is a traditional way of honoring Nookomis.

Nookomis Tibik Giizis Today

Nookomis manifests herself today in the practice of restorative justice and peace activism, in the healing of trauma and posttraumatic stress. Nookomis understands the power of cause and effect, for she is one of the keepers of time and all that occurs in time. She knows war begets more war. One lie, one cruel or ignorant action will set another in motion. Likewise she knows the power of kindness and how one generous act will set another in motion. She calls all to greater awareness. She shines with mindfulness: Be awake! Be aware! Be wise. She sings in dreams: "Peace and Harmony! Peace and Harmony! Peace and Harmony Among All Beings is the Greatest State of Harmony!"

Both men and women revere Nookomis. She teaches men to care for children and elders. She brings gentleness to their hearts. She calls them to keep balance within themselves in order to be an example of balance in their societies. She guides them by sharing her light equally. She teaches them that there is a balance of power in the relationships between men and women. And even today when the women gather on the full moon to do her ceremonies, the men prepare the food for the feast that will follow.[6]

The Story of Mindemoya: The Old Woman of the Mists

Just as Nookomis is beloved by the Anishinaabeg, so is Mindemoya, though she is perhaps less well known. Here is one story about her. It is said that long, long ago Mindemoya lived among the people. She was a hard worker and took care of a large extended family. Since misfortune had taken her young husband, she became the primary care provider. She hunted with the men and chopped wood for the fire. She hauled water and cooked with the women. She tanned hides and sewed clothing. She told the stories that needed to be told and did what needed to be done.

Then when her own family no longer required her care, she helped other families. She was always ready when illness or death struck unexpectedly. She would arrive unannounced and simply begin to do the necessary tasks to help out. She listened and understood. She knew which herbs to collect and how to prepare them. She cared for the ones everyone else had given up on. She tended to the most difficult pregnancies. The dying could count on her care. She did not look away. She was able to withstand the most challenging of circumstances. When starvation came near, she knew which roots to boil. When death came near, she sang the song to honor the last breath.

It is said that Mindemoya lived a very long life. She became stooped and blind in one eye. Yet she went on cheerfully lending a hand from village to village. And all who came upon her thanked her, for the stories of her good work had spread out in all directions. Mindemoya was, by all accounts, a good woman.

When she died, she took the Journey to the Next Land. There Mindemoya came upon the Red Gates of Epingishmook, which stand between this world and the next one. Before she passed through those gates, Gitchi Manitou spoke to her. Gitchi Manitou allowed most people to pass through the gates but stopped Mindemoya.

"Old Woman," Gitchi Manitou called out to her. "Before you pass through to the next world, I have something to offer you. I have been watching you. I have seen your tenacity and devotion. You never gave up. I watched how you gave all of yourself each day. You never held back. And you undertook each challenge with great joy. I admire you, Old Woman, and the great love you have expressed for the least fortunate. Mindemoya, what is the one thing I can do for you?"

The Old Woman paused. She wrapped her white shawl a bit more tightly across her shoulders. Then Mindemoya held up her chin and spoke. "*Chi miigwetch*, Gitchi Manitou, thank you, for your kind words. I can think of only one thing to ask of you but am afraid even you cannot grant this request."

"Old Woman!" Gitchi Manitou chided her. "There is nothing I cannot do. Speak truly what you hold in your heart, for you did so much for so many and never sought anything in return."

"That is it, exactly," the Old Woman responded. "I found joy in doing good work, and that is all I want. I want to return to the Earth, to the People, and be able once again to ease their burden and help them when they are in need."

"Very well, Mindemoya," replied Gitchi Manitou. "It is done. You may travel in your white shawl, in the gentle penetrating mists, coming and going wherever the people are in need for time eternity."

And so it is said that today Mindemoya can take many forms. She may arrive in as a little old woman who offers just what one needs: a look, a touch, a nod. She may stay awhile and care for the young or the elderly and ill. Disease does not frighten her. Suffering does not stop her. She arrives when there is danger or difficulty or despair. And when she is no longer needed, she disappears into the mist.

As mist, Mindemoya envelops each separate thing blurring any distinct differences. Mist is both air and water. It connects the waters of the earth with the air of the atmosphere, merging the realms of land and sky. Mindemoya wears the soft gauzy mist, easing anger, suffering, and pain. She erases the hard edges. She softens. She reconnects. Her power is a penetrating gentleness.

Consider her unique position. Mindemoya was able to win the respect of and thus negotiate with Gitchi Manitou, the Great Mystery, who serves as the ultimate authority over the dead and the living. She is awarded a unique ability and becomes one of the very few beings who travels freely between the dual realms of the *now* and *then,* the *here* and *there*. She is able to make this mystical journey betwixt and between without causing havoc among the living because her purpose is to serve the need of all that lives. Purpose and purposefulness, she teaches, are the ultimate power. In this way she urges each to find a true purpose and live it without distraction. Mindemoya appears and disappears mysteriously. She is not limited by time or place. She is not limited by a physical body or a single point of view. She is a force of consciousness, the very embodiment of love in action. As such, she is a powerful protection.

Mindemoya is alive in hospice workers and those who volunteer their time to help others. She sings with the Threshold Choirs that go to the bedside of the dying and sing. She is among those who suddenly appear and provide crucial life-saving assistance at the scene of crime or catastrophe. She is there amid the rubble, the drowning, the forgotten, the hungry. She lives in the hearts of rescue workers. She works in rape-crisis centers and battered women's shelters. She lives in the men and women who lend a hand and do not turn away from others' suffering. She is present in refugee camps and prisons, in places of despair and longing. She holds the hands of the tortured. And of those who die from this kind of pain, she accompanies them to the Red Gates of Epingishmook to insure their road to the next world is not fraught with difficulty even if their road in this world was.

Mindemoya sees with her blind eye into the human heart. She sees suffering even when it is masked by courtesy or shame. She is fearless in her expression of caring. She does not worry about becoming too involved. She does not become overly attached. Her ability to fulfill her purpose does not depend on others noticing her. She is perfectly lucid. She takes no offense. She just does what needs to be done and moves on to wherever she is next needed.

Age and Female Power

Mindemoya and Nookomis are postmenopausal female deities who live among and within people. Far from being seen as diminished because of their maturity, they are understood to be empowered by it. They are considered to be as beautiful, graceful, and fierce as the swan. Swan-feather fans may be used in their ceremonies for blessing. They are seen to be as strong and gentle as the doe. Deer rattles may accompany their songs. Of special importance is the softness of their faces, weathered by life, lined but tender and able to express all human emotions.

The tears of a grandmother are especially sacred. If a grandmother weeps openly, it is considered a blessing and all present will remain with eyes cast down and allow her to cry. It would be rude to stifle her, or give her a Kleenex to blow her nose, or even to reach out and hold her. Instead, one should sit respectfully as her tears fall. She teaches that feeling deeply is a blessed part of being alive. She shows by example what it is like to keep the heart soft. She teaches that there is no shame in expressing honest emotion openly among others if it is done with gentleness and respect.

The eyes of the female elders carry specific importance for dancing in their light is the life story of the people. When an elder female speaks, her voice is listened to above all others for it is understood that she does not speak from personal ego or for individual interest but for the welfare of future generations. Grandmothers are the wisdom-carriers for they hold the long view seeing into the heart of things. Grandmother speaks from her heart, for she is the heart.

The living grandmothers of today are understood to be spiritually connected to Nookomis and Mindemoya. The grandmothers may be seen as the living spokeswomen for these powerful spiritual beings. Grandmothers are seen as a source of guidance, for by their actions they indicate the correct path to take to restore right relations. As such, they are holders of the deepest wisdom of survival and continuity. They represent an old set of values in which people are placed above property; long-term health and welfare are more important than short-term gain; the good of the whole is placed above the good of the individual.[7]

The Desire of Each Granddaughter Is to Become a Grandmother

Nookomis and Mindemoya represent the most admirable female qualities. These are wisdom, generosity, forgiveness, patience, courage, beauty, love, and compassion. They are not passive beings but deeply active and engaged in living processes. It is in the daily enacting of these qualities that one maintains inner balance. Balance is beauty.

Wisdom is gained through keen observation over time. This is why these are elder beings and not youthful ones. Stories of Nookomis Tibik Giizis and Mindemoya teach how to sustain an ongoing relationship with the spirit. Though these divine entities may serve as intermediaries between human beings and the vast unseen forces who guide all being and becoming, humanity must seek contact with them in order to grow old and beautiful.

In this way Mindemoya and Nookomis may be represented on earth among the human family by a respected elder female, a grandmother in the traditional sense. For example, every birth requires the presence of an elder female. She may be the one to serve as the midwife or she may be in attendance alongside the midwife offering up the prayers necessary for a successful birth. She will greet the newborn and serve as a protective watchful eye over both mother and child.

The human grandmother who serves as the ambassador of the spiritual beings of Nookomis and Mindemoya does not turn away from difficulty or hardship. She pitches in and helps out no matter how dire the circumstances or the risk to herself. She has cultivated great stamina and endurance. In this way she may be compared to the elk. Elk teeth may adorn her clothing. She may wear elk teeth earrings or necklaces. An elk robe may rest upon her shoulders.

The love represented by Nookomis and Mindemoya is a powerful and sustaining kind of love. It is love for mate, children, grandchildren, community, tribe, nation, planet; love for soil, water, tree, forest, prairie, meadow, garden, wolf, bear, goose, sturgeon, cloud, rain, moon, sun; it is love for self tempered by love for family. Their love is expressed through action. Love is their emblem, and one symbol for it is the blueberry plant. Their goodness may be compared to the blueberry whose name, *min,* is also translated as "good." Blueberry's health-giving properties are well understood and this beautiful plant, source of sustenance, is seen as vital for a woman's health. A blueberry woman is a good woman for she has the ability to see clearly into another's situation and respond in kindness without pity, judgment, or expectation. A blueberry woman stores a little away for hard times. A blueberry woman is always prepared. She is generous and kind.

Through their actions, Nookomis and Mindemoya honor others, and in turn they are venerated as embodying the female ideal. To become a grandmother as wise and cherished as Nookomis, as kind and capable as Mindemoya, is the goal of any young girl raised on the old stories. She wants to be the powerful peacemaking Moon, the penetrating Mist, the Swan, the Doe, the Elk, the Blueberry Woman. If she is called to it she will learn to develop eyes that see the invisible, ears that hear the heart, and a voice that speaks truth. To come to the end of one's life able to serve the lives of others is the goal of the elder female. What she says and what she does will shape the generations beyond her.

Though as ancient as the moon and as mist, Nookomis and Mindemoya remain active beings, alive every time the moon shines and each time the mist rises. They are continuous and creative, able to manifest themselves in the modern world. They are available to assist. They respond to human need. To honor them, the Anishinaabeg may sing specific songs. They may dance, pray, and tell stories about the powerful gifts of Nookomis and Mindemoya.

Notes

1. The Anishinaabeg (also spelled Anishinaabek) include the "Three Fires" of the Ojibwe or Chippewa, the Potawatomi, and the Odawa or Ottawa.

2. Keewaydinoquay Peschel, also known as the Woman of the Northwest Wind, *mashkikikwe* (herbal medicine woman), author and educator. I served as her *oshkibewis* (helper) from 1979 to 1999.

3. See printed versions of this song in the *Miniss Kitigan Drum (MKD) Songbook*; also find the song with accompanying story in the MKD pamphlet, *Sisters of the Moon Shield*; also find song, story, and interpretation in Ann Filemyr's *Living at the Crossroads: the Intersection of Nature, Culture and Identity*; (Ann Arbor, MI: UMI Dissertation Services, 1995). The *Miniss Kitigan Drum Songbook* is self-published and distributed by the Miniss Kitigan Drum, a nonprofit organization founded by Keewaydinoquay Peschel in Michigan.

4. Eddie Benton-Banai, *The Mishomis Book* (St. Paul, MN: Indian Country Press, 1979), 16. Spellings of Anishinaabemowin words varies greatly as these words, transcribed from the oral language, reflect regional differences in pronunciation. A standardized orthography using a "double-vowel" system has

been introduced. See John D. Nichols and Earl Nyholm's A *Concise Dictionary of Minnesota Ojibwe* (Minneapolis: University of Minnesota Press, 1995).

5. Traditionally there were thirteen moons, so that when these names are applied to the twelve months of the nonlunar calendar year, they are only approximations. "Anishinaabemowin" is a term for the language in the language itself. Dictionaries often refer to it as Ojibwe. It is an Algonkian language of the Great Lakes. Various Algonkian languages are spoken along the St. Lawrence Seaway from the East Coast and across the northern Great Plains into the areas of the United States and Canada now called Sasketchewan and North Dakota. The dialect I was taught has spoken roots in northern Michigan.

6. There are many references to Nookomis in stories and poems inspired by the oral tradition. *Hiawatha* is one example. The process through which this poem entered American literature involves the storytelling, cultural knowledge, and literary talents of an Ojibwe woman. Henry Schoolcraft married Jane Johnston, and through this marriage gained great access to the Ojibwe world. He did not credit her or his extended Ojibwe family as he built his reputation as an ethnographer. His writing in "Algic Researches" was the basis for Longfellow's *The Song of Hiawatha* (1855). For a deeper examination of this and to read the poetry of Jane Johnston Schoolcraft, see Robert Dale Parker's *The Sound the Stars Make Rushing Through the Sky: The Writings of Jane Johnston Schoolcraft* (Philadelphia: University of Pennsylvania Press, 2007).

7. A wonderful modern example is found in the International Council of 13 Indigenous Grandmothers, founded in 2004. Thirteen elder women from the tribal peoples of the Americas, Africa, and Asia come together to pray and educate others about the need for healing and peaceful restoration of ecological and cultural life-giving practices. Various groups have hosted these gatherings. They have met with Gloria Steinem, Alice Walker, the Dalai Lama, the Bioneers, and others. The first Council Gathering was in the Catskills in 2004 and the sixth was in August 2009. For more see their Website, www.grandmotherscouncil.com, or Carol Schaffer, *Grandmothers Counsel the World: Women Elders Offer Their Vision for Our Planet* (Boulder, CO: Trumpeter, 2006).

Bibliography

Benton-Banai, Edward. *The Mishomis Book*. St. Paul, MN: Indian Country Press, 1979.

cwc, ed. *Miniss Kitigan Drum: Songs of the People*. May 17, 1994.

Filemyr, Ann. *Living at the Crossroads: The Intersection of Nature, Culture, and Identity*. Ann Arbor, MI: UMI Dissertation Services, 1995.

Johnston, Basil. H. *Mermaids and Medicine Women: Native Myths and Legends*. Toronto: Royal Ontario Museum, 1998.

Nichols, John D., and Earl Nyholm. *A Concise Dictionary of Minnesota Ojibwe*. Minneapolis: University of Minnesota Press, 1995.

"Min: Anishinaabeg Ogimaawi-minan" (Blueberry: First Fruit of the People). Collected and retold by Keewaydinoquay. Miniss Kitigan Drum pamphlet. 1978; 7th printing, 1985.

Parker, Robert Dale. *The Sound the Stars Make Rushing Through the Sky: The Writings of Jane Johnston Schoolcraft.* Philadelphia: University of Pennsylvania Press, 2007.

Peschel, Keewaydinoquay. *Puhpohwee for the People: A Narrative Account of Fungi Uses Among the Anhisnnabeg.* Dekalb: Northern Illinois University LEPS Press, 1998.

Schaffer, Carol. *Grandmothers Counsel the World: Women Elders Offer Their Vision for Our Planet.* Boulder, CO: Trumpeter, 2006.

"Sisters of the Moon Shields and the Eighteen Canoes." As told to Megisikwe by Keewaydinoquay. Miniss Kitigan Drum pamphlet, ca. 1993.

13

White Buffalo Calf Woman (Pte-san win-yan): The First and Second Coming

Arieahn Matamonasa-Bennett

To the indigenous people of the Americas, stories are sacred—they are *medicine* or forms of indigenous healing, which also includes rituals and ceremonial practices.

In contemporary times, as in the past, the people are not concerned with the exact dates or finding "evidence" to prove that the events in the story may have happened. What was—and remains—important are the messages, rituals, values, and guides for living in a sacred way that these stories provide. This is what gives them such longevity and enormous power.

The myths and stories of the indigenous people of North America are as varied as the geographic regions that they occupy. Each of the over 300 distinct remaining Native American cultures has its own cosmology and mythology informing people on how to live in relationship not only with each other but also with the natural world. Cosmology and myth have a critical influence on shaping societies and informing its people on what is good and what is evil. They provide a means for social cohesion and the transmission of cultural values from one generation to the next. Additionally, myths and cosmology determine and inform the members of a culture who can assume positions of leadership, power, and honor. While each Native American culture has its own sacred stories and worldview there are two

Figure 13.1 The Lakota people of the American plains honored White Buffalo Calf Woman, who brought spiritual insights and cultural awareness to them. She is still honored today, and her story told to exemplify respect toward women. (Copyright Hrana Janto.)

main themes or threads that are common to all of the stories: reverence for the Earth and all of creation, and reverence for the feminine.

The feminine principle is found throughout the creation stories and mythologies of Native people in the Americas, and the majority of principal spiritual figures and icons are female. Virtually all indigenous religions on this continent exhibit an abundant presence of feminine elements within their cosmologies.[1] There are numerous examples of the feminine as White Buffalo Calf Woman and Kanka (Lakota), Grandmother Turtle and Sky Woman (Iroquois), First Woman (Abanaki), Thought Woman (Laguna), Changing Woman (Dine), Spider Woman (Hopi), and Beloved Woman and Selu (Cherokee)—some of which are presented in this volume. None of the creation stories recorded by historians, or currently handed down in the oral tradition, have male figures as either creators or principal spiritual figures despite undergoing changes due to contact with Christian missionaries.[2]

Indigenous cultures view existence as a web of interconnected, interdependent relationships. Humankind is not the center of the web, merely a strand in it. All parts of creation are equally important and entitled to honor and respect. The creator, who is called by many names, dwells in all of creation. In creation myths, the creator is typically female or may be an animal relative with whom the group closely identifies. Earth is viewed as a living entity, and it is sacred. For Native people, saying, "Earth is our Mother" is not metaphorical, but literal. There are not concepts of domination and control of nature but rather, the *feminine* values of cooperation with, and receptivity to, the natural worlds are emphasized.

This chapter examines the story of Pte-san win-yan, White Buffalo Calf Woman of the Lakota, from not only the sociohistorical context, but also from the ways in which this story and its values continue to heal and sustain Lakota contemporary culture and its people. The story of White Buffalo Calf Woman is a living story, and not only are her teachings and ceremonies making a resurgence among the Lakota people offering healing and hope, they have provided hope and healing for people of all races and nations and for healing of the Earth as well. Pte-san win-yan told the people many hundreds of years ago that she would return to the people when they needed her in a time of great hardship and that she would come in a form that they would recognize. There is evidence that her spirit has already returned.

Background and Lakota History

The Lakota people were and remain *Pte O-Ya-te* ("Buffalo People"), as humans and buffalo are mythically part of the same people. Lakota oral history teaches that the Lakota came from Paha Sapa, the Black Hills in South Dakota, which are called "the heart of everything there is." Originally living underground, the ancestors emerged to the Plains where they relied on the buffalo to provide food, shelter, and clothing. They honored the buffalo as a relative, and special ceremonies reciprocated the gifts of life that the buffalo made possible. Originally, the dog was the closest ally and beast of burden for the people, but that radically changed in the 17th and 18th centuries when the horse was reintroduced to North America as a result of Spanish exploration. The Lakota, like the other Plains tribes, quickly integrated the horse into their life ways and they became highly mobile and nomadic.

Over thousands of years, the Lakota had developed a complex social system and code that allowed them to successfully and peacefully live as a highly interdependent cohesive society. The social code was taught and reinforced through stories, ceremony, and rituals at every stage of the lifespan. Gender roles were diverse and far more flexible than in European societies. Many Native and other scholars believe that the emphasis of the feminine at the heart of Lakota philosophy made equality between the sexes a given. Beatrice Medicine, a Sihasapa Lakota anthropologist, asserts that women were an active part of ritual life in the men's societies as well as having their own spiritual and social societies.[3] Women were highly valued in Lakota society, especially because of their roles as the primary caretakers and socializers of children.

That the Lakota valued women and the feminine is evidenced in the story of White Buffalo Calf Woman, who brought to the Lakota people the Sacred Pipe and the Seven Sacred Rites that are at the heart of their spiritual existence. However, as Native American scholar Vine Deloria asserts, the importance of White Buffalo Calf Woman was, and continues to be, the story itself along with the reception of the Sacred Pipe and ceremonies, rather than the woman herself as a personal object of salvation or adoration.

The First Coming: The Story of White Buffalo Calf Woman

While there are many versions of this story, depending on the teller, the themes and values transmitted remain constant. An Internet search will yield thousands of versions of this story, often told by people who are neither Lakota or knowledgeable of traditional Lakota oral history and culture. The story presented here is adapted and paraphrased from the version collected by Chief Arvol Looking Horse, who is the Nineteenth Generation Keeper of the Sacred White Buffalo Pipe of the Lakota, Dakota, and Nakota Great Sioux Nation. In a special edition publication for World Peace and Prayer Day, June 21, 2001, Chief Looking Horse compiled White Buffalo Teachings, which not only holds the story of White Buffalo Calf Woman, but also includes prophecies and calls for much needed healing.[4] Looking Horse called for healing not only the Lakota people, but for all people and the Sacred Mother Earth as well.

More than nineteen generations ago, Pte-san win-yan came to the Lakota, bringing the Sacred C'anupa (pipe) and the Seven Sacred Rites. During this time, the people were experiencing great hardships including starvation. Even though the people were still following the great buffalo herds, they were living out of balance and had forgotten the Creator. The buffalo herds were disappearing and scouts sent to look for the buffalo repeatedly returned empty-handed.

One day the scouts were returning to camp after another unsuccessful search and they saw a woman walking alone over a hill. They watched her in awe while wondering what she was doing alone in the middle of nowhere.

She was dressed in a beautiful white buckskin dress, and she carried a bundle in her arms. Because she was very beautiful, one of the scouts felt lust for her despite warnings from the other scout that she was obviously wakan (holy) and had been sent by the Great Spirit as an answer to their prayers for help.

The lustful scout refused to listen and as he approached the woman to touch her, a swirling cloud surrounded him, and when it lifted, his skeleton lay at her feet with a snake crawling from his skull.

The woman then pointed at the remaining scout, who was trembling with fear, and told him to go back to the people and tell them what he had witnessed. She told him to have the people build an altar out of sage and cherry branches and to put up a tipi. She promised that she would come to the people tomorrow from the West and that she would give them the great gift that was in her bundle. The scout, who was still fearful, thanked her for the message and ran back to the camp to tell the people what he had seen and heard. The people followed the instructions and prepared the altar and the tipi for her arrival.

The following day, as promised, the woman appeared to the people from the West. As she approached them, she held the bundle in her outstretched arms, and she sang a beautiful song that is still sung today. She walked clockwise around the altar made of sage and cherry branches. She then set her bundle down and opened it to reveal the Sacred C'anupa, the Sacred Pipe of Pipes that is still kept today.

The woman then instructed the people about following the way of the Sacred C'anupa. She told them that they should walk in a sacred way upon the Earth—that she is the grandmother and mother, and that she is sacred. She told them about the symbolism of the C'anupa—that the red stone bowl represented the blood of the People and the feminine, and that the wood stem represented the Tree of Life, the roots of the ancestors and the masculine. By connecting the stem and bowl together, the world above and below is connected. Through using the pipe a person could achieve connection and unity with Wakan Tankan (the Great Mystery). She instructed that the C'anupa should only come together for prayer and that the people should humble themselves and pray for life, peace, harmony, and happiness. She instructed that prayers should be presented to all of the sacred directions—the four cardinal directions, the Great Spirit above and the Mother Earth below.

Pte-san win-yan then gave the people the Seven Sacred Rites: (1) the I-ni-pi (Purification ceremony); (2) the Wi-wanyang wa-c'i-pi (Sun Dance ceremony); (3) the Han-ble-c'i-ya (Vision Quest ceremony); (4) the Hun-ka ka-g'a (Making of a Relative adoption ceremony); (5) the Ta-pa kah'-g'o-ya (Throwing of the Sacred Ball ceremony); (6) the Wi-yan I-na-j'in (Womanhood ceremony); and (7) the Na-g'i glu-ha (Keeping of the Spirit ceremony). All are still practiced to this present day.

Reflecting on Cultural Values

The story of White Buffalo Calf Woman, like other sacred stories, reflects traditional Lakota worldview and spiritual values. The story of White Buffalo Calf Woman provided more than a morality myth offering instructions for living a traditional life. The story contains instructions for the rituals and ceremonies she brought to the people that were and still remain key to Lakota spiritual existence. The C'anupa (pipe) ceremony she gave to the people provided the means to connect with the Great Mystery and achieve unity and oneness through prayer. In addition, she promised that through prayer, the C'anupa and the sacred sites and ceremonies, they could achieve connection to the Creator, along with peace, harmony, and happiness. That other personal bundles (pipes) could be made and carried by individuals as a means to connect with the original C'anupa speaks to the highly personal and individual spiritual relationship that was, and is still, possible in Lakota spirituality. By smoking this C'anupa, a person could achieve union and unity with all beings and things in the world and make personal contact with Wakan Tankan (the Great Mystery).

The Seven Sacred Rites she taught provided the people with ceremonies and right-of-passage rituals to mark and facilitate transition to important life-stages and provided the community with a means to create harmony, balance, and social cohesion. These ceremonies reaffirmed reverence and respect for the Mother Earth and for the feminine. When she first appeared to the scouts and one of them lusted after her with "bad thoughts" despite warnings from the other scout that she was obviously sacred or holy, he was turned into a pile of bones. She instructed the people that they should "walk in a sacred way upon the Earth—the grandmother and mother—and that she is sacred." In one of the Seven Sacred Rites, the *Wi-yan i-na-j'in* (Womanhood ceremony), young girls are celebrated by the entire community when they enter womanhood as well as receiving instructions on Lakota values and honoring the power inherent in menstruation, conception and childbirth. In the past, such young women were taught that they were so powerful during this time that they needed to isolate themselves and take care not to allow their power to interfere with other ceremonial activities.

Ceremonies were, and remain, critical in helping the people heal from loss, death, and grief. The *I ni-pi* (sweat lodge) purification ceremony provided a means for cleansing and renewal of the body and spirit and a means for letting go of the past. The *Hun-ka Ka-g'a* (Making of a Relative adoption ceremony) allowed a formal process to create and re-create and strengthen extended families. This ceremony not only honored the closeness of certain relationships but also replaced those who had previously died. The *Na-gi glu-ha* Spirit Keeping ceremony allowed family members to "keep" the spirit of the loved one for up to a year and then formally release their loved one and end the mourning period in a "spirit releasing" ceremony.

Respect for the Earth and for all living things was, and still is, central to Lakota worldview. Even in the act of hunting or gathering plants, there were prayers said and songs sung to reciprocate and honor the gifts from these relatives. In addition to honoring all of creation, praying and singing at sacred sites from Lakota oral history was, and is, central to spiritual life. In the story, she tells the people to honor sacred places, ceremonies, and sites, and gather at the sites to sing and pray.

Living these ceremonial and cultural values allowed the Lakota ancestors to prosper on the Plains for many successive generations. Highly adaptable to change, they endured climate changes, brutal winters, contact with explorers, invaders from many other nations, and other hardships, striving always to achieve harmony and balance with each other and all of life around them. Although White Buffalo Woman predicted future hardships along with the message of hope that she would come to the people again, the ancestors could not have predicted the level of devastation and loss that was to come with the start of the 19th century.

A Time of Great Darkness

The arrival, colonization, and eventual westward expansion of settlers from the newly formed America caused great upheaval and turmoil to the Lakota and other Plains people. Starting in the early 19th century, westward expansion increased competition for land and resources and caused warfare between Native nations that had previously coexisted in the West. Death from warfare and disease caused much loss and grief; however, it was the systematic federal policy to assimilate or annihilate the Lakota and other Plains tribes that brought a cycle of darkness that lasted almost 100 years.

The fact that genocide and atrocities occurred during the process of colonization in North America is well established, but the full scope and details of this are well beyond what could be covered here.[5] There are, however, several key aspects of historical events and policies that have particular relevance to this work and to the story of White Buffalo Calf Woman.

Death of the Buffalo Nation

When it became apparent that the Lakota were "hostile," in that they were resisting forced removal and refusing relocation to reservations, the mass slaughter of buffalo began. It was a military policy, key to the plans for colonization of the Plains, expansion of the cattle industry, establishment of American agriculture, and the construction of the railroads.[6] The purposeful near-extinction of the 50 million buffalo, which by the turn of the last century were estimated at 26 survivors (500 remained in Canada), mirrored what was happening with the *Pte O-Ya-te,* the Buffalo People. The mass killing of the buffalo had devastating effects on the Lakota both physically and spiritually. Restricted from hunting due to reservation boundaries and the absence of game, the Lakota men not only lost their primary cultural roles and identities, they and their families now had to depend on grossly inadequate government rations for sustenance. Spiritually, there was great loss and suffering having watched not only their human relatives but also their closest animal relatives massacred without the ability to honor and mourn their deaths in a proper ceremonial way.

As Winona LaDuke points out:

Many would argue that the ecological future of the Great Plains is intertwined with the psychological and spiritual relationship the prairies and the people of the prairies have with the buffalo and with American culture and mythology. Cattle culture's takeover of the prairie and the subsequent destruction of the buffalo herds is a multifaceted mistake and one whose significance is becoming increasingly apparent. At its foundation many would say it is a spiritual mistake: killing without reverence.[7]

Banning of Ceremony and the Seven Sacred Rights

Official federal policies towards Plains tribes from the mid-1800s until the middle of this last century were geared toward assimilation into majority culture. The boarding school system forcibly removed children from their families and sent them away to break the transmission of cultural values and identity. Christianity was also widely utilized as a tool for assimilation and acculturation. When it became apparent to U.S. officials and policymakers that their efforts to destroy Lakota culture through warfare, forced removal, and destruction of the buffalo were still not successful, policies were created that banned Native religion. This made the practice of Native American, and specifically Lakota traditional ceremony illegal until the American Indian Religious Freedom Act of 1978.[8] Additionally, confinement to reservation land prevented Lakota people from having access to many of their sacred sites.

Once Lakota ceremonies were prohibited, the Lakota people were prevented from openly transmitting cultural values and mores that were essential for the continuation and survival of the culture to following generations. The banning of traditional ceremonies also prevented both individual healing and community healing from the genocide and loss that had occurred. The absence of rituals to facilitate the mourning and healing process may have severely limited the resolution of grief and may have resulted in self-destructive behaviors. Many Native scholars assert that the Lakota people and many other Native people are suffering from disenfranchised grief, as well as the intergenerational transmission of grief from one generation to the survivors.[9]

Despite the banning of Lakota ceremonies, many Lakota took great personal risk to continue to hold and pass down the oral history and Seven Sacred Rites in secret. The spirit and ceremonies of White Buffalo Woman were passed down until the Lakota began asserting their rights to sovereignty and religious freedom in the wake of the American Indian movement of the 1970s. With an awareness of history and outrage at the injustices that their ancestors had suffered, new generations of Lakota were showing a renewed sense of pride in Native identity and an interest in learning traditional spirituality. This renaissance occurred just as the last elders, who knew the ceremonies and sacred rights, were dying. Had this not occurred, the story of White Buffalo Calf Woman and the Seven Rites and ceremonies would have died with them.

Today, in Lakota communities there are epidemic rates of alcoholism, suicide, homicide, domestic violence, rape, and child abuse. Many respected traditional Lakota men and women believe that the problems that plague the people today are the direct result of history and brutal colonization. Perhaps, even more important, many believe that the loss of traditional Lakota ceremony and spirituality that valued the Earth *and* women as sacred are the roots of these social problems. For Native scholars, mental health practitioners, and policymakers, it is critical to recognize the role of colonization and history in these problems. Concepts of intergenerational grief, disenfranchised grief, loss of traditional spirituality, and loss of cultural identity are critical for analyzing and understanding these serious social problems and toward developing solutions.[10]

The Second Coming: The Living Spirit of
White Buffalo Calf Woman

In 1994 a white buffalo calf named Miracle was born on a farm in Janesville, Wisconsin. For some Native elders, this represented the fulfillment of a prophecy about an impending apocalypse and environmental disasters. For most traditional Lakota people, however, it represented fulfillment of White Buffalo Calf Woman's promise to return and was a symbol of hope for the Buffalo Nation and the Buffalo People. The birth of the white buffalo calf was believed to signal the beginning of a new era with the promise of restoration and healing of both the Earth and the Nation. The groundwork for the healing and the restoration had already been prepared and many warrior men and women had carried the spirit of White Buffalo Calf Woman to the point where this new era is now within the realm of possibility. More than a symbol of a new era, there is evidence in many areas that the spirit and presence of White Buffalo Calf Woman is with the Lakota people.

The destruction of the great buffalo herds had devastating impacts on the prairie, the largest ecosystem in North America. Hundreds of native plant species were lost in the transition to industrial agriculture and cattle farming, and the Plains were stripped of the biodiversity of other native wildlife as well. Despite the mass killing and near extinction of the buffalo at the turn of the last century, the survivors have begun to repopulate the Plains through the hard work and dedication of many Native people including the Oglala Lakota Natural Resource Management, the Knife Chief Buffalo Project, the Seventh Generation Buffalo Cooperative, and individuals like Birgil Kills Straight and Rosalie Little Thunder. Currently, there are many community-based projects underway to restore and develop diverse herds and return the buffalo to the prairie ecosystem. As the herds grow, many believe that the Lakota's collective mental, physical, and spiritual health are restored as well. Many believe that the return of the buffalo may help the current ecologic and economic crisis now facing states in the West.

At the turn of the last century, it was popularly believed that Native Americans were a vanishing race. Like the buffalo, however, Native American populations are increasing and are one of the fastest growing minority groups. U.S. Census (2000) data estimated 4.3 million (1.5%) of the population as Native American. The Lakota (Sioux) population estimates were 153,000 with 2005–2006 data showing a 1% increase in population.[11]

White Buffalo Calf Woman Society: A Resurgence of Respect for Women

> Many winter-counts ago, a wakan (sacred) woman appeared among the Lakota people, bearing with her a truly marvelous gift. She was called the White Buffalo Calf Woman, and her gift is still with the Lakota people today—the sacred Cannunpa (pipe).
>
> The Pipe represents unity, truth, understanding, and peace to all who practice the Teachings of the Pipe. The White Buffalo Calf Woman Society strives to follow the teachings that were given to the Oyate (people) by the White Buffalo Calf Woman. Our goals are peace, understanding and improved quality of life for all people. Only if there is spiritual peace and focused determination within our hearts can we hope to share these goals with others. That through learning and caring, through desire and hard work, through concern and inspiration, the vision of the White Buffalo Calf Woman may become a reality for all people.[12]

The loss of traditional worldviews and cosmologies has been devastating to Native communities throughout North America, and increased cultural loss has paralleled the increase in numerous social problems including domestic violence. Clearly, the role that cosmology and patriarchal religion plays as far as influencing or condoning violence against women in Native and non-Native societies is not well understood.

Traditional Lakota values included honoring the feminine and respect for women. However, through the process of colonization, forced assimilation, and confinement to reservations, Lakota communities became increasingly threatening places for women and in many communities sexual assault and domestic violence/intimate partner violence have become the most serious health problems for women today.

The importance of understanding the beliefs and perceptions of Native American men regarding whether domestic violence and sexual assault are new problems brought on by colonization, or whether they existed historically as part of traditional Native culture, is paramount in light of current prevention and awareness initiatives. Currently, numerous domestic violence prevention programs and public awareness efforts in reservation communities across the United States and Canada are utilizing the concept that domestic violence is not "traditional." For example, Artichoker and Gullickson interviewed male and female Lakota Elders and spiritual leaders in

South Dakota, most of whom identified domestic violence as a problem brought on by colonization.[13] The slogan "Domestic Violence is not a Lakota Tradition—Women are Sacred" is currently being used as a means for raising public awareness of this problem on the reservation and nearby communities.

In 1977 the White Buffalo Calf Woman Society (WBCWS) was formed on the Rosebud Reservation in Mission South Dakota from a grassroots movement and signaled a new era of victim services and community outreach for preventing violence against women and children. The WBCWS has the distinction of being the first battered women's shelter for Native American women and the first shelter for women of color in the United States. It has become a model of what can be achieved through strong leadership. Today, the organization serves over 900 women and children each year and WBCWS has a very strong presence in the community. The WBCWS frequently conducts public service announcements and other events as an approach to ending the violence in Lakota families.[14]

The organization has incorporated traditional beliefs, stories (such as the teachings of White Buffalo Calf Woman), and cultural practices into its victim services. Additionally, it has influenced and developed public policies through strong victim-centered ordinances. For example, in April of 2004, Chief Arvol Looking Horse and 300 people from the community participated in a nineteen-mile walk to reclaim the sacredness of women and children through ceremony and prayer and to bring awareness of ending sexual violence in Lakota communities.

Tillie Black Bear, a founding member and now executive director, has received numerous honors and recognition for her work. In 2000 she received the Eleanor Roosevelt Human Rights Award and was designated one of President George Bush's "Thousand Points of Light." At the 1999 Millennium Conference in Chicago, she was honored among the ten individuals who were recognized as founders of the domestic violence movement in the United States. In 2005 she was a keynote speaker at the National Organization for Women Foundation's Women of Color and Allies Summit. Additionally, she was one of the founders of the National Coalition Against Domestic Violence and founding mother for the South Dakota Coalition Against Domestic Violence and Sexual Assault.

Under Black Bear's leadership, the White Buffalo Calf Woman Society provides life-saving services, community outreach, and education for addressing the problems of violence against Lakota women and children in a way that clearly carries her spirit and message. Currently, the organization is tackling the growing problem of teen suicide on the reservation and other serious social concerns.

Conclusions

Much has changed for Lakota people since the first coming of White Buffalo Calf Woman nineteen generations ago. The devaluing of indigenous worldviews, spirituality, and feminine values through the forces of colonization wreaked much devastation on both the Earth and the people. Like the buffalo, the Lakota people have proved to be survivors.

Traditional Lakota culture is adapting to life in the 20th century. The values of reciprocity, balance, harmony, and respect for the feminine—both the sacred Mother Earth and women—have relevance today not only for Lakota people, but for everyone. Values that promote peace and the healing of the planet are sorely needed. White Buffalo Calf Woman has returned to the Lakota people with a message of hope and healing. She has returned and is a living icon in the heart and spirits of those who not only carried her ceremonies and stories through indescribable hardship, oppression, and discrimination, but she is also living through those traditional people who are working tirelessly for the healing of the feminine on this planet.

Notes

1. V. Deloria, *God Is Red: A Native View of Religion* (Golden, CO: Fulcrum, 1994).

2. Ibid; R. Erdoes and A. Ortiz, *American Indian Myths and Legends* (New York: Pantheon Books, 1984).

3. Beatrice Medicine, "Warrior Women: Sex Role Alternatives for Plains Indian Women," in *The Hidden Half: Studies of Plains Indian Women*, ed. Patricia Albers and Beatrice Medicine (Lanham, MD: University Press of America, 1983).

4. A. Looking Horse, *White Buffalo Teachings*, compiled by H. Arden and P. Horn (Williamsburg, MA: Dreamkeepers Press, 2001).

5. V. Deloria, "Trouble in High Places: Erosion of American Indian Rights to Religious Freedom in the United States," in *The State of Native America: Genocide, Colonization, and Resistance*, ed. M. A. Jaimes (Boston: South End Press, 1992); V. Deloria, *Red Earth, White Lies: Native Americans and the Myth of Scientific Fact* (Golden, CO: Fulcrum, 1997); E. Duran and B. Duran, *Postcolonial Psychology* (Albany: SUNY Press, 1995); L. H. Legters, "The American Genocide," *Policy Studies Journal* 16, no. 4 (1988): 768–777.

6. W. La Duke, "Buffalo Nations, Buffalo People," in *All Our Relations: Native Struggles for Land and Life* (Cambridge, MA: South End Press, 1999).

7. Ibid. The ecological crisis to the prairie ecosystem that this destruction created remains to be fully realized and is explored in detail in *All Our Relations.*

8. M. A. Jaimes and T. Halsey, "American Indian Women: At the Center of Indigenous Resistance in North America," in *The State of Native America: Genocide, Colonization, and Resistance*, ed. M. A. Jaimes (Boston: South End Press, 1992).

9. K. J. Doka, *Disenfranchised Grief: Recognizing Hidden Sorrow* (Lexington, MA: D. C. Heath, 1989); M. Y. H. Brave Heart and L. M. De Bruyn, "The American Indian Holocaust: Healing Historical, Unresolved Grief," *American Indian and Alaska Native Mental Health Research* 8, no. 2 (1998): 60–82.

10. Brave Heart and De Bruyn, "American Indian Holocaust," 60–82.

11. U.S. Census Bureau, The American Indian and Alaska Native Population, http://www.census.gov/population/www/socdemo/race/censr-28.pdf (accessed December 28, 2008).

12. White Buffalo Calf Woman Society, Inc., http://www.wbcws.org (accessed December 28, 2008).

13. K. Artichoker and V. Gullickson, *Raising Public Awareness on Domestic Violence in Indian Country,* report published by the National Resource Center on Domestic Violence, 2003, http://www.vawnet.org/NRCDVpublications/TAPE/papers/NRCDV_Cangleska.php (accessed July 3, 2004).

14. White Buffalo Calf Woman Society.

Bibliography

Artichoker, K., and V. Gullickson. *Raising Public Awareness on Domestic Violence in Indian Country.* Report published by the National Resource Center on Domestic Violence, 2003. http://www.vawnet.org/NRCDVpublications/TAPE/papers/NRCDV_Cangleska.php.

Brave Heart, M. Y. H., and L. M. De Bruyn. "The American Indian Holocaust: Healing Historical, Unresolved Grief." *American Indian and Alaska Native Mental Health Research* 8, no. 2 (1998): 60–82.

Deloria, V. *God Is Red: A Native View of Religion.* Golden, CO: Fulcrum, 1994.

Deloria, V. *Red Earth, White Lies: Native Americans and the Myth of Scientific Fact.* Golden, CO: Fulcrum, 1997.

Deloria, V. "Trouble in High Places: Erosion of American Indian Rights to Religious Freedom in the United States." In *The State of Native America: Genocide, Colonization, and Resistance*, ed. M. A. Jaimes, 267–290. Boston: South End Press, 1992.

Doka, K. J. *Disenfranchised Grief: Recognizing Hidden Sorrow.* Lexington, MA: D. C. Heath, 1989.

Duran, E., and B. Duran. *Postcolonial Psychology.* Albany: SUNY Press, 1995.

Erdoes, R., and A. Ortiz. *American Indian Myths and Legends.* New York: Pantheon Books, 1984.

Jaimes, M. A., and T. Halsey. "American Indian Women: At the Center of Indigenous Resistance in North America." In *The State of Native America: Genocide, Colonization, and Resistance,* ed. M. A. Jaimes. Boston: South End Press, 1992.

La Duke, W. "Buffalo Nations, Buffalo People" In *All Our Relations: Native Struggles for Land and Life,* 311–344. Cambridge, MA: South End Press, 1999.

Legters, L. H. "The American Genocide." *Policy Studies Journal* 16, no. 4 (1988): 768–777.

Looking Horse, A. *White Buffalo Teachings.* Compiled by H. Arden and P. Horn. Williamsburg, MA: Dreamkeepers Press, 2001.

Medicine, Beatrice. "Warrior Women: Sex Role Alternatives for Plains Indian Women." In *The Hidden Half: Studies of Plains Indian Women,* ed. Patricia Albers and Beatrice Medicine. Lanham, MD: University Press of America, 1983.

White Buffalo Calf Woman Society, Inc. http://www.wbcws.org.

14

Wolves and the Divine Feminine: European and Native American Wolf Mythologies

Cristina Eisenberg

For nearly two millennia, humans have worked hard to push wildness to the outer edges of the psyche.[1] To many people today, the wolf symbolizes wildness and freedom from the constraints of city life. However, as recently as the mid-20th century, the majority of people in modern European-based societies saw the wolf as symbolic of evil and humans' bestial nature.[2] These notions originated in Europe, fanned by superstition, ignorance, and by the Roman Church, which was determined to repress wildness. By medieval times, humans were obsessed with wolf legends and widely believed in werewolves, characterized as troubled males. Nevertheless, underneath this dark, male-oriented association ran a powerful, life-affirming association between wolves and the divine feminine.

This duality can be traced to early humans, who made a connection between wolves and the crepuscular period—dusk and dawn. Wolves are most active during crepuscular periods, when they hunt and often howl. As a creature of the dawn the wolf represents enlightenment, light coming out of darkness. As a creature of the dusk, the wolf represents returning to fearful darkness. However, like all dualisms, "dark versus light" is false,

Figure 14.1 No "big bad wolf," the wolf goddess who appears in worldwide mythology connects humans to wild animal instinct. (Photograph by Cristina Eisenberg.)

because ultimately polar opposites merge. And as occurred with wolves, applying such a dualism can cause damage. The Greek word for wolf, *lukos*, has the same root as the Greek word for light, *leukos*. The Latin word for wolf, *lupus,* and the word for light, *lucis,* suggest an association with Lucifer, the Devil.[3] The Bible reflects this association, referring to Lucifer as "day star, son of the morning" (Isa. 14:12). Psychologist Karen House suggests an association with the twilight zone, or ecotone, of cultivated fields as they fade into the darkness of the forest and the crepuscular period when wolves hunt.[4]

Through the ages, humans have felt both attraction to and repulsion from wolves. These associations can be physiological, mythic, or habitat-related, and are deeply embedded in our culture.[5] Twentieth-century Spanish philosopher José Ortega y Gasset suggests that a parallel relationship between human subsistence hunters and their prey, and between wolves and their prey, causes this attraction.[6] These human hunters brought to the hunt a visceral desire to actively participate in the most intimate workings of wild nature. However, as humans turned from hunter-gatherer societies to agronomy and their population grew, the potential for conflict with wolves increased.

Most of the myths that follow contain archetypes. Rooted in prehistoric beliefs, in modern times they have been distilled to suit cultural needs. Psychologist Carl Jung defines *archetype* as a collective image, that is, common to at least whole peoples or periods of history. Normative of myth, archetypes express common human needs, instincts, and potentials present always and everywhere.[7] An archetypal image of the wolf is informed by positive and negative judgments made in regard to actual historical and ancestral experiences with wolves. These archetypes reside within what Jung termed the "collective unconscious." While the personal unconscious contains images that have at one time been conscious, the collective unconscious contains things that have never been individually acquired, but owe their existence to heredity.[8]

Late Pleistocene cave paintings in Europe, Asia, and North America provide evidence of the earliest archetypes of wolves. These petroglyphs, which date back to between 30,000 to 10,000 BCE, depict humans and wild animals engaged in acts of hunting and predation. Images of wolves hunting bison embody the concept of death and rebirth through ritual and the sanctity of the hunt.[9] The story of human metaphysical struggle with the wolf begins here, with these cave paintings. It is the story of humankind's alternating attraction and repulsion to this animal and of the inquiry into the nature of the universe and what it means to be human.

Researching wolf myths can be likened to following a trail through the woods that leads progressively deeper into collective mythologies. Many European wolf myths pertain to the dark side of human nature, inspired by the urges, dream images, and intuitive thoughts that dwell in the individual unconscious mind. European wolf myths inspired by the divine feminine provide an exception. Native American wolf myths address the positive aspect of human nature, featuring wolves as nurturing wise beings and guides. According to Jung, one should not negatively judge archetypes, myths, and dreams, but should accept them for what they can teach about human nature. Thus, the aim of one's life, psychologically speaking, should be to come to know one's other side, and thus both enjoy and control the full range of one's capabilities.[10]

European Wolf Myths Involving Women

The Greek god Apollo embodies humans' complicated association with wolves. The earliest evidence of this appears on coins minted in

Argos, his patron city, which date back to the fifth century BCE and bear images of wolves. According to myth, Apollo was born on Delos and fathered by Zeus. His mother, Leto, traveled to Delos with a pack of wolves, disguised as one of them to hide from Hera, Zeus's jealous wife. Apollo took the form of a wolf in battle, as recounted in the Aeneid. Thus he represents the wolf image of a powerful hunter, ruthless warrior, and strong force of nature. Wolves appear on many ancient images of Apollo. His temple at Argos commemorates a battle between a wolf and a bull, and another wolf appears at the most famous of his shrines, the Oracle of Delphi. However, the reverse side of this relationship is most evident at the Acropolis Lyceum, an ancient temple dedicated to Apollo as the patron of shepherds. Second-century AD Greek writer Pausanius tells of Apollo directing shepherds to put out poisoned meat to kill wolves.[11]

In *The White Goddess,* mythologist Robert Graves writes about wolf goddesses Artemis and Cerridwen. A Greek divinity known as the goddess of the hunt, Artemis is sometimes depicted with wolves at her side and has a benign association with them. The wolf goddess Cerridwen came to Britain between 2500 and 2000 BCE, with the Stone Age agriculturalists from North Africa. Both are also known as moon goddesses, and Graves credits this association with wolf characteristics such as howling at the moon, eye-shine, and a propensity to haunt wooded landscapes. In Celtic mythology the death-goddess the Morrigan shape-shifted into a red wolf to go into battle.[12]

The Wolf of Harvest Rites

The wolf figured in fertility rites involving the grain harvest in Brittany, Germany, France, and Slavonic countries. Referred to as the rye-wolf or the green-wolf rites, these proliferated from before the time of Christ and endured well into the medieval era.[13] In Brittany bonfires held on the first day of the summer season were lit just before the sun dipped below the horizon. When they died down, the Brotherhood of the Green Wolf chose a new chief or master. The new head of the brotherhood donned a long green mantle and tall green hat. The local priest said mass and then the brotherhood kindled another bonfire and had a feast. After the feast, they seized the past Green Wolf, threw him into the flames, and watched him burn to death. After midnight, the festivities ended and everyone behaved piously, singing church hymns. The next day the new Green Wolf was formally installed in office during a hand-bell ceremony. His primary tasks were to ensure a bountiful harvest and fertile fields come spring. In

France, when the grain was harvested, celebrants draped a flower garland around the last sheaf of grain in the fields, thought to contain the Rye-Wolf. It was burned or saved, depending on local tradition, to ensure fertility in the coming year.[14]

Werewolf Myths and the Divine Feminine

Twelfth-century fabulist and poet Marie de France wrote *lais*, narrative poems intended to be read aloud. In her *Lais du Bisclaveret,* she created a sympathetic werewolf character. Early Bretons called the werewolf Bisclaveret; in Normandy it was known as the *garwall,* and in the rest of France as *loup garou.*[15] A popular superstition held that a baby born with a caul about its head would grow up to become bloodthirsty, crafty, lucky, and swift of foot, and would turn into a wolf at night.[16] The tale of Bisclaveret goes as follows, translated and adapted by the author from the original French:

It is certain that since ancient times men have been transformed into wolves. These beasts are ferocious and live in the forests. Their rage is as great as their ferocity. There once was a lady from a good family who was in love with her husband, a baron. Every week he left her alone for three whole days, and during that time she had no knowledge of his activity, nor he of hers. In time she became unfaithful and took a knight as her lover.

Every time the baron returned to the castle, he would embrace her and demand to know all she had done in his absence, telling her that she must not keep any feminine secrets from him. She would press him about his actions, but he would not say what he had been doing. She grew increasingly anxious. Eventually, he confessed that when he left, he did so to turn into a "loup garou." He went on to tell her he had been one all his life, due to a curse. He told her he couldn't help himself, that he was unable to maintain human form for more than a few days at a time. When he assumed werewolf form, he went by the name of Bisclaveret. To revert to human form, all he had to do was put his clothes back on.

The lady grew frightened. The next time she saw her lover, she asked him to follow the baron into the woods and steal his clothes, so he couldn't turn back into a human. This the lover did and everyone presumed the baron was dead. The lady married her lover and he assumed the barony.

A year later, when the king was hunting in the part of the forest where Bisclaveret roamed, the king's dogs overtook Bisclaveret. The wolf took the king's stirrupped foot in his mouth and implored him to call off the dogs. Something about the wolf touched the king's sentiments, so he took the wolf home. Bisclaveret became the king's loyal companion and enjoyed the king's good graces. All the court treated Bisclaveret with respect and affection.

One day, the king invited his barons and vassals to visit court. The lady arrived with her new husband. The king asked her to account for what had happened to her previous husband. She could not provide a satisfactory answer. Bisclaveret entered the room. When he saw his wife, he went mad and bit her. He would have killed her, had the king not called him off. As it was, he bit off her nose. The king imprisoned the lady and her new husband and had them interrogated. The story of her betrayal was exposed. The king banished the unfaithful lady and gave the baron back his clothes, so he could regain human form. All of the king's court celebrated that justice had been done. The baron returned to his castle. The lady's future female children were cursed to be born without noses. This story is true, as told by the Bretons.[17]

Perhaps most striking about this story is its context. Written during a time when wolves were being actively slaughtered in Europe, it depicts the werewolf in a benign manner, an unwilling victim of a curse, and ends favorably for this creature.[18] The werewolf would not fare so well in subsequent tales. However, this story, albeit written by one of the earliest women writers in recorded history, carries a strong misogynistic message, characteristic of the medieval era.

An early 15th-century edition of Dante's *Divina Commedia* has as its only illuminations initials drawn in colored ink and wash on velum, embellished with gold leaf. Nevertheless, the drama of Dante's story comes through in the loops and swirls of the ornate Italian "bastarda" script. The first canto portrays a female wolf as a symbol of grief and fraud.

Last came a She-Wolf, her gauntness charged
With gnawing avarice, for she indeed
Had made life lean for many folk before.
In fear of her and of her aspect fierce
I lost the new born hope of the ascent.[19]

The *Malleus Maleficarum,* or the Hammer of Witches, a medieval manual for finding and killing witches, promulgated harmful myths about wolves and actively attacked the wild woman archetype and all things that eluded Christian norms. One of the first books ever printed, it became the Inquisition's primary instrument of inquiry. This book became so popular in Europe that it went through thirty printings. One of the most odious documents in all human history, it was written by Roman Church high clergy. Filled with sexual perversion and gore, this book came out of an era overhung by a pall of superstition and fear of the divine feminine.

The *Malleus Maleficarum* contains accounts of succubi, wolves who had been turned by demons into female form for the purpose of harming men in their sleep.[20] With the Roman Church's approval, this book caused the werewolf myth to gain such power that it became heretical *not* to believe in this creature's existence. The Spanish Inquisition, authorized by Pope Sixtus in 1478 CE, as well as the Roman Inquisition, authorized in 1542 CE by Pope Paul III, used the *Malleus Maleficarum* to condemn thousands of alleged witches and werewolves to burn at the stake. In doing so the church intensified the fear of women and fixed in the human imagination an image of the wolf as a ghoul and instrument of evil. This text had lasting impact. Through the 19th century, it lay on the bench of every judge and on the desk of every magistrate in Europe.[21] Thus the medieval wolf lurked somewhere in the half-light between the cultivated field and the dark of the forest, both metaphorically and in reality. Human fear of this creature persisted well into the 20th century.

Wolf-Mother Myths

The wolf-mother myth lies on the opposite end of the spectrum from werewolf myths that cast this animal in a negative light, and first appeared in the Roman story of Romulus and Remus. Early Roman coins show a she-wolf suckling the twins, as do Egyptian coins, and in Lycopolis, an ancient Greek city on the Nile delta, a temple featured a similar image.[22] Plutarch says Romulus and Remus were twin sons of a vestal virgin named Rhea, fathered by the war-god Mars. Rhea pleads with her father, the king of Alba, for her life. Rather than have her buried alive, the usual punishment for this type of indiscretion by a vestal, her father turns the infants over to a servant to be banished. The servant sets them afloat in the river on a small boat, which lands next to a fig tree. Two creatures related to Mars, a she-wolf and a woodpecker, feed the twins until a swineherd finds them and assumes their care. He names them Romulus and Remus, from the root *ruma,* which means wolf den. They grow up brave and strong. Romulus slays Remus in a dispute and then founds the city of Rome.[23]

The wolf-mother archetype also appears in the myth of St. Edmund. The illuminated manuscript that tells this tale harkens to the first half of the 12th century, from the Abbey of Bury St. Edmund, Suffolk, England. It narrates the life and martyrdom of St. Edmund, a mid-800s East Anglican king. A Danish king shoots Edmund with arrows and decapitates him for refusing to give up his Christian beliefs. After Edmund's death, his foes hide his head in the woods to prevent him from receiving a decent burial. A blue she-wolf finds St. Edmund's head in a thicket and guards it for one year. A particularly evocative illumination depicts the wolf curled protectively around St. Edmund's head, an adoring expression on her face. Her swollen nipples indicate she has been nursing pups.[24]

St. Edmund's supporters eventually find his head. The wolf relinquishes it, but accompanies it wherever it is taken. A series of folios show the she-wolf following St. Edmund's funeral procession, love and devotion on her face, tears in her eyes. She is deep blue, the color of the lapis lazuli crushed to make the pigment for these illuminations. It is the intense blue described as the color of dreams; the color of peace; the color of sadness; the color of hope—and the color the church associated with the Virgin Mary.[25]

The notion that wolves could raise human children became popular in Europe. Rousseau writes of the wolf-child of Hesse, discovered in 1344. Myths of this nature had such widespread credibility that in 1778 Swedish botanist Carl Linnaeus gave these children the taxonomical designation *Homo ferus.* Children allegedly raised by wolves tended to hate to wear clothing and had a fondness for raw meat. They sought darkness and howled. They peeled back their lips in grimaces, panted when hot, and ran about on all fours.[26] In all likelihood, they suffered from mental disorders such as autism or Down Syndrome; however, their behavior gave further credence to the wolf-mother myth. It may have arisen out of repressed human need to align ourselves with the wolf's positive attributes. If the wolf can be seen as a metaphor of human nature, the wolf-mother represents association with the dawn (*lukos*) and enlightenment.

A more contemporary wolf-mother myth comes from Kipling's *Jungle Book.* In one of these stories, wolves adopt Mowgli, a human boy.[27] This story became so popular that in 1967 Walt Disney Studios released an animated film version.

Little Red Riding Hood

The wolf of fairytales represents the perceptions of the individual unconscious mind and of Jung's collective unconscious, thus becoming a vehicle for expressing and sustaining sexual fantasies. Fairytales occur outside time, in a mythical land, often involving magic. The wolf appears in several fairytales, including "The Three Little Pigs," "The Seven Little Goats," and the Bohemian story "Toby and the Wolf."[28] "Little Red Riding Hood," so widespread that it is told on every continent and in every major language, contains more sexual imagery than any of the Germanic fairytales.

Katherine Orenstein characterizes "Little Red Riding Hood" as a misogynistic tale of male dominance and female victimization. Its main components include a young girl, a lascivious wolf, and a meeting in the woods. Yet parents continue to think the story simple and pass it on from one generation to the next, unaware of its history and significance. Over the years scholars have interpreted it in Freudian terms as the ego overcome by the id and as a vehicle for imparting sexual ethics. The plot contains polarities: good and evil, beast and human, male and female.[29]

The first written version of Little Red Riding Hood, *Conte de ma Mere L'Oye,* by Charles Perrault, dates back to 1697. Perrault tells it as the story about how the wolf eats Red Riding Hood. The woodcut that illustrates this story features a drooling, sharp-toothed beast leaning lasciviously over Little Red Riding Hood. As she reaches up to pet the wolf's muzzle in a placating gesture, the wolf touches her bodice.[30] Many versions of this story exist. In an 1840s version, her father rushes in to save her. In a 19th-century version from Brittany, the wolf puts grandmother's blood in a bottle, which he gives to Red Riding Hood to drink before killing her. In the Brothers Grimm version, called "Little Red Cap," the wolf eats Red Riding Hood and falls asleep. Huntsmen hear his snores, slit the wolf's belly, and free her. They then fill the wolf's belly with stones. James Thurber's 1930s version has Red Riding Hood pulling a pistol on the wolf and killing him.[31]

Native American Women and Wolves

Native Americans traditionally shared close personal associations with the wolf as a spiritual guide. They used this animal as a totem because of traits such as physical endurance, loyalty, and the ability to travel far.[32] To them the wolf represented an ideal. The Blackfoot Indians of the northern Rocky Mountains spoke of a harmonious life as "traveling the wolf trail."[33]

Myths about humans interacting with animals form the core of a totemic culture. The Lakota Sioux and other Plains tribes tell the story of "The Woman Who Lived with the Wolves," among other stories that encompass a world larger than humans. They are meant to teach about the gifts that can come from honoring the human kinship with the wolf. Details vary, according to who tells them, but their themes remain the same.[34] In this tale a heartbroken, angry woman leaves her village because her husband has brought home a second, younger wife. She travels to her relatives' village in late autumn and becomes lost. With no food, she must fend for herself or starve to death. In time a wolf family finds her and rescues her by leading her to shelter. They bring her fresh meat. As the season turns to winter, she learns to communicate with them by howling and barking. When spring comes, the wolves tell her that some of her kin are moving close. She leaves her wolf family and returns to her village. There she finds that everyone had assumed she was dead. Her family celebrates her return and names her The Woman Who Lived with the Wolves.[35]

In another version of this story, also ascribed to the Sioux, when the woman returns to her people she keeps her distance from them. She does not see her husband and no one says anything about him. A medicine man named White Bull feels threatened by her and challenges her to a duel of medicine skills. She wins the duel and her people rename her.[36] Other versions end with the woman turning into a wolf and returning to wolf society. In all of these interpretations, wolves save a woman from death by welcoming her into their society and teaching her their ways.

Originally collected in the summer of 1905 by writer Walter McClintock during a visit to a Blackfeet village at Two Medicine Lake in Montana, "Sits by the Door" is a story also known as "The Legend of the Friendly Medicine Wolf." It begins with a Blackfeet woman named Sits by the Door being taken prisoner by the Crow during a raid. They take her hundreds of miles deep into their territory. When the prisoner arrives, a Crow woman feels sorry for her and helps her escape. The Blackfeet woman searches for her people on the prairie, slowly starving in the process because food is scarce. As she nears death, a wolf comes and lies down next to her. The woman thinks he is just waiting for her to die, and will eat her, so she tells him her story. The following morning she wakes and finds a fresh-killed buffalo calf next to her. She eats it and becomes strong enough to resume her travels, although she is still weak. She has trouble walking, so the wolf walks next to her and supports her. They travel together in this manner for days, with the wolf continuing to bring her kills. By the time she reaches home, she feels as strong as she did before she left. She camps outside her village with the wolf, who was not welcome in her village. After a while the camp dogs run it off. The woman becomes sick and dies. After her death, the wolf sits and waits and waits for Sits by the Door for many years.[37]

Postmodern Wolf Myths: Women Who Run with the Wolves

Storytelling is the process of reinventing ourselves. William Kittredge likens stories to rafts, which one can ride or "lay out on a table like maps." Eventually they fail and have to be reinvented, because the world is too complex for forms to ever encompass it for long.[38] A new category of wolf mythology has been emerging since the early 1990s, born of contemporary humans' desire to reconnect with wildness. This may be called reconstructionist wolf mythology, because it borrows myths from various cultures and reshapes them to suit contemporary psychospiritual needs.

The modern therapist and author Clarissa Pinkola Estes provides the most literate and compelling example of reconstructionist wolf mythology. Here she uses storytelling to teach and heal as she attempts to reawaken ancestral, primal memories of other places, times, and long-suppressed ways of being. According to Estes,

> We are filled with a longing for the wild. . . . We are taught to feel shame for such a desire. We grew our hair long and used it to hide our feelings. But the shadow of Wild Woman still lurks behind us . . . no matter where we are, the shadow that trots behind us is definitely four-footed.[39]

Her study of wildlife biology inspired this work. She claims to have found many similarities between women and wolves: both are capable of being highly intuitive, intensely devoted to their pack, adaptable, stalwart, and brave. Yet both have been harassed and have become the targets of the hatred of those afraid of wildness. She presents the Wild Woman archetype as her own creation and then narrates the stories and myths that inspired this archetype. Her objective is to collect and preserve that which was in danger of being lost to women—their sense of wildness— and offer a new, emerging wolf/feminine mythology.

La Loba, or the wolf woman, is a central figure in Estes' reconstructionist mythology, whom she also refers to as the bone collector *La Huesera*. She draws this character from Southwestern, Spanish, and Aztec mythology, and mentions Na'ashje'ii Asdzaa (Spider Woman), the Navajo creation goddess, and Coatlique, the Aztec goddess of female self-sufficiency, the birth and death mother, portrayed giving birth in a squatting position, wearing a skirt made of skulls.[40] The closest European associations to Estes' conception of wolves and women are the goddesses Cerridwen and Artemis, Welsh and Greek respectively; the wild man's counterpart, the witch of the forest; and Native American myths that cast women as wives or helpers to wolves.[41] These myths correspond to the *La Loba* archetype, presented as Estes' reconstructionist creation, born of the postmodern feminist collective unconscious. All mythologies shape a culture. Since it was published in 1992, Estes' book has had a profound effect on women. Her idealized depiction of wolf nature fosters positive opinions of this animal and has empowered women.

The New Wolf

The images of the wolf that emerge from some European myths, such as the werewolf, are mostly malevolent and sinister, while wolf-mother myths such as Romulus and Remus and St. Edmund the Martyr provide exceptions. Native American myths are kinder to wolves. This chapter has traced the chronology of the development of wolf mythology that embraces the divine feminine. The true wolf lies somewhere between the wolf depicted in St. Edmund the Martyr and "The Woman Who Lived With the Wolves," and the lascivious wolf that devoured Little Red Riding Hood. Jung suggests all are equally valid aspects of a single complex archetype.

In the 21st century, people are drawn to a more benign wolf mythology, one that embodies what some call the "new wolf." Whether motivated by guilt, compassion, a need for reconciliation with wolves, or a biocentric acceptance of the divine feminine, this shift represents a tremendous leap forward—an evolution of the human spirit in which the concept of community is extended to life in all its forms. The more enlightened images presented in this review have led to a postmodern mythology that has helped strengthen human acceptance of wolves, acknowledgment of women's power and rights, and welcoming into culture the wildness these mythological elements represent.

Notes

1. Paul Shepard, *Nature and Madness* (Athens: University of Georgia Press, 1982).
2. Barry H. Lopez, *Of Wolves and Men* (New York: Touchstone Books, Simon and Schuster, 1978), 142.

3. Ibid., 209–211.

4. Karen M. House, "The Wolf Archetype," master's thesis, Prescott College, Prescott, AZ, 1998, 23.

5. Paul Shepard, *Thinking Animals: Animals and the Development of Human Intelligence* (Athens: University of Georgia Press, 1978), 1–3.

6. Jose Ortega y Gasset, *Meditations on Hunting* (New York: Charles Scribner's Sons, 1972), 28–31.

7. Carl G. Jung, *Man and His Symbols* (New York: Bantam, 1964).

8. Carl G. Jung, "The Archetypes and the Collective Unconscious," in *Collected Works*, trans. R. F. C. Hull (Princeton, NJ: Princeton University Press, 1936), 9:87–100.

9. Frances Klingender, *Animals in Art and Thought to the End of the Middle Ages* (Cambridge, MA: MIT Press, 1971), 3–27.

10. Carl G. Jung, *The Portable Jung* (New York: Viking Press, 1971).

11. Lopez, *Of Wolves and Men*, 271–272.

12. Robert Graves, *The White Goddess: A Historical Grammar of Poetic Myth* (1949; New York: Farrar, Straus and Giroux, 2001), 143, 222.

13. Joseph Campbell, *The Masks of God: Occidental Mythology* (New York: Viking Press, 1964), 456–504.

14. James George Frazer, *The Golden Bough* (New York: Macmillan, 1963), 519–521.

15. Marie de France, *Poisies de Marie de France*, trans. Cristina Eisenberg (Paris: Chasseriau et Hecart, 1175).

16. Norma Lorre Goodrich, *The Medieval Myths* (New York: New American Library, 1961), 156–157.

17. de France, *Poisies de Marie de France*.

18. Edward Topsell, *The History of Four-Footed Beasts and Serpents: Collected Out of the Writings of Conradus Gesner and Other Authors* (London: G. Sawbridge, 1658).

19. Dante Alighieri, *Divina Comedia*, Pierpont Morgan Library Manuscript MS M.0341. Provenance: written and illuminated in Italy, possibly in Venice, ca. early 15th century, canto 1.

20. Heinrich Kramer and James Sprenger, *Malleus Maleficarum: The Hammer of Witchcraft* (Germany:,1489), original manuscript, Special Reference Collections, New York Public Library, New York City.

21. Heinrich Kramer and James Sprenger, *Malleus Maleficarum: The Hammer of Witches*, ed. Montague Summers (New York: Dover Publications, 1971), *viii*.

22. D. Bernarde, *L'homme et le loup* (Paris: Berger-Levrault, 1981), 36.

23. Campbell, *The Masks of God: Occidental Mythology*, 313–319.

24. *Miscellany in the Life of St. Edmund,* Manuscript MS M 0736, Pierpont Morgan Library, New York City. Provenance: written and illuminated in the Abbey of Bury St. Edmunds between 1125 and 1135.

25. Campbell, *The Masks of God: Occidental Mythology*, 456–504.

26. Lopez, *Of Wolves and Men*, 242–248.

27. Rudyard Kipling, *Jungle Book*, reprint ed. (New York: Tor Books, 1992).

28. M. Novak, Z. Cerna, D. Stovickova, M. Stovickova, M. Kosova, V. Hulpach, M. Tvrdikova, J. Horak, O. Sirovatka, V. Stovicek, Z. Dubovska, M. Maly, and J. Tichy, *Fairy Tales of the World,* trans. O. Kuthanova, V. Gizzing, J. Eisler, and S. Finn (Prague: Artia, 1985).

29. Katherine Orenstein, *Little Red Riding Hood Uncloaked: Sex, Morality, and the Evolution of a Fairy Tale* (New York: Basic Books, 2003).

30. J. Barchilon, *Perrault's Tales of Mother Goose: The Dedication Manuscript of 1695, Reproduced in Collotype Facsimile, with Introduction and Critique* (New York: Pierpont Morgan Library, 1956).

31. Lopez, *Of Wolves and Men*, 264.

32. George Bird Grinnell, *Blackfoot Lodge Tales: The Story of a Primitive People* (Lincoln: University of Nebraska Press, 1962).

33. Dennis L. Olson, *Wisdom Warrior: Native American Animal Legends* (Minnetonka, MN: NorthWord Press, 1999), 2.

34. John Marshall, *On Behalf of the Wolf and the First Peoples* (Santa Fe, NM: Red Crane Books, 1996), 12–14.

35. Olson, *Wisdom Warrior.*

36. Lopez, *Of Wolves and Men*, 129–132.

37. Rick McIntyre, *The War Against the Wolf* (Stillwater, MN: Voyageur Press, 1995), 267–270.

38. William Kittredge, *The Nature of Generosity* (New York: Vintage Books, 2002), 9.

39. Clarissa Pinkola Estes, *Women Who Run with the Wolves: Myths and Stories of the Wild Woman Archetype* (New York: Ballantine Books, 1992), xiii.

40. Ibid., 196.

41. Graves, *White Goddess*, 222.

Bibliography

Barchilon, J. *Perrault's Tales of Mother Goose: The Dedication Manuscript of 1695, Reproduced in Collotype Facsimile, with Introduction and Critique.* 2 vols. New York: Pierpont Morgan Library, 1956.

Bernarde, D. *L'homme et le loup.* Paris: Berger-Levrault, 1981.

Campbell, Joseph. *The Masks of God: Occidental Mythology.* New York: Viking Press, 1964.

Campbell, Joseph. *The Masks of God: Primitive Mythology.* New York: Viking Press, 1959.

Dante Alighieri. *Divina Comedia.* Pierpont Morgan Library Manuscript MS M.0341. Provenance: written and illuminated in Italy, possibly in Venice, ca. early 15th century.

Estes, Clarissa Pinkola. *Women Who Run with the Wolves: Myths and Stories of the Wild Woman Archetype*. New York: Ballantine Books, 1992.

France, Marie de. *Poisies de Marie de France*, trans. Cristina Eisenberg. Paris: Chasseriau et Hecart, 1175.

Frazer, James George. *The Golden Bough*. New York: Macmillan, 1963.

Goodrich, Norma Lorre. *The Medieval Myths*. New York: New American Library, 1961.

Graves, Robert. *The White Goddess: A Historical Grammar of Poetic Myth*. New York: Farrar, Straus and Giroux, 2001.

Grinnell, George Bird. *Blackfoot Lodge Tales: The Story of a Primitive People*. Lincoln: University of Nebraska Press, 1962.

House, Karen M. "The Wolf Archetype." Master's thesis, Prescott College, Prescott, AZ, 1998.

Jung, Carl G. "The Archetypes and the Collective Unconscious." In *Collected Works*, trans. R. F. C. Hull, 9:87–100. Princeton, NJ: Princeton University Press, 1936.

Jung, Carl G. *Man and His Symbols*. New York: Bantam, 1964.

Jung, Carl G. *The Portable Jung*. New York: Viking Press, 1971.

Kipling, Rudyard. *Jungle Book*. Reprint ed. New York: Tor Books, 1992.

Kittredge, William. *The Nature of Generosity*. New York: Vintage Books, 2002.

Klingender, Frances. *Animals in Art and Thought to the End of the Middle Ages*. Cambridge, MA: MIT Press, 1971.

Kramer, Heinrich, and James Sprenger. *Malleus Maleficarum: The Hammer of Witchcraft*. Germany, 1489. Original manuscript, Special Reference Collections, New York Public Library, New York City.

Kramer, Heinrich, and James Sprenger. *Malleus Maleficarum: The Hammer of Witches*, ed. Montague Summers. New York: Dover Publications, 1971.

Lopez, Barry H. *Of Wolves and Men*. New York: Touchstone Books, Simon and Schuster, 1978.

McIntyre, Rick. *The War Against the Wolf*. Stillwater, MN: Voyageur Press, 1995.

Marshall, John. *On Behalf of the Wolf and the First Peoples*. Santa Fe, NM: Red Crane Books, 1996.

Miscellany in the Life of St. Edmund. Manuscript MS M 0736, Pierpont Morgan Library, New York City.

Nash, Roderick. *Wilderness and the American Mind*. 3rd ed. New Haven, CT: Yale University Press, 1982.

Novak, M., Z. Cerna, D. Stovickova, M. Stovickova, M. Kosova, V. Hulpach, M. Tvrdikova, J. Horak, O. Sirovatka, V. Stovicek, Z. Dubovska, M. Maly, and J. Tichy. *Fairy Tales of the World*. Trans. O. Kuthanova, V. Gizzing, J. Eisler, and S. Finn. Prague: Artia, 1985.

Olson, Dennis L. *Wisdom Warrior: Native American Animal Legends*. Minnetonka, MN: NorthWord Press, 1999.

Orenstein, Katherine. *Little Red Riding Hood Uncloaked: Sex, Morality, and the Evolution of a Fairy Tale.* New York: Basic Books, 2003.

Ortega y Gasset, Jose. *Meditations on Hunting.* New York: Charles Scribner's Sons, 1972.

Perrault, Charles. *Histoires du Temps Passe, ou, Les Contes de Ma Mere* (Little Red Riding Hood.) Brussels and London: Chez B. LeFrancq, 1697.

Shepard, Paul. *Man in the Landscape: A Historic View of the Esthetics of Nature.* College Station: Texas A&M University Press, 1991.

Shepard, Paul. *Nature and Madness.* Athens: University of Georgia Press, 1982.

Shepard, Paul. *Thinking Animals: Animals and the Development of Human Intelligence.* Athens: University of Georgia Press, 1978.

Topsell, Edward. *The History of Four-Footed Beasts and Serpents: Collected Out of the Writings of Conradus Gesner and Other Authors.* London: G. Sawbridge, 1658.

15

Sedna: Underwater Goddess of the Arctic Sea

Jacqueline Thursby

Sedna—also called Niviaqsiaq, Talilajuq, Nuliajuk, and many other names—is the ruling Inuit child-goddess of the deep eastern Arctic seas. Her domain is vast and spread throughout the great oceans of the north from the eastern Arctic Ocean to Baffin Bay and down to the Davis Straight and Hudson Bay in the south. In that icy world, the rhythmic and predictable seasons create shifting landscapes of snow and ice, and the enigmatic Sedna is said to have both given birth and to rule the underwater creatures living there. She is also believed to have influence over humans in the northern regions. Because of that belief, ceremonies and feasts have been held in her honor since ancient times. In the frigid ocean world of the far north, seal, walrus, varied fish, whale, and orca swim freely in the icy waters. Their origin, legends say, was from Sedna's hands, mutilated by her angry father.

Traditions hold that Sedna blesses the people of the northern lands with food from the sea if they live good lives and remember her. If not, her hair falls into tangles, her face becomes distorted, and she becomes very angry. She withdraws her blessing, their hunts yield nothing, and people starve to death. Part of the purpose of the feasts and ceremonies, more frequent and intense before Christianity came to the northern world in the 1800s, was to placate her anger. Some narratives represent her as a redemption figure, and there are those who still believe, wonder, and pay homage to her power.

Because the name Sedna is associated with an intensely cold region of the planet, one of the latest discovered planetoids has been named after her.

On 15 March, 2004, astronomers from Caltech, Gemini Observatory, and Yale University announced the discovery of the coldest, most distant object known to orbit the sun. The object was found at a distance 90 times greater than that from the sun to the earth—about 3 times further than Pluto, the most distant known planet.[1]

Because it is so cold, the planetoid was named Sedna = 2003 VB12, after the Inuit goddess of the northern seas. The planetoid, or minor planet, has an orbit of 10,500 years, and for the next seventy-two years it will be brighter and closer than it has been since the last ice age.[2]

Many variant stories are told of Sedna, who was born at the edge of the Arctic when the world was new. Inuit oral history is vast, and Sedna is represented in many narratives in oral tradition and continues to be represented in contemporary Inuit art. Stone carvings and paintings of the goddess continue to be created, but Inuit artists are often reluctant to explain the meaning of their versions of Sedna. Early tellers of her stories were select members of the Angakkuit,[3] who practiced a form of shamanism, and their stories were an important part of the Inuit culture before the Christian missionaries arrived. To explain the spiritual power of these shaman, the early 20th-century anthropologist Franz Boas wrote: "The persons, who can see the souls of men and of animals and who are able to visit Sedna, are called *angakut (angakkuit).*"[4] Shamanism still plays a part in the Inuit tradition, though "the representation of nonhuman beings [has largely] shifted from the context of shamanism to that of art."[5] Contact between the Inuit people and Western culture in the 20th century has altered their way of expressing parts of the culture, but there is evidence that some of the beliefs still remain.

Narratives and Variants

The story of Sedna begins in the ancient world, long before there were seals and walruses for the people to hunt. There were land animals for food including bears, wolves, reindeer, and birds like the wild geese, black ravens, fulmars or sea gulls, and cormorants.[6] Sedna's mother died while she was a young child, and Sedna grew up in an igloo near the seashore raised by her grandmother and her father Anguta, also called Isarrataitsoq.[7] Her father, a good hunter, provided caribou or bear meat for his family. They were usually well fed, but sometimes in spite of his efforts food became scarce and hunger was a familiar sensibility.

Some of the stories told about Sedna when she lived on the land describe things her father taught her for comfortable survival in the icy Arctic. She had to learn how to make fire by rubbing stones so that she could prepare and cook the game he provided. He taught her how to process animal skins for creating waterproof huts and making warm, fur-lined clothing and boots. When there was time, he would beat his drum with a certain rhythm and tell stories and sing songs about their ancestors and about the many land animals he hunted. He made tiny carvings for her that she kept close.

Sedna was very beautiful. When she reached her teens her father encouraged her to choose a man from their village to marry, but she refused because none of the men pleased her. This was a serious refusal because, in the far north, the gender roles and responsibilities were clearly delineated and important for survival: men hunted and brought home the raw materials, and women cooked and provided clothing using the game the men brought to them. After many years, Sedna's paternal grandmother died. The grandmother was a skilled cook and seamstress, and her skills had helped the family survive. At her death, the household work fell to Sedna. Because she was still unmarried, her father was eager for her to make a choice of a companion so there would be a son in the family to help him hunt and to take care of his needs in his old age.

In time she did marry, but that is where tension and conflict in the story became more serious. Some of the myths about Sedna suggest that she married a dog; others say that she married a fulmar, a type of seabird. The dog variant is connected to the arrival of an uncle whose wife was killed in an accident at sea and who came to his brother's igloo to recover from his own wounds suffered in the accident. He drove a sled pulled by excessively underfed dogs. Among the animals was a magnificent white animal named Sattu, the leader of the pack. When Sedna refused again and again to accept a man from the village for her husband, her father and uncle forced her to have the dog as her husband. They took Sedna and the big dog to an island and left them there. In spite of her supposed alliance with the dog, one of the human behaviors said to upset her most after she became an underwater goddess was bestiality. Her father, regretful about the banishment, took summer berries and vegetables to them and asked them to return to the village. But Sedna would not return.

The winter cycle arrived with its winds and howling threats, and her father had to leave the village to find meat in the wilderness. Because he had to hunt far away, he could no longer deliver food to the island. Sedna made a carrier for the dog and sent it swimming to the mainland for food twice a week. This continued until the uncle discovered that Sedna had produced a litter of dog-children. This angered him, so when the dog came to the mainland to forage for food the uncle gave it meat loaded with rocks. When the beautiful white animal tried to swim back to the island, he sank to the bottom of the sea and drowned. Sedna realized what had happened and agreed to move back to the mainland but she and her dog-children lived in a hut separate from her father's.

Sedna wanted revenge, so while her father was away on a hunt, she sent her dog-children to the uncle's starving sled dogs to provoke them. The sled dogs, in turn, chewed off her uncle's arms and legs and then dragged his body to the sea where fish ate the last of his body. The sled dogs ran away to the wild to join the packs of wolves who knew how to find food for their own survival. The dog-children returned to Sedna, and all of them were provided for by their grandfather's bounty though there was rarely enough food to really satisfy their hunger.

The story then changes into a variant with a fulmar husband, though in some stories the beautiful stranger is described as a loon.[8] Sedna first saw a handsome young man appear out of the heavy mist paddling gracefully in a seamless kayak. He had blue-black hair much like the shiny feathers of a raven, large round eyes, and snow-white teeth. She was immediately attracted to him, and he tempted her to go with him. He promised her luxurious wraps, a safe shelter, and all the food she would ever need. Her children were nowhere near, and he convinced her to immediately gather her few possessions, dress in her warmest furs, and join him in the kayak. They traveled smoothly over the choppy water, but when Sedna turned to ask him where they were going, there was no answer. She was alone in the rapidly moving kayak. Flying just overhead was a creature that seemed to be a bird and yet human, too. When they finally reached a mist-shrouded island, the creature landed and instantly transformed into the handsome young man.

Taking his beautiful bride by the hand, he led her to the pinnacle of a cliff and showed her their lofty and seriously windy home. It was in poor condition, and there was no food. He promised that she would have plenty of seafood provided by the droves of birds circling over head, and then he transformed himself into a bird once more and flew away. Though the birds did bring fish and other food from the sea, and even an occasional rabbit from the countryside, Sedna had no way to cook anything. Her food was always cold and raw. She mourned Sattu, her beautiful dog-husband, and she desperately missed their playful dog-children. Cold and unprotected, she wanted her father to rescue her. Far away, her father was thinking of her and wondering if he would ever see her again. He knew where she was, but it was some time before he could make a trip to Bird Island to visit his beloved daughter. At last he set out on the long journey to visit her. When she saw her father from afar, she scrambled down to the beach and begged him to take her home immediately while the bird-husband was away.

He helped her into his kayak, and they set off across the icy sea. The wind was blowing furiously, and soon the bird-husband, informed by the birds of his island that Sedna was in the kayak with her father, turned into human form again and took chase in his own fast-gliding kayak. He soon overtook Anguta and Sedna and tried to persuade her to join him. She refused, so he slowly raised his arms to the sky and they became wings. Before he could take flight, Sedna's father threw his spear, and the huge bird fell dead into the sea. The fulmar's followers, furious at the death of their leader, chased down Anguta's kayak. They caused the winds to become more violent, and Anguta became frightened. To lighten the boat and save himself, he threw Sedna into the sea. As she clung to the side of the kayak, he cut off her fingers. In some variants she returns, and he cuts her hands even further.

The blood that flowed from her wounds, either from the places where the fingers were cut, or where he stabbed her as she returned to try to cling to the boat, formed the myriad sea animals. Whales, seals, and all the other sea animals of the Arctic were born from her blood. According to some tales, Sedna commanded that the sea animals get her father and bring him to her. By raising a high tide, the animals swept him into the sea, and Sedna, her dog-husband, and her father all live in the depths of the Arctic Ocean. She has a house there, deep under the sea, and occasionally, when humans are behaving badly, she rises to the surface and may even pay an angry visit to someone who lives on the land.

Other myths say that when the storm passed, she climbed back into the kayak and ordered her father's dogs to eat his hands and feet. In that version he awakened violently angry and caused such an uproar that caused the earth to swallow all of them and took them to Adlivun (a place beneath earth and sea), and that is where they are to this day. There are still more versions of the story and also various theories about them. One suggests that Sedna's father killed her dog-husband and she in turn had the dog-children kill their grandfather. Then she sent the dogs out into the world to look out for themselves. That variant suggests that various races of humans and spirits originated from the dogs, including the Native Americans and the white people. It also prophesies that whites, probably whalers, would someday give gifts to Native American women living in the Arctic region; in particular, these gifts were given to the Inuit women.[9]

These gifts began to occur in the late 19th century when the first variant of the dog-husband/sea-woman was recorded.[10] "Young Inuit women would typically receive such [small] gifts in return for their services as seam-stresses, dancing partners and mistresses to white whalers on board the whaling ships."[11] The girls' fathers would provide the crews with fresh meat and iron for harpoon heads and provide for the mixed-blood offspring that the whalers left behind. "Sonne suggests that the development of the [Sedna] narrative may be of a relatively recent date and connected to trade and whaling activities. She considers the fulmar as well as the hands as sym-bols of trade relationships with foreigners."[12]

The Sedna Feast

There are also many variants of a Sedna feast in contemporary Inuit and Eskimo life. The celebrations range from entertainment and games to spirit-ual "visits" to Sedna by the shamanic *angakut* deep in the sea. They inquire if she will provide for the people, and are often rewarded with scoldings for their transgressions.[13] Patricia Monaghan wrote about the laws of Sedna:

> She was willing to provide for the people if they accepted her rules; for three days after their death, the souls of her animals would remain with their bodies, watching for violation of Sedna's demands. Then they returned to the goddess, bearing information about the conduct of her people. Should her laws be broken, Sedna's hand would begin to ache, and she would punish humans with sickness, starvation, and storms. Only if a shaman traveled to her country, Adlivun, and assuaged her pains would the sea mammals return to the hunters, which, if the people acted righteously, they did willingly.[14]

Another variant is the traditional belief of the Greenland Eskimos. They suggest that except for murderers, all dead humans eventually reach Adlipar-miut. It is located far away from Sedna's underwater home Adlivun (or Adlinden) and is a dark and forbidding place but not as bad as Adlivun. "In some myths it is said that spirits from Adlivun, dressed in old clothes, bring disease and death to their villages."[15] Sedna is considered present at some of these celebrations and not present at others, but when she does appear, it seems to mean that circumstances are grim for the people. The feast is not held at the same time of the year throughout the vast region, and one "text suggests that the Sedna feast was not celebrated on an annual basis, but only when bad weather or scarcity of game required it."[16]

Some versions of the feast include door-to-door hut visits, not unlike Irish mumming or American Halloween trick-or-treating, and the tradition in that practice is that the woman of the house, when she hears their band-like noise, awards them with "little gifts of meat, ivory trinkets, and articles of sealskin."[17]

Other variants of the feast include skits performed by two men, one dressed as a female and the other as a male, both wearing masks of skin. It is performed in a comic fashion with ill-fitting clothing. The "female" carries an *anautAq*, or snow-beating stick, and the "male" carries a *te-garut* or (short dog whip). The male character also has a phallic symbol attached, "a huge penis, grotesque in its effect, fashioned either of wood or of stuffed intestines."[18] Their presentation is slapstick, and gender behaviors during the interactive performance are traditional and specific. It is said that the shaman slips into a trance and slips down a tube to pay a visit to Sedna to appease her anger. Scholars of the Inuit have been unable to determine whether the shaman or only his spirit descends to the sea woman, and some versions of the visit mention "the expression *pullaalik*, someone who has a bubble (i.e., the bubble of air that contains the *tarniq*[words or language]), is used," rather than a human of flesh and bones.[19] Though these practices are seldom reenacted in their full scope and variation presently, the feasts or ceremonies are still held, and many ancient traditions are imitated and reinvented to meet the needs of contemporary life.

Sedna, the Newly Discovered Planetoid

A planetoid is a small celestial mass composed of rock and metal that moves around the sun primarily between the orbits of Mars and Jupiter. These small celestial bodies range in diameter from one mile to about 500 miles, and they are so small that a viewer is able to block out the sight of it with the head of a pin. Sedna, a planetoid, performs a highly eccentric orbit and resides well beyond the Kuiper belt, an area of the solar system beyond the planets. The objects within the Kuiper belt are largely made up of frozen volatile gases such as methane and ammonia, and these objects are not the same as an oort cloud, which is much more distant.

A March 2004 press release by California Institute of Technology titled "Most Distant Object in Solar System Discovered," states that Sedna is the most distant object orbiting Earth's sun.

This is likely the first detection of the long-hypothesized "oort cloud," a faraway repository of small icy bodies that supplies the comets that streak by Earth. Other notable features of Sedna include its size and reddish color. After Mars, it is the second reddest object in the solar system. It is estimated that Sedna is approximately three-fourths the size of Pluto. Sedna is likely the largest object found in the solar system since Pluto was discovered in 1930.

The elliptical orbit of Sedna is unlike anything previously seen by astronomers. However, it resembles that of objects predicted to lie in the hypothetical Oort cloud. The cloud is thought to explain the existence of certain comets. It is believed to surround the Sun and extend outward halfway to the star closest to the Sun. But Sedna is 10 times closer than the predicted distance of the Oort cloud. Brown said this "inner Oort cloud" may have been formed by gravity from a rogue star near the Sun in the solar system's early days.[20]

The Sea Goddess and Her Celestial Namesake

Susan Boulet suggests that Sedna, abused by her father and a child-goddess, will perhaps serve as a "true [mythic] balance between genders, races, and species."[21] She is a New World creature rather than a figure from Mediterranean antiquity. Some planets are numbered by astronomers and scientists who discover them, but the large and most familiar planets of the solar system are named for Greek or Roman divinities, and other than Venus and Earth all have been given male names. Boulet suggests that there may be parallels of meaning in the planetoid Sednas's orbit:

> Right now, and for the next 72 years, she is growing closer and brighter than she's been since the last ice age. . . . That Sedna is now being made known to our collective unconsciousness at the beginning of the 21st century suggests that the threshold period of the next 72 years will witness a refocusing on the rights of women, their children, and the environment. Such a resurgence is cause for much hope.[22]

Just as scientific descriptions of the newly discovered planetoid vary, the mythic sea-goddess Sedna has also been described in many ways. Though she was said to be a beauty in her early years, the time under the sea may have changed her. "In some descriptions, Sedna is fat, hideous, and ill-tempered. She is also depicted as a giant with one eye. In another description, her hands are like seals' flippers."[23]

Contemporary Views

James Houston, an author and illustrator of many books that depict the landscape of the Arctic and its strong independent people, also produced and directed several documentary films of the Arctic and its people. He is credited with bringing Inuit art to the attention of the world. His son, John Houston, an author and cinematographer raised in Cape Dorset located in the South Baffin region of Nunavut, Canada, made three films referred to as an "Arctic trilogy" "connecting Inuit beliefs, and practices to his own personal quest for truth."[24] The second film of the trilogy, *Nuliajuk: Mother of the Sea Beasts*, is the story of Sedna. All three of John Houston's Arctic films have won multiple awards.

Michael P. J. Kennedy also contributed to this quest for meaning in regard to Sedna in an effort to recapture and represent this multifaceted legend. Kennedy's work discusses the reality of Inuit life in the latter half of the 20th century. The Sedna narrative has been present in oral history among the people of the North extending from the Baffin Bay region to East Greenland and on to Siberia, and some contemporary versions suggest that Sedna was sexually abused by her father as well as mutilated.[25]

Whatever the variant, whatever her appearance, Sedna continues to be a respected and honored goddess in the icy eastern Arctic. "In 2002, Peter Suvaksiuq from Arviat related, 'I don't know anything about who has power over the sea animals. Just last year there was something seen by many people in Arviat with arms and long hair and a tail like a fish.' "[26] Though long thought by many scholars to be a part of the forgotten Inuit past, she is still a part of lived experience.

> Recent research on Inuit oral tradition shows that encounters with nonhuman beings are still very central to Inuit experience. Many elders can relate stories about their encounters with nonhuman beings. . . . Therefore, the representations of the sea woman and other sea people not only reflect traditional beliefs but may well express contemporary beliefs and experiences.[27]

"Even though the rules of the past (*pittailiniit*) have been replaced by rules of Christian conduct and Canadian law, Inuit are still very much aware of the need to respect those nonhuman beings in the world."[28] Sedna and her powerful story live and continue to be reimagined and retold through recent carving and other arts—art that provides continuity of ancient legends and beliefs in a contemporary context.

Notes

1. M. E. Brown, "Sedna," California Institute of Technology: Division of Geological and Planetary Sciences Web site, 2004, 1–8, http://www.gps.caltech.edu/~mbrown/sedna (accessed November 12, 2009).

2. Ibid.

3. Plural, the spelling varies.

4. Franz Boas, "Second Report on the Eskimo of Baffin Land and Hudson Bay," in *Notes Collected by Captain George Comer, Captain James S. Mutch, and Rev. E. J. Peck, Bulletin of the American Museum of Natural History* 15, no. 2 (1907): 433.

5. Frédéric Laugrand and Jarich Oosten, *The Sea Woman: Sedna in Inuit Shamanism and Art in the Eastern Arctic* (Fairbanks: University of Alaska Press, 2008), 1.

6. John Houston's Arctic Trilogy: *Songs in Stone: An Arctic Journey Home* (1999), a tribute to the artists of Cape Dorset, Nunavut; *Nuliajuk: Mother of the Sea Beasts* (2002), the myth of Sedna, the ancient sea goddess; and *Diet of Souls* (2004), which explores the Inuit relationship with animals and the environment.

7. David Leeming, *The Oxford Companion to World Mythology* (New York: Oxford University Press, 2005), 349.

8. Jane Yolen, ed., *Favorite Folktales from Around the World* (New York: Pantheon Books, 1986), 106.

9. Carolyne Larrington, ed., *The Woman's Companion to Mythology* (London: Pandora, 1997), 182.

10. Birgitte Sonne, "The Acculturative Role of Sea Woman: Early Contact Relations Between Inuit and Whites as Revealed in the Origin Myths of the Sea Woman," in *Meddelelser om Grønland, Man and Society* 13 (1990): 1–34.

11. Larrington, ed., *Woman's Companion to Mythology*, 182.

12. Sonne, "The Acculturative Role of Sea Woman," 52.

13. Franz Boas, "The Eskimo of Baffin Land and Hudson Bay," quoted in Laugrand and Oosten, *The Sea Woman*, 94.

14. Patricia Monaghan, *The Encyclopedia of Goddesses and Heroines* (Santa Barbara, CA: Greenwood, 2009).

15. Patricia Turner and Charles Russell Coulter, *Dictionary of Ancient Deities* (New York: Oxford University Press, 2001), 16.

16. E. J. Peck, Anglican Church of Canada/General Synod Archives/Peck Papers M56-1, Series 33, no. 12, quoted in Laugrand and Oosten, *The Sea Woman*, 103.

17. Peck, quoted in Laugrand and Oosten, *The Sea Woman*, 96.

18. Knud Rasmussen, quoted in Laugrand and Oosten, *The Sea Woman*, 104.

19. Laugrand and Oosten, *The Sea Woman*, 62.

20. "Most Distant Object in Solar System Discovered," California Institute of Technology Web site, 2004–2005, 1–2, http://www.spitzer.caltech.edu/Media/releases/ssc2004-05/release.shtm (accessed March 17, 2009).

21. Susan Boulet, personal communication, March 16–17, 2004.

22. Ibid.

23. Turner and Russell Coulter, *Dictionary of Ancient Deities*, 418.

24. Laugrand and Oosten, *The Sea Woman*, 13.

25. Michael P. J. Kennedy, "The Sea Goddess Sedna: An Enduring Pan-Arctic Legend from Traditional Orature to the New Narratives of the Late 20th Century," in *Echoing Silence: Essays on Arctic Narrative*, ed. J. Moss (Ottawa: University of Ottawa Press, 1997), 211–230.

26. Jarich Oosten and Frédéric Laugrand, eds., "Inuit Qaujimajatuqangit: Shamanism and Reintegrated Wrongdoers into the Community," in *Inuit Perspectives on the 20th Century* (Iqaluit: Nunavut Arctic College, 2002), 4:12.

27. Ibid.

28. Laugrand and Oosten, *The Sea Woman*, 133.

Bibliography

Boas, Franz. "The Eskimo of Baffin Land and Hudson Bay." In *Notes Collected by Capt. George Comer, Captain James S. Mutch, and Rev. E. J. Peck. Bulletin of the American Museum of Natural History* 15, no. 1 (1901): 1–370.

Boas, Franz. "Second Report on the Eskimo of Baffin Land and Hudson Bay." In *Notes Collected by Captain George Comer, Captain James S. Mutch, and Rev. E. J. Peck. Bulletin of the American Museum of Natural History* 15, no. 2 (1907): 371–570.

Boulet, Susan. "Sedna, Goddess of the Arctic Seas—and Our Tenth Planet." http://www.mythinglinks.org/ip~northamerica~Sedna.html.

Brown, M. E. "Sedna." 2004. Division of Geological and Planetary Sciences Web site, California Institute of Technology. http://www.gps.caltech.edu/~mbrown/sedna.

California Institute of Technology. "Most Distant Object in Solar System Discovered." 2004–2005. http://www.spitzer.caltech.edu/Media/releases/ssc2004-05/release.shtml.

Kennedy, Michael P. J. "The Sea Goddess Sedna: An Enduring Pan-Arctic Legend from Traditional Orature to the New Narratives of the Late 20th Century." In *Echoing Silence: Essays on Arctic Narrative*, ed. J. Moss, 211–230. Ottawa: University of Ottawa Press, 1997.

Larrington, Carolyne, ed. *The Woman's Companion to Mythology*. London: Pandora, 1997.

Laugrand, Frédéric, and Jarich Oosten. "Quiviasukvik: The Celebration of an Inuit Winter Feast in the Central Arctic." *Journal de la Société des Américanistes* 88 (2002): 203–226.

Laugrand, Frédéric, and Jarich Oosten. *The Sea Woman: Sedna in Inuit Shamanism and Art in the Eastern Arctic*. Fairbanks: University of Alaska Press, 2008.

Leeming, David. *The Oxford Companion to World Mythology*. New York: Oxford University Press, 2005.

Monaghan, Patricia. *The Encyclopedia of Goddesses and Heroines*. Santa Barbara, CA: Greenwood, 2009.

Oosten, Jarich, and Frédéric Laugrand, eds. "Inuit Qaujimajatuqangit: Shamanism and Reintegrated Wrongdoers into the Community." In *Inuit Perspectives on the 20th Century*. Vol. 4. Iqaluit: Nunavut Arctic College, 2002.

Rasmussen, Knud. "Intellectual Culture of the Iglulik Eskimos." In *Report of the Fifth Thule Expedition, 1921–1924*. Vol. 7 (1). Copenhagen: Gyldendalske Boghandel, 1929.

Rudinger, Joel. *Sedna—Goddess of the Sea*. Huron, OH: Cambric Press, 2006.

Sonne, Birgitte. "The Acculturative Role of Sea Woman. Early Contact Relations Between Inuit and Whites as Revealed in the Origin Myths of the Sea Woman." *Meddelelser om Grønland, Man and Society* 13 (1990): 1–34.

Turner, Patricia, and Charles Russell Coulter. *Dictionary of Ancient Deities*. New York: Oxford University Press, 2001.

Yolen, Jane, ed. *Favorite Folktales from Around the World*. New York: Pantheon Books, 1986.

16

Spider Woman: Creator and Destroyer

Marion W. Copland

"A steel spider rising seven and a half feet in the center of the Guggenheim's Frank Lloyd Wright rotunda welcomes visitors to the Louise Bourgeois retrospective that opened there on June 25, 2008." The *New Yorker*'s "Goings on About Town" column perceptively labeled the exhibit "Spider Woman," commenting that whatever art movements Bourgeois may have been aligned with, "she is best known for her spiders." The announcement goes on to describe both the giant spider and its kin as "menacing steel arachnids." But the *New York Times*' art critic, Carol Vogel, tells viewers that Bourgeois's "spider sculptures . . . are a symbol of her mother . . . a [woman as] deliberate, clever, patient, soothing, reasonable, dainty, subtle, indispensable, neat and useful as a spider." The *New York Review of Books*' Sanford Schwartz admits the spiders "can seem primarily threatening" even though the artist recognized them as "embodiments of industriousness" and of a hard "fought-for balance."[1]

Native American cultures of the Southwest as well as across the Americas saw in the spider exactly the qualities Bourgeois saw. To them the spider is female, kindly, creative, industrious, persistent, qualities that allow her to achieve balance in challenging environments. Many researchers have been *On the Trail of Spiderwoman*, like Carol Patterson-Rudolf, who wrote a book of that title, finding traces of her passage in the *Petroglyphs, Pictoglyphs, and Myths of the Southwest.* Inspired by Navajo weaver and storyteller Sarah Natani's version of how Spider Woman gave the Navajo the gift of weaving, collaborators Kelly Bennett and Ronia Davidson began exploring the recurrence of the spider as a unifying thread in the literature of Native American cultures. Their anthology, *Spider Spins a Story,* includes legends from fourteen Native American cultures including the Kiowa, Zuni, Cherokee, Hopi, Lakota, and Muskogee.[2]

Traditional Wisdom Juxtaposed to Modern Sentiment

Despite their diverse customs and habitats, these Native American legends share Bourgeois's vision of the spider's industriousness, creativity, and spiritual balance. Lois Duncan reinforces this vision by retelling of a Navajo tale of a girl who "learns from Spider Woman how to keep her life in balance by respecting boundaries" and its account of "why Navajo blanket weavers include a spirit pathway in their creations to this day."[3]

In contrast to the Native American view, most contemporary urban gallery goers will find the Guggenheim spiders alien and threatening, related rather to the giant figures of 1940s horror movies and the archetype of feminine evil, the Black Widow, than to the figure Louise Bourgeois has made the muse of her long "daring and dangerous" career.[4] Based on observations that the Black Widow spider, one of North America's two poisonous species, frequently dines on her successful mates, the archetype of the Black Widow has darkened the reputation of women and spiders and their mythic counterparts. The archetype is old and pervasive: many critics, for instance, have commented that the spider appears as an image of evil in Dostoevsky's work.

In his novel *The Possessed* Dostoevsky's Stravrogin dreams of a little red spider who in turn becomes the ruling metaphor of a contemporary Canadian theater piece, *la petite araignee rouge,* in 2003. In contrast to this association with evil, the folk culture of late 19th-century Devonshire records that the red spider may bring either curse or blessing depending on how a human being treats the spider. When treated well, the spider has the power to spin money in the pocket of its benefactor. However, when Hillary Nanspian in *Red Spider,* an 1887 novel by folklorist Sabine Baring-Gould, unwittingly squashes a red spider in his pocket, his action brings disastrous consequence to his family and neighbors. Late in the 2009 animated film *Coraline,* based on a novel by Neil Gaimon, the rejected Other Mother metamorphoses into a terrifying invocation of the Black Widow, suggesting the continued power of that negative association.

Demonizing of Species Results from Separation from Nature

Some commentators see the perceptual divide between menacing Black Widow and benevolent Grandmother Spider as a symptom of 21st-century Euro-American culture's separation from nature. In *The Infinite in the Small*, for instance, Joanne Luack explains that "the demonizing of any species depends on the perception and belief in our separateness from other animals and tangent belief in their evil and amoral intent." Projecting malevolence onto the female spider or foolhardiness onto the male doesn't serve to better the human-spider relationship. What would better it, Lauck suggests, is "allowing certain mysteries [like Bourgeoise's spiders] to evolve in our nonholistic, fearful imagination" until they displace "our anxiety about spiders with information that gives us strategies for coexisting with them."[5]

Refocusing might begin with the 14th-century Scottish legend of Robert the Bruce. As the Bruce recovers from a wound, he observes a spider reweaving her web each time it is destroyed, teaching him that the essence of a great leader is patience and perseverance. Clearly she is for him not a menace but a teacher, even a healer, suggesting again that the legend and lore of modern European cultures retain vestiges of an earlier preanthropocentric cultural perception of the spider in which the spider is seen more as Grandmother Spider than Black Widow.

Spider as Creator of the World and Patron of Arts

For many indigenous peoples, as for Bourgeois, the spider is both the creator of the world, its habitats, and its inhabitants and also the patron of the arts that celebrate and imitate the spider's creativity and skill. The Ghanaian Anansi, the most familiar of African and African American spider figures, in addition to his trickster exploits, "spun the raw material out of which human beings were created."[6] Although he is male and like all tricksters essentially amoral, Anansi belongs more to the family of Grandmother Spider than of the archetypal Black Widow. Likely Ghanian culture was, either by nature or after contact with colonial cultures, essentially male-oriented.

Two variations of Spider Woman or Grandmother Spider exist among the Indians of the American Southwest. In the Navajo and Hopi versions, although she remains responsible for the emergence of people from one world to the next, she is seen as the assistant of a male creator, usually the sun. In an alternate Pueblo version, which Paula Gunn Allen believes to be the original and least influenced by colonial interpreters' versions, remaining more animistic than anthropocentric, people are believed to be born of the earth, and Spider, "identified with a figure known as 'Spider Woman or

Thinking Woman,'" is herself the creator.[7] Kivas or houses of worship in the area always possess a central opening or spider hole in memory of her crucial role in the survival of the people. In this guise, she becomes the principal figure in Leslie Marmon Silko's novel *Ceremony*, and, through that incarnation, enters the consciousness of modern Americans:

> Thought-Woman, the spider,
>   named things and
> as she named them
>   they appear.[8]

Pueblo Ts'its'tsi'nako ("Thought-Woman") controls the webs and tangled threads that Tayo, Silko's human protagonist, must untangle to find balance or harmony. Old Ka'oosh, the Pueblo healer, speaks to Tayo of the fragility of Earth, defining fragility as a word "filled with the intricacies of a continuing process," one possessing "a strength inherent in spider webs woven across paths through sand where early in the morning the sun becomes entangled in each filament of the web." Telling the story of that continuing process, explains the old man, is "the responsibility of being human."[9]

During one of his most essential encounters, as Tayo seeks the ceremony that evokes this evolutionary process he encounters Spider Woman at a spring in a narrow canyon. The spider "drank from the edge of the pool, careful to keep the delicate egg sac on her abdomen out of the water. She retraced her path, leaving faint crisscrossing patterns in the fine yellow sand. He remembered stories about her," how she knew ways to end the drought.[10]

The relationship between Grandmother Spider and rain, found in *Ceremony*, may be as basic to Euro-American culture as to the American-Indian cultures of the Southwest. The children's chant and finger game, "The Itsy Bitsy Spider," which illustrates that relationship, seems to date only from the 19th century yet, like the legend of Robert Bruce, grows from deeper cultural roots. The spider's climb up the water-spout seems to cause the rain that washes her out, but her climbing of the silken line she spins out of herself and the almost automatic hand-motions that accompany the chanting of the rhyme by young singers has the feel of ritual. Anthropocentric Euro-American scholars have "view[ed] the lyrics [of the Itsy Bitsy Spider] as an Absurdist metaphor of Albert Camus' interpretation of the Sisyphus myth," seeing the similarity between her climbing and reclimbing the spout and his repeated pushing of the stone up the hill.[11] More likely, both myths share the same rooting in the elemental wisdom of the Darwinian world.

Whether stories bringing Spider Woman back to life are as seemingly simple as this children's rhyme or as complex as Silko's novel, they endorse the qualities Bourgeois shapes into her spider sculptures, speaking of an animistic world in which humans, rather than constituting the web of life, recognize themselves as but one strand in Spider Woman's web—not the whole story, but, as Silko's Tayo recognizes, part of a world "made of stories, the long ago, time immemorial stories. . . . It was a world alive, always changing and moving . . . like the motion of the stars across the sky."[12] Once Silko's Tayo has that insight, he is ready to discover how to participate in the pattern:

> He cried with the relief he felt at finally seeing the pattern, the way all the stories fit together—the old stories, the war stories, their stories—to become the story that was still being told. He was not crazy, he had never been crazy. He had only seen and heard the world as it always was: no boundaries, only transitions through all distances and time.[13]

In this ongoing story, people still emerge into the present world through the *sipapu* (the kivas' opening) where Spider Woman and her female offspring wait to teach them the patterns of living, the balance that will allow them to survive. Spider Woman's daughters, frequently appearing as sisters, are responsible for working out the ceremonial details reflected in surviving ceremonial dances and rituals and in the feminine architecture of the kiva and in the patterns of agriculture still practiced among traditional peoples in the Southwest and, equally, in the ceremony Silko's Tayo discovers and in the rhythms of "Itsy, Bitsy Spider."[14]

The Ancient Spider-Creator

The antiquity of this matrilineal version of the Spider Woman myth is suggested by its parallels to the "mythology of the tribes inhabiting Nauru Island in the South Pacific [whose] . . . world was created by Areop-Enap, or Ancient Spider."[15] Among the giant figures "dug into Earth's surface 2,000 years ago by the Inca people of Nazca Peru . . . is a spider, by far the largest spider image in the world . . . [measuring] 160 feet across." An even older spider image was "drawn by an unknown prehistoric artist on the wall of [a] cave in Gasalla Gorge Spain."[16] Spiders are among the pantheon of predators carved in the massive 11,000-year-old megaliths now being excavated at Gubekli Tepe, six miles from the ancient city of

Urfa in southeastern Turkey. Although no one is sure what these ancient images mean or why they were made, these figures, which predate Stonehenge by some 6000 years, in all likelihood "represent the root beliefs . . . of the neolithic people who, after the erection of Gubekli Tepe, went on to settle the Fertile Crescent." The creatures depicted there, the spider among them, hold the secrets of the web of human settlement on earth.[17]

It seems likely each of these ancient images represents a strand of the wide-spun mythology of Spider Woman. And as evidence mounts for the early and widespread travel of humans by sea, the likelier the relationship of widespread spider traditions to the archaic Spider Woman becomes. The matrilineal Spider Woman and her daughters seem akin, then, less to the classical and therefore essentially patriarchal figure of the Greek Arachne than to the far older figures of the Moirai or Fates, remnants of the myth of similar indigenous peoples.

> In the oldest myths, the spider is associated with the triune Great Goddess, as spinner, measurer, and cutter of life. In Hindu mythology, the spider represented Marja, virgin aspect of the Triple Goddess . . . the Spinner sitting at the hub of the Wheel of Fate. As the weaver of the web of illusion—maya—she also created life from her own substance."[18]

> In Borneo the spider is also a strong creative figure. There is a legend there that Mother Spider spun a huge web that covered the whole world including the original tree, then with the help of an insect larvae she was able to stimulate the tree to produce human beings from its leaves.[19]

In the pre-Columbian Teotihuacan or Mayan civilization of what is now Mexico, a fresco shows a spider attended by two smaller figures. The robes they wear identify them as goddesses. The larger figure's nosepiece, "equipped with what appear to be arachnid-like fangs," identifies her with "the underworld, darkness, the earth, water, war, and possibly even creation itself." Other animals commonly associated with the same powers—the jaguar and owl, and spiders themselves—are either shown in the background, on her clothing, or hanging from her arms. Significantly, these powerful and dangerous, but not evil, figures share many of the traits found in the Grandmother Spider of the Pueblo and Navajo, but "no one is really sure which culture she originally came from, or how exactly she passed from one to the other."[20]

Spider as Spinner of Fate and Creator of Patterns

The Greek Fates—Clotho, Lachesis, and Atropos—

spin out life, measure it, and cut it. They are often depicted carrying . . . instruments of spinning . . . [and] are sometimes thought
of as goddesses of both birth and death because of the non-linear
aspect of the spun thread of life. They present a theological problem in relation to the question of whether the [patriarchal gods]
Thor, Zeus, or in modern terms, Fate or God, has ultimate control
over life and death.[21]

In Silko's *Ceremony,* because the modern world has both lost faith in
those gods and lost the original patterns taught by Spider Woman, her
human protagonist must rediscover, with Thinking Woman's help, the
patterns or webs of survival.

It is potentially tragic, then, that in patriarchal modern cultures spiders
have become female destroyers instead of female creators and saviors. In
nature, when the Black Widow occasionally consumes her mate, it is in the
service of her role as mater-creator, reabsorbing or recycling life as she does
silk. In the patriarchal anthropocentric vision that characterizes much of
Euro-American culture, the Black Widow is seen only as "menacing," a
negative figure of deception, greed, and selfishness, of destruction rather
than creation. Unlike Native American poet and writer Sherman Alexie,
who in *The Summer of the Black Widows* acknowledges spiders as the source of
his poems and stories, Euro-American children are brainwashed to react to
the spider's presence, however neighborly her gesture of sitting nearby may
be, as does Little Miss Moffett in her entomologist father's 16th-century
poem of the same name: they run away.

Sue Hubbell confirms in *Broadsides from the Other Orders* that Euro-
Americans are inveterate bug haters, and, although spiders are not
insects, they are tarred with the same brush.[22] In fact, as Richard J.
Leskosky points out:

Spiders make particularly effective big bugs [in horror movies],
since they already occupy a significant place in the panoply of
human fears. . . . Probably the most horrific scene in any big bug
film is the penultimate shot of *The Fly* (1958), when the human-
headed fly, caught in the spider web of a particularly huge spider,
screams at the approach of the arachnid, "Help me! Help me!"

The natural order is subverted in so many ways in this shot that it overwhelms any objections the logical mind might have to the scene.[23]

Examples abound, from the apparently indefatigable delight readers of the cartoon *Garfield* take in his squashing perfectly affable spiders with a rolled-up newspaper to *Kingdom of the Spiders*, where "tarantulas mutate after coming into contact with a new crop-dusting spray and seek humans for food" to the myriad of mysteries, novels, and movies like *Kiss of the Spider Woman* that allude in their titles and imagery to the Black Widow with its Freudian connections to the feminine only in its Western demonized form of witchcraft and evil.[24] In contrast, positive feminine spider figures are few and far between.

Spider Woman: Comix, Not Comic

The Marvel Comics universe contains a number of Spider Woman characters, descended from a comic book published by Harry 'A' Chesler Comics in 1944. The best known of such characters, Jessica Drew, is the daughter of a bioengineer. Accidentally exposed to uranium radiation (or, in a 2005 version inspired by *The Fly*, a laser containing the DNA of a mixed species of spider) and therefore condemned to an excruciating death, Jessica's only hope to survive is her father's experimental spider venom. Forty years later, still seventeen, she emerges from her coma to find herself in possession of spider-like powers.

Falling into evil company reflected in her code name, Arachne, she joins a host of other comic-book spiderwomen as a version of the deadly Black Widow. Even Spider Girl, Spiderman Peter Parker's daughter, emerges during her teenage year as a negative figure like Jessica Drew before her.[25] Both Jessica Drew and Spider Girl, however, evolve to use their powers positively, and the spidermen and -women of the 21st century, despite the gender difference, embrace the positive aura of the original archaic Spider Woman goddess.

This positive Spider Man is anchored in a number of cultural traditions that recognize essentially positive and complex male spider images, the most familiar being the African Ashanti trickster figure Anansi. Like most trickster figures, Anansi weaves together the good and the bad, truth and trick, life and death. It is perhaps proof of this relationship that among Ashanti Obeah faithful in the Caribbean, Anansi comes to be known as Aunt Nancy, a sex change perhaps more related to habitat than language evolution. But there exists as well a male spider akin to the devious Black Widow in such works as Mary Howitt's well-know 1831 poem "The Spider and the Fly" or H. G. Wells' *The Valley of the Spiders*.

Visionary artists like Bourgeois are easing Euro-American culture toward an essentially feminist, positive view of the spider. Examples, as mentioned earlier, include the legend of the 14th-century Scottish hero-king Robert the Bruce, a tale that may owe something to the biblical tale of David escaping the vengeful Saul with the help of swift spinning spiders whose webs obscure the cave entrance where David hides. Concealed by the web of an equally industrious spider, Mohammad is also said to have escaped pursuers as he fled Mecca, and "a 12th-century Japanese hero . . . is also supposed to have been saved by a spider spinning a web across the opening of a hollow tree he was hiding in."[26]

Charlotte's Web and Other Contemporary Spider-Friendly Works

Contemporary literary and artistic works seeking to recapture the ancient spirit of the Spider Woman creator weave together names and titles not often linked in modern critical theory. E. B White's *Charlotte's Web*, usually passed over by critics as a children's classic, is equally as important as novelist Nicholas Christopher's magnificent and demanding *A Trip to the Stars*. Charlotte A. Cavatica, a New England orb-spinning spider the size of a gumdrop, spins webs that save Wilbur from the fate of most pigs, but in the long run also teaches him that death is a natural and essential part of life. Although she must leave him after laying her eggs, every spring thereafter some of Charlotte's descendants hatch and stay to spin their webs in the doorway of Wilbur's barn, making it, Wilbur thought, "the best place to be . . . with the changing seasons, the heat of the sun, the passage of the swallows, the nearness of rats, the sameness of sheep, the love of spiders, the smell of manure, and the glory of everything."[27]

Christopher's novel focuses on a species of trapdoor spider (*Ummedia stallarum*) indigenous to the world of the southwestern Grandmother Spider. The spider's black abdomen is "sprinkled silver like a night sky filled with stars" and its venom is used in both Hopi and Zuni purification rituals to "reduce the human soul to its rarest elements, stripping away all that is false, illusory, or fearful." Those carrying the spider's venom are said to be "obsessed with . . . stargazing"; others "become master architects—like the spider" whom the Zuni believe created the universe. The stars are, they believe, "her eggs. From each . . . springs a warrior who will eventually drop to earth."[28]

Christopher ties this Zuni belief to the Boru of North Vietnam, animists who display tattoos of their totem animals, one of which is "a red spider, finely drawn . . . , complimented by a concentric web. . . . At the center of the web was a silver star." Later it is revealed that the Boru see the heavens as "a gigantic circular [or orb] web in which the stars had been caught like flies."[29] Ancient petroglyphs found in Costa Rica reflect this tradition, showing webs that have been seen as maps of the heavens.[30]

More and more fossil evidence suggests that spiders have been spinning their silk on Earth at least since "the Devonian (350–420 million years ago)—long before even the dinosaurs," making them "among the first terrestrial species."[31] By the time plants and insects diversified, spiders were weaving their complex webs out of spinnerets on the undersides of their bodies. The strength of this amazingly resilient substance, waterproof and elastic, is lauded by the poet Robert Frost in his "The Silken Tent." Some species produce up to eight different kinds of silk, each adapted to particular uses, but all 50,000 species of spiders produce silk draglines five times stronger than steel, which anchor them to their habitat and even allow them to disperse by sailing through the air.[32]

Young adult novels like Jenny Nimmu's *The Snow Spider Trilogy*, Gregory Maguire's *Seven Spiders Spinning*, K. A. Applegate's Animorph spin-off *The Android*, Colin Wilson's four-volume evolutionary *Spider World*, and Vernor Vinge's *A Fire Upon the Deep* and its prequel *A Deepness in the Sky* reawaken the original positive energy of Spider Woman much as do *Charlotte's Web* and *A Trip to the Stars*. In Maguire, an archeological dig discovers seven deadly Siberian snow spiders from before the dawn of time frozen in a glacier. By a series of coincidences they invade a classroom in Vermont, but instead of the anticipated horror movie outcome, the spiders find an appreciative welcome and prove beneficial rather than deadly. Similarly in Applegate's *The Android*, Marco, an arachnophobe, morphs into a wolf spider[33] and thereby learns to appreciate the creature's special sensory acumen, predatory gifts, and relationship to nature:

> it's all the thousands of tiny hairs that really get the spider brain's attention. They sense every subtle clue in the wind. Every minor movement in every direction.
>
> And all of a sudden it felt like the whole world was moving: leaves, pine needles, the dirt beneath my claw-tipped eight legs, bugs in the dirt, moles under the ground, birds in the air.[34]

Wilson's humans, in a future world where insects and spiders have evolved into giants, supplanting humans as the ruling species, live as prey. But through the four volumes readers see humans develop from seeing the spiders as totally alien to accepting the possibility of a cooperative peaceful existence. In Vigne's novels the spiders who rule Arachna are, as one reviewer put it "the most lovable arachnids in American literature since *Charlotte's Web*."

While E. B. White, a series of young adult novels, Leslie Silko, Nicholas Christopher, and Louise Bourgeois may seem strange web-masters, they and others like them are opening the way to revision Spider Woman in her more positive manifestations or, at least, to recognize how her Grandmother Spider manifestation balances her seemingly menacing manifestations as Black Widow or Anasasi Noir, the Obeah of the Caribbean Islands, or Matlacihuatler Mujer enredador, the dangerous entangling spider woman of the Mexican Chiapus highlands.[35]

In these incarnations Spider Woman is not the opposite of life, but the essential warp that weaves the woof of life into being. The creator Grandmother Spider of the American Southwest spins the world out of herself as real spiders spin their silk, but she cannot spin without first, like Anasazi Noir or the Black Widow, consuming, reabsorbing, or recycling the life and web (or mate) she has already spun. So fortified, she is able to spin it anew. Unlike most modern mythic figures, such archaic goddess figures are complex, combining what to Western logic seem incompatible dualities, light and dark, life and death.

Although medieval Europeans associated spiders with witches, these may not have been wholly negative associations. Barbara G. Walter says, "The folk-tale of The Spider and the Fly suggested the once widespread belief that flies are souls in search of a female entity to eat them and give them rebirth," evidence of Grandmother Spider's role as recycling creator.[36] Perhaps, without realizing it, modern humans already acknowledge Spider Woman as creator and sustainer of life. Common terms like "the web of life" carry with them "the understanding that all beings are sustained in myriad ways by the places in which they live and in ways that are not always self-evident."[37]

In her *Buffalo Gals, Won't You Come Out Tonight*, Ursula Le Guin's nonhuman rescuers of a human child, sole survivor of a plane crash in the American Southwest, instinctively know "the person she needs to find is Grandmother." Grandmother's house "was underground . . . and the Grandmother was there at the center, at her loom. She was making a rug or blanket of the hills and the black rain and the white rain, weaving in the lightning. As they spoke, she wove."[38] She advises the child that it is safe to return to her own people (modern humans) because, even if she doesn't realize it yet, her experience with Coyote and the other animals has taught her how to live well: "Go on, little one, Granddaughter,' Spider said. 'Don't be afraid. I'll be there too, you know. In your dreams, in your ideas, in dark corners in the basement. Don't kill me, or I'll make it rain.' "[39]

Spiders have been weaving themselves into the dreams of non–Native Americans at least since Jonathan Edwards who, as a boy, marveled at the activities of a web-spinning spider.[40] Thoreau saw magic rather than the sophistry commonly associated with them from the time of Plato in the web-work of spiders.[41] The work of South American writers, as David Spooner points out, is equally rich with spider and web imagery. Sooner goes on to argue that although physical evolution links humans to other primates, cultural evolution provides links to the more ancient heritage of insects and their arachnid kin. The word *imagination*, he says, has at its root "imago" which is used equally to refer to a phase in the development of insects and the development of the creative functions of the mind. Thoreau's interest in insects developed into what Spooner describes as a sociobiological view of man's place in nature that is certainly in harmony with the views of the indigenous peoples who first recognized the significance of Spider Woman.[42]

Art emerged, after all, as "a way for people to order their psyches and keep their minds clear . . . relate their lives to other powers and other lives in the universe," skills recognized as necessary "for health in the individual and the tribe." Spider Woman, in one manifestation or another, has been credited with the creation of the first alphabet, hailed as the patron of language and writing, and as the source of "medicine—creativity, intelligence, industry, and [echoing Bourgeois] patience."[43] She has even been seen as the totem of the World Wide Web, the modern dream of worldwide connection facilitated by its powerful search spiders. As poet/anthropologist Dave Aftandilian puts it, Spider Woman has

> from the beginning of days
> . . . patiently watched and waited,
> sifting the winds with [her] sparkling snare,
> . . .
> at home in the center
> of air, water, and earth,
> of the time before time and days yet to come,
> you spin a new prayer each day
> and when it flags later, care-worn and tattered.
> you spin it again, and again.[44]

Notes

1. "Goings on About Town," *New Yorker*, June 25, 2008, 8; Carol Vogel, "The Week Ahead: Art," *New York Times*, June 22, 2008, Arts and Leisure, 2; Sanford Schwartz, "Daring and Disturbing," *New York Review of Books*, October 23, 2008, 32.

2. Jill Max, ed. *Spider Spins a Story: Fourteen Legends from Native America* (Flagstaff, AZ: Northland, 1998), http://jillmax.com/Spider/html (accessed September 10, 2008).

3. "Spinning Spider Stories," www.learnnc.org/lp/pages/405 (accessed September 10, 2008).

4. Schwartz, "Daring and Disturbing," 31.

5. Joanne Elizabeth Luack, *The Voice of the Infinite in the Small* (Boston: Shambhala, 2004), 53, 215.

6. "Spinning Spider Stories"; see also Paul Hillyard, *The Book of the Spider: From Arachnophobia to the Love of the Spider* (London: Hutchinson, 1994), 15–39.

7. David Leeming, *Oxford Companion to World Mythology* (New York: Oxford University Press, 2005), 85, 365–366.

8. Leslie Marmon Silko, *Ceremony* (New York: Viking, 1977), 1.

9. Ibid., 2, 38.

10. Ibid., 94.

11. In Native American legends she emerges as both a Promethean character providing the world with light and fire and rain: see www.ilhaeaii.net/~story/lore 120.html and www.ferrum.edu/applit/bibs/tales/firstfire.html (both accessed September 16, 2008).

12. Silko, *Ceremony*, 95.

13. Ibid., 246.

14. Leeming, *Oxford Companion to World Mythology*, 120.

15. Luack, *Voice of the Infinite in the Small*, 33.

16. "Spiders and Man," http://www.earthlife.net/chelicerata/s=man.http (accessed September 20, 2008).

17. Andrew Curry, "The World's First Temple," *Smithsonian*, November 2008, 54, 68.

18. Luack, *Voice of the Infinite in the Small*, 216.

19. "Spiders and Man."

20. Crystalinks, "Teotihuacan Spider Woman," www.crystalinks.com/mayan spiderwoman.html (accessed September 16, 2008).

21. Leeming, *Oxford Companion to World Mythology*, 132–133.

22. Sue Hubbell, *Broadsides from the Other Orders: A Book of Bugs* (New York: Random House, 1993), 158–159.

23. Richard J. Leskosky, "Size Matters: Some Bugs on the Big Screen," in *Insect Poetics*, ed. Eric C. Brown (Minneapolis: University of Minnesota Press, 2006), 336–337.

24. Luack, *Voice of the Infinite in the Small*, 8.

25. "Spider Woman," Wikipedia, http://en.wikipedia.org/wiki/Spider-Woman, and "Spider Woman (comics), Comicvine, the Comic Book Encyclopedia, http://comicvine.com/spider-woman/1453 (both accessed September 20, 2008).

26. Mary Howitt, "The Spider and the Fly" (1821), www.earthlife.net/chelicerata/s-man.html (accessed October 3, 2008).

27. E. B. White, *Charlotte's Web* (New York: Harper and Row, 1952), 183.

28. Nicholas Christopher, *A Trip to the Stars* (New York: Dial Press, 2000), 22, 167.

29. Ibid., 400, 421.

30. "Chasing Birds with Charlie: A Sacred Site," www.jackmaryete.com/Travel/Americas/CostaRica/CBWC1.html (accessed September 16, 2008).

31. Crystalinks, "Teotichuacan Spider Woman."

32. "Amazing Arachnids: Neurophilosophy," http://neurophilosophy.word press.com/2006/09/28/amazingarachnids (accessed September 9, 2008).

33. K. E. Applegate, *Animorphs: The Android* (NewYork: Scholastic, 1997), 57.

34. Ibid., 68.

35. Lewis Hyde, *Trickster Makes the World: Mischief, Myth, and Art* (New York: Farrar, Straus, and Giroux, 1998), 338–339.

36. Barbara G. Walter, *The Woman's Encyclopedia of Myths and Secrets* (San Francisco: Harper and Row, 1983), 958.

37. Lyanda Lynn Haupt, *Pilgrim on the Great Bird Continent: The Importance of Everything and Other Lessons from Darwin's Lost Notebooks* (Boston: Little, Brown, 2006), 158.

38. Ursula Le Guin, *Buffalo Gals, Won't You Come Out Tonight* (San Francisco: Loose Press, 1996), 37, 150.

39. Ibid., 151.

40. David Spooner, *The Insect Populated Mind: How Insects Have Influenced the Evolution of Consciousness* (London: Hamilton Books, 2005), 134.

41. Tony Tanner provides an excellent discussion of the spider web in American literature in his *Scenes of Nature, Signs of Men* (New York: Cambridge University Press, 1987).

42. Spooner, *The Insect Populated Mind*, 11, 132.

43. Luack, *Voice of the Infinite in the Small*, 220, 227.

44. David Aftandilian, "Spider Woman," *NILAS Newsletter* (Summer 2008): 40. Reprinted with permission.

Bibliography

Aftandilian, David. "Spider Woman." *NILAS Newsletter* (Summer 2008): 40.
Alexie, Sherman. *The Summer of Black Widows.* New York: Hanging Loose Press, 1996.
Allen, Paula Gunn. *Grandmothers of the Light: A Medicine Woman's Source Book.* Boston: Beacon, 1991.

Allen, Paula Gunn. *The Sacred Hoop: Rediscovering the Feminine in American Indian Traditions.* Boston: Beacon, 1986.

Applegate, K. E. *Animorphs: The Android.* New York: Scholastic, 1997.

"Art: Spider Woman." In "Goings On About Town." *New Yorker,* June 30, 2008, 8.

Barratt, Amy. "The Devils Lacking Detail." *Montreal Mirror,* www.montrealmirror .com/ARCHIVES/2003/11203/theatre.html (accessed July 14, 2010).

Carmean, Kelli. *Spider Woman Walks This Land: Traditional Cultural Properties and the Navajo Nation.* Walnut Creek, CA: AltaMira Press, 2002.

Christopher, Nicholas. *A Trip to the Stars.* New York: Dial Press, 2000.

Crystalinks. "Spider Fossils." www.crystalinks.com/fossilspiders.html (accessed September 16, 2008).

Crystalinks. "Teotihuacan Spider Woman." www.crystalinks.com/mayanspider woman.html (accessed September 16, 2008).

Curry, Andrew. "The World's First Temple?" *Smithsonian.* November 2008, 54–68.

Duncan, Lois. *Ill. Shonto Begay. The Magic of Spider Woman.* Singapore: Scholastic, 1996.

Haupt, Lyanda Lynn. *Pilgrim on the Great Bird Continent: The Importance of Everything and Other Lessons from Darwin's Lost Notebooks.* New York: Little, Brown, 2006.

Hillyard, Paul. *The Book of the Spider: From Arachnophobia to the Love of the Spider.* London: Hutchinson, 1994.

Howitt, Mary. "The Spider and the Fly." 1821. http://www.earthlife.net/cheli cerata/s-man.htr (accessed October 3, 2008).

Hubbell, Sue. *Broadsides from the Other Orders: A Book of Bugs.* New York: Random House, 1993.

Hyde, Lewis. *Trickster Makes the World: Mischief, Myth, and Art.* New York: Farrar, Straus and Giroux, 1998.

Landsong, Robin. "Grandmother Spider Weaves the Universe." http://landsong .net/landsong-medicine-art-gallery (accessed September 14, 2008).

Lauck, Joanne Elizabeth. *The Voice of the Infinite in the Small: Revisioning the Insect-Human Connection.* Boston: Shambhala, 2004.

Le Guin, Ursula. *Buffalo Gals, Won't You Come Out Tonight.* San Francisco: Roc, 1990.

Lee, Nathan. "Portrait of a Haunted Artist Who Befriended Giant Spiders." *New York Times,* June 25, 2008. http://movies.nytimes.com/2008/06/25/ movies/25loui.html?ref=movies (accessed June 26, 2009).

Leeming, David. *Oxford Companion to World Mythology.* New York: Oxford University Press, 2005.

Leskosky, Richard J. "Size Matters: Bug Bugs on the Big Screen." In *Insect Poetics,* ed. Eric C. Brown, 319–341. Minneapolis: University of Minnesota Press, 2006.

Maguire, Gregory. *The Hamlet Chronicles: Seven Spiders Spinning.* New York: Harper-Trophy, 2005.

Max, Jill, ed. *Spider Spins a Story: Fourteen Legends from Native America.* Flagstaff, AZ: Northland, 1998, http://jillmax.com/Spider/html (accessed September 10, 2008).

Moffett, Thomas. "Little Miss Moffett." www.librarysupport.net/mothergoose society/rhymes/littlemissm.html (accessed September 12, 2008).

Nimmu, Jenny. *The Snow Spider Trilogy.* New York: Troll Communications, 1991.

Patterson-Rudolph. Carol. *On the Trail of Spiderwoman: Petroglyphs, Pictographs, and Myths of the Southwest.* Santa Fe, NM: Ancient City Press, 1997.

Reichard, Gladys A. *Spider Woman: A Story of Navajo Weavers and Chanters.* New York: Macmillan, 1934.

Schwartz, Sanford. "Daring and Disturbing." *New York Review of Books,* October 23, 2008, 31–33.

Silko, Leslie Marmon. *Ceremony.* New York: Viking, 1977.

"Spiders and Man." http://www.earthlife.net/chelicerata/s-man.htr (accessed September 20, 2008).

"Spider-Woman (comics). Comicvine, the Comic Book Encyclopedia. http://www.comicvine.com/spider-woman/1453 (accessed September 20, 2008).

"Spider-Woman." Wikipedia, http://en.wikipedia.org/wiki/Spider-Woman (accessed September 20, 2008).

"Spinning Spider Stories." http://www.learnnc.org/lp/pages/405 (accessed September 20, 2008).

Spooner, David. *The Insect Populated Mind: How Insects have Influenced the Evolution of Consciousness.* London: Hamilton Books, 2005.

Tanner, Tony. *Scenes of Nature, Signs of Men.* New York: Cambridge University Press, 1987.

Vinge, Vernor. *A Deepness in the Sky.* New York: Tor Books, 1998.

Vinge, Vernor. *A Fire Upon the Deep.* New York: Tor Books, 1992.

Vogel, Carol. "The Week Ahead: Art." *New York Times,* June 22, 2008, Arts and Leisure, 4.

Walker, Barbara G. *The Woman's Encyclopedia of Myths and Secrets.* San Francisco: Harper and Row, 1983.

Wells, H. G. "The Valley of the Spiders." http://arthursclassicnovels.com/arthurs/wells/valleyspiders10.html (accessed October 3, 2008).

White, E. B. *Charlotte's Web.* New York: Harper and Row, 1952.

Wilson, Colin. *Spider World: A Quartet.* Vol. 1: *The Tower.* Charlottesville, VA: Hampton Books, 2001.

Wilson, Colin. *Spider World: A Quartet.* Vol. 2: *The Delta.* Charlottesville, VA: Hampton Books, 2001.

Wilson, Colin. *Spider World: A Quartet.* Vol. 3: *The Magician.* Charlottesville, VA: Hampton Books, 2001.

Wilson, Colin. *Spider World: A Quartet.* Vol. 4: *Shadowland.* Charlottesville, VA: Hampton Books, 2003.

17

The One and the Many: The Return of the Goddess in Contemporary American Novels

Kathleen L. Nichols

One characteristic of postmodern American fiction is the invention of ecofeminist stories celebrating the "goddess tradition, nature theology, indigenous spirituality, and immanence rather than transcendence."[1] This trend is especially notable in recent novels by black and Native American women writers like Toni Morrison, Leslie Marmon Silko, and others who construct a contemporary "feminine divine" based on the remnants of early Gnostic-Christian, African, and indigenous American goddess traditions that, historically, were suppressed by the male-dominated religions of western civilization. One result of this attempted erasure, according to ecofeminist theory, has been the parallel exploitation of nature (gendered as female) and the subjugation of women in society, as well as the domination of "others" on the basis of race, class, and imperialistic power.

This contemporary interest in resurrecting ancient goddess traditions is apparent in Morrison's *Paradise* (1997) and Silko's *Gardens in the Dunes* (1999), to take two fairly recent novels by well-known writers. As different as these novels are in most respects, they share a somewhat similar plot line. An orphaned child-heroine of mixed racial heritage is adopted by well-intentioned whites who take her on a long, transcontinental journey introducing her to western patriarchal culture. By the end of the novel, the displaced heroine returns, literally or spiritually, to her maternal "home," but the divine feminine she finally embraces is a revision of her first culture's goddess tradition. It has been modified by traces of the divine feminine encountered in other cultures during the heroine's travels and by the changing requirements of the heroine's modern world and self. In this increasingly multicultural age, often cut off from direct access to traditional cultures, the heroine must construct her own individualized path to a re-envisioned goddess capable of bridging cultural and ethnic differences as well as of healing and empowering modern women.

In Morrison's novel, the heroine is Consolata, whose mixed origins may include some combination of African, Portuguese, and Indian descent. An abused street child living on garbage in a Brazilian city, she is "abducted" by a group of nuns led by the white Reverend Mother Mary Magda, who bring her to the United States where the nuns will be running a Catholic boarding school in western Oklahoma to educate and "save" displaced Native American girls. Years later, after all the Native American girls have gone and Mary Magda is dying, the school—named "the convent" by the neighboring town—becomes a refuge attracting four unrelated women outcasts severely wounded by modern society.[2] After the death of Mary Magda, the grieving Consolata undergoes an awakening. Vaguely remembering the Candomblé culture of her Afro-Brazilian childhood, she creates new rituals dedicated to a goddess she may have partially invented called Piedade, who helps heal the convent women.

In counterpoint to this convent story is the chronicle of their nearest neighbors, seventeen miles away in the all-black town of Ruby run by civic and religious (Protestant) patriarchs who, years earlier, undertook a biblical "exodus" away from the racism exhibited by white society and by lighter-skinned blacks. Having created a pure all-black "paradise," as the title ironically implies, in western Oklahoma, the patriarchs cannot cope with the social and political changes of the post–civil rights era, changes that disrupt the supposed unity of Ruby. Violence finally erupts as the Ruby patriarchs scapegoat the highly unconventional convent women, invade their female refuge, and presumably murder them all. The reader is left in the final scene with an alternate paradisiacal image of a Consolata-like daughter-figure reposing her head in the maternal lap of Piedade, a black oceanic goddess-figure singing a song of "solace."[3]

The Search for Gnosis

As suggested by the novel's unnamed epigraph from the third-century Gnostic poem "Thunder, Perfect Mind," one source Morrison drew upon for Consolata's story is the Gnostic-Christian myth about Sophia, goddess of wisdom, as interpreted by modern scholars like Elaine Pagels, whose work has influenced the development of contemporary theories of the divine feminine. Based on studies of the fifty-two ancient Gnostic scrolls discovered in 1945 at Nag Hammadi in Egypt, Pagels describes several Gnostic "prequels" to the biblical Genesis story. In one version, the narrative begins with an earlier divine dyad consisting of "the Great Father" and "Sophia, the Great Mother" and their two children, daughter Sophia and son Christ. In this paradigm, the story of the daughter's fall and awakening illustrates a central Gnostic belief about "the fragmentation and reintegration of the soul."[4]

Although the Gnostic texts are various, complex, and often abstract, the basic Sophia myth has been conveniently summarized as follows:

> The mother Sophia gave birth to a daughter, the image of herself, who lost contact with her heavenly origin, and in her distress and sorrow brought the earth into being, and became entangled and lost in the chaotic realm of darkness that lay beneath the realm of light. . . . She was condemned to wander in this dark labyrinth, "endlessly searching, . . . laboring her passion into matter, her yearning into soul."
>
> . . . [T]he Virgin Mother Sophia, in response to her daughter's call, sends her son to rescue his sister. Her son is Christ . . . who descends into the darkness . . . to awaken his sister to remembrance of her true nature.
>
> . . . As the soul awakens, she becomes aware of her indwelling spirit, personified by Christ, who says to her: "I am thou and thou art I. . . ." (620–622)

As many scholars have pointed out, "gnosis" refers to a kind of intuitive knowledge or insight that is the goal of the Gnostic quest and attained by the transformed daughter Sophia when she realizes "the divine consciousness within" (624). Prior to that insight, Sophia or the soul is often described as "sleeping, blind, or drunk"—in other words, not in a state of "sin" but rather in a state of spiritual unconsciousness or ignorance. At death, as awakened soul, daughter Sophia will be guided "home" to be reunited with the Great Mother Sophia (622).

Consolata's Story as Neo-Gnostic

In many ways, Consolata's story of her separation from her divine origins—Brazil and the mother goddess Piedade—is a neo-Gnostic version of the Sophia myth. After thirty years under Mary Magda's tutelage, Consolata suspects that something is missing from her life of obedience, duty, and denial of the flesh. The beginning of her awakening occurs when she happens to view the "reckless joy" of the public festivities in the near-by all-black town of Ruby where "she heard a faint but insistent Sha sha sha. Then a memory of just such skin and just such men dancing with women in the street to music beating like an infuriated heart" surfaces.[5] As a result of these fragmented memories, presumably of Afro-Brazilian street carnivals, Consolata engages in a secret but passionate affair with a man from Ruby. When he finally breaks off the affair in disgust at the excesses of her passionate longings, Consolata realizes that what her sexual hunger was expressing was her desire "to go home" to that "loud city full of glittering black people" (226). After Reverend Mother dies, the grieving Consolata understands that her devotion was not to Jesus and his mother, but to the flesh and blood human being named Mary Magda who had cared for her.

Abandoned again, Consolata finally recognizes what the Gnostics would call the duality of the earthly and the divine, or what the Reverend Mother would have labeled the division of flesh and spirit, but to the Gnostic that gap is a wound that needs to be healed rather than a desirable polarization that preserves, through separation and transcendence, the purity of the spirit. Consolata will eventually conclude that one should "never break them in two. Never put one over the other. Eve is Mary's mother. Mary is the daughter of Eve" (263). Before Consolata arrives at this insight about the spiritual located within the physical, however, her story draws heavily on Gnostic imagery to express her sense of being "entangled and lost in the chaotic realm of darkness." She is literally becoming "blind" and is "sleeping" a lot and getting "drunk" in the convent's dark cellar where she spends most of her time. These common Gnostic metaphors stand for her condition of spiritual ignorance and sense of displacement from her lost "home."

Just as Sophia's radical alienation is cured when her "brother" Christ descends to the dark place and rescues her by asserting their spiritual twinship, as it were ("I am Thou and Thou art I"), so Consolata receives a visit one evening in the convent garden from a mysterious male who somewhat resembles herself; they both have tea-colored hair and green eyes covered in reflecting sunglasses. However, this guide is a new kind of rescuer in that he seems to combine the qualities of both Christ the brother and her former human lover—a union of divine love and human love: "Suddenly he was next to her without having moved . . . flirtatious, full of secret fun. . . . He took off his [sun]glasses then and winked, a slow seductive movement of a lid" (252). This is Consolata's moment of gnosis or knowledge when she realizes that she does, indeed, know him, just as he claims. He is the projection of her own divine spirit. He is she and she is he.

Revelation of the New Consolata

This moment of neo-Gnostic knowledge and unity completely transforms Consolata who becomes "like a new and revised Reverend Mother" (265). She invents new rituals to heal her "disciples," the four homeless and hurting women who have been living at the convent. Consolata proclaims, "I will teach you what you are hungry for" and proceeds to create a picture of a paradisiacal Brazil-of-the-imagination, replete with a goddess whose name "Piedade," in Portuguese, translates as mercy or compassion (262):

> She told them of a place where white sidewalks met the sea and fish the color of plums swam alongside children. She spoke of fruit that tasted the way sapphire looks and boys using rubies for dice. Of scented cathedrals made of gold where gods and goddesses sat in the pews with the congregation. . . . Then she told them of a woman named Piedade who sang but never said a word. (263–264)

This magical place is the "home" she was longing for earlier—on one level, her maternal origins in Brazil with its pleasurably sensuous memories based on nature and, on another level, her divine maternal origins represented by the Great Mother, Sophia from whom Consolata was separated at birth and with whom she, as the daughter Sophia, is reunited in death, as is described on the last page of the novel: "[S]olace . . . is what Piedade's song is about . . .; the unambivalent bliss of going home to be at home—the ease of coming back to love begun" (318).

Since there is no identifiable goddess named Piedade and it is unlikely that Consolata spent years in the Oklahoma wilderness studying ancient texts of Gnosticism, which was condemned as a heresy by the early fourth-century Christians, the reader has to assume that Consolata's image of the goddess derives, in part, from a combination of her own love for "mother" Mary Magna and Mary Magna's devotion to the orthodox interpretation of the Virgin Mary. And, indeed, Morrison has carefully constructed that final image in the novel—the adult child lying in the lap of the idealized mother—as a deliberate revision of Michelangelo's famous statue *Pietà*, which depicts the grieving Virgin Mary holding the lifeless body of her crucified son. However, Morrison's pietà differs in several significant ways. First, the sacrificed child is a daughter who is happy to be reunited with the missing mother, and, second, Piedade is described as being "black as firewood" (318).

The Tradition of the Black Madonna

Perhaps with that last detail, Morrison means to evoke the European tradition of the Black Virgin. The standard explanation for the many dark-toned statues of the Virgin Mary that were discovered during the Middle Ages is that the dark image links the Virgins with the Gnostic or pre-Christian lunar goddess of wisdom whose color is black.[6] Conversely, Consolata's Gnostic quest began with her awakening memories of her early childhood in Brazil, a country that can certainly lay claim to any number of Virgin Mothers, one common title for her being *Nossa Senhora de Piedade* (Our Lady of Mercy). It can also boast having one of the world's most famous dark-skinned Madonnas, namely, *Nossa Senhora da Conceicao Aparecida* (Our Lady of the Conception Who Appeared). She is Brazil's patron saint and "queen," and the legend connected with her shrine in San Paulo explains that a 17th-century statue of her was lost at sea and, nearly seventy years later, dredged out of the depths by three humble fishermen whose nets, it is claimed, were also suddenly and miraculously filled with fish.[7] Consolata's black and maternal Piedade is also identified with aquatic settings and imagery: "We sat on the shore. She bathed me in emerald water. . . . Piedade had songs that could still a wave, make it pause in its curl listening to language it had not heard since the sea opened."[8] However, Consolata's conflation of her recent recollections of Reverend Mother Mary Magna with her vague childhood memories of numerous Brazilian Madonnas will not entirely answer the question of who is this Piedade who sings in the primal language of nature.

The missing connection can be found in the African-Brazilian religions like Candomblé which are based on the worship of imported African nature deities called *orishas* (spelled *orixás* in Portuguese). Prominent among those orixás was the Yoruban water goddess named Yemanjá (also spelled Yemojá, Yemaya, Iemanjá, La Sirene, Yemalla) who, as a consequence of the Atlantic slave trade, traveled to America along with the enslaved West Africans. As a result of that journey, Yemanjá evolved from an African river deity and creator of most of the Yoruban orixás into an

expansive Brazilian goddess of the ocean who is sometimes credited with
the creation of all life. Since worshiping African gods was forbidden in
Portuguese-Catholic Brazil, the slaves ensured the survival of their Yoruban beliefs by using the veneration of their slave-masters' Catholic saints
and other religious figures as masks for hiding their orixá worship. This
practice of syncretization led to Yemanjá, mother of all, becoming associated with the Virgin Mary who shares special feast days with the African
deity. Indeed, at the entrance to the Church of Nossa Senhora de Piedade,
worshipers are first greeted by a statue of Yemanjá.[9] In Morrison's novel,
the dark-skinned mother-goddess Piedade is a composite of all these various strands.

Neither Candomblé nor Yemanjá is directly mentioned in Morrison's
novel, but as the author has noted in interviews, the inspiration for the
deadly confrontation between the Rubyite patriarchs and the convent
women came from a newspaper article about a group of men supposedly
murdering some Brazilian nuns rumored to be practicing Candomblé.[10]
Although that report proved to be inaccurate and Morrison has taken
many liberties with the story, she has clearly tried to introduce elements
somewhat suggestive of African-derived orixá worship into her novel.
For instance, while Morrison never relates much about the background
of the Rubyite midwife Fairy DuPres, she does note that the DuPres
family lived in Louisiana, the home of several syncretized African-Carib-
bean religions. As it turns out, Fairy DuPres taught everything she knew
to the younger Lone DuPres who, orphaned and alone like the young
Consolata, had been adopted, in this case, by the DuPres family traveling
with the black Protestant "exodusters" heading for the Oklahoma pan-
handle. It is Lone DuPres—midwife, herbalist, mind-reader, lay priestess,
and, some would say, witch—who acts as a teacher or guide directing the
development of Consolata's awakening consciousness, thus unofficially
"initiating" her into a kind of African-derived philosophy and practice.

Spirit Possession in African Syncretic Religions

In general, African-derived syncretic religions practice spirit-possession. The devotees participate in ceremonies featuring drums, music, and
dancing that move an appropriate orixá to come down and take possession of the dancer. The result is a trancelike or ecstatic union of human
and divine that infuses the dancer with axé, or the sacred vital energy of
the nature deity.[11] In Morrison's novel, variations on these beliefs occur.
Sensing that the middle-aged Consolata is spiritually "gifted," Lone begins

training her in nature-based spirituality by teaching her natural medicine while also pointing out the limitations of Consolata's church-trained beliefs that separate the "sinful" flesh from the saving spirit: "Don't separate God from His elements. He created it all. You stuck on dividing Him from His works. Don't unbalance His world."[12] At first, Consolata resists such ideas, knowing that the church views "magic" as evil, but when confronted by the body of a teenager just killed in a car accident and urged on by Lone's commands to "Go inside him. Wake him up," Consolata finds herself suddenly performing a remarkable act described in terms that sound very much like spirit-possession, with Consolata being the conductor of the revitalizing sacred energy: "She stepped in. . . . Inside the boy she saw a pinpoint of light receding. Pulling up energy that felt like fear, she stared at it until it widened. Then more, more, so air could come seeping, at first, then rushing rushing in. . . . [The teenager] opened his eyes, groaned and sat up" (245). Despite her guilty feelings, a desperate Consolata also prolongs the life of the dying Mary Magna by repeatedly "stepping in" or "seeing in" (i.e., "insight"), as she renames it, for seventeen days straight—until the Reverend Mother asks to be allowed to die (247).

After the later visits of the neo-Gnostic green-eyed messenger-god in the convent garden, the awakened Consolata emerges not only as a "new and revised Reverend Mother," but also as what might be considered a freelance version of a Candomblé *mãe de santo* or spiritual leader of her own syncretized nature cult devoted to the worship of Piedade, the new composite mother goddess. To heal the "broken" women who found refuge at the convent, Consolata invents innovative rituals of renewal that are a combination of the Catholic confessional and modern group therapy (222). These rituals are periodically accompanied by Consolata's "sermonettes," as it were, on the sacredness of the united body and spirit and the fantastical beauty of "a woman named Piedade, who sang but never said a word."

Initially, Consolata directs the women, who are silent, naked, and encircled by a ring of candles in the dark womb-space of Consolata's cellar bedroom, to outline their bodies lying on the floor and then to fill the templates with pictorial symbols not of their "sins," but of the emotional garbage and self-loathings of their lives. The next stage fuses a kind of confessional, free-associational style of storytelling with Consolata's unique version of empathetic participation or "stepping in": "That is how the loud dreaming began. How the stories rose in that place. Half-tales and the never-dreamed escaped from their lips. . . . And it was never important to know who said the dream or whether it had meaning. In spite of or because of their bodies ache, they step easily into the dreamer's tale." Morrison adds that this "loud dreaming . . . is no different from a shriek" (264).

The Rain-Dance as Gnostic Baptism

The culmination of this healing process is an unplanned "baptism" or "blessing" in the form of a rain-dance in the convent garden. Like the dry land, the healing women welcome the "longed for rain." Led by Consolata, the group "entered it and let it pour like balm on their shaved heads and upturned faces." Morrison describes "the rapture of holy women dancing in hot sweet rain" and the "enchantment" they feel as "the irresistible rain washed [their fears] away" (283). The point of this extended passage is easily deciphered by most readers: nature is symbolically cleansing and blessing them. However, the passage gains in resonance if it is also read in the context of nature-based orixá-worship. The descending rain that "irresistibly" fills the dancing women with "rapture" could just as readily describe the experience of possession by a water orixá at a Candomblé dancing ceremony. And this orixá could very well be Oshún (spelled "Oxum" in Portuguese), the deity of the inland fresh or "sweet" waters and daughter of the sea goddess Yemanjá. In one of her functions, Oxum is the evaporating water that forms clouds over the ocean (Mother Yemanjá) and is blown inland to fall, as rain, upon the land, the rivers of which all lead back to the sea (Yemanjá) with whom Oxum reunites.[13] In other words, this is an African-derived version of the Gnostic daughter Sophia, or soul, separated from and being reunited with the Great Mother Sophia.

What happens next in the novel has been a point of debate among scholars. The reader is startled and appalled when this scene of Oxum-like possession is immediately followed by the completion of the brutal massacre of the convent women by the Rubyite patriarchs who, having been held in frozen suspension since the opening pages of the novel while Morrison flashed the reader back to the events leading up to this shocking scene, finish what they began. Afterward, the Rubyites try to regroup back in town, but permanent divisions have erupted and destroyed the unity of this earthly "paradise" which, now at cross-purposes, proliferates different and competing stories of justification to explain what happened, and why, and—most amazing of all—how the bodies disappeared without a trace.

Morrison leaves the reader even more puzzled by adding five short "extra" scenes showing the five dead women alive and functioning somewhere—but where? For example, the novel's final image is the revised pietà of the reunited Consolata and Mother Piedade, but the junk and waste of civilization littering the nearby seashore do not fit the conventional image of a transcendent paradise or Heaven, but rather some polluted place "down here"—that is, on earth. And while the other four women are shown making brief contacts with selected members of their birth families, they act more like materialized ghosts, or perhaps ancestral spirits called "revenants" who sometimes visit the living,[14] except that the women seem largely indifferent to their kin and are soon moving on to the "far country" referred to earlier by Consolata's Gnostic messenger—a place that exists in the space somewhere between life and death where they have unfinished work to complete. But what is the work that remains to be done? This magical realist ending cries out for explanation.

A "visionary" or "mythic" reading of this magical realist ending is possible if readers take their cue from W. B. Yeats's apocalyptic poem "The Second Coming." This well-known poem proposes a cyclical view of history, with the end of the great Egyptian era signaled by the appearance of the Virgin Mary traveling by donkey toward Bethlehem and the birth of Jesus representing the start of the new 2000-year Christian era, the demise of which is foreshadowed at the end of the poem by the arrival of another "shaggy beast . . . / slouch[ing] toward Bethlehem"—the approach of a new historical cycle, in other words.[15] That space between the present and future eras is where these postmodern revenants may be "located." These dead-but-living convent women are preparing to take on the unfinished task of constructing a differently imagined "paradise" down here on earth, one that functions under the sign of Mother Piedade whose latest "adopted" spiritual daughter, Pallas "Truelove," one of the transformed convent women, is last seen striding purposefully forward while confidently carrying a spear in one hand and gently cradling in her other hand her infant son named Divine—an appropriate image of the new and evolving definitions of the sacred feminine for the future.[16]

Ecofeminist Themes in Morrison and Silko

Implicit in Morrison's novel are some additional ecofeminist themes. One could trace, for instance, the increasing alienation of the Rubyite patriarchs who begin to view nature primarily as a financial asset signaling the patriarchal God's approval of Ruby's separatist "paradise," which labels "others" as witches and difference as evil when the convent women, tolerated or ignored for years, begin to form a new synthesis of past traditions of the feminine divine. Another ecofeminist concern touched on by Morrison is the history of the Euro-American imperialistic conquest and destruction of Native American culture and the environment, all in the name of a patriarchal God and his supposed law of "Manifest Destiny." Morrison, for instance, briefly reminds the reader that the land on which the town of Ruby was built was originally Arapaho country, implying a contrasting attitude toward nature. Morrison also took care to name Mary Magna's Oklahoma school "Christ the King School for Native Girls"—a subtle reminder of the role the Catholic Church played in assisting and justifying the Spanish conquest of Native tribes on both the North and South American continents. However, a more in-depth treatment of the intersections of Native American and ecofeminist goddess themes can be found in another contemporary novel, *Gardens in the Dunes* by the Laguna Pueblo writer Leslie Marmon Silko.

Two ecofeminist concerns more fully explored in Silko's novel are the respect for both women and nature inherent in earth-based spiritualities rooted in ancient and indigenous goddess traditions and the patriarchal domination of and violence against both women and nature exhibited by imperialism and capitalism in western civilization.[17] These themes are developed through the typical neo-Gnostic plot, as it has been labeled here, which is doubled in Silko's novel, set in the late 19th century, the era that witnessed the demise of the traditional Native American ways of life. For the purposes of this novel, Silko invented an ancient Sand Lizard tribe that she loosely based on a number of lost tribes once living along the Colorado River between Arizona and California.

In Silko's first plot, Indigo is the young Native American heroine who is orphaned and taken away from the place of her maternal origins by a white married couple who embarks on a transcontinental tour of unusual gardens. During the journey, the homesick Indigo collects seeds from the gardens and searches for evidence of the Native American messiah (and his mother and wife) revealed at the Ghost Dance ceremony she participated in back home. By the end of the novel, Indigo returns to her reconstituted maternal home represented by the new madonna-child dyad, namely, her mixed-race older sister and her baby living in the maternal gardens in the dunes. The second intertwining plot is the story of Hattie, the privileged white woman who, before she married and "adopted" Indigo, was a student of the Gnostic gospels and, as a result of the transcontinental tour, discovers that her true spiritual home to which she needs to return is to be found in the Old European gardens of the goddess maintained by her Aunt Bronwyn in England and by her professor friend Laura in Italy. Splitting off from Hattie's plot is that of her husband,

Edward, who as a child was emotionally "orphaned" by indifferent and frequently absent parents. His adult plant-collecting obsession will carry the main burden of the destructive imperialistic-capitalistic theme in this novel.

The Indigenous Garden as Paradise

Gardens are the central metaphor of this novel which opens with a detailed description of an unusual indigenous "paradise" that, like Morrison's novel, radically revises the conventional biblical myth of the Garden of Eden." We are told that "all over the sand dunes, datura blossoms round and white as moons breathed their fragrance of magic."[18] This magical spot is a place of refuge for Grandma Fleet and her granddaughters Sister Salt and Indigo, ages thirteen and nine, respectively, who are the last surviving members of the ancient Sand Lizard tribe. Silko blends typical elements from Native American myths to give her fictional tribe an "authentic" feel and believable oral history, but also introduces themes important to contemporary ecofeminists, such as the sacred interconnections among all human and nonhuman life:

> [T]he old gardens had always been there. The old-time people found the gardens already growing, planted by the Sand Lizard, a relative of Grandfather Snake, who invited his niece to settle there and cultivate her seeds. Sand Lizard warned her children to share: Don't be greedy. The first ripe fruit . . . belongs to the spirits of our ancestors, who come to us as rain; the second ripe fruit should go to the birds and wild animals. . . . A few choice . . . plants were simply left . . . [to] return to the earth. . . . Old Sand Lizard insisted her gardens be reseeded that way. (17)

In the beginning of the novel, a descendent of Grandfather Snake resides by the desert pool and is respectfully greeted every morning by the three women. When Grandma Fleet dies of old age early in the novel, she is buried in a "burrow" she dug under the apricot trees she planted so that she would become "food" for the plants and continue living in their blooming and fruiting cycles (52). As such, Grandma Fleet becomes a kind of "earth mother," somewhat in the tradition of the Native American Corn Mother goddess, perpetually renewing the dune refuge every spring.

This indigenous paradise contains all the basic elements, and more, of a Garden of Eden, with the exception of the missing human male. It has three Eves, a small orchard of fruit trees, knowledge gained, and a serpent. However, in this garden they receive only helpful knowledge about how to keep the trees (and other plants) thriving so that they can eat the fruits and participate in the life-death-renewal cycle represented by the trees of life, and instead of a serpent tempting them into sin, Grandfather Snake functions more like a primal life force that created the garden and provided the means by which humans, plants, animals, and the earth, working together, can survive and thrive in what would otherwise be the barren desert of a "paradise lost."

The Missing Adam?

The Adam figure, however, is not really missing. Instead of depicting an evil serpent, Silko supplies an Adam who splits and multiplies into the male "aliens" or "destroyers," as Indigo puts it—referring presumably to the Spanish conquistadors, gold prospectors, U.S. military, and reservation police—who periodically invade the general region, sometimes even the remote garden refuge, bringing with them "bloodshed and cruelty," "hunger and suffering," and "disease and fever," the "evils" of imperialistic western civilization, in other words, that intrude upon and threaten the Native American way of life (17, 63). Those same "evil" forces are responsible for the disappearance of the girls' mother who never returns and for the later capture of the girls themselves. Sister Salt ends up pregnant, working as a laundress at a large construction site, a place rampant with entrepreneurial greed, that is destroying the ecosystem along the Colorado River as they build the Parker Canyon Dam and dig an aqueduct rerouting water into southern California. Indigo gets temporarily "adopted" by Hattie and Edward Palmer after escaping from the enforced assimilation required at a Christian boarding school not unlike Mary Magna's Christ the King School for Native Girls in Morrison's novel.

Gardens as Locations for the Great Goddess

For the descriptions of the gardens visited by Indigo and the Palmers during their European tour, Silko seems to have drawn liberally from the theories advanced by archaeomythologist Marija Gimbutas. Gimbutas's studies of the Neolithic sculpture and art of ancient European, Near Eastern, and Mediterranean civilizations—what Gimbutas calls "Old Europe"—led her to hypothesize the existence of a peaceful, matrilinear pre-Indo-European culture permeated with signs of the worship of the great goddess: "Her power was in water and stone, in tomb and cave, in animals and birds, snakes, and fish, hills, trees, and flowers. Hence the holistic and mythopoeic perception of the sacredness and mystery of all there is on Earth."[19] As Gimbutas and others have noted, some of the symbols of the great goddess are the moon, rivers, water vessels, birds, eggs, and mother bears, all of which refer to the goddess as the creator and sustainer of all life. Most significant for this novel is the image of the goddess as a serpent which, annually shedding its skin and awakening from hibernation each spring, is particularly associated with the waters of rebirth or renewal.[20]

Remnants of that Old European goddess worship are preserved in and around all the gardens Hattie, Edward, and Indigo visit in England and Italy. Hattie's Aunt Bronwyn, who believes that plants have souls, is restoring an old Norman abbey and its gardens, which include one featuring ancient sacred stones that she believes have the ability to dance after midnight. Outside the gardens she allows an old Celtic breed of white cattle whose crescent horns bear the sign of the lunar goddess the free run of her property. An ecofeminist-activist, she protects migrating toads, "incarnations of the primordial Mother," trying to cross the busy road and takes action to save the region's ancient giant oaks and stones (homes of the faeries) which had survived the early Christian church's war on the Druids, but are soon to be destroyed by "earthmoving teams carv[ing] wide scars in the bellies of the hills overlooking the river" to make way for some modern capitalist's "mansion of gigantic misproportions."[21]

In Italy Professor Laura proves to be the true, albeit "fictional," predecessor of Gimbutas. Laura's overgrown wild garden contains ancient statues of the half-human/half-horse centaurs peeking through the untrimmed tree branches, a snaky-haired Medusa head "big as a cookstove," and a fat, nude Bacchus astride a tortoise (291). Another garden blooms with hundreds of black gladioli, black being "the color of fertility and birth, the color of the Great Mother," Laura explains (298). Hattie calls the black flowers, carefully hybridized by Laura herself, the "little madonnas" (300), and Indigo associates them with the flocks of shiny blackbirds that preceded the appearance of the Indian messiah and his divine mother at the Ghost Dance back home in the American desert. In the rain garden, the visitors are taken with the numerous statuettes of snake-headed women with double-snake limbs nursing snake babies at their human breasts, and Laura tells her guests the legend of the snake-goddess, appearing human by day, but transforming at night into a luminous "big white snake wearing a crown" and accompanied by "legions of smaller snakes, all dancing with her" by the forest lake (302).

Each character reacts differently to Laura's garden of the snake goddess, as is indicated by their respective dreams that reveal their basic orientations to the sacred feminine and nature. Edward's response is completely negative. Subconsciously fusing the black color and African origins of Laura's gladioli with her snake-goddess images, he has a nightmare of "giant African snakes in [his] bed" (306). Although that image would seem, at first glance, to refer to sexual fears that have produced his long-term impotency problems, the mysterious origin of that problem is his earlier Brazilian orchid-collecting expedition which Silko relates to the global issue of white imperialism, especially in nonwhite countries, by suggesting parallels with Joseph Conrad's anti-imperialistic novel *Heart of Darkness*. Silko's revision of Conrad implies that Edward's experience on the Pará River in the Amazonian jungles partakes of the same corruption and destruction by capitalistic-imperialism that Conrad portrayed through his greedy white ivory-hunters along the Congo River in the African jungles.

Silko's version of Conrad's story begins with the seemingly innocent purpose of collecting specimens of rare Brazilian orchids. Edward knows that "Sun priests of the Maya reputedly held the orchid sacred because it invariably bloomed on the autumnal equinox," but his commercial interests outweigh any concern for the orchid's habitat or cultural significance: "Flowers of the gods! He could imagine the ads in magazines now" (373). What is gradually revealed is that the lucrative possibilities of the orchid-mania sweeping through western civilization have motivated a group of rich investors to gain control of the orchid market by burning down the remaining orchid fields after Edward collects his prime specimens. Trying to escape the fire, Edward breaks his leg, which provides him an excuse for his impotency, and is left for dead by the other members of the expedition who were also using his project to hide their own illegal activities—collecting the rubber-tree specimens needed to revitalize the rubber plantations in Britain's Far Eastern colonies. What is more, the entire project seems to have been secretly approved by a collaboration of British and American government officials and well-known botanical institutions. Edward unexpectedly survives, but then is the only one arrested for smuggling by the Brazilian authorities, and he loses most of his own investment in the project when, after his release, a three-day storm destroys the orchid specimens he still has in his possession.

This failed project marks the beginning of the end for Edward. Never again does he have a successful expedition, but he fails to recognize that his participation in the destruction of the rare wild orchid "paradise" is what rendered him spiritually impotent as far as nature is concerned as well as unable to physically consummate his marriage with Hattie, who wants to have children. He has, in effect, been cursed by the nature gods, but fails to understand it even when his next expedition is aborted by hurricane-like storms and he is confronted in the marketplace by the mysterious and frightening figure of the "Black Indian of Tampico":

> Suddenly a huge blue face appeared in the window and Edward could not help but jump back. The old woman's long tangled hair and her ample chest and arms all had been painted a bright blue that emphasized the woman's Maya features. . . . Her glittering black eyes fastened on his and he felt beads of sweat form above his lip and across his forehand.

The sailors believe she is the daughter of "the African spirits and the Maya spirits" who cause storms when angered (89, 90).

Edward is particularly bothered by the feeling that this angry manifestation of a multicultural storm goddess "knew him and she had hated him for a long time" (90), and with the failures of his next two expeditions, the last one resulting in his death, the reader is, indeed, left with the uncanny sense that an angry goddess has worked out an exemplary revenge on this representative capitalist-imperialist for his "crimes" against nature and women. However, at his death, a strange pietá emerges as Edward's fading consciousness fuses his orchid expedition memories with the blue-face of the Black Indian of Tampico, creating Silko's version of Morrison's Mother Piedade: "He drifted off on the Pará River once more, his head rested on gardenia blossoms in the big Negress's lap in the canoe; when he looked up at her face it was sky blue"—a surprising image of reconciliation with the dark maternal in death (429).

Neo-Gnosticism in the Novel

The neo-Gnostic themes of the novel are most obviously developed in Hattie's contrasting response to the garden of the snake goddess. As a young single woman preparing for an academic program of advanced studies, Hattie had proposed writing a thesis on "The Female Principle in the Early Church" based on her research of the old texts of the Gnostic heretics who taught her about "the Illumined Ones, those to whom Jesus appeared and whom he instructed in secrets not revealed" to the church authorities and who introduced her to "the Mother as the mythic eternal Silence and Grace, who is before all things and is incorruptible Wisdom, Sophia" (231, 100–101). The results of this scandalous thesis proposal were that it was rejected on the grounds of "unreliable" sources, her fellow student tried to sexually assault her because he assumed that "freethinkers" are also "libertines," and Hattie sought refuge from both in a marriage with Edward Palmer.

Hattie's awakening consciousness as she progresses from depression and self-doubt to illuminated revelation is facilitated by the breakthrough insight she experiences after viewing Laura's gardens. Like Morrison's Consolata after she loses Mary Magna or daughter Sophia lost in the darkness, Hattie sleeps a lot after she loses her place in academe, but she is visited by a dream of glowing lights that puzzle her. In England, directed by her subconscious instincts, she finds herself sleepwalking in Aunt Bronwyn's garden of the ancient sacred stones where she hears a knocking sound and feels enveloped by a luminous light: "Hattie felt such joy she wept" (250). Later, after touring Laura's garden of the snake goddess and hearing Laura's tale about the white snake goddess who is surrounded by a dazzling light, Hattie is able to make a half-conscious connection that transforms the "sinful" snake of Christianity into the lifegiving symbol of the goddess:

> Hattie drifted off to sleep recalling the pictures and statues of the Blessed Virgin Mary standing on a snake. Catechism classes taught Mary was killing the snake, but after seeing the [snake goddess] figures in the rain garden, she thought perhaps the Virgin with the snake was based on a figure from earlier times" (306).

Hattie's complete breakthrough occurs in a climatic scene that encompasses three unorthodox revisions of traditional Christianity: the neo-Gnostic, the folk-Christian, and the Native American messianic. In Corsica on the last leg of their European tour, Hattie, the privileged white woman, and Indigo, the Native American child, join a group of Corsican peasant families who, much to the dismay of the orthodox Church authorities, have gathered before a local schoolhouse wall where the peasants joyously witness the shining image of the Virgin Mary. Simultaneously, Indigo sees glittering snowflakes swirling around Ghost Dancers amid whom appear the Indian messiah and his mother, while the fully awake Hattie, "her heart beating faster," witnesses "a faint glow" that "grew brighter with a subtle iridescence that steadily intensified into a radiance of pure color that left her breathless, almost dizzy" (321). What links these three responses is that they all focus on the "feminine principle" historically subordinated or suppressed by orthodox Christianity, yet all three groups image that principle differently, depending on their cultural and class backgrounds. The Corsicans free the Virgin Mary from the institutional constraints of the Church—that subordinates her to her son, and Indigo's messiah and mother are Native Americans who are co-equal and bring the message of renewal rather than sin and repentance. Hattie's vision is the most abstract, but represents the light of personal illumination that leads to gnosis, or Sophia-Wisdom.

To Silko, this multicultural revelation scene embodies an important lesson about maintaining cultural differences even while recognizing the commonalities of different spiritual traditions. That sameness-within-difference will be demonstrated in Hattie's and Indigo's choices by the end of the novel. Hattie will finally decide that her true spiritual home is in the gardens of "Old Europe," so she will return to England to live with her Aunt Bronwyn and maintain her friendship with Laura and her Italian gardens of the snake goddess. In contrast, Indigo will heed the call of the Big Snake for her to return home to the maternal gardens in the dunes, the dream she had after touring Laura's snake goddess garden.

The Goddess's Paradise Found

The final image of the novel is not "paradise found," but rather "paradise renewed and revised." Indigo discovers that Old Snake has died a victim of senseless destruction by "evil" intruders who have also chopped down Grandma Fleet's apricot trees. However, she is reunited with the new mother-child dyad—the mixed-race Sister Salt and her mixed-race baby—and there are signs that the desert garden is renewing itself, a process aided by the human inhabitants. Old Snake's "beautiful daughter" appears and drinks at the same desert pool, new sprouts begin growing from the healthy roots in the sandy soil over Grandma Fleet's grave, and soon the gardens are flourishing with a new crop of the "little madonnas," the innumerable African gladioli hybridized in Italy and now being bred by Indigo who discovers that they are not only beautiful and symbolic, but also edible (419). And this process of renewal is all taking place under the celestial sign of the snake goddess, a Native American presence Indigo had not remembered until her return to the dune gardens of Grandma Fleet: "Yes, the eye of the big snake was watching out for them—that's what Grandma said. The wide band of bright stars was her belly and chest, though of course she was much too big to be seen from earth" (323).

As suggested by the novels of Morrison and Silko, contemporary writers are greatly attracted to goddess themes and exhibit considerable knowledge about a number of different cultural traditions that they often freely mix and match. These goddess themes may also be combined with feminist or multicultural analyses of the role of gender and race in society or with ecological concerns about the destructive values of western civilization, which continues to exploit or subordinate women, nature, and "others" in the name of progress and profit. The neo-Gnostic plot identified in Morrison's and Silko's novels is one contemporary response to these concerns, but the fictional goddesses created do not simply repeat the past. To rewrite the Sophia-story of the soul's loss of and search for its maternal home, magical realist texts by contemporary novelists explore women's spirituality by employing eclectic, syncretic, and multicultural approaches to the construction of new manifestations of the Great Mother.

Notes

1. Greta Gaard and Patrick D. Murphy, introduction to *Ecofeminist Literary Criticism: Theory, Interpretation, Pedagogy*, ed. Gaard and Murphy (Urbana: University of Illinois Press, 1998), 3.

2. Toni Morrison, *Paradise* (New York: Plume, 1997), 3.

3. Ibid., 318.

4. Anne Baring and Jules Cashford, *The Myth of the Goddess: Evolution of an Image* (London: Penguin Books, 1991), 619. Subsequent page numbers appear in the text.

5. Morrison, *Paradise,* 226. Subsequent page numbers appear in the text.

6. Baring, *Myth of the Goddess*, 647.

7. "Our Lady of Aparecida," http://marypages.com/LadyAparecida.htm.

8. Morrison, *Paradise*, 285.

9. Zita Nunes, *Cannibal Democracy: Race and Representation in the Literature of the Americas* (Minneapolis: University of Minnesota Press, 2008), 171–172.

10. La Vinia Delois Jennings, *Toni Morrison and the Idea of Africa* (Cambridge: Cambridge University Press, 2008), 71.

11. Ibid., 169.

12. Morrison, *Paradise*, 244. Subsequent page numbers appear in the text.

13. "Iemonja/Olukun," http://www.swarthmore.edu/Humanities/ychirea1/yemaya.html#yemaya.

14. Shirley A. Stave, "The Master's Tools: Morrison's Paradise and the Problem of Christianity," in *Toni Morrison and the Bible: Contested Intertextualities*, ed. Shirley A. Stave (New York: Peter Lang Publishing, 2006), 227.

15. W. B. Yeats, "The Second Coming," in *The Collected Works of W. B. Yeats*, Vol. 1: *The Poems*, ed. Richard J. Finneran (New York: Scribner, 1997), 189.

16. Morrison, *Paradise*, 311.

17. Mary Magoulick, "Landscapes of Miracles and Matriarchy in Silko's *Gardens in the Dunes*," in *Reading Leslie Marmon Silko: Critical Perspectives through Gardens in the Dunes,* ed. Laura Coltelli (Pisa, Italy: Pisa University Press, 2007), 21; and Terre Ryan, "The 19th-Century Garden: Imperialism, Subsistence, and Subversion in Leslie Marmon Silko's *Gardens in the Dunes*," *Studies in American Indian Literatures* 19, no. 3 (Fall 2007): 115.

18. Leslie Marmon Silko, *Gardens in the Dunes: A Novel* (New York: Simon and Schuster, 1999), 15. Subsequent page numbers appear in the text.

19. Baring, *Myth of the Goddess*, 105.

20. Ibid., 49–71.

21. Silko, *Gardens in the Dunes,* 243, 237. Subsequent page numbers appear in the text.

Bibliography

Baring, Anne, and Jules Cashford. *The Myth of the Goddess: Evolution of an Image.* London: Penguin Books, 1991.

Gaard, Greta, and Patrick D. Murphy, eds. *Introduction to Ecofeminist Literary Criticism: Theory, Interpretation, Pedagogy.* Urbana: University of Illinois Press, 1998.

"Iemonja/Olukun." http://www.swarthmore.edu/Humanities/ychirea1/yemaya.html#yemaya (accessed July 15, 2010).

Jennings, La Vinia Delois. *Toni Morrison and the Idea of Africa.* Cambridge: Cambridge University Press, 2008.

Magoulick, Mary. "Landscapes of Miracles and Matriarchy in Silko's Gardens in the Dunes." In *Reading Leslie Marmon Silko: Critical Perspectives through Gardens in the Dunes,* ed. Laura Coltelli, 21–36. Pisa, Italy: Pisa University Press, 2007.

Morrison, Toni. *Paradise.* New York: Plume, 1997.

Nunes, Zita. *Cannibal Democracy: Race and Representation in the Literature of the Americas.* Minneapolis: University of Minnesota Press, 2008.

"Our Lady of Aparecida." http://marypages.com/LadyAparecida.htm (accessed July 15, 2010).

Ryan, Terre. "The 19th-Century Garden: Imperialism, Subsistence, and Subversion in Leslie Marmon Silko's Gardens in the Dunes." *Studies in American Indian Literatures* 19, no. 3 (Fall 2007): 115–132.

Silko, Leslie Marmon. *Gardens in the Dunes: A Novel.* New York: Simon and Schuster, 1999.

Stave, Shirley A. "The Master's Tools: Morrison's Paradise and the Problem of Christianity." In *Toni Morrison and the Bible: Contested Intertextualities,* ed. Shirley A. Stave, 215–231. New York: Peter Lang Publishing, 2006.

Yeats, W. B. *The Collected Works of W. B. Yeats,* Vol. 1: *The Poems,* ed. Richard J. Finneran. New York: Scribner, 1997.

18

Audre Lorde's Seboulisa: Muse for the Death Journey

Sharon L. Barnes

When confronted with her own mortality in the form of a malignant tumor in her breast, which later developed into metastatic breast cancer, Audre Lorde set out to record her reactions in poetry, essays, and a journal which she published in two editions, *The Cancer Journals* in 1980 and *A Burst of Light* in 1988. The thoughts recorded in the journals and in her late poetry range from diatribes against the medical establishment's emphasis on prosthesis to meditations on the meaning of living with an intimate knowledge of death. Lorde's late work extends and broadens themes that consumed her early work, giving her political activism in the areas of rights for people of color, for women, and for lesbians and gays an urgency and clarity that mark the power of her vision, what Alice Walker called "her cool stare back into the eyes of death."[1] Though as Lorde said, "I would never have chosen this path," the result of her open-eyed confrontation of death and dying is more than a record; it is a challenge, a set of insights that offer all those who follow her words a model for expanding the spiritual, political, and personal meaning of our lives.[2]

Lorde's late poetry offers not only some truly excellent modern feminist ruminations on death, but also a unique window on Lorde's spiritual vision, particularly how Lorde focused on the African goddess Seboulisa as the muse of her death journey, and how she fused her use of Seboulisa with other African goddesses in a fairly traditional African/indigenous "ancestor worship" practice with a more unique, personal pantheon that included

Figure 18.1 The American poet Audre Lorde employed an African goddess, Sebou-lisa, as an alter-ego in her work. (Photograph courtesy Spelman College.)

herself and other powerful women in what can be seen as her "mathematics" of spirituality. It is these two points, the presence of Seboulisa as a spiritual partner in the death journey, and the presence of not only the African ancestors in herself, but also other strong women and earlier versions of herself, that make her late poems a magnificent challenge to those of us who read and use her work.

Lorde first traveled to Africa in 1974 and, partly as a consequence of that experience, became a lifelong student of African goddess spirituality. According to Alexis De Veaux's biography of Lorde entitled *Warrior Poet*, Lorde felt that she had found a spiritual center in Dahomey. De Veaux explains:

> There, in the synthesis of Yoruba and Dahomean deities, she found what she believed was the religion of her foremothers and her spiritual connection to them. She found Seboulisa, the goddess of Abomey . . . who was worshipped as "the mother goddess of all." She found Oshumare, the Yoruba rainbow-snake deity, who signified unity between aggression and compassion. Oshumare was also known as *Da Ayido Hwedo* to the Fon people of Dahomey, for

whom the deity signified the union of female and male energies. . . . She found Mawu-Lisa, the highest deity of the Fon, whose combination of female (*Mawu*) and male (*Lisa*) aspects represented the union of the Moon and the Sun as a Fon ideal.

For Lorde, the spiritual knowledge of Dahomey revealed the connections binding the deities of Dahomey to the Yoruba pantheon, which had traveled with and been transformed by the spiritual practices of African captives throughout the African diaspora.[3]

De Veaux's conclusion, that Lorde spiritually "construct[ed] her own version of "Africa reblended" once she got back home, is borne out in much of her poetry, particularly in the poems she wrote about death and dying.[4] This reading of Lorde is affirmed by Jacqueline de Weaver in *Mythmaking and Metaphor in Black Women's Fiction*; in her exploration of Greek mythology in black women's writing, de Weaver notes Lorde's use of African mythology as well: "A striking example of the triangle of traditions emerges in the poetry of the poet Audre Lorde, who consciously reclaims mythological figures from West Africa as living entities in her poems, written from a Black-American as well as a feminist point of view."[5] Lorde not only embraced the West African mythological figures in her work, but also feminist icons and other strong women, including herself.

Immediately after her mastectomy in 1978, Lorde expressed a desire to create an archive of her physical and emotional responses to her illness as a part of her political calling to break silences, to "piece together that chunk of my recent past, so that I, or anyone else in need or desire, can dip into it at will if necessary to find the ingredients with which to build a wider construct. That is an important function of the telling of experience."[6] It is this "use" of her experience that comes not just from her perception of herself as a writer, but also from her developing personal theology, through the African/indigenous traditions of ancestor honoring.[7] As explored in *African Religion: The Moral Traditions of Abundant Life*,

> it is not possible to grasp the meaning of the religious foundations of Africa without going through the "thought-area" occupied by the ancestors. . . . The operating principle is that of presence. The ancestors, though dead, are present and continue to influence life in their erstwhile communities on earth; indeed, they are expected to do so. The presence of the dead is assumed and invoked when the life of the tribe is threatened with disaster."[8]

Lorde's final volume of poems, entitled *The Marvelous Arithmetics of Distance*, contains some of the pieces that establish a "mathematics" that utilizes but goes beyond the traditional African/indigenous concept of the presence of the ancestors in daily life to a self-conscious calling of not just familial or genetic ancestors, but of feminist activist peers and other ancestors for use in the final phase of her earthly journey. In the spiritual mathematics Lorde invokes when her life is threatened, the power of the ancestors takes on a feminist, personal, and Americanized twist; she summons and utilizes Seboulisa and other African deities to be sure, but she also consistently calls upon powerful women from her various American communities, as well as all previous aspects of herself, her life experiences, and the various and sometimes conflicting identities that made up her life, for help. This mathematics fascinates, challenges, moves, and spiritually nourishes her and, ultimately, her readers, which is part of Lorde's intended "use" of her work.

Essays and journal entries reveal the strength of Lorde's commitment to speaking her truth about both life and death as a part of her politics of transformation, offering a demonstration her growing devotion to Seboulisa as a spiritual anchor. Lorde wants to use the time that she has left to document the way of her passing, for use by others later, just as she had challenged readers earlier through her coming out about her sexuality and about her breast cancer and mastectomy. She begins to understand that, long after readers can no longer hear her actual voice, we will continue to seek her written counsel, just as she is summoning Seboulisa and other strong women for her journey. A journal entry from several years into her illness takes up the theme of her literary estate and ties it, as Lorde so often does, to issues of speech, politics, living life fully and openly, and her community. Especially relevant in this particular entry is her entreaty to Seboulisa, the goddess who she understands as the muse for her death-journey.

November 6, 1986
New York City

Black mother goddess, salt dragon of chaos, Seboulisa, Mawu. Attend me, hold me in your muscular flowering arms, protect me from throwing any part of myself away.

Women who have asked me to set these stories down are asking me for my air to breathe, to use in their future, are courting me back to my life as a warrior. Some offer me their bodies, some their enduring patience, some a separate fire, and still others, only a naked need whose face is all too familiar. It is the need to give voice to the complexities of living with cancer, outside of the tissue-thin assurance that they "got it all," or that the changes we have wrought in our lives will insure that cancer never reoccurs. And it is a need to give voice to living with cancer outside of that numbing acceptance of death as a resignation waiting after fury and before despair.

There is nothing I cannot use somehow in my living and my work, even if I would never have chosen it on my own, even if I am livid with fury at having to choose. Not only did nobody ever say it would be easy, nobody ever said what faces the challenges would wear. The point is to do as much as I can of what I came to do before they nickel and dime me to death. . . .

So I feel a sense of triumph as I pick up my pen and say yes I am going to write again from the world of cancer and with a different perspective—that of living with cancer in an intimate daily relationship. Yes, I'm going to say plainly, six years after my mastectomy, in spite of drastically altered patterns of eating and living, and in spite of my self-conscious living and increased self-empowerment, and in spite of my deepening commitment to using myself in the service of what I believe, and in spite of all my positive expectations to the contrary, I have been diagnosed as having cancer of the liver, metastasized from breast cancer.

This fact does not make my last six years of work any less vital or important or necessary. The accuracy of that diagnosis has become less important than how I use the life I have.[9]

In this entry, Lorde's integration of the issues that have preoccupied her early writing is stunningly complete. Conscious of the need to attend to her emotional well-being regardless of her physical health, aware of the importance of not just her words but her presence on the women who have looked to her for guidance and strength, Lorde is also connecting with the strength that such sharing engenders in her. Bent on "using" the pain as well as the pleasure in her life, she will use her resistance to death just as she has used her resistance to the cultural push toward the false universalization of difference, toward plasticized eroticism, and toward collusive silence, as an opportunity to seek and speak truth from within. And of course, such a truth will be shared, "in the service of what I believe," the creation of a new, "more possible" world. Such sharing is also an invitation to her readers to take up the practice for ourselves, to invoke her energy as we read, speak, and share her words, for strength when we are embattled, or in danger, or simply in need of spiritual sustenance.

Several of Lorde's poems take up and integrate the themes of the journals: the significance, the difficulty, and the transformative potential of speaking in and to the face of death, the value of meeting experiences fully, head on, and the necessity of seeing her spiritual connection to women engaged in revolutionary transformation. Looking at the close of her life open-eyed, Lorde speaks what she sees and feels as a means of experiencing it all, even the pain, more fully. Given Lorde's commitment to complete and "deep feeling in all aspects of our lives," as explained in her essay "Uses of the Erotic: The Erotic as Power," her extension of this eros even to her own death is not surprising.[10] Exploring death is as much a part of her power and political responsibility as is her experience of great joy, so she wants to meet the experience without the "looking away" that she believes characterizes so much of "european-american" emotional experience. She states this aim beautifully in the preface to her final poem, "Today is Not the Day," where she notes that she cannot just sit by and watch herself dying, "staring death in her face" and only ask for a new name to call it, a way to avoid what is happening. Rather, she claims, she is not afraid to say baldly that she is dying; however, she asserts, she does "not want to do it/looking the other way."[11]

The self-examination and extension of this analysis to political transformation that readers have grown so accustomed to in Lorde is not shelved in her poetic ruminations on death. In fact, her exploration of silence continues as she examines how an intimate awareness of death influences her speech. Particularly moving in its awareness of her mortality and in its merciless investigation of her power to speak is the poem "Seasoning," which was published in 1978, just a year after Lorde's initial biopsy. She opens with the self-interrogating question, "What am I ready to lose in this advancing summer?" which indicates both her growing awareness of the limitations of her time on earth, for an advanced summer is quick to give way to fall and winter, and her knowledge that such awareness imposes decisions upon her about what is important and necessary in her life.[12] Her immediate response to the thought of her days trickling away is typical of Lorde in its personally demanding expectation of herself as a political warrior-poet; she must "chew up time" (259), enjoying every last moment just as she must investigate how her experiences are influencing her ability "to speak the truths for which I am still seeking."[13] As she consumes time, she asserts, each individual moment will "expand" in what she calls "an emotional mathematic" that encompasses the sensory details of every single moment since her birth.[14]

Especially remarkable because it was written early after Lorde's initial investigation of her mortality so movingly documented in her essay, "The

Transformation of Silence into Language and Action," "Seasoning" incorporates several of the themes that continued to dominate Lorde's thinking, the difficulty and importance of speech, the political necessity of fully experiencing the sensual, erotic moments of life, and, significantly, the "use" of her earlier "selves" in the work that remains for her to do. In these opening lines where she expresses her desire to consume the time she has left in an expansive way that allows her to taste, feel, and smell her own history, Lorde's "emotional mathematic" connects her past to the present so that each moment, lived and experienced to its fullest, brings her past to bear on her present and, ultimately, connects Lorde to what she elsewhere called the powerful wellspring of women's emotional experience, which she experiences as political, personal, and spiritual nourishment. Thus Lorde rejects the "european-centered" powerlessness associated with illness and death in favor of an African-based, feminist-inflected, woman-centered celebration of the power that awareness of mortality brings. This articulation of the complex equation of interactions—the "mathematics"—of past and present, including in Lorde's conception her past selves and the lives of her spiritual sister-warriors before her, remained a useful metaphor for Lorde until the end of her life.

While in "Seasoning" the mathematic includes moments of her own life, later works expand this spiritual equation even further. In the poem "October," Lorde prays to Seboulisa for help in "remember[ing] what I have learned" and in "attend[ing] with passion these tasks at my hand for doing," and analyzes her mortality in terms of her work.[15] She asserts that some spirits live on in water, some in the entrails of a snake, and since she exists on a "wild bridge," suspended between life and death, she wonders, "how shall I return?" Here, questioning how her spirit will live is an interrogation not only of the afterlife, but also of the meaning and value of her work. She prays to Seboulisa for the gifts of physical and spiritual nonviolence and asks that she not die before she learns the name of the tree she is sitting under, evidence of her balancing between spiritual concerns and an ongoing earthly interest in the natural world. Along with her focus on observing, experiencing, and speaking about the world around her, the world of her senses, Lorde is conscious of her own legacy as a writer, and just as she vowed early in her career to "never leave her pen lying in someone else's blood" (360), here she prays for Seboulisa to carry her heart to a shore that her feet "will not shatter" (346). She is concerned about how her work impacts others and how it will represent her after she is dead. Expressed as an entreaty to Seboulisa to "not let [her] die/still/needing to be a stranger" (346), Lorde prays for help in maintaining intimacy with herself, her work, and those to

whom her work connects her. Such an entreaty demonstrates Lorde's awareness of connection as significant to her spiritual vision, established here
through her awareness of eminent death.

Of the many examples of this strategy in Lorde's late poetry, the poem
"Call" is especially interesting because it offers a powerful example of the
spiritual and contemporary activist "ancestor summoning/honoring" strategy
and also because it is a beautiful, but not very well-known poem by Lorde.
"Call" is a prayer to the "Rainbow Serpent, Aido Hwedo" (418), whom
Lorde defines as "a representation of all ancient divinities who must be worshipped but whose names and faces have been lost in time" (419). In "Call"
Lorde provides a powerful example of the two spiritual strategies outlined
here, the summoning of Seboulisa and other deities as death muse, and the
"mathematics" of their spiritual energy combined with her own and that of
other powerful women, for use by her and, by extension, by those of us who
come after her and read her words. In the poem, she conflates her past and
present with the experiences of other powerful women, including "the
woman who scrubs the capitol toilets" (417), anonymous sons and daughters,
Oya, Seboulisa, Mawu, Afrekete, Rosa Parks, Fannie Lou Hamer, Assata
Shakur, Yaa Asantewa, her mother, and Winnie Mandela. This poem also
discusses her writing as part of her spiritual calling, hoping her life will be
"worth its ending" (418), that the commitment she has made to speaking her
truth, that the risks she has taken—for she has "offered up" (418) safety—
will be part of a positive transformation of the world she is preparing to leave
behind, even as she understands her role in the struggle to make it better.[16]

"Call" opens with an invocation and an acknowledgment of the history
that has been lost, or to be more precise, robbed, as she calls to the Aido
Hwedo, "holy ghost woman" who has been "stolen out of [her] name"
(417). Taking care to respect the ancestors, even those whose names and
faces we can no longer remember, Lorde asserts that we must summon all
of the entities and energies that are necessary for the work that we must do.
Praying that we "not shatter any altar" as we piece together our personal
and spiritual histories, Lorde creates a caring, feminist, egalitarian scenario in
which women warriors are creating spiritual weapons from "scraps of our
histories" that will be hybrid versions of those ancestral histories as we come
together in community with each other. Not in vaulted cathedrals, but "on
worn kitchen stools and tables," women will gather to remember and honor
the ancestors, who she implies have never really been forgotten, even if
we no longer know their faces (417). Not only does she invoke the holy
ghost mother, but she understands that she and, by extension, we too are
holy, descendants of the Mother, like "your sister's youngest daughter," and

we are all listening. Lorde calls the goddess as she assures her that neither she nor her descendants have forgotten to worship her; thus we are all calling, claiming, as Lorde does in a chorus at the end of each stanza: "Aido Hwedo is coming."

Turning her focus toward her own personal circumstances, and recognizing the significant changes that are eminent on her horizon, Lorde names herself "a Black woman turning," toward death, it is clear. Reviewing the dangers of her experience, from external "seductions" to internal, "self-slaughter," Lorde notes that women both "war" and "endure" as we strive for spiritual and political wholeness, for "we do not choose all our rituals." Lorde affirms connection as an important aspect of her spiritual vision, for she has "offered up the safety of separations" in this "call" and in her work, political and poetic. Asserting her identity as a Black woman who is struggling with her mortality, "stripped down/and praying," Lorde once again calls "Aido Hwedo" to help her in the death journey and in the political work with which she's been engaged, and she also recalls her past experience, as she prays that "her whole life has been an altar/worth its ending." Even those women who are not yet connected to this ancient spirituality are included in Lorde's vision, as she asserts that she "may be a weed in the garden" of those women "still/trapped in their season," but they, too, call out the name of Aido Hwedo, summoning her. Citing Thandt Modise, "winged girl of Soweto," an anti-Apartheid activist, Lorde also recalls the political component of this spiritual journey (417, 418).[17]

The call closes with a confluence of Lorde's spiritual, political, and poetic impulses, calling powerful women, from feminist and political activists to her mother, and recommitting herself to her work of breaking silence. Using the communal "we," Lorde reminds us that we are "learning by heart/what has never been taught." As we invoke the ancient Goddess by her various names, "Oya Seboulisa Mawu Afrekete," we also simultaneously mourn those who have given in to despair and silence under patriarchy, who are "lost to the false hush of sorrow," while celebrating and summoning those women who have not given in: "Rosa Parks, Fannie Lou Hamer" (American civil rights activists), "Assata Shakur and Yaa Ansantewa" (exiled Black Panther activist and exiled Queen of the Ashanti people in Ghana), "my mother and Winnie Mandela" (Lorde's own mother, mentioned with the then-wife of South African liberation leader Nelson Mandela) (418, 419). Invoking all, Lorde calls Aido Hwedo, older versions of herself, and her feminist foremothers and daughters in a call that is at once a cry for help in her transition through death and a summons to those of us who continue this, her work.[18]

With all these figures "singing in her throat," Lorde makes use of their spiritual energy on her own "fire-tongued" journey. While she entreats the Mother for a loosening of her tongue or a lighter burden, Lorde continues to assert the coming of Aido Hwedo, "the holy ghosts' linguist," noting that "one iron silence" has already been broken, in this call (418, 419). Fittingly, Lorde ends her "Call" with a return to her work as a poet, a seer and a speaker who condemns silence, for, as she has consistently asserted—most famously in "The Transformation of Silence into Language and Action"— "there are so many silences to be broken."[19]

Aido Hwedo is coming.

Notes

Portions of this chapter are adapted from Sharon L. Barnes, "Marvelous Arithmetics: Prosthesis, Speech, and Death in the Late Work of Audre Lorde," *Women's Studies* 37, no. 7 (January 2008): 769–789. Reprinted by permission of the publisher (Taylor & Francis Ltd., http://www.tandf.co.uk/journals).

1. Alice Walker, *Anything We Love Can Be Saved: A Writer's Activism* (New York: Random House, 1997), 82.

2. Audre Lorde, *The Cancer Journals* (San Francisco: Spinster's Inc., 1980), 77.

3. Alexis DeVeaux, *Warrior Poet: A Biography of Audre Lorde* (New York: Norton, 2004), 151.

4. Ibid., 151.

5. Jacqueline de Weaver, *Mythmaking and Metaphor in Black Women's Fiction* (New York: St. Martin's Press, 1991), 26.

6. Lorde, *Cancer Journals*, 53.

7. Thank you to the participants of the "International Women and Spirituality Conference" (Cleveland Spring 2009), for this phrase, solving the language puzzle of moving conceptually from the common African tradition of "ancestor worship" to a hybrid version more fitting Lorde's spiritual practice.

8. Laurenti Magesa, *African Religion: The Moral Traditions of Abundant Life* (Maryknoll, NY: Orbis Books, 1997), 48.

9. Audre Lorde, *A Burst of Light: Essays* (Ithaca, NY: Firebrand Books, 1988), 111–112.

10. Audre Lorde, *Sister Outsider: Essays and Speeches* (Freedom, CA: The Crossing Press, 1984), 57.

11. Audre Lorde, *The Collected Poems of Audre Lorde* (New York, Norton, 1997), 471.

12. Ibid., 259.

13. Lorde, *Sister Outsider*, 41.

14. Lorde, *Collected Poems*, 259.

15. Audre Lorde, "Uses of the Erotic: The Erotic as Power," in *Sister Outsider*, 54.

16. Lorde, *Collected Poems*, 346.

17. An online history of Nelson Mandela offers a brief biography of "Thandi" Modise, a young, anti-Apartheid activist in the 1970s, who is most likely the referent here: "THANDI MODISE: As a teenager, Thandi Modise crossed the borders into Angola to train as a guerilla soldier for the emerging military wing of the ANC, Umkonto we Sizwe (MK). Having undergone military and political training, she was the first woman sent back to fight and organize in the townships. Her fellow soldiers named a machine gun 'The Thandi' in her honor. Modise has recently served prominent roles in the ANC, the Women's League, and Parliament" (Radio Diaries, Inc.)

18. Danuta Bois, "Yaa Asantewaa," Distinguished Women of Past and Present, 1998, http://www.distinguishedwomen.com/biographies/yaa-asantewaa.html (accessed June 5, 2009).

19. Lorde, *Sister Outsider*, 44.

Bibliography

Bois, Danuta. "Yaa Asantewaa." Distinguished Women of Past and Present, 1998. http://www.distinguishedwomen.com/biographies/yaa-asantewaa.html (accessed June 5, 2009).

DeVeaux, Alexis. *Warrior Poet: A Biography of Audre Lorde*. New York: Norton, 2004.

de Weaver, Jacqueline. *Mythmaking and Metaphor in Black Women's Fiction*. New York: St. Martin's Press, 1991.

Lorde, Audre. *A Burst of Light: Essays*. Ithaca, NY: Firebrand, 1988.

Lorde, Audre. *The Cancer Journals*. San Francisco: Spinster's Inc., 1980.

Lorde, Audre. *The Collected Poems of Audre Lorde*. New York: Norton, 1997.

Lorde, Audre. *Sister Outsider: Essays and Speeches*. Freedom, CA: Crossing Press, 1984.

Magesa, Laurenti. *African Religion: The Moral Traditions of Abundant Life*. Maryknoll, NY: Orbis Books, 1997.

Radio Diaries, Inc. "Mandela: An Audio History," http://www.radiodiaries.org/mandela/mpeople.html (accessed June 5, 2009).

Walker, Alice. *Anything We Love Can Be Saved: A Writer's Activism*. New York: Random House, 1997.

19

Sekhmet in America: The Heart of the Sun

Anne Key

The setting sun shines through the doorway of a temple, illuminating a large black statue. Footsteps sound as the priestess enters. She arranges wood and grasses in the fire pit, then lights candles and incense. The searing heat of the desert day quickly gives way to the cool, star-lit evening, and she looks over the hill to the place where the moon will rise. Dust and noise herald the arrival of cars; voices and laughter punctuate the desert silence. The temple fills, the fire is lit, and the ritual to the Egyptian goddess Sekhmet in the American desert begins.

Founded in 1993, the Temple of Goddess Spirituality Dedicated to Sekhmet is one of the most established goddess temples in the United States. The temple, its features, and its story certainly hearken to ancient times. In keeping with the tradition of honoring deities with capital construction and clergy, the Temple of Goddess Spirituality Dedicated to Sekhmet was built through the benefaction of one whose life had been profoundly affected by a deity.

Genevieve Vaughan, philanthropist, feminist, peace activist, and author of the theory of the Gift Economy, was on a tour in Egypt with her husband in 1965. In Karnak in front of one of the great black statues of Sekhmet, her guide advised Genevieve that if she wanted something, she should ask the goddess and then offer her a promise. Knowing nothing of Sekhmet but having been unable to conceive, Genevieve asked for a child and promised in exchange to build the goddess a temple. Genevieve

Figure 19.1 In the American Southwest, an adobe structure built beside a nuclear test site honors the Egyptian goddess Sekhmet. Founded as a result of a personal vow, the temple attracts women and men from around the world for meditation and social action. (Photograph by Anne Key.)

conceived her first child within the week and went on to have three daughters. She never forgot her promise.[1]

Two decades later, while Genevieve was participating in peace and anti-nuclear demonstrations, the dream of building a temple in honor of Sekhmet took hold. She commissioned the design and construction of the Temple of Goddess Spirituality Dedicated to Sekhmet at a site frequently used by peace activists, only a few miles from the Nevada Nuclear Test Site. From its inception, Genevieve's intent was to establish a ritual space dedicated to honoring Sekhmet and other manifestations of the divine female; to engender an environment where women are spiritual leaders; and to create a setting devoted to the mothering principles of the Gift Economy, an economic theory that takes mothering as its example for a model of interchange, moving beyond the pattern of exchange to a paradigm of gift. She funded a priestess to live on the land and lead ritual. Her gift is a literal and figurative oasis in the desert.

In the Egyptian iconography, the goddess Sekhmet has the head of a lioness and the body of a woman (see Normandi Ellis's chapter in volume 1). Her name "Sekhmet" is derived from *sekhem*, meaning power, and *et* referring to female and thus means "female powerful one." Though Sekhmet is often characterized as a warrior goddess, she can more expansively be viewed as the manifestation of power, particularly female power. Her ancient symbolism and myths reverberate in her modern manifestation in the Nevada desert.

Symbolism and Meaning in Ancient and Modern Statuary

Exhibited in museums all over the world, the most famous representations of Sekhmet are statues carved from black stone that are truly larger-than-life at over seven feet tall. In some she is seated on a throne; in others she stands tall, holding a scepter. In all of these statues she is regal and commanding, the corporeal manifestation of female power. The figures are mesmerizing; they radiate an aura of noble authority and serene majesty.

These Egyptian statues of Sekhmet are carved from diorite, a black igneous stone. This fire-wrought rock hearkens to another of her names, "The Lady of the Flame." For Egyptians, the color black connoted two complementary aspects of the underworld—fertility and death. Black symbolized Egypt itself, as the word for black (*kem*) is the root for the name of its people (*kememu*/black people) and the land (*Kemet*/black land). The high iron content in Egyptian diorite not only gives the stone its black color but also adds to the sediment that contributes to the Nile's renowned fertility. The link of the color black with fertility was underscored with the rich fertile black soil the Nile delivered with its annual inundation of the land.

Signifying the powerful properties of fertility and death, black stone was often used for statues with healing, magical, and regenerative properties.[2] As the "Lady of Enchantments," Sekhmet is closely tied to magic and healing. A large solar disc balances on her head, identifying Sekhmet as a sun goddess and recalling her name "The Lady of the Horizon." In front of the solar disc is the uraeus, a rearing cobra poised to strike. The uraeus embodies the idea of power, power ready at a moment's notice, power that is as unstoppable as a cobra's strike. In this way, the uraeus harnesses and focuses the immense power of the sun.

The prominent snout and whiskers proclaim Sekhmet a lion, not a cat. The round ears atop her head are alert, and her wig and ceremonial collar emphasize her association with royalty. Sekhmet's face is encircled with a ruff, represented by small triangles like rays of the sun. This ruff, a typical feature of the lioness, should not be confused with the large mane of the male lion.[3]

A rosette pattern is inscribed on her nipples. The rosette has been associated with Regulus, the "shoulder star" of the constellation Leo as well as the pattern of the shoulder hair of lions. As the rosette is found on contemporaneous statues of other goddesses and women, it may represent the broader association with regeneration.[4] Its placement on the nipples coupled with its solar and stellar motifs emphasizes the rosette as a symbol with a strong maternal connection with life, rebirth and divine feeding.[5] On Sekhmet, the rosette is a reminder of the manifold aspects of female power, including regeneration and nurturance.

Sekhmet holds an ankh, the symbol of life that commonly represents the life force inherent in such things as water, food, and breath. The ankh is an intrinsically female symbol. This association is plainly evident in some ankhs that have a pubic triangle directly below the crossbar, with a dividing line down the base to differentiate legs.[6] In this instance, the circle of the ankh is undoubtedly the womb, with woman as the source of life and creation. The ankh is also a solar disc, reflecting the sun's life-giving properties and emphasizing Sekhmet's powers of creation.

Marsha Gomez, a Mexican/Native American artist, created the statue of Sekhmet inside the temple in Nevada, modeling it after the traditional seated Sekhmet, with a few differences reflecting her modern emanation. The statue of Sekhmet inside the temple in Nevada is seated. She is black and shining with her ears alert, the corporeal manifestation of female majesty and power. An ankh is clasped in her left hand; rosettes are inscribed on her nipples, hearkening to her name "Mother of All." With the head of a lioness and a woman's body, Sekhmet fittingly embodies all that is animal, human, and divine. Gomez captured her very human nature in the size of the statue. Instead of being larger than life, she is life-sized, a constant reminder of the divine within. Her very human and female nature is also exemplified in her bare breasts, one slightly larger than the other.

A poem examines the full aspect of female power embodied by Sekhmet:

She is Divine Connection
The Human Animal
The Woman Lion Snake
Birth Death Mother Healer Destroyer.

She is Sekhmet
Power Woman
The Sun.[7]

Names and Manifestations

The names and epithets of the ancient deities preserve their various characteristics. There are over a hundred Egyptian epithets attributed to Sekhmet, illustrating her multivalent representations: from healer to warrior, from protector and nurturer to bringer of disease. As the "Lady of Life" and the "Lady of Pestilence," Sekhmet was recognized as the origin of both healing and illness. She was the uncontrollable power of pestilence and disease, for diseases were her messengers. Moreover, she was the only force strong enough to resist them: "The sun goddess was evoked in times of illness because she was an all seeing eye able to detect the cause of illness, a mirror reflecting the soul's disease."[8] The clergy of Sekhmet, the "Uab," were famed as healers and surgeons, attributed with a comprehensive knowledge of the heart and circulation. The heart reflected the solar attributes of regeneration, and heart scarabs were placed on the chest of the deceased to manifest the revitalizing powers of the sun and to aid the transformation of the deceased.

As a deity who was named "More Powerful than the Gods," Sekhmet was the manifestation of power. She was considered the protector of royalty, in both maternal and political notions. She conceived the ruler, which positioned her as the protective mother.[9] For Queen Hatshepsut, Sekhmet embodied the power of a ruling female. And it was as the Eye of Ra that she was a symbol of heroism and strength, one who could protect the ruler in the face of rebellion.

In many instances, rulers both female and male regarded Sekhmet as the premier standard for power. In a flattering tribute, one ruler's power and influence in foreign lands were compared to "Sekhmet in a year of pestilence."[10] Other common examples of praise were comparisons such as "He is Sekhmet to foes who tread on his frontier" and he was "like Sekhmet in Her moment of rage."[11]

As with all spiritual traditions, the culture, land, history of the deity, and the supplicants themselves co-create the form and patterns of honoring. In the instance of the Nevada temple, the modern overlay of feminist goddess spirituality blends with ancient Egyptian rites in the honoring of Sekhmet. The priestesses of the Temple of Goddess Spirituality Dedicated to Sekhmet conceive new rites for this ancient goddess. Weaving the Egyptian names and epithets for Sekhmet into the modern Wicca format of calling the directions at the beginning of a ritual, Dr. Candace Kant, a priestess of the temple, created this Call of the Directions:

> In the South we call you, Sekhmet, Lady of Flame, whose essence is fire, Eye of the Sun. Powerful one who empowers us, ignite this sacred space with the embers of courage and strength.
>
> In the East we call you, Sekhmet, Lady of Fragrance, the Source of the Words of Power, at whose wish the arts were born. Fly into this sacred space with the hot desert wind and breathe into us your inspiration and laughter.
>
> In the West we call you, Sekhmet, Lady of Enchantments, who controls the waters of life. Flow into this sacred space, bring your healing waters. Let us drink deeply of your love.
>
> In the North we call you, Sekhmet, Mother of all the Gods who makest sound our bones. Mistress of life, Ancient One, root this sacred space in the rich soil of your protection.
>
> Above we call you, Sekhmet, Goddess of the Galaxies, Sparkling one, Keeper of the Divine Order, the Light beyond Darkness. Illuminate this sacred space.
>
> Below we call you, Sekhmet, Great One of the Place of the Appearance of Silence, Guide and Protectress from the perils of the Underworld, Guardian of the Gates of Life and Death; the Darkness beyond Light. Enfold us in this sacred space.
>
> Within we call you, Sekhmet, Lady of the Place of the Beginning of Time, One who was before the Gods were. Encircling one; Bringer of wisdom, awaken within us this sacred space.[12]

The priestesses of the temple compile contemporary names and epithets of Sekhmet. These names reflect the modern manifestations of this ancient goddess: "Reminder of the Sweetness of Life," "She Who Walks on Forests of Red Rose Petals," "She Who Is the Precious Flame of Hope," "Lady of the Silent Roar Within," "Truthseer," "She of Regal Clarity," "Heart of the Sun," and "The Elixir of Life."[13]

From Queen Hatshepsut to the modern supplicant in Nevada, the image and presence of Sekhmet evoke a multitude of highly individual responses to the idea of female power personified by a lioness. In a survey conducted by the temple inquiring about their views of Sekhmet, many responded that they, like the ancient Egyptians, connect with her power:

> I envision Her as a fierce lioness, whose body can take on the bright glare of the midday sun, gaining her the title Lady of

Flame. Another title that resonates is One Before Whom Evil Trembles. Righteous indignation, retribution, and justice are Her strengths.

I understand Her power and ask her to devour my discouraged feelings. I am not totally comfortable with Her. Yet.

I see and understand Sekhmet as a living force that carries the passions of huge cat, hot wind, internal growth and transformation. She has fed on parts of me that are no longer appropriate in my life. Things that are given or offered to Sekhmet are truly gone from my life. She has eaten my silence and my know/no it all at different times.

Some experience her power in a distinctly feminine aspect, as mother and protector:

I see her as motherly, protective, but not soft and gentle. She is an initiator of change. She presides over transitions and passages. She has absolutely no tolerance for illusion and falsehood. She is a bringer of truth and justice. If you ask her for something, and you really want it, and you are willing to be dedicated to what you want, work at it and make sacrifices, she will help you, although not always in the way you expected.

Sekhmet to me is strength and protection, the powerful lioness who protects her loved ones fiercely. She is beauty in the feline/feminine form and helps me to see those qualities within myself and others. She is about transformation and focus.

I see Sekhmet primarily as a strong protector willing to stand up for me and help me stand up for myself. I think about Her facing the test site calmly waiting for the time that someone will begin to see the error of the trends today and stop them, before She feels that She needs to do so. I'm not sure if I would have been patient for so long.[14]

As well, her priestesses have unique connections with her different aspects. Candace Ross, the fourth woman to serve as the temple priestess, describes her:

Sekhmet is 'She who was before the gods were.' She is 'Mom,' She is 'All.' She is the Heart of the Universe, the Great Cosmic Mother. Her power, Her beauty, love and compassion stretch beyond what any of us can define.[15]

And Candace Kant, also a priestess, describes her first encounter with Sekhmet at her temple:

> The temple was the most alive and sacred place I had ever experienced. I visited with a lizard who came to look me over. I sat on a large rock and watched the Earth breathe. I went inside and sat on the floor next to the west portal and gazed upon the face of Sekhmet. I knew I had seen Her before, but I didn't know when. She filled me with an overwhelming sense of peace and love.[16]

Temples Ancient and Modern

Sekhmet is featured prominently in the Temple of Mut at Karnak, near Luxor. It is at Karnak and the mortuary temple of Amenhotep III where the majority of her black majestic statues reside. Presently, some 200 statues of Sekhmet are *in situ* at Karnak, although there were over 700 there during excavations in the 19th century.[17] It is speculated that originally 730 of these giant diorite statues of Sekhmet were created, two for each day, granting protection each day and each night of the year.

Hatshepsut (1472–1457 BCE), the long-reigning female pharaoh, built the Temple of Mut at Karnak. During Hatshepsut's reign, Mut and Sekhmet were closely connected. "Hatshepsut demonstrated her veneration of this goddess (Mut), who characterized female possession of supreme authority by building her a temple of her own to the south of the Temple of Amun at Karnak." At Karnak, Mut is seen as the power and integrity of the state, as "female royal power deified."[18]

Encircling the three sides of the southernmost end of the Temple of Mut is an Isheru, a sacred crescent-shaped lake. Isherus were found throughout Egypt in association with the veneration of lioness goddesses, though the lake at the Temple of Mut is the only surviving one.[19] The Isheru may have served as a place to attract lions with the promise of water, or possibly even to accentuate that many of these lioness goddesses are associated with water. The Temple of Mut, rebuilt and expanded a number of times, was in use from the 13th century BCE until the Ptolemaic Dynasty (ending 330 BCE).

With the same thoughtfulness and attention to detail as the ancient temples, the Temple of Goddess Spirituality Dedicated to Sekhmet was built with spirituality, the landscape, and the environment in mind. The temple is an eco-friendly straw-bale structure, with four doorways open to the directions and a roof open to the sky. The open roof is crisscrossed with copper tubes filled with crystals in the shape of a seven-petaled lotus, forming a yantra-like image overhead.[20] This open-air temple is perfectly suited for the desert, allowing those who come to be fully immersed in the natural environment while sitting in a chapel-like setting.

Near the temple is a spring, calling to mind the sacred Isherus of ancient Egypt. Surrounded on three sides by property owned by the federal Bureau of Land Management, the temple and grounds are entwined together within the natural desert landscape, with mesquite and cactus, coyotes and jackrabbits. In spring, the intensely vivid fuchsia flowers of the pancake cactus lend their hue to the otherwise olive foliage. Rainfall is sparse, usually measuring less than five inches per year, and its rare arrival is heralded by the unforgettable scent of the creosote bush, whose fragrance instills a sense of refreshed hope. Unobstructed horizons set the stage for stunning daily sunrises and sunsets, and the night sky opens the cosmos to full view. The harsh yet rich desert landscape, the life-giving spring, and the brilliant sun echo the multiple aspects of Sekhmet. But it is the surrounding additional installations that deepen the temple's meaning.

Less than twenty miles northwest of the temple is the Nevada Test Site, where mushroom clouds from atomic testing were once celebrated and the risks of radiation repeatedly ignored. Due east lies a large prison complex, and to the north is Creech Air Force Base and over 4000 square miles of bombing range. The ground-shaking, window-rattling booms of exploding bombs and jets often disrupt the deep silence of the desert. Yucca Mountain, a proposed nuclear waste dump site, is just a bit farther north. Finally, forty miles south of the temple is Las Vegas, that monument to materialism and arguably the leader in the commodification of women's bodies.

In this beautiful temple, the statue of Sekhmet sits in the south corner, facing north and looking out toward the Nevada Test Site. The location of the temple is a testament to the modern manifestation of Sekhmet, for this sacred place dedicated to peace is in a place where one can never forget war.

Ancient Myths, Modern Reverberations

Relatively few myths mention Sekhmet, and the ones that do so mention her in her guise as the Eye of Ra. Of the many goddesses that manifested as the Eye of Ra, Sekhmet was the most notable. In ancient Egyptian, *Ra* was the word for the sun, and so the Eye of Ra was "the

Eye of the Sun." In this light she could be seen as a solar goddess, as in her name "The Sun Goddess of the Ennead," the Ennead being a group of ancient Egyptian deities. The Eye of Ra, considered stronger than all other deities, was always a goddess and was often seen in leonine form. The Eye was associated with a number of female deities, including Sekhmet, Hathor, Tefnut, Mut, Maat, Bastet, and Wadjet.

Just as the human eye sees with light and is the portal through which light enters the body, so the Eye of Ra was associated with the powers of the sun: light and creation as well as fire and the forces of destruction. Conversely, just as the human eye is associated with water through its salty tears, so the Eye is associated with water, especially the creative forces of salty water found in the ocean, the womb, and the tear.

Three myths about the Eye interweave and overlap, sharing characteristics and differences. They are all found in different texts, so these myths should not be seen as linear or congruent; however, they do provide an interesting and fuller portrait of the Eye and Sekhmet. In the first two myths, the Eye leaves Egypt. The Eye creates humanity in the first myth and sets out to destroy humanity in the third. The Eye's return to Egypt in the second and third myths is heralded with fanfare and joyous festivities.

In the first of these three myths, this version from the Book of Smiting Down Apophis, the Eye leaves Egypt following the deities Tefnut and Shu. Upon her return, the Eye is enraged to find that Ra created another Eye to take her place. Her tears of rage and grief form human beings. Ra then places the Eye on his forehead as the uraeus, where it rules over everything.[21]

In the second myth, often referred to as "The Distant Goddess," the Eye leaves Egypt and goes south to Nubia. Ra realizes that he is powerless without his Eye, so he sends an emissary to convince the Eye to return. Through much storytelling, cajoling, and charm, the Eye is persuaded to return. Upon the Eye's return, everyone rejoices and a great festival is given in her honor.[22] According to one text, upon return the Eye "has come to rest and has stopped in Isheru in Her form of Sekhmet." The Eye can be seen as the first feminine being, and the ensuing festival upon her return in both this myth and the following was celebrated as "the welcoming of a beneficial force for all of Egypt."[23]

The myth most commonly associated with Sekhmet is referred to as "The Destruction of Humanity" and is from the Book of the Heavenly Cow found on the walls of royal tombs from the 19th and 20th dynasties. This myth is considered to be one of the oldest Egyptian narratives. The

"Destruction of Humanity" myth opens with a group of humans rebelling against Ra, the aging solar god. Ra brings together a council of elder deities for advice. Among those attending is his Eye, who created humans. Nun, the primeval chaos, suggests that Ra send his Eye out against the humans who rebelled against his authority. The Eye, in the form of Hathor, goes to slay the human rebels that have fled to the desert. She slaughters the rebels and then returns to Ra, saying that she "overpowered mankind, and it was agreeable to my heart." And it is here that "Sekhmet came into being." Realizing that Sekhmet will destroy the rest of humanity, Ra has a change of heart.

Ra commands his chief priest to grind red ochre to mix with 7000 jars of barley beer being brewed by women. On the eve of Sekhmet's planned destruction of humanity, the intoxicating draught is completed and poured into the fields where she will arrive. In the morning, Sekhmet arrives to find the fields brimming with the red liquid. Seeing her own reflection in the flooded plains, she is delighted and drinks her fill. She is then too intoxicated to even recognize humans.[24] Ra greets her with the words "Twice welcome in peace, O Charming One" and decrees that every year women will brew intoxicating draughts for a great feast in her honor.[25]

Variants of "The Destruction of Humanity" myth exist, with different deities and different rebellions, which causes this narrative to be viewed as a repeating pattern of events.[26] This Egyptian myth shares a similarity with many mythologies from other cultures throughout the world wherein the deities that created humans ultimately destroyed them because they were dissatisfied with their creation, supporting the principle that a deity that is powerful enough to create life is also powerful enough to destroy it. And in this Egyptian myth, power resides with female deities. The power of Sekhmet is beyond the male gods' control; she is a force of nature, wild and indiscriminate.

Egyptians reenacted the myth of "The Destruction of Humanity" in an annual festival held in the first month of the year after the flooding of the Nile. These feasts are well documented at the Temple of Mut during the reign of Hatshepsut and well into the Ptolemaic era. The temple inscriptions reveal continual singing, dancing, drinking, and music-making as acts of propitiation of Mut in her form as Sekhmet.[27]

This New Year festival occurred after the hottest days of summer had finally ended, the rains arrived, and the Nile flooded. Ochre-colored beer flowed during an ecstatic ritual of propitiation to the power of the female divine.[28] The flooding of the Nile brought the promise of the continuation of life in an annual cycle. The early floods would flush more clay, silt, and sand down the river, creating rich and fertile sediment. With the mythic identification of the Nile and menstruation, this festival certainly honored the many aspects of female power.[29]

The New Year festival was one of the principal transition periods for the ancient Egyptians. Sekhmet was invoked and propitiated because her immense power could be wielded in many directions. A recitation of a spell called "The Book of the Last Day of the Year" was performed over a piece of cloth, which was then worn as an amulet during the days leading up to the New Year. Prayers were recited to gain the protection of Sekhmet, and tokens of Sekhmet and Bastet were liberally bestowed.

The rituals held at the Temple of Goddess Spirituality Dedicated to Sekhmet do not attempt to reconstruct the Egyptian rites. Instead, the temple observes solar and lunar holidays: solstices, equinoxes, cross-quarter days, full and new moons. Mother's Day and Earth Day are also celebrated in ritual. In some years the temple holds a special ceremony in honor of Sekhmet, "The Heart of the Sun." This ritual is held on the cross-quarter day between summer solstice and fall equinox, corresponding to the New Year celebration in ancient Egypt. In a mixture of ancient and modern traditions, Sekhmet is honored with a procession, song, dance, and offerings.

This invocation reflects the multivalent aspects of Sekhmet:

Sekhmet, You are the Great Mother.
I know you by your infinite love;
I know you by your fierce strength.
You are the ecstasy of the Earth;
You are the song of Spirit;
You are the fire of the Cosmos;
You are the tears of Life.[30]

At the temple, Sekhmet as well as other goddesses are honored. Sitting across from Sekhmet in the south is a large statue entitled "Madre del Mundo." Madre del Mundo has a distinctively indigenous North American face and cradles the world in an embrace. She was created in 1988 to sit at the Nevada Test Site. Representations of goddesses from cultures worldwide sit in places of honor throughout the temple, illustrating the pervasive figure of the divine female.

Sekhmet manifests in the Nevada desert as the protector of the divine order, as female power. A commemorative engraving in front of Sekhmet in the temple urges those that come to embrace the power of Sekhmet: "May woman take our power and be strong as the lioness giving birth to the future. A promise kept by Genevieve Vaughan."

The Heart of the Sun

She was called "Mother in the Horizon of the Sky," "Sun Goddess," and "Lady of the Flame." The sun is the life force of the planet, but as is apparent in the desert, its intensity also burns life away. Sekhmet holds the uncontrollable energies of life and death, creation and destruction, illness and health.

Yet, in spite of Sekhmet's fearsome powers, she was never demonized. "A goddess such as Sekhmet is a reflection of the ancient Egyptian's sense that the universe is an awesome and dangerous place, ruled by unpredictable powers beyond human control."[31] As the embodiment of female power, she was revered, propitiated, and called upon as an ally. Amid the dry heat of the desert and the water of a sacred spring she unites the red rage and the black fecundity, the hunter and the mother, the creator and the destroyer. She is the Lady of Life, bringing the power of healing to her home in the American desert.

In ancient times and present, her return is celebrated.

Notes

1. See Genevieve Vaughan, "My Journey with Sekhmet: Goddess of Power and Change," *SageWoman* 42 (Summer 1998). Read more about the Gift Economy at her Web site: www.gift-economy.com.

2. Richard Wilkinson, *Symbol and Magic in Egyptian Art* (New York: Thames and Hudson, 1994), 110; Arielle P. Kozloff, and Betsy M. Bryan, *Egypt's Dazzling Sun: Amenhotep III and His World* (Cleveland, OH: The Cleveland Museum of Art in cooperation with Indiana University Press, 1992), 142.

3. Kozloff and Bryan, *Egypt's Dazzling Sun*, 225.

4. Marija Gimbutas, *The Living Goddesses*, ed. Miriam Robbins Dexter (Berkeley: University of California Press, 1999), 137.

5. Danièle Michaux-Colombot, "The Rosette in Nubian Cultures," paper presented at the 11th International Conference for Meriotic Studies, Vienna, Austria, September 1–4, 2008.

6. Richard Wilkinson, *Symbol and Magic in Egyptian Art* (New York: Thames and Hudson, 1994), 160.

7. Anne Key, "Invocation to Sekhmet," in *The Heart of the Sun: An Anthology in Exaltation of Sekhmet*, ed. Anne Key and Candace Kant (Bloomington, IN: Goddess Institute Publishing/iUniverse, Inc., 2010).

8. Patricia Monaghan, *Oh Mother Sun! A New View of the Cosmic Feminine* (Freedom, CA: The Crossing Press, 1994), 60.

9. Richard H Wilkinson, *The Complete Gods and Goddesses of Ancient Egypt* (New York: Thames and Hudson, 2003), 181.

10. William Kelly Simpson, trans. "The Story of Sinuhe," in *The Literature of Ancient Egypt*, ed. Simpson (New Haven, CT: Yale University Press, 2003), 54–66.

11. Miriam Lichtheim, *Ancient Egyptian Literature: A Book of Readings*, vol. 2 (Berkeley: University of California Press, 1973), 200, 62.

12. Candace Kant, "Call to Sekhmet," in *The Heart of the Sun*, ed. Key and Kant.

13. Names of Sekhmet can be found on the Web site for the Temple of Goddess Spirituality Dedicated to Sekhmet: http://www.sekhmettemple.com.

14. Survey developed by a team of anthropologists and sociologists from the College of Southern Nevada, conducted electronically by author; unpublished, results on file, 2006.

15. Candace Ross, personal communication, January 15, 2009.

16. Candace Kant, personal communication, February 18, 2009.

17. Kozloff and Bryan, *Egypt's Dazzling Sun*, 225.

18. Barbara Lesko, *The Great Goddesses of Egypt* (Norman: University of Oklahoma Press, 1999), 137–138.

19. Jennifer Pinkowski, "Egypt's Ageless Goddess: A Modern Pilgrim Visits the Temple of Mut," *Archeology* 59, no. 5 (2006): 45–49.

20. A *yantra* is a geometric figure used as an aid to meditation in the Hindu tradition.

21. Joseph Kaster, *The Wisdom of Ancient Egypt* (New York: Barnes and Noble, 1968), 55–56.

22. Normandi Ellis, *Feasts of Light: Celebrations for the Seasons of Life Based on the Egyptian Goddess Mysteries* (Wheaton, IL: Quest Books, 1999), 58.

23. Lesko, *Great Goddesses of Egypt*, 145.

24. Edward F. Wente Jr., trans., "The Book of the Heavenly Cow," in *Literature of Ancient Egypt*, ed. Simpson, 289–292.

25. Kaster, *Wisdom of Ancient Egypt*, 70.

26. Geraldine Pinch, *Egyptian Mythology: A Guide to the Gods, Goddesses, and Traditions of Ancient Egypt* (New York: Oxford University Press, 2004), 125.

27. Pinkowski, "Egypt's Ageless Goddess," 45–49.

28. Ibid.

29. Jaana Toivari-Viitala, *Women at Deir el-Medina: A Study of the Status and Roles of the Female Inhabitants at the Workmen's Community during the Ramesside Period* (Leiden: Nederlands Instituut voor Het Nabije Oosten, 2001), 162; Judy Grahn, *Blood, Bread, and Roses: How Menstruation Created the World* (Boston: Beacon Press, 1993), 225.

30. Key, "Invocation to Sekhmet."

31. Jocelyn Almond and Keith Seddon, *Egyptian Paganism for Beginners: Bring the Gods and Goddesses into Daily Life* (St. Paul, MN: Llewellyn Publications, 2004), 133–134.

Bibliography

Almond, Jocelyn, and Keith Seddon. *Egyptian Paganism for Beginners: Bring the Gods and Goddesses into Daily Life*. St Paul, MN: Llewellyn Publications, 2004.

Ellis, Normandi, trans. *Awakening Osiris: A New Translation of the Egyptian Book of the Dead*. Grand Rapids, MI: Phanes Press, 1988.

Ellis, Normandi. *Feasts of Light: Celebrations for the Seasons of Life based on the Egyptian Goddess Mysteries*. Wheaton, IL: Quest Books, 1999.

Gimbutas, Marija. *The Living Goddesses*. Ed. Miriam Robbins Dexter. Berkeley: University of California Press, 1999.

Grahn, Judy. *Blood, Bread, and Roses: How Menstruation Created the World*. Boston: Beacon Press, 1993.

Kant, Candace. "Call to Sekhmet." In *The Heart of the Sun: An Anthology in Exaltation of Sekhmet*, ed. Anne Key and Candace Kant. Bloomington, IN: Goddess Institute Publishing/iUniverse, Inc., 2010.

Kaster, Joseph. *The Wisdom of Ancient Egypt*. New York: Barnes and Noble, 1968.

Key, Anne. "Invocation to Sekhmet." In *The Heart of the Sun: An Anthology in Exaltation of Sekhmet*, ed. Anne Key and Candace Kant. Bloomington, IN: Goddess Institute Publishing/iUniverse, Inc., 2010.

Kozloff, Arielle P., and Betsy M. Bryan. *Egypt's Dazzling Sun: Amenhotep III and His World*. Cleveland, OH: The Cleveland Museum of Art in cooperation with Indiana University Press, 1992.

Lesko, Barbara. *The Great Goddesses of Egypt*. Norman: University of Oklahoma Press, 1999.

Lichtheim, Miriam. *Ancient Egyptian Literature: A Book of Readings*. Vol. 2. Berkeley: University of California Press, 1973.

Michaux-Colombot, Danièle. "The Rosette in Nubian Cultures." Paper presented at the 11th International Conference for Meriotic Studies, Vienna, Austria, September 1–4, 2008.

Monaghan, Patricia. *Oh Mother Sun! A New View of the Cosmic Feminine*. Freedom, CA: The Crossing Press, 1994.

Pinch, Geraldine. *Egyptian Mythology: A Guide to the Gods, Goddesses, and Traditions of Ancient Egypt*. New York: Oxford University Press, 2004.

Pinkowski, Jennifer. "Egypt's Ageless Goddess: A Modern Pilgrim Visits the Temple of Mut." *Archeology* 59, no. 5 (2006): 45–49.

Simpson, William Kelly, trans. "The Story of Sinuhe." In *The Literature of Ancient Egypt*, ed. William Kelly Simpson, 54–66. New Haven, CT: Yale University Press, 2003.

Toivari-Viitala, Jaana. *Women at Deir el-Medina. A Study of the Status and Roles of the Female Inhabitants at the Workmen's Community during the Ramesside Period.* Leiden: Nederlands Instituut voor Het Nabije Oosten, 2001.

Vaughan, Genevieve. "My Journey with Sekhmet, Goddess of Power and Change." *SageWoman* 42 (Summer 1998).

Wente, Edward F., Jr., trans. "The Book of the Heavenly Cow." In *The Literature of Ancient Egypt*, ed. William Kelly Simpson, 289–298. New Haven, CT: Yale University Press, 2003.

Wilkinson, Richard H. *The Complete Gods and Goddesses of Ancient Egypt.* New York: Thames and Hudson, 2003.

Wilkinson, Richard H. *Symbol and Magic in Egyptian Art.* New York: Thames and Hudson, 1994.

20

Artemis as Protectress of Female Mysteries: Modern Worship in the Dianic Tradition in America

Denise Saint Arnault

Over the shadowy hills and windy peaks . . . [Artemis] draws her golden bow, rejoicing in the chase, and sends out grievous shafts. The tops of the high mountains tremble and the tangled wood echoes awesomely with the outcry of beasts: earthquakes and the sea also where fishes shoal. But the goddess, with a bold heart, turns every way, destroying the race of wild beasts: and when she is satisfied and has cheered her heart, this huntress who delights in arrows slackens her supple bow and goes to the great house of her dear brother . . . there to order the lovely dance of the . . . (Muses) and . . . (Graces). There she hangs up her curved bow and her arrows, and . . . leads the dances.[1]

Worship of the goddess Artemis spanned vast geographical regions, cultures, and epochs, from the thousand-breasted Artemis of Ephesus in Turkey (3000–200 BCE), to the early winged Artemis found in Sparta (eighth century BCE),[2] to the stylized and urbane Roman Diana of Italy

Figure 20.1 The Artemis Sanctuary at Vravrona (35 kilometers northeast of Athens, Greece) was a regional center of pilgrimage for women and girls for more than 300 years. (Courtesy of Denise Saint Arnault.)

(third century CE). Unfortunately, it is beyond the scope of this chapter to examine the similarities and differences between these forms in terms of cultural influences, religious migration, or other dispersion patterns. Here, the focus will be to examine the activities that may have occurred in the Artemis temples established by the Athenian political center in Greece between 700 and 400 BCE. There, scholars agree that women engaged in female-exclusive religious activities organized around the specific life cycle events in the temples in Greece.

While Artemis cared for boy children and animals, she was specifically a goddess who guarded women as they moved through life transitions. Within the Wiccan religious movement in America, a feminist branch honors the goddess as the primary and unitary source of all. Many practitioners of these groups hold exclusively female religious activities that celebrate the female body as a reflection of the goddess, and the seasons as a reflection of her aspects, from conception through menarche, maturity, cronehood, and death. Artemis is an extremely important goddess in this feminist religion since it is *she* who presides over the mysteries of the female body. The links between this mythos of Artemis and contemporary goddess-centered cosmology have ignited the spirits of women for decades, providing cosmological and legendary evidence and validity to their religious form. These are the mythological underpinnings for women who aim to claim and reclaim their right to practice a religion in which their fundamental and unique biological being is honored as divine and holy, in segregated space—a right protected by the goddess herself.

Artemis as the Goddess of Women's Mysteries

Artemis was a goddess who moved and transformed across time (from 3000 BCE to the 300 CE) and across vast regions (from Turkey in the east across southern Europe). Using Artemis's images, motifs, and temple locales in Greece between 700 and 400 BCE, this examination focuses on the smallest slice of a vast religious field by painting a conceptual picture, not a linear one, and by exploring common threads that relate to one contemporary goddess religion.

Temples were established at boundaries and edges. Artemis was the inviolable goddess of the wild. There are no accurate counts of the numbers of Artemisian temples throughout Greece during this period; however, estimates are in the hundreds. Because she was the goddess of the wilderness, her temples were established at the margins of the centralized provinces. Artemis's temples were also established on remote edges of marshes, lakes, hillsides, and sacred streams. One source of evidence about the function of Artemis temples in Greek society was these geographic placements.

> On the right [of the road from Argos to Arkadia, Argolis] is Mount Lykone, which has trees on it, chiefly cypresses. On the top of the mountain is built a sanctuary of Artemis Orthia (of the Steep). . . . Saron built the sanctuary [at Troizenos, Argolis] for Artemis Saronis by a sea which is marshy and shallow, so that for this reason it was called the Phoibaian lagoon. . . . Artemis called Daphnaia (of the laurel). By the sea is a temple of Artemis Diktynna on a promontory, in whose honor they hold an annual festival.[3]

Artemis temples varied in size and were regional in their character. Central or local governments constructed and maintained these temples, and sponsored women-specific activities at them. Cole and others have hypothesized that these locales, along with the sheer number of temples throughout Greece, indicate that the Greek government considered Artemis a remote but important protector of the people.[4] Her guardianship occurred at these edges, where she claimed dominion. Cole focuses on how the Greek government may have established Artemis temples at the margins and edges of their established territory to symbolically protect the borders of their lands. As the protectress of the wild spaces, and as the guardian at the edges, Artemis protected the Athenian people where they were most vulnerable from invasion.

Cole's argument is convincing; Artemis temples can be analyzed from a political and economic perspective as carrying strategic importance. However, Herodotus, and Pausanias recorded primarily women-festivals or other types of women-specific community events at most of these temples.[5] Indeed, while little is known about what happened at Artemis's temples, symbols and art from them suggests that activities were related to women's transitions. By establishing goddess temples, the Greek polis was not only safeguarding its sovereignty, but was also sponsoring a social form that entitled women to spaces that focus on female-specific religious activities.

In day-to-day life in the Greek world, local people may have vague knowledge about the strategic and political rationale for governmental sponsorship. However, it is likely that the priestesses who served at these temples felt passion and desire in their service to their goddess. Certainly, the women who traveled to these temples with offerings of their faith were moved by a psychological and spiritual motivation beyond the political desires of the Greek polis. Such women may well have passionately practiced their faith, beseeching Artemis for protection for a successful birth, or sending their daughters to her temples for transitional rituals. These women and girls were engaged in religious and symbolic relationship with Artemis. They hoped, prayed, and gave offerings from true devotion.

Temples Relate to the Biological Aspect of Womanhood

The next important variable is that the symbology contained in Artemis temples was in most cases primarily or exclusively about women, and activities that are documented in them were about female-specific life issues, including the safety of the young, the transition of girls into women, childbirth, and, in some places, transition into marriage. One Artemis temple that has engendered enthusiastic scholarship and debate is the Artemis sanctuary at Vravrona, now Brauron. Located about fifty miles outside of Athens, this temple is of interest for several reasons. It is near Athens, has enjoyed a thorough excavation in the 1940s–1960s, and has stone tablet remains (both in Vravrona and the Acropolis) that document the offerings that women brought for the goddess. There were also myths as well as historic writings about it.[6]

In Greek mythology, a priestess of Artemis, Iphigenia, was credited as having established the temple at Vravrona. During the Trojan War, Agamemnon had offended Artemis, and she punished him with ill winds. Myth suggests that Iphigenia was to be killed by her father in exchange for favorable winds. In some versions of the myth, Artemis intervened by replacing Iphigenia with a female deer. Artemis also proclaimed that Iphigenia would henceforth act as priestess of Artemis's temple in Tauris, north of the Black Sea. In a later myth, Iphigenia's brother, Orestes, traveled to Tauris to search for the statue of Artemis. He was also captured, but Iphigenia recognized him, and they escaped. With the help of the goddess Athena, Iphigenia was told to establish, preside over, and become entombed at the Temple at Vravrona. Iphigenia had an important role in mythology and at the temple and legend says her tomb stands there.

Excavations have found textile offerings, mirrors, jewelry, and other items such as garment pins were found in the sacred spring at the temple. There is evidence that this temple enjoyed an established system of religious activities from 700 through 400 BCE, when it was destroyed by invasion. There is also evidence that the Greek government had slated this temple for reconstruction in the late fourth century BCE. The evidence suggests that this temple had an altar, an inner space for priestesses (cella), a house for maidens, a gymnasium, a wrestling school, and a stable, as well as a sacred spring and a cave tomb.[7] It was well known throughout Greece that these were female-specific activities:

> The Pelasgians dwelt at that time in Lemnos and desired vengeance on the Athenians. Since they well knew the time of the Athenian festivals, they acquired fifty-oared ships and set an ambush for the Athenian women celebrating the festival of Artemis at Brauron. They seized many of the women, then sailed away with them and brought them to Lemnos to be their concubines.[8]

Artemis's Connection to Childbirth

Written documents, pottery, artwork, and stone engravings have been interpreted to indicate that women gave offerings of their weavings and textiles to Artemis to ensure a healthy birth. This affirms Artemis as specifically a goddess who provided protection and care to a woman during childbirth. One wonders if other childbirth-related rituals, spells, or activities might have occurred at this and other Artemis temples.

> Seldom is it that Artemis goes down to the town. . . . I [Artemis] will visit (these cities) only when women vexed by the sharp pang of childbirth call me to their aid—even in the hour when I was born the Moirai (Fates) ordained that I should be their helper, forasmuch as my mother suffered no pain either when she gave me birth or when she carried me in her womb, but without travail put me from her body.[9]

And, in a beautiful poem to Artemis:

> [Artemis Prothyraia] labour pains are thy peculiar care. In thee, when stretched upon the bed of grief, the sex, as in a mirror, view relief. Guard of the race, enbued with gentle mind, to helpless youth benevolent and kind; benignant nourisher; great nature's key belongs to no divinity but thee. . . . Thine is the task to loose the virgin's zone and thou in every work art seen and known. With births you sympathise, though pleased to see the numerous offspring of fertility. When racked with labour pangs, and sore distressed the sex invoke thee, as the soul's sure rest; for thou Eileithyia [Artemis] alone canst give relief to pain, which art attempts to ease, but tries in vain. Artemis Eileithyia, venerable power, who bringest relief in labour's dreadful hour; hear, Prothyraia and make the infant race thy constant care.[10]

Her Connection to Maidenhood and Menarche

Another function of this temple was related to the maturation of girl children. Early writings suggest that female-specific rituals were held annually or possibly every four years. Determining what ceremonies or rituals took place at the Temple of Vravrona requires examining both the depictions on the vases that were found at the temple, as well as the documented choruses and poetry about the events. In both the vases and the poems, females in a group competed in contests or races, processed to an altar, carried or wore garlands, and participated in choral performances. These age differences among the women and among the girls, as well as the use of torches, suggest that at least some of the events took place at night.[11]

Women playing the bear used to celebrate a festival for Artemis [at Brauron]. . . . The reason was that a wild she-bear [sacred to Artemis] used to come to the . . . Phlauidoi and spend time there; and she became tamed and was brought up with the humans. Some virgin was playing with her and, when the girl began acting recklessly, the she-bear was provoked and scratched the virgin; her brothers were angered by this and speared the she-bear, and because of this a pestilential sickness fell upon the Athenians. When the Athenians consulted the oracle [the god] said that there would be a release from the evils if, as blood price for the she-bear that died, they compelled their virgins to play the bear.[12]

While records are not consistent, there are suggestions that girls between the ages of five and ten years old participated in these festivals, which have been interpreted to be maturation rites. These were unlikely to be specific to menstruation, since the girls were probably too young. In addition, the facilities at this temple and written evidence suggest that the girls also stayed at the temple complex to engage in religious service. It is not known how long the girls stayed, if their mothers stayed with them, what the full purpose of this pilgrimage was, or how many girls would come. Some speculate that the girls who went would have been from the families of the elite in Athens, while most report that all girls would have been obliged to go at some time. One legend states that "Girls playing the bear used to celebrate a festival for Artemis dressed in saffron robes; not older than 10 years nor less than 5 . . . the Athenians decreed that no virgin might be given in marriage to a man if she hadn't previously played the bear for the goddess."[13]

This mythology and archeological evidence suggest that the girls ran races and wore the pelt of a bear, dancing with torches around an altar to Artemis. The wildness of these rituals leaves the imagination flying. One wonders what it would mean to a six- or seven-year-old girl to march over fifty miles to a remote temple and to become engaged in enactments for the goddess and her priestesses. These pre-menarche rites could have served a host of psychological and spiritual purposes.

Women's Religion in a Misogynous Culture

Several authors have focused on the misogyny of the Greek culture during this archaic period. It has been speculated that there were only a few roles that a woman could play in society. Indeed, Pomeroy maintains that these were the only options for a female in this society.[14] Records from Greek medical text, as well as writings by Plato and Socrates, espouse the view that women are fundamentally inferior to men, wild in their nature, and prone to insanity.[15] Women were outside of the enculturation or domestication of ordered society; they were wild, untamed, unclaimed, and unconstrained. Artemis's temples were also at the margins of society, and women went to these places to relate with this untamed and wild goddess. Whatever the political and social benefits this had for the patriarchal society, women knew themselves as apart from men, different because of their biology, experiencing their unique and specific religious rites apart from men. Artemis, living on the edge, outside of the center, cared for and protected the wild and the vulnerable: her women.

Dianic Tradition in America

I am Nature, the universal Mother, mistress of all the elements, primordial child of time, sovereign of all things spiritual, queen of the dead, queen also of the immortals, the single manifestation of all gods and goddesses that are. My nod governs the shining heights of Heaven, the wholesome sea-breezes, the lamentable silences of the world below. Though I am worshipped in many aspects, known by countless names, and propitiated with all manner of different rites, yet the whole round earth venerates me.[16]

A branch of the American Wiccan tradition referred to as the Dianic tradition does not embrace the concept of sacred duality of male and female as the most important cosmological principle, an important principle to other Wiccan traditions.[17] Rather, they understand that the goddess is the primary source of all, that both the female and the male biological forms arise from the goddess. She is the sacred and unified divine being, sovereign and inviolable, fundamental and complete. Her dominion is all that is; all of the elements, the heavens, sea, earth, and universe are *her*. She has a million aspects or facets. She can be seen in all that is and is known by a myriad of different names, roles, faces, perspectives, and cultures. However, her essence is singular and holistic. Everything comes from her and returns to her.

The namesake for the Dianic tradition is Artemis-Diana because of her specific female-centered cosmology. Her wildness—in the sense that she cannot be claimed, tamed, or in any way ruled—is the essence of the understanding of the goddess in the Dianic tradition. Artemis-Diana is not defined by another, and unflinchingly exemplifies all of the desired attributes of people of *both* genders: strength and tenderness; vengeance and pity; power and grace; beauty and terror. These attributes are equally and fully juxtaposed in her mythology and her symbolism. So, too, in Dianic tradition there is a spiritual, psychological, symbolic, and collective emphasis on the wholeness and completeness of a woman outside of her relationships with others. This emphasis serves to assist her on claiming or regaining access to all of a woman's complete being. Woman, as goddess, is fully formed, complete and supremely capable of all attributes, regardless of how these attributes have been *culturally* distributed to specific genders.

In addition, Artemis-Diana is completely female-identified. She rejects domination by men, seeking instead to serve nature, animals, the young, and women. She does not engage in the politics of men and lives entirely outside of their control. She is not in any way aggressive to men: her focus is on her women. However, she will retaliate against any man or woman who violates her laws: protection of the weak and vulnerable; clarity in one's own sanctity and purity; or unauthorized intrusion into her sovereign domain. As in Artemis's myths, Dianics believe that they have the sovereign right to their own space. They identify *with* women, identify in the world *as* women, and focus their energies *on* women. There is no issue with their relationships with men, since most Dianic practitioners maintain relationships with their fathers, sons, husbands, brothers, lovers and others. However, they are not defined by, or identified by, these relationships. Most Dianic practitioners would likely also claim as their focus the security of, protection of, and stewardship of, nature, children, girls, and women.

Finally, but perhaps most important, Artemis-Diana was a goddess focused on the biological specificity of the female. Her sanctuaries were claimed by women as specific to women, and to the biological reality of the female body. The mysteries of being born into a female body were her mysteries. As the guardian of the wild and vulnerable, she cared for the girl-child during her transition into womanhood. She also cared for the woman who suffered the dangerous state of pregnancy and childbirth, taking pity on her by easing her pain. Or, Artemis would take mercy on her if the circumstances required by releasing a woman with her golden arrow.

So it is with Dianic practitioners. Being born into the female body is the foundation of commonality among women, and the focus is on the distinct spiritual mysteries of this separate biological sex. In that specific body-knowledge, women share commonality and spiritual mystery. Religious rituals specific to the mysteries arising from the biological reality of being female are the birthright of any woman, granted and protected by the goddess herself. Dianic practitioners celebrate the earth, her seasons, the elements and all that is, as manifestations or aspects of her totality. In religious rituals, they honor the mysteries of being a female throughout the year by symbolically overlaying the life-cycle of a female over the seasons of the year. In this way, celebrations of spring may be the celebrations of the mysteries of maidenhood, even as celebrations of the winter are celebrations of the mysteries of the hag.

The goddess is all that is, and is known by 10,000 names and faces. She is essential, unitary, and total in herself. However, women can understand the goddess only by relating to her aspects, and one such aspect that has taken hold in the consciousness of modern witches is the face of Artemis-Diana. In her mythology and cosmology, women and Dianic practitioners can find motifs and symbolism indicating a female birthright to have separate, sacred space to celebrate uniquely female mysteries.

Notes

1. Hesiod, *Homeric Hymns, Epic Cycle, Homerica,* trans. H. G. Evelyn-White, Loeb Classical Library 57 (Cambridge, MA: Harvard University Press, 1914), Homeric Hymn 27 to Artemis.

2. M. S. Thompson, "The Asiatic or Winged Artemis," *Journal of Hellenic Studies,* 29 (1909): 286.

3. Pausanias, *Guide to Greece* (Cambridge, MA: Harvard University Press, 1918), 2.24.5, 2.30, 3.24.9.

4. S. G. Cole, *Landscapes, Gender, and Ritual Space.* (Los Angeles: University of California Press, 2004).

5. Pausanias, *Guide to Greece*; see also Herodotus, *Histories* (Cambridge, MA: Harvard University Press, 1922).

6. L. Papadimitriou, "The Sanctuary of Artemis at Brauron," *Scientific American* 208, no. 6 (1963): 110.

7. Ibid.

8. Herodotus, *Histories* (Cambridge, MA: Harvard University Press, 1922), 6:138.

9. Callimachus, *Hymns and Epigrams in Lycophron and Aratus,* Loeb Classical Library 129 (London: William Heinemann, 1921), Hymn 3 to Artemis.

10. Orpheus, *The Hymns of Orpheus,* trans. by T. Taylor (Los Angeles: Philosophical Research Society, 1981[1792]), Orphic Hymn 2 to Prothyraia.

11. R. Hamilton, "Alkman and the Athenian Arkteia," *Hesperia* 58, no. 4 (1989): 449.

12. Herodotus, *Histories* (Cambridge, MA: Harvard University Press, 1922), Arktos e Brauroniois.

13. Ibid.

14. S. B. Pomeroy, *Goddesses, Whores, Wives, and Slaves: Women in Classical Antiquity* (New York: Schocken Books, 1995).

15. H. King, "Bound to Bleed: Artemis and Greek Women," in *Images of Women in Antiquity*, ed. A. K. Cameron (London: Routledge, 1993), 109–127.

16. Apuleius, *The Golden Ass* (New York: Farrar, 1951), 264.

17. R. Barrett, *Women's Rites, Women's Mysteries: Intuitive Ritual Creation* (Woodbury, MN: Llewellyn, 2007); Z. Budapest, *The Holy Book of Women's Mysteries* (San Francisco: Weiser Books, 2007); S. Mountainwater, *Ariadne's Thread: A Workbook of Goddess Magic* (Berkeley: Crossing Press, 1991).

Bibliography

Apuleius. *The Golden Ass.* New York: Farrar, 1951.

Barrett, R. *Women's Rites, Women's Mysteries: Intuitive Ritual Creation.* Woodbury, MN: Llewellyn, 2007.

Budapest, Z. *The Holy Book of Women's Mysteries.* San Francisco: Weiser Books, 2007.

Callimachus. *Hymns and Epigramsin, Lycophron and Aratus,* Loeb Classical Library 129. London: William Heinemann, 1921.

Cole, S. G. *Landscapes, Gender, and Ritual Space.* Los Angeles: University of California Press, 2004.

Hamilton, R. "Alkman and the Athenian Arkteia." *Hesperia* 58, no. 4 (1989): 449–472.

Herodotus. *Histories.* Cambridge, MA: Harvard University Press, 1922.

Hesiod. *Homeric Hymns, Epic Cycle, Homerica.* Translated by H. G. Evelyn-White. Loeb Classical Library 57. Cambridge, MA: Harvard University Press, 1914.

King, H. "Bound to Bleed: Artemis and Greek Women." In *Images of Women in Antiquity*, ed. A. K. Cameron, 109–127. London: Routledge, 1993.

Mountainwater, S. *Ariadne's Thread: A Workbook of Goddess Magic.* Berkeley: Crossing Press, 1991.

Orpheus. *The Hymns of Orpheus.* Translated by T. Taylor. Los Angeles: Philosophical Research Society, 1981.

Papadimitriou, L. "The Sanctuary of Artemis at Brauron." *Scientific American* 208, no. 6 (1963): 110–120.

Pausanias. *Guide to Greece.* Cambridge, MA: Harvard University Press, 1918.

Pomeroy, S. B. *Goddesses, Whores, Wives, and Slaves: Women in Classical Antiquity.* New York: Schocken Books, 1995.

Thompson, M. S. "The Asiatic or Winged Artemis." *Journal of Hellenic Studies* 29 (1909): 286–307.

21

American Goddess: A Modern Apotheosis

Michael B. MacDonald

Since the 1970s America has inherited Britain's place as the world center of modern paganism.[1] One of America's significant contributions to neo-paganism is the transformation of Wicca into a feminist spiritual practice. Some American feminist witches have suggested that the roots of witchcraft may be found in goddess polytheism. American goddess worship seems to differ, however, from other named-goddess worship elsewhere in the world, in that the goddess of much American paganism has no single name or identity. She is, as Starhawk wrote, "the cycle of birth, growth, death, and regeneration."[2] Marion Green wrote of contemporary paganism, "What you accept in terms of deity will be entirely your business."[3] Exploring the development of goddess worship in the United States since 1970 will show how this nonhierarchical, nondogmatic, spiritual practice has developed into very personal and community spiritual practices that celebrate the goddess.

Why Paganism, Why the Goddess?

From a long line of British neo-pagan writings that stretches back to the middle of the 19th century, American neo-paganism was constructed upon a rich heritage. There are a wide variety of reasons neo-paganism has taken root in America since the 1960s. For some adherents, neo-paganism represents a break with traditional Judeo-Christian traditions.

Neo-paganism offers a spiritual practice that fits with their personal point of view. Some take inspiration from an introduction to American Indian (First Nations in Canada) earth-based spiritual traditions that revere mother earth. For still others, like Margot Adler, it is the realization of lost traditions and a search for roots.[4] There are yet other reasons, because there are as many types of neo-pagan practices as there are practitioners. The antihierarchical nature of many neo-pagan beliefs means that there is little in the way of central organization and therefore little dogma that defines Wicca. If there is a dogma at all in neo-paganism it could be described as the witches creed or Wiccan Rede, "If it harms none, do what you will." It is precisely the lack of a solid description that is the best description.

In America a connection between Wicca and feminism has developed. Second-wave feminist Wicca practitioners see the witch as a misunderstood yet powerful traditional female practitioner made ugly by popular Christian and monotheistic culture as part of a centuries-long oppression of women. Margot Adler explains this connection vividly:

> Consciousness-raising provided an opportunity for women (some of them for the first time) to talk about their lives, make decisions and act upon them, without the presence of men. Women used such groups to explore their relations with women, men, work, motherhood and children, their own sexuality, lesbianism, their past youth, and the coming of old age. Many women began to explore their dreams and fantasies; sometimes they tentatively began individual and collective psychic experiments.[5]

Others, like Macha NightMare, had already been active in consciousness raising community work and brought those skills to newly forming spiritual communities.[6] Starhawk wrote that the symbol of the goddess has "given us a deep sense of pride in women's ability to create and sustain culture."[7] In a variety of ways and for a variety of reasons during the late 1960s and throughout the 1970s women and women's groups both overtly political and singularly spiritual embraced Wicca.

Connecting Witchcraft with the Past

Some Wiccans sought to connect witchcraft with an even earlier spiritual practice. Merlin Stone spent a decade researching traditional women's beliefs and made the claim that Hebrews suppressed goddess-based traditions and women clergy (see Daniel Cohen's chapter in volume 2).[8] She argued that goddess-worshiping societies had been overthrown by god-worshiping societies, a female spiritual order violently replaced by a male spiritual order.[9] Archeologist Marija Gimbutas wrote, "We are still living under the sway of that aggressive male invasion and only beginning to discover our long alienation from our authentic European Heritage— gylanic, nonviolent, earth-centered culture."[10]

Some practitioners of witchcraft see themselves as priestesses of a goddess whose image was perverted by Judeo-Christian propaganda. In keeping with the diversity inherent in paganism, some practitioners use "witch" and "priestess" interchangeably. Some writers have argued that Wicca has been a continuous traditional practice that has focused its attention on the worship of the goddess. In a few cases authors have claimed goddess worship is a recent creation based upon a feminine spiritual archetype. But in all cases, goddess worship has been described as a direct political protest against a misogynistic, mainstream, environmentally destructive, god-worshiping society. In short, modern American feminists have created a domestic and politically charged spiritual practice called goddess worship.

Paths to the Goddess

The diversity witnessed in contemporary goddess spirituality could be understood as networks of paths upon which one can make her way across geographical, conceptual, and spiritual territories. Choosing one path or another will lead the traveler to different experiences. At the end of the journey, though, some experiences of "journeying" may be shared but do not have to be shared. So it is with a journey to the goddess.

A journey to contemporary goddess spirituality takes on many forms and has many stories. There is no official way to become a pagan and no official face of the goddess. But some paths are well worn and others are brightly marked. Some books, like travel maps, help to lead the uninitiated along "a way." Other practitioners choose personal experience and gut instinct as the basis for their journey. No choice is the correct choice. The following are a few well-marked paths to the goddess.

Folklore, Mythology, and Archeology

Joseph Campbell popularized the notion that mythology springs from a very basic experience and that the hero has "a thousand faces." Campbell suggested that world mythology should be understood comparatively, meaning that all of the stories found in the mythologies of the world tell more or less the same stories. When these stories are appreciated side by side, he noted, the reader will come to understand the richness of the human experience and human similarity.[11] Campbell influentially asserted the notion of the first goddess or earth goddess as philosophically, psychoanalytically, or structurally obvious. He wrote that the goddess was associated with agricultural societies in the ancient world, including Mesopotamia and the Egyptian Nile, and that the goddess was the "personification of the energy that gives birth to forms and nourishes forms."[12] He built upon Carl Jung's notion of the archetype and suggested that the goddess, as archetypal woman, represented creator and destroyer, womb and tomb, and thus united good and bad and was understood as both the personal giver of life (one's own mother) and the universal giver of life (the earth).

Marija Gimbutas's groundbreaking and controversial studies of the goddess would become the scientific foundation for something more concrete than Campbell's thesis. Gimbutas argued, with archeological evidence to support her, that ancient civilizations worshiped the goddess. Her research provided a connection to ancient tradition. Gimbutas suggested that in Neolithic Europe and Anatolia—in the era between 7000 and 3000 BCE—religion focused on the wheel of life and its cyclical turning. She argued that this spirituality saw birth, nurturing, growth, death, and regeneration, as well as crop cultivation and the raising of animals as the foundation of its religious practice, not the blood sacrifice and individual worship that "religions of the book" would later venerate.[13] The people of this era pondered untamed natural forces, as well as wild plant and animal cycles, and they worshiped goddesses, or a goddess, in many forms.[14] Gimbutas's ideas, which fit directly the Wiccan mythology of the ancient goddess, were immediately and enthusiastically accepted as proof of the preeminence of the goddess.

Gimbutas and Campbell discuss the wide variety of goddess figurines that have been found in gravesites, arguing that these figures are representations of the goddess used as a personal divinity. This connection between archeology and mythology is an important path for contemporary feminists. Proof from archeology and mythology that a polytheistic goddess-worshiping society existed, and was geographically diverse, peaceful, and sexually egalitarian, would prove that contemporary misogyny and hierarchy are not a natural form of social organization. If the contemporary social order is not natural, then it is also changeable.

Dianic Tradition

Zsuzsanna Budapest is important in the early development of goddess worship in America. After fleeing the Hungarian revolution of 1956 Budapest, a descendant of a Hungarian people with their own folkloric witch tradition, arrived in America.[15] Budapest founded the Susan B. Anthony Coven No. 1 on the Winter Solstice of 1971.[16] By spring equinox of 1972 Budapest had written the manifesto for the group that outlined goddess worship for the coven. In it she wrote,

> We believe that feminist witches are women who search within themselves for the female principle of the universe and who relate as daughters to the Creatrix. We believe that, just as it is time to fight for the right to control our bodies, it is also time to fight for our sweet woman souls. . . . We believe that the Goddess-consciousness gave humanity a workable, long-lasting, peaceful period during which Earth was treated as Mother and women were treated as Her priestesses. We believe that women lost supremacy through the aggressions of males who were exiled from the matriarchies and formed the patriarchal hordes responsible for the invention of rape and the subjugation of women. . . . Our immediate goal is to congregate with each other according to our *ancient woman-made laws* and to remember our past, renew our powers, and affirm our Goddess of the Ten Thousand Names."[17]

The central themes of goddess worship outlined for the first time in manifesto form informed some of the goddess worship that followed.

The Dianic tradition is a women-only spiritual practice that looked to a number of sources for its inspiration (see Denise Saint Arnault's chapter in this volume). Members of the Susan B. Anthony Coven No. 1 brought different experiences and histories and helped shape the character and practice of not only the coven but goddess worship in general. These members brought spiritual practice learned from Native American, astrology, academic theology, and engaged feminist politics, and interest and experience with neo-pagan witchcraft. Budapest articulated the relationship between contemporary witchcraft and the historic relations "thealogical" practices had with theology organizations: "Before white people were Christianized, before Europe was taken by the sword of the Byzantine Empire, before Rome extended its imperial grasp around Western Europe, white people followed a native European nature religion."[18]

Eco-feminism and Reclaiming

Starhawk, an important thealogian[19] and writer, helped found the San Francisco–based Reclaiming tradition. The Reclaiming Collective began after publication of Starhawk's highly influential *The Spiral Dance* in 1979; subsequent editions have become the most important Wiccan publications of the late 20th century and a guide for the 21st century. Starhawk emphasized the environmental and political aspects of goddess worship, as expressed by Reclaiming's Principles of Unity:

> The values of the Reclaiming tradition stem from our understanding that the earth is alive and all of life is sacred and interconnected. We see the Goddess as immanent in the earth's cycles of birth, growth, death, decay, and regeneration. Our practice arises from a deep, spiritual commitment to the earth, to healing, and to the linking of magic with political action.[20]

Starhawk provided links among ecology, feminism, and paganism, connections that are vital in the Reclaiming tradition. This connection has remained one of the primary characteristics of Reclaiming and much American witchcraft in general. Reclaiming differs from the Dianic tradition in a number of ways, but two of the most important are that it was open to men and women early on, and that Reclaiming has a strong ecological politics.

One of the hallmarks of Reclaiming is that there is no central organization. Many groups use rituals that Reclaiming has created without necessarily identifying themselves with the Reclaiming tradition. Many goddess-celebrating communities use Starhawk's *Spiral Dance* and Budapest's *Book of Women's Mysteries* to inform their thealogy but do not call themselves Dianic or Reclaiming. What does bind most pagans together is the use of ritual and magic.

Ritual and Magic

Ritual and magic are central to goddess worship. A predominant belief in goddess worship is that magic is the transformation of consciousness. For an eco-feminist pagan, the transformation (magic) that is needed can be created through the practice of rituals[21] designed to transform the world into a "sensuous and living world."[22] This transformation is designed to "re-enchant" the world.[23] The ritual process for the community is designed to transform the world for those who enact the ritual. The Californian countercultural writer Theodore Roszak suggested that "the way forward is inevitably the way inward," and American Wicca have been working with ritual and magic to chart this path.[24]

The Mists of Avalon

The first four paths to the contemporary American goddess have impacted a great many people, but arguably the fourth path has done more to pique the interest of people and draw them to one or more of the other paths. The American novelist Marion Zimmer Bradley's celebrated novel *The Mists of Avalon*, and the subsequent *Avalon* series by Bradley and Diana L. Paxson, created a goddess-centered universe. Bradley retold the Arthurian legend from the point of view of the story's female characters. Her approach gave the women in the story a voice for the sake of contemporary women. She wrote, "Restoring Morgan and the Lady of the Lake to real, integral movers in the drama is, I think, of supreme importance in the religious and psychological development of women in our day."[25] The *Avalon* series plumbs the stories of the Roman conquest of Europe and tells the tales of this period from the point of view of important and often-silenced historical female characters.

The *Avalon* series continues to play an important role in introducing the idea of goddess worship to new generations. In much the same way Campbell and Gimbutas make claims for prehistory, Bradley and Paxson make claims against a male-dominated European history. Their stories are a spiritually sensitive, feminist retelling of history with the contemporary female reader in mind. The *Avalon* series, though a work of fiction, is an important historical reclamation project that may lead people to "reach out for the gentler reign of Goddess-oriented paganism to lead them back to a true perception of the spiritual life of the Earth."[26]

Our Goddess of Washington State

What follows is a single local account and must be only one among many possible accounts of contemporary goddess worship in North America. Mela was the spiritual elder for a small goddess community that met for nearly three decades on the property in rural Washington State she called New Avalon.[27] The morning after summer solstice 2008 she passed away after a two-year battle with cancer. At a ritual circle for winter solstice in December 2008 her name was called, for the first time, as the community's personal goddess. This is her story.

Mela, by her own account, accidentally discovered goddess worship while living in Santa Barbara, California, in the early 1980s. She had worked as a model in Los Angeles during the late 1960s–1970s, and by the 1980s she had discovered the *Mists of Avalon*. In Guinevere she felt she discovered her archetypal personality. She felt that she knew Avalon and that somehow the story spoke to her in ways that she could not fully understand. She felt she was living the tragedy of Guinevere, forever torn between two men and two lives. She lived one life for the camera and another life for her spirit. But the magic of Guinevere and the Lady of Avalon touched her deeply and did not let go.

By the early 1980s she was introduced to goddess worship by an acquaintance who sang a single line, "We come from the goddess and to her we shall return, like a drop of rain, running to the ocean."[28] The song astonished Mela and changed her life. She asked her friend where that song was from and her friend responded, "Goddess rituals . . . would you like to do a goddess ritual?" Within a week they had organized a number of women into a group in Santa Barbara and began regular rituals. Using a mixture of Starhawk's process and self-designed goddess rituals, they set out to ritualize the beauty of being women and to discover the magic in their lives. This experience led Mela on a path of learning she would follow for over thirty years.

She and a number of friends relocated to Washington State a few years later to more fully experience the seasons they were celebrating. In this new space she became central to community ritual. When, by chance, the facilitator for a ritual circle that she had organized could not attend, Mela was forced for the first time to take the lead in a ritual. Nervously, she did what she had to do, and her experience was so positive that she felt that she should continue to organize and lead ritual circles.

Mela was able to continue her learning by attending workshops and circles organized by elder women. She attended a gathering in California that had a great impact on her. She was transformed into a feminist at a large circle organized by Starhawk and Reclaiming Tradition. She heard Marija Gimbutas speak and what she had been studying and thinking came together. She had heard a song about the Burning Times and saw a National Film Board of Canada documentary that detailed the history of women's persecution.[29] Mela claimed that after the event she understood feminism for the first time and felt her devotion to the goddess deepen.

The Community Grows

For years Mela's circles were only open to women, but later men were permitted to join. The circles grew larger year after year, and more people were brought to each of the summer and winter solstice ceremonies. The rest of the ritual calendar, however, was celebrated by only a small group of local practitioners. By the late 1990s people were traveling from all over the United States and western Canada to be at New Avalon for the yearly summer and winter solstices. Mela and New Avalon had become the ritual center for a goddess community.

So it continued for years, until sickness made it impossible for Mela to continue. Throughout her sickness volunteers, messages, prayers, and money from the community helped sustain her and her husband. The community rallied around her and assisted her throughout her sickness. After her passing, many people gathered to celebrate Mela's life and rebirth into the mystery of the goddess. Mela had become for each member of the community a personal connection to the mystery of the goddess. She led the way upon a difficult path that the rest of the community would inevitably follow.

Today, New Avalon, like Bradley's Avalon, has disappeared into the mists. Mela's ritual space is no longer available for public gathering. Many have started smaller local groups closer to their homes. Mela's practice and teachings are being explained to new ritual participants. Mela's words and expressions are being distributed as the wisdom of the goddess; everyone is blessed with a "circle of love, light, and protection."[30] Mela, Our Goddess of Washington State, is one example of a personal manifestation of a feminist goddess in America.

"We are not the first, nor the last"

Z. Budapest wrote, "Come with me to the Temple, close your eyes, and then open them again. I will show you images of the Goddesses created before us by Goddess worshipping people. We are not the first, nor the last. And even if we are the first women to turn to worship themselves and *their own creativity in the Goddess,* then more glory to us."[31] The act of creativity in the experience of the sacred is central to the contemporary worship of the goddess. Since the 1960s a growing number of North Americans have been turning toward a personalized relationship with goddess spirituality. This relationship has taken a variety of forms but what is central to all experiences of the spirit is the ritual. The experience of the ritual is an active and engaged relationship that transcends the perceived separation of outside and inside. The ritual act is the engagement with the experience of the sacred, of the intuition that the goddess is there. John Dewey wrote, "There is something mystical associated with the word intuition. . . . Although there is a bounding horizon, it moves as we move. We are never wholly free from the sense of something that lies beyond."[32] The act of ritualizing a relationship with the goddess is an attempt to move beyond what is most physically obvious so that one may get closer to the mystery on the other side of perception; it is just out of reach.

The spiritual quest is as old as humanity. For millennia, humans have actively cultivated a relationship with the mystery of life and death. These mysteries have inspired spiritual practices and informed social order. Neo-paganism may represent a philosophical and spiritual return to a relationship with the natural world. Martin Heidegger claimed that religion is "a poetic experience of the world as something sacred and deserving of reverence."[33] The worship of the goddess shows that the act of creation and regeneration, of birth, maturity, and death, is the natural order of life but one that must be rooted in the natural environment. In some way humanity may be, in this period of environmental and political uncertainty, feeling the necessity to find a way to a balanced spiritual, political, and natural world. It does not hurt to remember that "before the gods existed, the woods were sacred, and the gods came to dwell in these sacred woods."[34]

Notes

1. Margot Adler, *Drawing Down the Moon: Witches, Druids, Goddess-Worshippers, and Other Pagans in America* (London: Penguin Books, 1979), 233–236; and Ronald Hutton, *The Triumph of the Moon* (New York: Oxford University Press, 1999), 17 and 341.

2. Starhawk, *The Spiral Dance: A Rebirth of the Ancient Religion of the Great Goddess* (San Francisco: Harper San Francisco, 1989), 13, 16–17.

3. Marion Green, *Wild Witchcraft: A Guide to Natural, Herbal, and Earth Magic* (London: Collins Publishers, 2002), 103.

4. Ibid., 27.

5. Adler, *Drawing Down the Moon*, 184.

6. Macha NightMare, telephone interview with author, Edmonton, AB, September 22, 2009.

7. Starhawk, *Spiral Dance*, 91.

8. Merlin Stone, *When God Was a Woman* (London: Virago Limited, 1976), 2.

9. A number of works deal with this issue. I feel that the following are the most succinct. Marija Gimbutas, *The Language of the Goddess* (New York: HarperCollins, 1989), xx–xxi; see also Marija Gimbutas, *The Living Goddesses*, ed. Miriam Robbins Dexter (Berkeley: University of California Press, 1999), 124. Also Shahrukh Husain, *The Goddess: Power, Sexuality, and the Feminine Divine* (Ann Arbor: University of Michigan Press. 2003), 6; Judith Ochshorn, "Goddesses and the Lives of Women," in *Women*

and Goddess Traditions: In Antiquity and Today, ed. Karen L. Torjesen and Karen Jo King (Minneapolis: Fortress Press, 1997), 378; Juliette Wood, "The Concept of the Goddess," in *The Concept of the Goddess,* ed. Sandra Billington and Miranda Green (New York: Routledge, 1996), 9.

10. Gimbutas, *Language of the Goddess,* xxi.

11. Joseph Campbell, *The Hero with a Thousand Faces* (Princeton, NJ: Princeton University Press, 1949), 3.

12. Joseph Campbell, *The Power of Myth: with Bill Moyers,* ed. Betty Sue Flowers (New York: Anchor Books, 1988), 209–210.

13. This is a name used to distinguish text-based religious practices like Judaism, Christianity, and Islam from non-text based and, in contemporary Western usage, usually pagan spiritual practices. A great deal could be made of this distinction through the lens of communications theory especially that of Harold Innis's *Empire and Communications* (1972) and the later work of Marshal McLuhan and Neil Postman.

14. Gimbutas, *Living Goddesses,* 3.

15. Zsuzsanna Budapest, *The Holy Book of Women's Mysteries* (San Francisco: Red Wheel/Weiser, 2007), 291–311.

16. Susan B. Anthony was a prominent civil rights leader and an important 19th-century women's rights advocate.

17. Budapest, *Holy Book of Women's Mysteries,* 1–2.

18. Ibid., xv–xxii, 265.

19. "Thealogian" is a word that many women, following Carol Christ, use in place of "theologian." Replacing the "o" with an "a" signals the difference between a male theology and a female thealogy, the study of goddesses. Thea is the Greek for Goddess.

20. Starhawk, *Spiral Dance,* 6.

21. For the sake of brevity I have used the work *rituals* to suggest a collection of approaches to life. Here I am thinking of Starhawk when she wrote, "Magic teaches us to be aware that we are viewing the world through a frame, warns us not to confuse it with ultimate reality or mistake the map for the territory. Moreover, part of our magical discipline is to make conscious choices about which frame we adopt." Starhawk, *The Earth Path: Grounding Your Spirit in the Rhythms of Nature* (New York: HarperCollins, 2005), 30. This matrix of conscious choices I am referring to with the work *ritual.* All readers will not share this overly open definition and therefore one may choose to think of ritual as a special physically enacted set of protocols. However, I argue that this is already how we live our lives. The question is, therefore, whose rituals are we enacting?

22. Stanley Jeyaraja Tambiah, *Magic, Science, Religion, and the Scope of Rationality* (New York: Cambridge University Press, 1990), 17. Thanks to David Lertzman (David Adam) for this reference. David is a celebrated bard and scholar whom I am fortunate to call a brother.

23. Morris Berman, *The Reenchantment of the World* (Ithaca, NY: Cornell University Press, 1981).

24. Theodore Roszak, *Unfinished Animal: The Aquarian Frontier and the Evolution of Consciousness* (New York: Harper and Row, 1975), 239.

25. Marion Zimmer-Bradley, "Thoughts on Avalon," 1986, http://www.mzbworks.com/thoughts.htm (accessed July 13, 2010).

26. Ibid.

27. I have written more about the ritual practice at New Avalon in "Singing Me Into the Land," *Vis-à-Vis: Explorations in Anthropology* 9, no. 1 (2009): 58–69.

28. "We All Come from the Goddess" a Goddess chant by Z. Budapest. This is one of the most famous and widely sung chants.

29. *Burning Times*, National Film Board of Canada, dir. Donna Read, 1990, 56 min 10 sec. Part 2 of a three-part series: *Goddess Remembered, Burning Times*, and *Full Circle*.

30. A general blessing used at New Avalon.

31. Budapest, *Holy Book of Women's Mysteries*, 313.

32. John Dewey, *Art as Experience* (New York: Capricorn Books, 1934), 193.

33. John D. Caputo, "Heidegger and Theology," in *The Cambridge Companion to Heidegger*, ed. Charles B. Guignon (New York: Cambridge University Press, 1993), 283.

34. Gaston Bachelard, *The Poetics of Space*, trans. Maria Jolas (New York: Orion Press, 1964), 186.

Bibliography

Adler, Margot. *Drawing Down the Moon: Witches, Druids, Goddess-Worshippers, and Other Pagans in America*. London: Penguin Books, 1979.

Bachelard, Gaston. *The Poetics of Space*. Translated by Maria Jolas. New York: Orion Press, 1964.

Berman, Morris. *The Reenchantment of the World*. Ithaca, NY: Cornell University Press, 1981.

Budapest, Zsuzsanna. *The Holy Book of Women's Mysteries*. San Francisco: Red Wheel/Weiser, 2007.

Burning Times. National Film Board of Canada. Donna Read, Director, 1990.

Campbell, Joseph. *The Hero with a Thousand Faces*. Princeton, NJ: Princeton University Press, 1949.

Campbell, Joseph. *The Power of Myth: with Bill Moyers*. Edited by Betty Sue Flowers. New York: Anchor Books, 1988.

Caputo, John D. "Heidegger and Theology." In *The Cambridge Companion to Heidegger*, ed. Charles B. Guignon. New York: Cambridge University Press, 1993.

Dewey, John. *Art as Experience*. New York: Capricorn Books, 1934.

Gimbutas, Marija. *The Language of the Goddess*. New York: HarperCollins, 1989.

Gimbutas, Marija. *The Living Goddesses*, Edited by Miriam Robbins Dexter. Berkeley: University of California Press, 1999.

Green, Marion. *Wild Witchcraft: A Guide to Natural, Herbal, and Earth Magic*. London: Collins, 2002.

Husain, Shahrukh. *The Goddess: Power, Sexuality, and the Feminine Divine*. Ann Arbor: University of Michigan Press. 2003.

Hutton, Ronald. *The Triumph of the Moon*. New York: Oxford University Press, 1999.

MacDonald, Michael. "Singing Me into the Land." *Vis-à-Vis: Explorations in Anthropology* 9, no. 1 (2009): 58–69.

Ochshorn, Judith. "Goddesses and the Lives of Women." In *Women and Goddess Traditions: In Antiquity and Today*, ed. Karen L. Torjeson and Karen Jo King. Minneapolis: Fortress Press, 1997.

Starhawk. *The Earth Path: Grounding Your Spirit in the Rhythms of Nature*. New York: HarperCollins, 2005.

Starhawk. *The Spiral Dance: A Rebirth of the Ancient Religion of the Great Goddess*. San Francisco: Harper San Francisco, 1979.

Stone, Merlin. *When God Was a Woman*. London: Virago Limited, 1976.

Roszak, Theodore. *Unfinished Animal: The Aquarian Frontier and the Evolution of Consciousness*. New York: Harper and Row, 1975.

Tambiah, Stanley Jeyaraja. *Magic, Science, Religion, and the Scope of Rationality*. New York: Cambridge University Press, 1990.

Wood, Juliette. "The Concept of the Goddess." In *The Concept of the Goddess*, ed. Sandra Billington and Miranda Green. New York: Routledge, 1996.

Zimmer-Bradley, Marion. "Thoughts on Avalon." 1986. http://www.mzbworks .com/thoughts.htm.

22

Deae ex Machina: Goddesses from a Machine

Kyle Glasgow

Goddesses in video games? How can that be? Do not goddesses have to do with nature, not technology? Do they not encourage connection with others, home, and hearth, rather than the use of virtual flame-throwers to eliminate zombies? Should they not exist in the warmth of human touch, instead of in the molded plastic of a controller, mouse, or keyboard? Many people in religious, spiritual, and academic fields view the emergence of video games with their violent, highly sexualized content as antithetical to the image of the nurturing, warm, and yielding divine feminine. But goddesses are everywhere, even in a microchip, much as Robert Pirsig suggested when he said that Buddha was just as home in a microchip as anywhere else.[1]

A goddess can be said to represent certain abstract and profound characteristics of the human experience. Goddess energies emerge in lover or maiden, mother and crone as well as a fourth, more active aspect, the daughter.

The mother aspect of the goddess is the best known and explicated of the four aspects. Traditionally associated with sustenance and fecundity, the mother is paradoxically also concerned with destruction. Perhaps the best-known embodiment is that of Kali, Hindu goddess of the cycle of creation and destruction. Kali is the representation of ultimate reality, the knowing and acceptance of death as necessary for life to continue.[2]

Figure 22.1 Venus de Carnage. (Venus picture by Jastrow [Marie-Lan Nguyen]. Gatling gun picture by Shane T. McCoy. Public domain images combined by Kyle Glasgow.)

The daughter represents the goddess in the form of a young, athletic woman, archetypically the Amazon or woman warrior. As explained by Ann Ulanov, "The feminine structured as Amazon produces a personality which is self-contained and independent."[3] She is "the warrior-maiden-adventurer" and the goal-directed, assertive Artemis as described by Jean Shinola Bolen.[4] While the daughter aspect of the goddess may elicit sexual desire in those around her, she is not interested in sexuality or relationship; that province is for the lover.

The lover represents not just the physical pleasure, beauty, and desire of the divine feminine, but also the warmth and connection felt by one person for another. Bolen weaves these two aspects together when she writes, "Growth of trust and love, and a gradual reduction in inhibition, precedes the 'evocation' or birth of Aphrodite, heralded by the first orgasm in lovemaking and a new desire for physical intimacy."[5]

Finally, there is the crone. Bolen calls this the "Hestia aspect" after the Greek goddess of hearth and home. This aspect represents the wisdom and knowledge of the goddess. "She is like an elder that has seen it all, and has come through with her spirit undampened and her character tempered by experience."[6] Both the lover and the crone seek connection. While the lover seeks to establish warm and physical connections between people, the crone seeks a connection with the divine to be of service.

Each of these expressions of the divine feminine can be found in video games. Some aspects of the goddess exist in video games in the form of characters. Some aspects of the goddess are present within the actual design of the video games in terms of certain qualities or abilities available to the player. If one were to take David Kinsley's interpretation of the goddess Kali as representative of ultimate reality, it is not a far stretch to imagine the virtual world created as goddess herself. Indeed, video games were birthed from the imaginations of programmers and have come from single players competing against each other on the same console to the Massively Multiplayer Online Role Playing Games (MMORPGs) that provide the opportunity to connect with others regardless of physical location and to cooperatively work toward common goals.

A Brief History of Video Games

Spacewar, the first interactive video game (1962), enabled two players to control opposing spaceships in an attempt to destroy each other with missiles. The video-game industry itself began in 1971 with a coin-operated ("coin-op") version of Spacewar introduced alongside pinball machines in arcades. The first home-console system was released within a year and featured the now-infamous Pong game, the video game that began the consumer market since it allowed people to use their televisions as the screen. In 1977 the Commodore PET and Apple II were commercially released and video games began to be played on computers. As personal computers developed greater power, they began to connect to each other and to the nascent Internet. As video-game graphics quality improved, visual representations of people gradually became more recognizable. Meanwhile, Internet use was growing steadily. By 1997 the ability to play graphical computer games with people from all over the world became possible. This resulted in the 1997 release of Ultima Online and the birth of the MMORPG genre.[7] Today video-game goddesses can be found on home computers and video-game consoles connected to the Internet. Goddess energy exists in the graphics, the storyline, and in the very act of playing the game. Today digital expressions of the goddess are everywhere.

Characters and Avatars: Distinctions

While early video games had crude graphics, the art has become more and more refined over time, resulting in a more immersive experience for the player.[8] Players control super-powered digital playing pieces variously known as characters, toons (short for "cartoon," a reference to the animated nature of the pieces), or avatars. For purposes of this chapter, a *character* is a static image that the player has little or no ability to alter in appearance, skill, or ability, much like a character in a book. For example, Ms. Pacman is a video-game character. The player can maneuver her around the screen but cannot change her appearance, speed, or size. *Avatars*, by contrast, are highly customizable and can embody the characteristics of the player, including characteristics of the goddess within. The word comes from the Sanskrit and references the descent of a divinity into human form; it can mean a literal incarnation of a deity, an embodiment (as of a concept or philosophy) or an electronic image that represents and is manipulated by a computer user (as in a computer game).[9]

The last definition was popularized by Neal Stephenson's seminal novel about cyberspace, *Snow Crash*.[10] Although the term *avatar* had been used in earlier video games and online communities, Stephenson's novel cemented the meaning for the representation of persons online.[11] As such a representation, the avatar allows the player to form connections with other avatars. In this way a player who embodies a certain goddess energy can express that divinity in ways that he or she could not in "real life."

Video-game genres include shooters, role playing or adventure games, fighting games, driving games, strategy games, and combinations thereof. This chapter focuses on shooters—role-playing games and fighting games—because they typically have human or humanoid avatars that provide a physical representation of goddesses as well as storylines and settings most conducive to channeling goddesses.

In shooter games, the video-game character uses a gun or other weapon to eliminate targets on the video screen. Role-playing games (RPGs) involve a detailed storyline and allow the player to develop the skills and abilities of his or her avatar. Fighting games have the player take control of a character to fight other players or computer opponents using combinations of button pushes/joystick moves. In shooter and fighting games, the player typically takes control of an already created character with fixed characteristics. The player can make few, if any, modifications. In contrast, RPGs often allow players to design their own characters and to modify the characters over time.

The Four Aspects of the Goddess on Screen

As discussed previously, four aspects of the goddess occur in video games: mother, daughter, lover, and crone (two of these are present *in* the game, two *are* the game). In video games, the aspects of the goddess most prevalent as playable characters are the daughter and the crone. The mother and the lover, while rarely expressed as playable characters, are present in both content and process. With the advent of the Internet and the spread of multiplayer games, the mother and the lover have come to life through the nurturing and loving relationships formed while playing games with others. For while it is true that some players simply tolerate the relationships necessary to play MMORPGs, far more players will say that playing the game is simply a backdrop for connecting with their online-communities.[12] These two energies are also utilized in the actual design of the game, where they are expressed not as playable characters but, rather, in the way the player connects to the game.

The mother can be thought of as the game itself. The game provides the framework through which the character encounters the cycle of life, death, and rebirth. In a sense, a video game allows the player to express the mother energy, especially in RPGs where the player creates characters and endows them with certain abilities and aspects. Thereafter the player nurtures and grows the characters throughout the life of the game. Many players have described feeling a connection with their characters. And yet while players may feel connected to what they have birthed and grown, in a video game this connection is without the earthy, physical, warmth of the true mother goddess. The connection is a transitional one, much like the connection a child has with a doll. After all, that is why it is called a game.

Much in the same way that Patricia Monaghan posits that the image of the lover goddess is present in advertising only to provide a connection to the object being sold, so to the lover is present in almost every video game involving human or humanoid-looking female characters.[13]

She exists not as a person to connect with in a warm, tender or passionate way, but as a way to connect *to* the character and thereby the game. Hence most female characters in video games are curvaceous, sexualized representations of the lover rather than the lover herself. The lover aspect involves more than just surface attraction. It exists as a way for people to enter into a union to bring forth something or someone previously unknown.

By and large the two aspects of the goddess most often represented in video games are the daughter and the crone. The daughter, as a playable character, appears in video games as the heroine, almost always in the guise of her warrior self. As an avatar, the daughter exists as a warrior also, able to be filled with the intentionality of the player. The crone is usually present in video games as a healer, witch, cleric, or similar magical being. Almost no video games portray the crone as a playable character. Sometimes she appears as the enemy, other times as a guide to the main character. However, no other avatar is more sought after in the MMORPG world than the crone. It is in the connection with other players where her skills and abilities to aid others are invaluable. Indeed very few adventures begin in the MMORPG world without the question "Who is healing?" being answered first.

How Characters and Avatars Appear in Games

As a character the daughter was first epitomized by the protagonist Samus Aran in the 1986 console game Metroid. Samus was portrayed as a humanoid figure in futuristic metal armor who hunts space pirates and aliens led by a Mother Brain; here mother energy is present not as a character, but as a concept. Every indication was made to refer to Samus as male, including references to the character in the U.S. version of the instruction manual. If the player won the game in under two hours—a feat that requires days if not weeks of playing to master the skills necessary—Samus removed her metal armor and waved to the player while wearing a pink bikini. Metroid had "one of video gaming's most famous endings: Samus' garish space armor fell away and thousands of pre-teen boys had to come to grips with the fact Mother Brain had just been wasted by a cootie-infested girl."[14] Samus is one of the most well-known and admired characters in video-game history.[15] In a genre filled with muscle-bound male heroes saving helpless women, Samus was the perfect representation of the daughter's concern with exerting her own power while saving the universe.

Despite the innovation of Samus, characters in early video games remained primarily male and the games themselves featured male-centered themes. This was also the case in the fighting-game genre. It was here that adolescent males spent much of their time going virtually *mano a mano* against other players through the use of video-game characters. That was until Chun-Li appeared in *Street Fighter II*.[16] Chun-Li, the first female fighting-game character, remains one of the most popular video-game characters.[17] This is not primarily because she looked good on screen (although she did) but because of the combat moves the player could use with her. Whereas many of the male characters had varying degrees of strength and "power" moves, Chun-Li was the finesse character, meaning the character's primary abilities were speed and accuracy. Finesse, however, did not mean she was a pushover. Well played, Chun-Li could easily defeat other players of equal skill. Her daughter energy resulted in quick kicks, jumps, and other archetypal moves repeated throughout the development of video games and even film.[18] She was Artemis the huntress, a daughter who consorted with men only to remind them that they are not the sole owners of physical prowess. The player who chose Chun-Li would have access to that energy and, if he or she knew how to use it well, could quickly crush a lesser skilled player playing a more powerful character.

The final daughter energy present as a character is personified in the sometimes-controversial character Lara Croft from the *Tomb Raider* series. Lara Croft appears wearing tight-fitting shorts with holsters strapped to each leg, giving the illusion of a pair of garters. Her hair was often pulled back in a braid, she sometimes wore librarian glasses, and her breasts were apparent in a tight-fitting top. Despite this fetishistic appearance, Lara was a unique video-game character in that she did not act like a woman in a video game usually acted.[19] She was independent, strong, capable, smart, aggressive, and at times brutal. This brutality fueled some of the controversy. Men characters were supposed to be brutal and to shoot people with guns. But a voluptuous young woman with guns was supposed to wear a bikini and smile. Lara Croft represented an emerging dynamic in video-game goddesses: the daughter energy wrapped up in the lover's garb. A player falls in love with her appearance and forms an attachment to the character based on visual beauty. But despite the lovely packaging, there is no lover's energy here. Rather, the player is utilizing the daughter energy to exude power over a virtual world and to win.

Goddesses as Avatars, Avatars as Goddesses

Unlike static characters controlled by a player but constrained by the characteristics imbued by the game's programmers, avatars are graphical representations of players that are not only controlled by but also created by the player. With the rise of the Internet as a medium of connection between players, there emerged the possibility of these pixilated progenies meeting and journeying together. While there are many types of online games, the MMORPG is the most goddess-friendly. Individual players create individual avatars. These games are also socially driven; a player's success often relies on cooperation with other players.[20] There are two ways the goddess energy is present in MMORPGs: first, as an intentional design by the developer, and second, through the interactions of the players.

Most MMORPGs involve the creation of an avatar, with the player choosing attributes such as strength, intelligence, or dexterity, for example; skills like healing, magic, or weaponry; gender; and appearance. The game designers establish the attributes available. Interestingly, the choice of gender often has a much smaller effect on the capabilities of the avatar than the choice of skills or abilities. Through the amalgamation of choices made by the player, the form of the avatar expresses the force of the goddess energy.

The four main types of avatars in MMORPGs are the warrior, thief, magic-user, and healer. The warrior provides the brute physical force necessary to overcome physical dangers; the thief makes use of trickery and stealth to achieve goals; the magic-user relies on arcane knowledge to master the environment; the healer exists to provide support to all the other characters. The daughter energy is present in the warrior and to a lesser extent the thief. The crone energy manifests itself in the magic-user and, most significantly, in the healer.

Unlike in shooter games, the daughter manifestation in MMORPGs is similar to static characters, although the player does control certain characteristics of the avatar. The warrior and the thief types in MMORPGs derive their power and influence in the physical realm of the game. With the addition of the magic-user and the healer however, the crone energy becomes critical.

The crone form in MMORPGs becomes important because players have the ability to coordinate their efforts in an attempt to achieve a larger goal. In this way connections are formed. With the establishment of connections comes the necessity of assistance and protection. In MMORPGs when individual players join together to accomplish a goal, they are called a group or party within the MMORPG culture. The crone establishes a connection between the physical avatars and the spiritual or mystical realm. Using this power as the form of a magic-user, the crone energy can attack threats to their party in much the same way that Athena would devastate the enemies of Athens. But the most important form of crone energy in MMORPGs is the healing avatar.

Healer avatars exist almost exclusively for the benefit of the other players. It should be noted also that this is crone energy, not form; a player could create a male healer and still embody the crone energy. The excitement of being a healer comes from the connection to others—a decisively feminine energy. The ability of the healer to repair injury or to even bring other avatars back after death is invaluable in combat. While many players choose the glorious path of warriors, thieves, or magic-users, those who pick the humble, quiet path of the crone-powered healer are often female in "real life" away from the computer. While playing a healer avatar might be less adrenaline producing, it is one of the most sought-after classes when creating a party. After all, avatars represent an enormous amount of time and energy. To be successful, however, one has to stay alive. As an intentional design of MMORPGs, the healer is the embodiment of the crone energy. In addition to this the crone serves as a virtual way to help other players. In this way a player can channel goddess energy to connect with other players in a way not available to them otherwise.

There exist in video games aspects of the divine feminine. Perhaps in no other medium is the divine feminine allowed full expression. In video games, female characters capable of defending themselves and exerting power over others are not viewed as unusual; in fact, the use of female avatars is quite common.[21] It is ironic that the pleasing physical form of the lover, undoubtedly used to engage players, can give rise to an appreciation of the other aspects of the goddess. Whether it is through the static characters in a console video game or a player-generated avatar, the divine feminine might be disguised, but is always ever present.

Notes

1. Robert Pursig, *Zen and the Art of Motorcycle Maintenance* (New York: Bantam, 1975), 16.

2. David Kinsley, *Hindu Goddesses: Visions of the Divine Feminine in the Hindu Religious Tradition* (New Delhi: Motilal Banarsidass, 1999), 130.

3. Ann Belford Ulanov, *The Feminine in Jungian Psychology and in Christian Theology* (Chicago: Northwestern University Press, 1971), 205.

4. Madonna Kolbenschlag, *Kiss Sleeping Beauty Good-Bye* (New York: Bantam, 1979), 8; Jean Bolen, *Goddesses in Everywomen: A New Psychology of Women* (New York: Harper Perennial, 1985).

5. Ibid., 240.

6. Ibid., 113.

7. Steve Butts, "Ultima Online: Kingdom Reborn Preview," IGN, http://pc.ign.com/articles/759/759391p1.html (accessed September 26, 2009).

8. John Suler. "Psychology of Avatars." Psychology of Cyberspace. http://www-usr.rider.edu/~suler/psycyber/psyav.html (accessed September 26, 2009).

9. Merriam-Webster's Online Dictionary, s.v. "avatar," http://www.merriam-webster.com/dictionary/avatar (accessed January 17, 2009).

10. Neil Stephenson, *Snow Crash* (New York: Bantam, 1992).

11. Randall Farmer, "Social Dimensions of Habitat's Citizenry," http://www.crockford.com/ec/citizenry.html (accessed January 17, 2009).

12. Kyle Glasgow, "Being-With Online in a Massively Multiplayer Online Role-Playing Game," PsyD diss., Farmington Hills, MI: Center for Humanistic Studies, 2003.

13. Patricia Monaghan, *The Goddess Path: Myths, Invocations and Rituals* (St. Paul: Llewellyn Publications, 1999).

14. Nadia Oxford, "One Girl Against the Galaxy: 20 Years of Metroid and Samus Aran," 1up.com, http://www.1up.com/do/feature?pager.offset=0&cId=3152658 (accessed September 26, 2009).

15. "Top 10 Videogame Characters," *Electronic Gaming Monthly*, no. 198 (December 2005), http://www.1up.com/do/feature?cid=3145545 (accessed January 17, 2009).

16. Knites, "Chun-Li: The First Lady of Video Games," Retrojunk, http://www.retrojunk.com/details_articles/569 (accessed January 17, 2009).

17. D. F. Smith, "Top 25 Street Fighters: The Final Five," IGN, http://stars.ign.com/articles/895/895030p3.html (accessed January 17, 2009).

18. Wikipedia, s.v. "Chun-Li," http://en.wikipedia.org/wiki/Chun-Li#Films (accessed October 4, 2009).

19. Helen Kennedy, "Lara Croft: Feminist Icon or Cyberbimbo? On the Limits of Textual Analysis," Game Studies, http://www.gamestudies.org/0202/kennedy (accessed September 26, 2009).

20. Glasgow, "Being-With Online."

21. Nick Yee, "The Demographics of Game Choices," The Daedalus Project, http://www.nickyee.com/daedalus/archives/print/001558.php (accessed September 26, 2009).

Bibliography

Bolen, Jean Shinoda. *Goddesses in Everywoman: A New Psychology of Women*. New York: Harper Perennial, 1985.

Butts, Steve. "Ultima Online: Kingdom Reborn preview." IGN, 2007. http://pc.ign.com/articles/759/759391p1.html (accessed September 26, 2009).

Cocker, Guy. "Lara Croft Earns Guinness World Record." GameSpot UK, 2006. http://uk.gamespot.com/news/6147291.html (accessed September 26, 2009).

Electronic Gaming Monthly. "Top 10 Videogame Characters." *EGM*, no. 198 (December 2005). http://www.1up.com/do/feature?cid=3145545 (accessed January 17, 2009).

Farmer, F. Randall. "Social Dimensions of Habitat's Citizenry." 1996. http://www.crockford.com/ec/citizenry.html (accessed January 17, 2009).

Glasgow, Kyle. "Being-With Online in a Massively Multiplayer Online Role-Playing Game." PsyD diss., Farmington Hills, MI: Center for Humanistic Studies, 2003.

IGN. "Chun-Li Biography." http://stars.ign.com/objects/142/14221626_biography .html (accessed September 26, 2009).

Kennedy, Helen W. "Lara Croft: Feminist Icon or Cyberbimbo? On the Limits of Textual Analysis." *Game Studies*, no. 2 (December 2002). http://www .gamestudies.org/0202/kennedy (accessed September 26, 2009).

Kent, Steven. "Alternate Reality: The History of Massively Multiplayer Online Games." GameSpy, 2003. http://archive.gamespy.com/amdmmog/week1/ index.shtml (accessed September 26, 2009).

Kinsley, David R. *Hindu Goddesses: Visions of the Divine Feminine in the Hindu Religious Tradition.* New Delhi: Motilal Banarsidass, 1999.

Knites. "Chun-Li: The First Lady of Video Games." Retrojunk, 2009. http://www .retrojunk.com/details_articles/569 (accessed January 17, 2009).

Kolbenschlag, Madonna. *Kiss Sleeping Beauty Good-Bye.* New York: Bantam, 1979.

Monaghan, Patricia. *The Goddess Path: Myths, Invocations and Rituals.* St. Paul: Llewellyn Publications, 1999.

Pirsig, Robert. *Zen and the Art of Motorcycle Maintenance.* New York: Bantam, 1975.

Oxford, Nadia. "One Girl Against the Galaxy: 20 Years of Metroid and Samus Aran." 1up.com, 2006. http://www.1up.com/do/feature?pager.offset=0& cId=3152658 (accessed September 26, 2009).

Schleiner, Anne-Marie. "Does Lara Croft Wear Fake Polygons? Gender and Gender-Role Subversion in Computer Adventure Games." *Leonardo* 34, no. 3 (2001). http://www.jstor.org/stable/1576939 (accessed September 26, 2009).

Smith, D. F. "Top 25 Street Fighters: The Final Five." IGN, 2009. http://stars .ign.com/articles/895/895030p3.html (accessed January 17, 2009).

Stephenson, Neil. *Snow Crash.* New York: Bantam Dell, 1992.

Suler, John. "Psychology of Avatars." Psychology of Cyberspace, 1996. http://www -usr.rider.edu/~suler/psycyber/psyav.html (accessed September 26, 2009).

Ulanov, Ann Belford. *The Feminine in Jungian Psychology and in Christian Theology.* Evanston, IL: Northwestern University Press, 1971.

Yee, Nick. "The Demographics of Game Choices." The Daedalus Project, 2003. http://www.nickyee.com/daedalus/archives/print/001558.php (accessed September 26, 2009).

Yee, Nick. "The Demographics of Gender-Bending." The Daedalus Project, 2003. http://www.nickyee.com/daedalus/archives/print/000551.php (accessed September 26, 2009).

About the Editor and Contributors

PATRICIA MONAGHAN is professor of interdisciplinary studies at DePaul University in Chicago and Senior Fellow at the Black Earth Institute in Wisconsin. She is the author of more than a dozen books, including *The Encyclopedia of Goddesses and Heroines* (Greenwood) and *The Red-Haired Girl from the Bog* (New World Library). She is an officer of the Association for the Study of Women and Mythology. Monaghan has published four books of poetry and has won numerous prizes for her literary work, including a Pushcart Prize.

DAVE AFTANDILIAN is assistant professor of anthropology at Texas Christian University and co-chair of the American Academy of Religion's Animals and Religion Consultation. He is the co-editor of *What Are the Animals to Us? Approaches from Science, Religion, Folklore, Literature, and Art*. His research and teaching focus on the intersection of nature and culture, especially human-animal interactions as expressed in stories, art, and religion. He is also keenly interested in issues of food and justice.

MUNYA ANDREWS is an Indigenous woman of Bandaiyan (Australia). Her people are the Bardi and Nyul Nyul who live on the Dampier Peninsula in the Kimberley region of northern Australia. A lawyer and anthropologist, Munya is enthralled by science, mythology, and comparative religions and is intrigued by the ways in which these disciplines interact and inform the other. Author of *The Seven Sisters of the Pleiades*, she examines various world mythologies on this famous star cluster and explores the links between science and spirituality. Munya teaches Aboriginal Dreamtime as a way of maintaining her people's language and cultural traditions in a world where Indigenous peoples struggle to assert their unique status of Indigeneity.

SHARON L. BARNES is associate professor of interdisciplinary and special programs at the University of Toledo in Toledo, Ohio, where she teaches developmental writing, women's studies, and honors multicultural literature. In addition to her work on Lorde, she is interested in other 20th-century American feminist poets and feminist activism against violence against women.

MARION W. COPLAND is a lecturer at Humane Society University and emerita professor of English at Holyoke Community College. Her primary research interests are in literature and art that foregrounds more-than-human animals as protagonists, narrators, and major characters. She is the co-editor of *What Are the Animals to Us? Approaches from Science, Religion, Folklore, Literature, and Art* and the author of *Charles Eastman (Ohiyesa)* and *Cockroach*.

MAX DASHU teaches global women's history and goddess traditions. In 1970 she founded the Suppressed Histories Archives to research female shamans, mother-right cultures, and the history of domination. Drawing on her collection of over 15,000 slides, she presents visual talks at universities, conferences, museums, and community centers. She is completing the first volume of *The Secret History of the Witches*, which looks at priestesses, oracles, goddesses, and ceremony in ancient Europe.

KAREN DILLON currently teaches in the English department at Indiana University, Bloomington. She specializes in 20th-century American literature and cultural studies, with an interest in the intersection of racial and national identity. Her dissertation focuses on representations of twins in American literary, visual, and popular culture.

CRISTINA EISENBERG is a Boone and Crockett Fellow and a PhD candidate in forestry and wildlife at Oregon State University. She holds a master's degree in environmental studies from Prescott College and is the author of *The Wolf's Tooth: Keystone Predators, Trophic Cascades, and Biodiversity*. She is a wolf biologist, editor, and scholar-advisor to the Black Earth

Institute, an interdisciplinary think-tank. Cristina is actively engaged in ecological restoration that supports sustainability of wildlife communities and of the human spirit.

ANN MEGISIKWE FILEMYR currently serves as Dean of the College of Contemporary Native Arts at the Institute of American Indian Arts in Santa Fe and is also a poet, photographer, speaker, and workshop leader. She had a twenty-year apprenticeship with a mashkikikwe, Keewaydinoquay, a traditional herbal healer in the Anishinaabeg culture of the Great Lakes. She studies and teaches traditional approaches to plant- and earth-based medicines, women's spirituality, creativity, and deepening self-awareness through writing and image-making. She has worked for twenty years in higher education with a special interest in innovative curriculum design interweaving the arts with experiential learning, service learning, and personal reflection.

BARBARA FLAHERTY holds a master's degree in culture and spirituality from Holy Names College. For twenty years she worked with Alaskan Native elders and healers facilitating village healing intensives using Inuit and cross-cultural mythological motifs. She is a published poet and essayist, winner of the Drogheda Amergin Poetry Award, and the author of two books, *Holy Madness* and *Do It Another Way*. Barbara is the founding companion of the Fourth Order of Francis and Clare, a transfaith community.

KYLE GLASGOW conducted his dissertation research on gaming and gaming communities. He works at a Detroit nonprofit organization devoted to the provision of mental health services for older adults. He is also a writer, educator, and clinical supervisor.

LANIER GRAHAM has published widely on world art and spirituality, and has been teaching world art, world religions, and world mythology for many years. He teaches at California State University, East Bay. His *Goddesses in Art* has been printed in four languages.

PATRIZIA GRANZIERA is a professor of art history at the University of Morelos, Cuernavaca, Mexico. She earned her PhD in art history from the University of Warwick (England). Her research focuses on the iconography of gardens and landscapes and the divine feminine. She has published widely on this topic in journals such as the *Journal of Intercultural Studies, Garden*

History, Landscape Research, and *World Christianity.* She has recently completed a book on *The Image of the Divine Feminine in Mexico: Aztec Goddesses and Christian Madonnas.*

MARGARET GROVE is a field researcher specializing in the rock art paintings and the mythology of the Aboriginal people of Northern Territory and Arnhem Land areas of Australia. Her explorations take her to all parts of the world where rock paintings exist, such as France, Spain, Africa, Baja Sur Mexico, Peru, and Brazil. She writes articles and takes photographs for magazines such as *Archaeology Magazine* and is referenced in a vast compendium of books. Her photographs are shown in curated shows around the world. She is a retired professor of archaeomythology.

ANNE KEY is an adjunct faculty member in women's studies and religious studies at the College of Southern Nevada and is cofounder of Goddess Institute Publishing. She was Priestess of the Temple of Goddess Spirituality Dedicated to Sekhmet, located in Nevada, from 2004 to 2007; her memoir is in process. She is co-editor of *The Heart of the Sun: An Anthology in Exaltation of Sekhmet.* Anne resides in Hood River, Oregon.

MICHAEL B. MACDONALD is a postdoctoral fellow in Canadian folk music at the University of Alberta, where he teaches courses on popular music and the popular music industries. His areas of research include folk festivals, social movements, and popular music with emphasis on the relationship between art, community, and the cultural industries. He has published articles and given public lectures on the politics of folk music, cultural sustainability, and the aesthetics of cultural and social ecology. He continues to produce albums and ethnographic videos and has toured widely as a musician.

SYLVIA MARCOS researches and writes on gender/women's issues in ancient and contemporary Mexico. She has been Visiting Professor on Gender in Mesoamerican Religions at Claremont Graduate University since 1996. She has conducted extensive ethnohistorical research on the construction of gender and sexuality in both indigenous and colonial religious culture. She is the author of *Taken from the Lips: Gender and Eros in Mesoamerican Religions* and *Women in Indigenous Religions: Perspectives from Asia, Australia, and the Americas.*

ARIEAHN MATAMONASA-BENNETT is a Native American scholar, licensed clinical psychologist, and assistant professor at DePaul University School for New Learning in Chicago. She holds a PhD from Fielding

Institute. Her areas of scholarship and research include diversity and cultural sensitivity in clinical practice and research with Native people. Her work supports the preservation of traditional indigenous cultures and the inclusion of traditional healing in psychotherapy for the treatment and prevention of addiction and interpersonal violence.

KATHLEEN L. NICHOLS is a professor of English at Pittsburg State University in Kansas, where she teaches a variety of courses in American literature, including a course on "The Goddess in Myth and Literature." A founder of the PSU Women's Studies Program, she was the program coordinator and taught women's studies classes until her recent semiretirement. She has published articles on women writers such as Sarah Orne Jewett, Willa Cather, Anne Sexton, and Gwendolyn Brooks, on earlier American women playwrights, and on Native American myths, narratives, and songs.

KERRY NOONAN is a folklorist who studies women and vernacular religion; in graduate school she studied with mentors who are internationally renowned in the fields of Celtic Studies and Afro-Caribbean Studies, resulting in her interest in Grande Brigitte. Her research areas also include modern neopaganism, feminist spirituality, Catholic charismatics, and cyber-religion. She is an assistant professor at Champlain College in Vermont.

JORDAN PAPER is Professor Emeritus in Religious Studies Programs at York University in Toronto and a Research Fellow at the Centre for Studies in Religion and Society at the University of Victoria. A comparative religionist, he specializes in Chinese and Native American traditions, focusing on female spirituality. His books include those on the above topics, as well as polytheistic theology and the mystic experience. During his career, he has held offices in all of the major American, Canadian, North American, and international religious studies associations.

DENISE SAINT ARNAULT is associate professor in nursing and anthropology at Michigan State University. She is an anthropologist who focuses on women's studies, especially gender and cultural meanings in Asian and Native American communities. She has also studied Japanese deities, priestesses in Japan and Korea, the mother goddesses of Turkey, and the goddesses Hekate and Artemis.

JACQUELINE THURSBY is a professor of folklore and English at Brigham Young University and has taught at Idaho State University, the University of Toledo, and Bowling Green State University. She has published widely, authoring books and articles on various aspects of folklore, American culture, and English pedagogy. She edited a special edition of *Western Folklore* and serves on the editorial board for the *Utah English Journal*. She is currently Director of English Education at BYU and teaches classes in mythology, folklore, and English pedagogy.

Index